Gordon

Gordon

The Career of
Gordon of Khartoum

The Complete Text of the
Original 2 Volume Edition

Demetrius Charles Boulger

LEONAUR

Gordon: the Career of Gordon of Khartoum
by Demetrius Charles Boulger

Originally published in 1896 in two volumes under the title
The Life of Gordon

FIRST EDITION

Leonaur is an imprint of Oakpast Ltd

ISBN: 978-1-84677-678-6 (hardcover)
ISBN: 978-1-84677-677-9 (softcover)

http://www.leonaur.com

Publisher's Note

The views expressed in this book are not necessarily
those of the publisher.

Contents

Preface

As so many books of a more or less biographical nature have been written about General Charles Gordon, it is both appropriate and natural that I should preface the following pages with a statement of a personal character as to how and why I have written another.

In the year 1881 I told General Gordon that I contemplated describing his career as soon as I had finished writing my *History of China*. His laughing reply was:

"You know I shall never read it, but you can have all my papers now in the possession of my brother, Sir Henry Gordon."

My history took a very long time to write, and the third volume was not published until April 1884, when General Gordon was hemmed in, to use his own words, at Khartoum.

For over two years General Gordon's papers and letters remained in my custody, and they included the Equator and Soudan correspondence, which was so admirably edited by Dr Birkbeck Hill in that intensely interesting volume, *Colonel Gordon in Central Africa*. The papers relating to China and the Taeping Rebellion were freely used in my history. To them I have the privilege of adding in the present volume an authoritative narrative of the events that followed the execution of the Taeping Wangs at Soochow, and of thus rendering tardy justice to the part taken in them by Sir Halliday Macartney. Among the contents of the large portmanteau in which all these documents were stored, I noticed a thick bundle of letters, in somewhat faded handwriting, and an examination of their contents showed me that they were of the deepest interest as relating to the important events of the Crimean War, and to the first seven years of Gordon's service in the Army. I at once went to Sir Henry Gordon, who honoured me with his friendship and confidence in no less a degree than his distinguished and ever-lamented brother, and begged of him permission to publish them. He at once gave his consent, which was ratified by the late Miss Augusta Gordon, the hero's favourite sister. The letters appeared in July 1884, under the title of *General Gordon's Letters from the Crimea, the Danube, and Armenia.* In the proper place I have told what Kinglake, the historian of the war, thought of them and their author.

In the rush of books that followed the fall of Khartoum, no favourable opportunity for carrying out my original purpose presented itself; and, indeed, I may say that the anonymous biographical work I performed during the course of the year 1885 would have filled a large-sized volume. Moreover, the terrible events of the fall of Khartoum, and the failure of the relieving expedition, were too close at hand to allow of a just view being taken of them, and it was necessary to defer an intention which I never abandoned. It seemed to me that the tenth anniversary of the fall of Khartoum would be an appropriate occasion for the appearance of a Life claiming to give a complete view and final verdict on the remarkable career and character of the man, with whom his own friendly inclination had made me exceptionally well acquainted.

In 1893, therefore, I began to take steps to carry out my project, and to the notification of my intention and the application for assistance in regard to unpublished papers, I received from several of the principal representatives of the Gordon family encouraging replies. But at this time both Sir Henry Gordon and Miss Gordon were dead, and I discovered that the latter had bound her literary executrix, Miss Dunlop, a niece of General Gordon's, by a promise not to divulge the bulk of the unpublished papers during her lifetime. I am happy to say, however, that Miss Dunlop, without accepting any responsibility for what I have written, has with the greatest possible kindness read these pages, and assisted me to attain complete accuracy in the facts, so far as they relate to family and personal matters, but excluding altogether from her purview all military and political topics. For that co-operation, unfortunately restricted by the condition of the promise to Miss Gordon, I avail myself of this opportunity to express my grateful thanks; and I am also indebted to Miss Dunlop for the youthful unpublished portrait of Gordon which forms the frontispiece of this volume, and also for that of the house in which he was born.

When I was first confronted with the difficulty that the unpublished papers would not be accessible to me, I contemplated the abandonment of my task; but a brief consideration made me conclude that, even without these documents, I had special knowledge, derived from

Sir Henry Gordon and many other sources, that would enable me to deal with all the more important passages of General Gordon's life. The result must be judged from the *Life* itself; but I have not sought to make any partisan attack on anyone, although, when I have felt compelled to criticise and censure, I have done so with a full sense of responsibility as well as with reluctance. I may be pardoned the confidence I express when I say that I am sure nothing in the unpublished documents will affect the main conclusions to which I have come on the Khartoum mission, its inception and disastrous close.

I am permitted by the courtesy of the proprietors of *The Times* to reproduce in these pages the several articles and letters which originally appeared in the columns of that paper.

It is a personal matter, of no interest except to myself, but I should like to state that the work would have been out much sooner but for a long and serious illness.

Demetrius C. Boulger
29th August 1896

CHAPTER 1

Birth and Early Life

Charles George Gordon was born on 28th January 1833, at No. 1 Kemp Terrace, Woolwich Common, where his father, an officer in the Royal Artillery, was quartered at the time. The picture given elsewhere of this house will specially interest the reader as the birthplace of Gordon. It still stands, as described by Gordon's father in a private memoir, at the corner of Jackson's Lane, on Woolwich Common.

The name "Gordon" has baffled the etymologists, for there is every reason to believe that the not inappropriate connection with the Danish word for a spear is due to a felicitous fancy rather than to any substantial reality. There is far more justification for the opinion that the name comes through a French source than from a Danish. The Gorduni were a leading clan of Caesar's most formidable opponents, the Nervi; a Duke Gordon charged among the peers of Charlemagne; and the name is not unknown at the present day in the Tyrol. The "Gordium" of Phrygia and the "Gordonia" of Macedonia are also names that suggest an Eastern rather than a Northern origin. History strengthens this supposition and entirely disposes of the Danish hypothesis. The first bearer of the name Gordon appeared in Scotland at far too near a date to the Danish descents upon that country to encourage the view that he was a member of that most bitterly hated race. Nowhere were the Danes more hated or less successful than in Scotland, yet we are asked to believe that the founder of one of the most powerful families in that kingdom belonged to this alien and detested people. The silence itself of the chronicler sufficiently refutes the idea that the first Gordon was a renegade or a traitor, as he must have been if he were a Dane.

In all probability the first Gordon, who helped Malcolm Canmore, and received in return a large grant of lands in Berwick, which became known as the Gordon country, was one of the many Norman knights attracted to the Court of Edward the Confessor. Accepting for the occasion the popular legendary version of Shakespeare, rather than the corrected account of modern historians, he may be supposed to have found his way north to the camp of Siward, where the youthful and exiled Scotch Prince had sought shelter from Macbeth, and it is no undue stretch of fancy to suggest that he took his part in the memorable overthrow of that usurper at Dunsinane, and thus obtained the favour of his successor. The growth of the Gordon family in place and power was rapid. To the lands on the borders was soon added the Huntly country on Deeside, where Aboyne Castle now stands, and in a very short period the Gordons ranked among the most powerful and warlike clans of Scotland. As Sir Walter Scott wrote of Adam Gordon, in words which might be appropriately applied to the subject of this biography:

'Tis a name which ne'er hath been dishonour'd,
And never will, I trust—most surely never
By such a youth as thou!

Be its remote origin what it may, no name has appeared more prominently or more honourably in the British Army Lists during the last century and a half than that of Gordon. One of the most famous of our regiments bears and has nobly upheld the name. In honourable and friendly rivalry with the equally numerous and equally distinguished clans of Grant and Cameron, the Gordons have figured on every battlefield from Minden to Candahar, thus establishing at the same time the political wisdom of Chatham, who first turned the Highlanders from a cause of danger into a source of strength, and the military ardour and genius of their own race. Thus it came to pass that the spirit of remote warlike ages was perpetuated, and that the profession of arms continued to be the most natural one for any bearer of the name Gordon. It is not surprising, therefore, to find that the practice of his nearest relations, as well as the traditions of his race, marked out Charles Gordon for a soldier's career.

Passing over an uncertain connection with the General Peter Gordon, who rose high in the Russian service under Peter the Great, the nearest direct ancestor of whom we can speak with absolute confidence was Charles Gordon's great-grandfather David Gordon, who served as a lieutenant in Lascelles' regiment of foot—afterwards the 47th Regiment—at the battle of Prestonpans. Although the majority of the clans were still loyal to the Stuarts, it seems from this that some of them had entered the Hanoverian service probably in that most distinguished regiment, the First Royal Scots, which a few years before Culloden had fought gallantly at Fontenoy. At Prestonpans David Gordon had the bad fortune to be made prisoner by the forces of Charles Edward, and he found on the victorious side the whole of the Gordon clan, under the command of Sir William Gordon of Park, a younger son of the Earl of Huntly. As he was able to claim kindred with Sir William, David Gordon received better treatment than he might have expected, and in a short time was allowed to go free, either on an exchange of prisoners or more probably on his parole. This incident is specially interesting, because, after making every allowance for the remoteness and vagueness of the old Highland custom of cousinship, it seems to bring Charles Gordon's ancestry into sufficiently close relationship with the main Gordon stem of the Huntlys. After his release David Gordon does not appear to have taken any further part in the war which terminated at Culloden, and he emigrated shortly afterwards to North America, where his death is recorded as having taken place at a comparatively early age at Halifax in the year 1752.

That he came of gentle blood is also proved by the fact that the Duke of Cumberland stood sponsor to his son, who bore the Duke's names of William Augustus. This second Gordon, of the particular branch that has interest for us, also entered the army, and held a commission in several regiments. The most memorable event in his life was his taking part in Wolfe's decisive victory on the heights of Abraham. In 1773 he married a lady, Miss Anna Maria Clarke, whose brother was rector of Hexham in Northumberland, and by her had a family of four daughters and three sons. Of the latter, two died at an early age, and only the youngest, William Henry, born in 1786, survived to manhood. He is especially interesting to us, because he was the father of General Gordon.

Like his father and grandfather, William Henry Gordon chose the profession of a soldier, and entered the Royal Artillery. He saw a great deal of active service, being with his corps in the Peninsula and at Maida, commanding at a later period the Artillery at Corfu and Gibraltar, and attaining before his death in 1865 the rank of Lieutenant-General. He was also connected with the Woolwich Arsenal as Director of the Carriage Department. He has been described as an excellent officer if a somewhat strict disciplinarian, and his firm character of noble integrity lived again in his sons. He married, in 1817, Elizabeth, the daughter of Samuel Enderby, a merchant whaler, one of those west country worthies who carried on the traditions of Elizabeth to the age of Victoria. It would not be possible to present a complete picture of Gordon's mother, and therefore none will be attempted here; but all the available evidence agrees in describing her as a paragon of women, and as having exercised an exceptional influence over her children. Gordon himself bore the most expressive testimony to her virtues and memory when, long years afterwards, he closed an exordium on the filial affection due to a mother with the outburst—"Oh! how my mother loved me!"

Such in brief were the forebears of the hero who comes next after Nelson in national veneration. To understand him and his career, it must be remembered that he came of a gallant race, with a quick sense of honour, seeing clearly the obvious course of duty, and never hesitating in its fulfilment. These qualities were not peculiar to the man, but inherited from his race, and as they had never been contaminated by the pursuit of wealth in any form, they retained the pristine vigour and fire of a chivalrous and noble age. What was personal and peculiar to Charles Gordon had to be evolved by circumstance and the important occurrences with which it was his lot to be associated throughout his military and public career, but his soldierly talent and virtue must be mainly assigned to the traditions and practice of his ancestors.

Of the five sons of General William Henry Gordon and Elizabeth Enderby, Charles George Gordon was the fourth. His eldest brother, Henry William Gordon, born in 1818, had entered the army, first in the 8th Regiment, and transferred in a short time to the 59th, when, at the early age of ten, Charles Gordon was sent off to school at Taunton. The selection of this school in the western country was due to the head-master, Mr Rogers, being a brother of a governess in the Gordon family. Little is known of his early childhood beyond the fact that he had lived, before he was ten, at Corfu, where his father held a command for some years. The Duke of Cambridge has publicly stated that he recollects, when quartered at Corfu at this period, having seen a bright and intelligent boy who occupied the room next to his own, and who subsequently became General Gordon. At Taunton Gordon remained during the greater part of five years, enjoying the advantages of one of the most excellent grammar schools in the West of England, and although he failed to make any special mark as a scholar, I find that, whether on account of his later fame or for some special characteristic that marked him out from the general run of boys, his name is still remembered there by something more than the initials cut upon his desk. If he distinguished himself in anything it was in map-making and drawing, and he exhibited the same qualifications to the end of his career. How careful and excellent the grounding at Taunton school must have been was shown by the fact that, after one year's special coaching at Mr Jefferies' school at Shooter's Hill, Gordon passed direct into the Royal Military Academy at Woolwich. It is noteworthy that during the whole of the period we are now approaching, he never showed the least tendency to extravagance, and his main anxiety seems to have been to save his parents all possible expense, more especially because they had a large family of daughters. To the end of his life, and in each successive post, Gordon was the slave of duty. At this time, and during the years that follow, down to the Chinese campaigns, his guiding thought was how to save his family the smallest expense on his account, and yet at the same time to hold his head high, and to show himself worthy of his race.

Gordon entered the Royal Military Academy at Woolwich in 1848, when he had not completed his sixteenth year, and during the four years he remained there he gave some evidence of the qualities that subsequently distinguished him, at the same time that he showed a lightness of disposition which many will think at strange variance with the gravity and even solemnity of his later years. Among his fellow-students he was not distinguished by any special or exclusive devotion to study. He was certainly no bookworm, and he was known rather for his love of sport and boisterous high spirits than for attention to his lessons or for a high place in his class. More than once he was involved in affairs that, if excusable and natural on the score of youth, trenched beyond the borders of discipline, and the stories of life at the Academy that he recited for many years after he left were not exactly in harmony with the popular idea of the ascetic of Mount Carmel.

As the reader treasures up the boyish escapades of Nelson and Clive, so will enduring interest be felt in those outbreaks of the boy Gordon, which made him the terror of his superiors. They are recorded on the unimpeachable evidence of his elder brother, and some of them were even narrated by Gordon himself to his niece nearly thirty years after they happened. Sir Henry is the writer.

Charles Gordon with a brother (William Augustus) more unruly than himself, finding the time hang heavily upon their hands during the vacation, employed themselves in various ways. Their father's house (at Woolwich) was opposite to that of the Commandant of the Garrison, and was overrun with mice. These were caught, the Commandant's door quietly opened, and the mice were transferred to new quarters. In after life (that

15

is in 1879, when in the Soudan) Charles Gordon wrote to one of his nieces: 'I am glad to hear the race of true Gordons is not extinct. Do you not regret the Arsenal and its delights? You never, any of you, made a proper use of the Arsenal workmen as we did. They used to neglect their work for our orders, and turned out some splendid squirts—articles that would wet you through in a minute. As for the crossbows we had made, they were grand with screws. One Sunday afternoon twenty-seven panes of glass were broken in the large storehouses. They were found to have been perforated with a small hole (ventilation), and Captain Soady nearly escaped a premature death; a screw passed his head, and was as if it had been screwed into the wall which it had entered. Servants were kept at the door with continual bell-ringings. Your uncle Freddy (a younger brother) was pushed into houses, the bell rung, and the door held to prevent escape. Those were the days of the Arsenal.'

But what Charles Gordon considered as his greatest achievement was one that he in after years often alluded to. At this time (1848) the senior class of Cadets, then called the Practical Class, were located in the Royal Arsenal, and in front of their halls of study there were earthworks upon which they were practised from time to time in profiling and other matters. The ins and outs of these works were thoroughly well known to Charles Gordon and his brother, who stole out at night—but we will leave him to tell his own story. He says: 'I forgot to tell——of how when Colonel John Travers of the Hill Folk (he lived on Shooter's Hill) was lecturing to the Arsenal Cadets in the evening, a crash was heard, and every one thought every pane of glass was broken; small shot had been thrown. However, it was a very serious affair, for like the upsetting of a hive, the Cadets came out, and only darkness, speed, and knowledge of the fieldworks thrown up near the lecture-room enabled us to escape. That was before I entered the curriculum. The culprits were known afterwards, and for some time avoided the vicinity of the Cadets. I remember it with horror to this day, for no mercy would have been shown by the Pussies, as the Cadets were called.'

After he entered the Academy the same love of fun and practical joking characterised him. Sir Henry writes:

After he had been some time at the Academy and earned many good-conduct badges, an occasion arose when it became necessary to restrain the Cadets in leaving the dining-hall, the approach to which was by a narrow staircase. At the top of this staircase stood the senior corporal, with outstretched arms, facing the body of Cadets. This was too much for Charlie Gordon, who, putting his head down, butted with it, and catching the officer in the pit of the stomach not only sent him down the stairs, but through the glass door beyond. The officer jumped up unhurt, and Gordon was placed in confinement and nearly dismissed.

Upon another occasion, when he was near his commission, a great deal of bullying was going on, and in order to repress it a number of the last comers were questioned, when one of them said that Charlie Gordon had on one occasion hit him on the head with a clothes brush. The lad admitted it was not a severe blow; nevertheless Charlie Gordon was for this slight offence put back six months for his commission, which turned out well in the end, since it secured for him a second lieutenancy in the Royal Engineers in place of the Royal Artillery.

This alteration in the branch of the service to which he was attached was due to his own act. He decided that, as his contemporaries would be put ahead of him, he would work for the Engineers instead of the Artillery.

Even to the end of his life there were two sides to his character. Private grief, much disappointment, and a long solitary existence, contributed to make him a melancholy philosopher, and a sometimes austere critic of a selfish world, but beneath this crust were a genial and generous disposition that did not disdain the lighter side of human nature, a heart too full of kindness to cherish wrath for long, and an almost boyish love of fun that could scarcely be repressed. If this was the individual in his quieter and contemplative moods, an energy that never tired, and a warlike spirit that only needed the occasion to blaze forth, revealed the man of action. It may be pronounced a paradox to say so, but to the end of his life the true Gordon was more of the soldier than the saint.

Even in the midst of his escapades at the Academy, something of the spirit of the future hero revealed itself. However grave the offence or heavy the punishment, he was never backward in taking his share—or more than his share—of the blame for any scrape into which he and his friends were brought by their excessive high spirits. On more than one occasion his ardour and sense of justice resulted in his being made the scapegoat of worse offenders, and it seems probable that he generally bore more than his proper share of the blame and punishment for acts of insubordination. But there were limits to his capacity of suffering and sense of guilt, and when one of his superiors declared that he "would never make an officer," he touched a point of honour, and Gordon's vigorous and expressive reply was to tear the epaulettes from his shoulder and throw them at his superior's feet. In this incident the reader will not fail to see a touch and forecast of greatness. He was ever willing to pay the penalty of youthful indiscretion, but he was sensitive to the reproach of honour, and his exuberant spirits detracted in no respect from his sense of the nobility of his profession. His earnestness saved him from the frivolity into which a light heart and good health might have led him, and compensated for his disinclination to devote all his spare time to the severer studies of his college.

On June 23rd, 1852, nearly four years after he entered the Royal Military Academy, Charles Gordon passed out with the rank of second lieutenant in the Royal Engineers. Notwithstanding some remissness in his work, he had passed through all his examinations—"Those terrible examinations," as he said long years afterwards—"how I remember them! Sometimes I dream of them,"—and in accordance with the regulations in force he was sent to Chatham for the purpose of completing there his technical training as an engineer officer. Chatham, as is well known, is the Headquarters of the Royal Engineer Corps, to which it stands in the same relation as Woolwich to the Artillery. There Gordon remained until February 1854, constantly engaged on field work and in making plans and surveys, at which his old skill as a draughtsman soon made him exceptionally competent. This kind of work was also far more congenial to him than the cramming at the Academy, and he soon gained the reputation of being an intelligent and hard-working subaltern. In the month named he attained the grade of full lieutenant, and on taking his step he was at once ordered to Pembroke Dock, then one of the busiest naval depots and most important military arsenals in the country. The war clouds were already lowering over Eastern Europe, and although all hope of maintaining peace had not been abandoned, arrangements were in progress for the despatch, if necessary, of a strong naval and military expedition to the Black Sea.

At Pembroke, Gordon was at once employed on the construction of the new fortifications and batteries considered necessary for the defence of so important a position, and in one of his letters home he wrote:

I have been very busy in doing plans for another fort, to be built at the entrance of the haven. I pity the officers and men who will have to live in these forts, as they are in the most desolate places, seven miles from any town, and fifteen from any conveyance.

Seclusion and solitude had evidently no charms for him at that period. In another letter about this time he wrote expressing his relief at being "free from the temptations of a line regiment," and concluded with the self-depreciatory remark that he was "such a miserable wretch that he was sure to be led away." In yet another letter from Pembroke, written not many weeks after his arrival, he reveals something of the deep religious feeling which was no doubt greatly strengthened by his experiences in the Crimea, and which became stronger and more pronounced as years went on. In writing to his favourite sister in the summer of 1854, he gives the following interesting bit of biographical information:

You know I never was confirmed. When I was a cadet I thought it was a useless sin, as I did not intend to alter (not that it was in my power to be converted when I chose). I, however, took my first sacrament on Easter Day (16th April 1854) and have communed ever since.

Charles Gordon was still occupied on the Pembroke fortifications when war broke out with Russia on the Eastern Question. His father was at the time stationed at Gibraltar in command of the Royal Artillery, and was never employed nearer the scene of hostilities during the war. But his two elder brothers were at the front—the eldest, the late Sir Henry Gordon, at Balaclava, where he served in the Commissariat, and the next brother, the late General Enderby Gordon, with his battery under Lord Raglan. At the battle of the Alma, fought on 20th September 1854, Enderby Gordon specially distinguished himself, for he worked one of the two guns of Turner's Battery, which exercised such a decisive influence on the fortunes of the day. Readers of Kinglake's *History* will remember that it was the flank fire of these two guns which compelled the Russian battery of sixteen guns on the Causeway to retire and thus expose the Russian front to our attack. It is a little curious to find that while one brother was thus distinguishing himself in the first battle of the war, another was writing from Pembroke Dock as follows: "—— says there were no artillery engaged in the battle of the Alma, so that Enderby was safe out of that." Enderby Gordon also distinguished himself at Inkerman, where he acted as *aide-de-camp* to General Strangeways. He subsequently earned the reputation of a good officer during the Indian Mutiny, and when he died he had, like his father, attained the rank of Lieutenant-General, and received besides the Companionship of the Bath. One character-istic incident has been recorded of him. As he commanded a column in India, he had only to ask for promotion to obtain it; this he declined to do, because he would thus have stepped over a friend.

In General Gordon's own letters from the Crimea there are fre-quent references to his eldest brother, Henry Gordon, a man of whom it may be said here that the best was never publicly known, for during a long and varied career, first in the combative branch of the army as an officer of the 59th Regiment, and then as a non–combative of-ficer in the Ordnance Department, he showed much ability, but had few opportunities of special distinction. In several of General Gor-don's transactions Sir Henry was closely mixed up, especially with the Congo mission; and I should like to say, of my own knowledge, that he was thoroughly in sympathy with all his projects for the suppres-sion of the slave trade, had mastered the voluminous Blue Books and official papers, from the time of Ismail to the dark days of Khartoum, in so thorough a manner that the smallest detail was fixed in his brain, and had so completely assimilated his brother's views that an hour's consultation with him was almost as fertile a source of inspiration as it would have been with the General himself. I believe that the original cause of Sir Henry's influence over his brother was that he disclaimed having any, and that he most carefully avoided any attempt to force his advice on his younger brother, as so many of our elders deem to be their right and prerogative. General Gordon was a bad listener to ad-vice at any time or from anyone. He acted almost entirely on his own judgment, and still more on his own impulse. His first thoughts were his best thoughts, or, perhaps, as Tennyson says, "his third thoughts, which are a maturer first." Sir Henry knew the ingrained and unalter-able character of his brother, and adapted himself to it, partly through affection and partly through admiration, for in his eyes Charles Gor-don was the truest of heroes. No man ever possessed a truer or more solicitous friend than General Gordon found in him. Sir Henry was thoroughly devoted to him and his interests, and carried out all his wishes and instructions to the very letter.

Having said this much about the relations between Gordon and his brother, it would be an inexcusable omission to pass over the still more striking sympathy and affection that united him with his sisters. From his first appointment into the service he corresponded on religious and serious subjects with his elder sister, the late Miss Gordon, who only survived her brother a few years, with remarkable regularity, and as time went on the correspondence became more, rather than less constant, and in his letters to her were to be found his most secret thoughts and aspirations. Most of the letters from the Crimea were addressed to his mother; but, in an interesting volume published in 1888, Miss Gordon presented the world with the remainder of her brother's letters, spread over thirty active and eventful years. One of General Gordon's most cherished objects, resembling in that, as in other respects, Lord Lawrence, was to add to the comfort of his sisters, and when he left England on his last fatal mission to Egypt, his will, made the night before he left for Brussels, provided that all he possessed should be held in trust for the benefit of his well-beloved sister, Mary Augusta, and that it was to pass only on her death to the heirs he therein designated. It is not necessary to enter into fuller particulars on this subject, but it may be proper to say that his affection for his other sisters was not less warm or less reciprocated. Of his six sisters, of whom two alone survive, it is only necessary to refer here (in addition to Miss Gordon) to the youngest, who married Dr Andrew Moffitt, who was not merely head medical officer with the Ever Victorious Army, but Gordon's right-hand man in China. Dr Moffitt was a man of high courage; on one occasion he saved Gordon's life when a Taeping attempted to murder him in his tent, and an English officer, who served with the Force, has described him in these two lines: "He was imbued with the same spirit as his future brother-in-law; he was a clever Chinese scholar and an A1 surgeon." Dr Moffitt, who received a gold medal and order, besides the Red Button of a Mandarin, from the Chinese Government for his brilliant services against the Taepings, died prematurely. To say less about these family relations would be an omission; to say more would be an intrusion, and they may be left with the reflection that as no one who knew him will dispute the depth and the strength of General Gordon's sentiments as a friend, his feelings towards the members of his own family cannot well be impugned.

Some account of the personal appearance of General Gordon will be deemed necessary, and may be appropriately given at this stage, although the subject is a dangerous one, because so very few people form the same impression about any one's appearance. There has been much discussion as to General Gordon's exact height, and I have been to much pains to obtain some decisive evidence on the subject. Unfortunately no such records as to height, etc., are kept about officers, and my search proved fruitless, more especially as the records at Woolwich for the period required were destroyed by fire some years ago. The best evidence I have obtained is that of General Gordon's tailors, Messrs Batten & Sons, of Southampton, who write: "We consider, by measurements in our books, that General Gordon was 5 ft. 9 in." As he had contracted a slight stoop, or, more correctly speaking, carried his head thrown forward, he looked in later life much less than his real height. The quotations at the end of this chapter will show some difference of opinion. His figure was very slight, but his nervous energy could never be repressed, and he was probably stronger than his appearance suggested. The suggestion of delicate health in his look and aspect, arising, as he was led to believe, but erroneously, from *angina pectoris*, or some mysterious chest pain, may have induced a belief that he was not robust, but this seems to have been baseless, because throughout his life, whether in the trenches of Sebastopol, the marshes of the Yangtse delta, or the arid plains of the Soudan, he appears to have equally enjoyed excellent health.

The only specific mention of serious illness was during his stay in the Soudan as Governor-General, when the chest pains became acute. These were at length traced to an enlarged liver, and perhaps the complaint was aggravated by excessive smoking. In the desert, far removed from medical aid, he obtained much relief from the use of Warburg's Tincture.

In his ordinary moods there was nothing striking about the face. The colour of the eye was too light—yet the glance was as keen as a rapier, and, as the little Soudan boy Capsune, whom he had educated, said, "Gordon's eyes looked you through and through"— the features were not sufficiently marked, the carriage of the man was too diffident and modest to arrest or detain attention, and the explanation of the universal badness of the numerous photographs taken of him at all stages of his career is probably to be found in the deficiency of colouring and contrast. Everything in his appearance depended on expression, and expression generally baffles the photographer. Perhaps the least objectionable of all these portraitures is the steel plate in Dr Birkbeck Hill's volume on *Gordon in Central Africa*, and that not because it is a faithful likeness, but because it represents a bust that might well be imagined to belong to a hero. It was only when some great idea or some subject in which he was interested seized his imagination that one could perceive that the square jaw denoted unshakable resolution, and that the pale blue eye could flash with the fire of a born leader of men. In tranquil moments no one would have been struck by a casual glance at his face, but these were rare, for in congenial company, and with persons he trusted, Gordon was never tranquil, pacing up and down the room, with only brief stops to impress a point on his listener by holding his arm for a few seconds, and looking at him intently to see if he followed with understanding and interest the drift of his remarks, lighting cigarette after cigarette to enable him to curb his own impetuosity, and demonstrating in every act and phrase the truth of his own words that "inaction was intolerable to him." Such was the man as I recall him on the all too few occasions when it was my privilege and good fortune to receive him during his brief visits to London of late years, and to hear from him his confidential views on the questions in which he took so deep an interest. One final remark must be hazarded about the most remarkable point after all in General Gordon's personality. I refer to his voice. It was singularly sweet, and for a man modulated in a very low tone, but there was nothing womanish about it, as was the case with his able contemporary Sir Bartle Frere, whose voice was distinctly feminine in its timbre. I know of no other way to describe it than to say that it seemed to me to express the thorough and transparent goodness of the speaker, and the exquisite gentleness of his nature. If angels speak with the human voice, Gordon's tone must have borne affinity to theirs.

In completing this subject it may be appropriate to quote a few of the more important and interesting descriptions of his personal appearance, contributed by those who had opportunities of seeing him.

An officer, who served with General Gordon in China, describes his first interview with him in the following words:

C—— introduced me to a light-built, active, wiry, middle-sized man of about thirty-two years of age, in the undress uniform of the Royal Engineers. The countenance bore a pleasant frank appearance, eyes light blue, with a fearless look in them, hair crisp and inclined to curl, conversation short and decided. This was Major C. G. Gordon.

General Sir Gerald Graham who, to use his own words, was Gordon's "school-fellow at Woolwich, his comrade in the Crimea and China, and for many years past a more or less regular correspondent," has put on record the following interesting description of the hero, and it should not be forgotten that, excepting his companion, Colonel Donald Stewart, and Mr Power, General Graham was the last Englishman to see General Gordon in this world.

Not over 5 feet 9 inches in height, but of compact build, his figure and gait characteristically expressed resolution and strength. His face, although in itself unpretending, was one that in the common phrase 'grew upon you.' Time had not streaked with grey the crisp, curly brown hair of his youth and traced lines of care on his ample forehead and strong clear face, bronzed with exposure to the tropical sun. His usual aspect was serene and quiet, and although at times a ruffling wave of un-controllable impatience or indignation might pass over him, it did not disturb him long. The depth and largeness of Gordon's nature, which inspired so much confidence in others, seemed to afford him a sense of inner repose, so that outer disturbance was to him like the wind that ruffles the surface of the sea, but does not affect its depths. The force and beauty of Gordon's whole expression came from within, and as it were irradiated the man, the steady, truthful gaze of the blue-grey eyes seeming a direct appeal from the upright spirit within. Gordon's usual manner charmed by its simple, unaffected courtesy, but although utterly devoid of self-importance he had plenty of quiet dignity, or even of imperious authority at command when required. With his friends he had a fund of innocent gaiety that seemed to spring from his impulsiveness, while his strong sense of humour often enabled him to relieve his impatience or indignation by a good-natured sarcasm.

Two further descriptions by men who served under him at Graves-end in the interval between the Taeping War and the first mission to the Soudan will suffice to complete the personal impressions that may help the reader to form some idea of the appearance of General Gordon. The first is from the pen of Mr W. E. Lilley, who brought out a special volume on Gordon at Gravesend.

In Colonel Gordon's appearance there was nothing par-ticularly striking. He was rather under the average height, of slight proportions, and with little of the military bearing in his carriage, so that one would hardly have imagined that this kindly, unassuming gentleman was already one who had at-tracted the notice of his superiors by his courage and zeal in the Crimean War, and who had won lasting renown by subduing in China one of the greatest revolts the world had ever seen. This last exploit had gained for him the name by which he was from that time best known, *viz*. "Chinese Gordon." The greatest characteristic of his countenance was the clear blue eye, which seemed to have a magical power over all who came within its influence. It read you through and through; it made it impossible for you to tell him anything but the truth, it inspired your confidence, it kindled with compassion at any story of distress, and it sparkled with good humour at anything really funny or witty. From its glance you knew at once that at any risk he would keep his promise, that you might trust him with anything and everything, and that he would stand by you if all other friends deserted you.

The other impression, formed under precisely the same circumstances, is that of Mr Arthur Stannard, recorded in the *Nineteenth Century* of April 1885.

> The next moment I was looking into Chinese Gordon's eyes. What eyes they were! Keen and clear, filled with the beauty of holiness, bright with an unnatural brightness, their expression one of settled feverishness, the colour blue-grey as is the sky on a bitter March morning. In spite of the beautiful goodness of his heart and the great breadth of his charity, Gordon was far from possessing a placid temperament or from being patient over small things. Indeed his very energy and his single-mindedness tended to make him impatient and irritable whenever any person or thing interfered with his intentions or desires. . . . For a man of his small stature his activity was marvellous—he seemed able to walk every one else off their legs over rough ground or smooth. . . . In Gordon strength and weakness were most fantastically mingled. There was no trace of timidity in his composition. He had a most powerful will. When his mind was made up on a matter it never seemed to occur to him that there could be anything more to say about it. Such was his superb confidence in himself!

When Gordon had been only a few months at Pembroke Dock he received orders to proceed to Corfu, and believing it to be due to his father's request, he wrote: "I suspect you used your influence to have me sent there instead of to the Crimea. It is a great shame of you." But the Fates were to be stronger than any private influence, for four days after he wrote those lines he received fresh orders directing him to leave for the Crimea without delay in charge of huts. It seems that the change in his destination was due to Sir John Burgoyne, to whom he had expressed the strongest wish to proceed to the scene of war. On 4th December 1854, he received his orders at Pembroke, on the 6th he reported himself at the War Office, and in the evening of the same day he was at Portsmouth. It was at first intended that he should go out in a collier, but he obtained permission to proceed *via* Marseilles, which he pronounced "extremely lucky, as I am such a bad sailor." This opinion was somewhat qualified later on when he found that the Government did not prepay his passage, and he expressed the opinion pretty freely, in which most people would concur, that "it is very hard not to give us anything before starting." He left London on the 14th December, Marseilles in a French hired transport on the 18th, and reached Constantinople the day after Christmas Day. He was not much struck with anything he saw; pronounced Athens "very ugly and dirty," and the country around uncommonly barren; and was disappointed with the far-famed view on approaching Constantinople. The professional instinct displayed itself when he declared that the forts of the Dardanelles did not appear to be very strong, as, although numerous, they were open at the rear and overlooked by the heights behind. On 28th December Gordon left Constantinople in the *Golden Fleece* transport conveying the 39th Regiment to Balaclava. The important huts had not yet arrived in the collier from Portsmouth, but they could not be far behind, and Gordon went on in advance. The huts, it may be added, were built to contain twenty-four men, or two captains and four subalterns, or two field-officers or one general, and the number of these entrusted to the charge of Gordon was 320. These reinforcements were the first sent out to mitigate the hardships the British Army underwent during a campaign that the genius of Todleben and the fortitude of his courageous garrison rendered far more protracted and costly than had been anticipated.

CHAPTER 2

The Crimea, Danube and Armenia

Charles Gordon reached Balaclava on New Year's Day, 1855. He found everyone engaged in foraging expeditions, that the siege of Sebastopol excited no interest, that the road from the bay to the hill was like a morass, and that a railway to traverse it was being slowly laid down. Gordon remained about three weeks at Balaclava assisting in the erection of huts, and in the conveyance of some of them to the front. When this task was accomplished he was himself ordered to the trenches, where his work could not fail to be more exciting and also more dangerous than that upon which up to this he had been engaged.

Before following him it will be useful to summarise the leading events that had taken place in the Crimea up to this date. War between England and France on the one side, and Russia on the other, was finally declared in March 1854, the allied forces landed in the Crimea early in September 1854, and the first battle was fought on the Alma stream on the 20th of that month. In that battle 60,000 allied troops—20,000 English, 40,000 French—attacked 120,000 Russians in a strong and well-chosen position. The result was a brilliant victory for the allies, and there is no doubt that it was mainly won by the dashing attack of the English Infantry. The losses were—French, 60 killed and 500 wounded; English, 362 killed and 1620 wounded, thus furnishing clear evidence as to the force which bore the brunt of the engagement. The Russian loss was computed to be not less than 6000, or double that of the allies.

As the allied forces advanced towards Sebastopol the Russian Army assumed the offensive. The brilliant and never-to-be-forgotten Cavalry charges on 25th October, of the Light and Heavy Brigades, under Cardigan and Scarlett respectively, at Balaclava in the valley that stretched at the foot of the hills overlooking the bay of that name, had not merely vindicated the reputation of English horsemen for dash and daring, but had done something—at excessive cost, it is true—to clear the advance for the whole army. When the Russians, assuming in their turn the offensive, attacked our camps on the heights of Inkerman, they were repulsed with heavy loss on both sides, and with the result that more than six months elapsed before they again ventured to show any inclination to attack in the open field, and then only to meet with fresh discomfiture on the banks of the Tchernaya.

The battle of Inkerman was fought in the early morning of 5th November, and again the brunt of the fighting fell on the English army. The Russian General, Todleben, subsequently stated that he reluctantly decided to attack the English camp instead of the French, because "the English position seemed to be so very weak." Here again the losses give no misleading idea of the proportionate share of the two allied armies in the struggle. While the Russian loss was put down in all at 11,000 men, the French lost 143 killed and 786 wounded; the English, 597 killed and 1760 wounded.

The opinion has been confidently expressed that if a rapid advance and attack had been made on Sebastopol immediately after Inkerman, the fortress would have been easily captured; but both before and during the siege the Russians made the best use of every respite the Allies gave them, and this lost opportunity, if it was one, never recurred. It will thus be seen that some of the most interesting incidents of the war had passed before Gordon set foot in the Crimea, but for an engineer officer the siege and capture of the fortress created by Todleben under the fire of his foes presented the most attractive and instructive phase of the campaign.

At this time the French army mustered about 100,000 men, the British about 23,000, and the Russian garrison of Sebastopol 25,000. In addition, there was a covering army, under the Grand Dukes and General Liprandi, which, despite its losses at Inkerman, was probably not less than 60,000 but the successive defeats at Alma, Balaclava, and Inkerman had broken the confidence of the troops and reduced their leaders to inaction. The batteries were nearly completed when Gordon reached the front, and a good deal had already been written and said about the hardships of the soldiers. Gordon was a man of few wants, who could stand any amount of fatigue, and throughout his life he was always disposed to think that soldiers should never complain. Writing as late as 12th February 1855, when the worst of the winter was over, he says:

There are really no hardships for the officers; the men are the sufferers, and that is partly their own fault, as they are like children, thinking everything is to be done for them. The French soldier looks out for himself, and consequently fares much better.

Something of the same conclusion had been forced on him when on board the French transport between Marseilles and Athens when he wrote:

The poor French soldiers, of whom there were 320 on board without any shelter, must have suffered considerably from cold; they had no covering, and in spite of the wet, cold, and bad weather, they kept up their health however, and their high spirits also, when our men would have mutinied.

And again, later on:

We have capital rations, and all the men have warm clothing, and more than enough of that. They of course grumble and growl a good deal. The contrast with the French in this respect is not to our advantage.

It must in fairness be remembered that the worst of the maladministration was over before he reached the scene, and that he came with those reinforcements, not merely of men, but still more especially of supplies, which ended "the winter troubles," and converted them into the sanguine hopes and views of the spring.

Gordon was not long in the trenches before he came under fire, and the account of his first experience of real warfare may be given in his own words:

The night of February 14th I was on duty in the trenches, and if you look at the plan I sent you and the small sketch enclosed I will explain what I had to do. The French that night determined to join their sentries on their right and our sentries on our left, in advance of their and our trenches, so as to prevent the Russians coming up the ravine, and then turning against our flank. They determined to make a lodgement in the ruined house marked B on the sketch, and to run a trench up the hill to the left of this, while I was told to make a communication by rifle-pits from the caves C to the ruined house B. I got, after some trouble, eight men with picks and shovels, and asked the captain of the advance trench to give me five double sentries to throw out in advance. It was the first time he had been on duty here; and as for myself, I never had, although I kept that to myself. I led forward the sentries, going at the head of the party, and found the sentries of the advance had not held the caves, which they ought to have done after dark, so there was just a chance of the Russians being in them. I went on, however, and, though I did not like it, explored the caves almost alone. We then left two sentries on the hill above the caves, and went back, to get round and post two sentries below the caves. However, just as soon as we showed ourselves outside the caves and below them, bang! bang! went two rifles, the bullets hitting the ground close to us. The sentries with me retired in a rare state of mind, and my working party bolted, and were stopped with great difficulty. What had really happened was this: It was not a Russian attack, but the two sentries whom I had placed above the caves *had fired at us*, lost their caps, and bolted to the trench. Nothing after this would induce the sentries to go out, so I got the working party to go forward with me. The Russians had, on the report of our shots, sent us a shower of bullets, their picket not being more than 150 yards away. I set the men to work, and then went down to the bottom of the ravine, and found the French in strength hard at work also. Having told them who we were, I returned to the trench, where I met Colonel —— of the 1st Royals. I warned him if he went out he would be sure to be hit by our own sentries or the Russians. He would go, however, and a moment afterwards was hit in the breast, the ball going through his coats, slightly grazing his ribs, and passing out again without hurting him. I stayed with my working party all night, and got home very tired.

In further illustration of the confusion prevailing in the trenches at night, he mentions in the same letter that while trying to find the caves he missed his way, and "very nearly walked into the town by mistake."

This was the more surprising because Gordon's intimate knowledge of the trenches was remarkable and well known. The following testimony given by Sir Charles Staveley affords striking proof that this reputation was not undeserved:

I happened to mention to Charlie Gordon that I was field officer for the day for command in the trenches next day, and, having only just returned from sick leave, that I was ignorant of the geography of our left attack. He said at once, 'Oh! come

30

down with me to-night after dark, and I will show you over the trenches.' He drew me out a very clear sketch of the lines (which I have now), and down I went accordingly. He explained every nook and corner, and took me along outside our most advanced trench, the bouquets (volleys of small shells fired from mortars) and other missiles flying about us in, to me, a very unpleasant manner, he taking the matter remarkably coolly.

The late Sir George Chesney, a very competent and discriminating witness, gives evidence to the same effect:

> In his humble position as an Engineer subaltern he attracted the notice of his superiors, not merely by his energy and activity, but by a special aptitude for war, developing itself amid the trench work before Sebastopol in a personal knowledge of the enemy's movements *such as no other officer attained.* We used to send him to find out what new move the Russians were making.

The next incident of the siege described by Gordon occurred about a week after his *baptême de feu* in the caves. While the French were somewhat deliberately making at Inkerman a battery for fifteen guns, the Russians, partly in a spirit of bravado, threw up in a single night a battery for nearly twenty guns immediately opposite, at a distance of not more than 600 yards from the French. As this was made in the open ground, it was a defiance which could not be tolerated, and the French accordingly made their arrangements to assault it. Kinglake has graphically described the surprise of the French when they discovered this "white circlet or loop on the ground," and the attempt made by three battalions, with two other battalions in reserve, to capture it. A battalion of Zouaves, under the command of Colonel Cere, carried it in fine style, but the Russian reserves came up in great force, and their own reserves "declining to come to the scratch," as Gordon laconically put it, the Zouaves were in their turn compelled to fall back, with a loss of 200 killed. Encouraged by this success, the Russians gave the French another surprise a few days later, throwing up a second battery 300 yards further in advance of the first "white circlet." These two batteries, mounting between them, according to Kinglake, twenty-two guns, were finally strengthened and equipped by 10th March, and although the French talked much of storming them, nothing was done, much to Gordon's disgust. It was while these operations were in progress that Charles Gordon had a narrow escape of being killed. A shot from one of the Russian rifle-pits "as nearly as possible did for me," he wrote; "the bullet was fired not 180 yards off, and passed an inch above my nut into a bank I was passing." His only comment on this is very characteristic: "They are very good marksmen; their bullet is large and pointed."

This was the first but not the last escape he had during the siege. One of his brothers, writing home some three months later, a few days before the assault on the Redan, wrote as follows:

> Charlie has had a miraculous escape. The day before yesterday he saw the smoke from an embrasure on his left and heard a shell coming, but did not see it. It struck the ground about five yards in front of him and burst, not touching him. If it had not burst it would have taken his head off.

Of this later shave Gordon himself says nothing, but he describes a somewhat similar incident, which had, however, a fatal result.

> We lost one of our captains named Craigie by a splinter of a shell. The shell burst above him, and by what is called chance struck him in the back, killing him at once.

During the three months March, April, and May, the siege languished, and Gordon apologises for the stupidity of his letters with the graphic observation: "It is not my fault, as none of the three nations—French, English, or Russian—will do anything."

At the end of May, however, there was a renewal of activity. General Pelissier succeeded to the French command, and, unlike his predecessors, made it his primary object to act in cordial co-operation with the English commander. He was also in favour of an energetic prosecution of the siege, with the view to an early assault. All the batteries were by this time completed, and 588 guns, with 700 rounds in readiness for each gun, were opposed to the 1174 in the Russian fortress. It only remained to utilise this terrific force, and at last orders were given for the commencement of what was known as the third bombardment. After nearly two days' incessant firing the French stormed the Mamelon and two advance redoubts. These were successfully carried and held, at the same time that the English stormed a position called the Quarries, close under the formidable Redan. Of this bombardment Gordon gives in one of his letters a very good description:

> On the 6th we opened fire from all our batteries. I was on duty in the trenches. I could distinctly see the Russians in the Redan and elsewhere running about in great haste, and bringing

up their gunners to the guns. They must have lost immensely, as our shot and shell continued to pour in upon them for hours without a lull. Never was our fire so successful. Before seven we had silenced a great many of their guns, while our loss was very small—only one man killed and four wounded. I was struck slightly with a stone from a round shot and stunned for a second, which old Jones has persisted in returning as wounded. (It was, notwithstanding, a real wound.) However, I am all right, so do not think otherwise. Our fire was continued all night, and the next day until four o'clock, when we opened with new batteries much nearer, and our fire then became truly terrific. Fancy 1000 guns (which is the number of ourselves, the French, and Russians combined) firing at once shells in every direction. On our side alone we have thirty-nine 13" mortars. At half-past five three rockets gave the signal for the French to attack the Mamelon and the redoubts of Selingkinsk and Volhynia. They rushed up the slope in full view of the allied armies. The Russians fired one or two guns when the French were in the embrasures. We then saw the Russians cut out on the other side, and the French after them, towards the Malakoff Tower, which they nearly reached, but were so punished by the guns of this work that they were obliged to retire, the Russians in their turn chasing them through the Mamelon into their own trenches. This was dreadful, as it had to be assaulted again. The French, however, did so immediately, and carried it splendidly. The redoubts of Volhynia and Selingkinsk were taken easily on our side. In front of the right attack a work called the Quarries had to be taken, which was done at the same time as the Mamelon. The Russians cut out and ran, while our men made their lodgement for our fellows. We were attacked four times in the night, but held the work. If we had liked to assault, I am sure we should have taken the place with little loss, some of our men being close to the Redan. The French took twenty guns and 400 prisoners, and found the Mamelon so traversed as to have no difficulty in making their lodgement. We were driven from the Quarries three times in the night, the Russians having directed all their efforts against them. Our loss is supposed to be 1000 killed and wounded. Nearly all our working party had to be taken for fighting purposes. The attacking columns were 200 strong; one went to the right, and the other to the left of the Quarries. The reserve consisted of 600 men. The Russians fought desperately.

A further week was occupied with a heavy but desultory bombardment, but at last on 17th June what is known as "the fourth bombardment" proper began, and after it had continued for about twenty-four hours, orders given for the assault to be made by the French on the Malakoff and the English on the Redan on the 18th June, a date ever memorable in military annals. The silence of the Russian guns induced a belief that the allied fire had overpowered theirs, and in consequence orders for the attack were given twenty-four hours sooner than had been intended. Kinglake, in his exhaustive History, has shown how this acted adversely on the chances of the assault, because the Russian gunners had really only reserved their fire, and also especially because the Redan, which we had to attack under the original arrangement between Lord Raglan and General Pelissier, had hardly suffered any damage from the bombardment. General Gordon's long account of this memorable assault will long be referred to as a striking individual experience:

I must now commence my long story of our attempted assault. To take up my account from 14th June, which was the last letter I wrote to you, Seeley, my fellow-subaltern at Pembroke, arrived on the 15th, and joined the right. On the evening of the 16th it was rumoured we were to commence firing again in the morning. I was on duty on the morning of the 17th, and I went down at half-past two a.m. At 3 a.m. all our batteries opened, and throughout the day kept up a terrific fire. The Russians answered slowly, and after a time their guns almost ceased. I mentioned in my report that I thought they were reserving their fire. (If this view had only been taken by the Generals, especially Pelissier, a dreadful waste of life would have been averted, and the result might have proved a brilliant success.) We did not lose many men. I remained in the trenches until 7 p.m.—rather a long spell—and on coming up dined, and found an order to be at the night attack at twelve midnight on June 17 and 18. I was attached to Bent's column, with Lieutenants Murray and Graham, R.E., and we were to go into the Redan at the Russians' right flank. Another column, under Captain de Moleyns and Lieutenants Donnelly and James, R.E., was to go in at the angle of the salient; and another under Captain Jesse, Lieutenants Fisher and Graves, was to go in at the Russian left flank. We passed along in our relative positions up to the advanced trench, which is 200 yards from the Redan, where we halted until the signal for the attack should be given from the eight-gun battery, where Lord Raglan, Sir G. Brown, and General Jones were.

About 3 a.m. the French advanced on the Malakoff Tower in three columns, and ten minutes after this our signal was given. The Russians then opened with a fire of grape, which was terrific. They mowed down our men in dozens, and the trenches, being confined, were crowded with men, who foolishly kept in them instead of rushing over the parapet of our trenches, and by coming forward in a mass, trusting to some of them at least being able to pass through untouched to the Redan, where of course, once they arrived, the artillery could not reach them, and every yard nearer would have diminished the effect of the grape by giving it less space for spreading. We could then have moved up our supports and carried the place.

Unfortunately, however, our men dribbled out of the ends of the trenches, ten and twenty at a time, and as soon as they appeared they were cleared away. Some hundred men, under Lieutenant Fisher, got up to the abattis, but were not supported, and consequently had to retire.

About this time the French were driven from the Malakoff Tower, which I do not think they actually entered, and Lord Raglan very wisely would not renew the assault, as the Redan could not be held with the Malakoff Tower in the hands of the Russians. Murray, poor fellow, went out with the skirmishers of our column—he in red, and they in green. He was not out a minute when he was carried back with his arm shattered with grape. Colonel Tylden called for me, and asked me to look after him, which I did, and as I had a tourniquet in my pocket I put it on. He bore it bravely, and I got a stretcher and had him taken back. He died three hours afterwards. I am glad to say that Dr Bent reports he did not die from loss of blood, but from the shock, not being very strong.

A second after Murray had gone to the rear, poor Tylden, struck by grape in the legs, was carried back, and although very much depressed in spirits he is doing well. Jesse was killed at the abattis—shot through the head—and Graves was killed further in advance than any one. We now sat still waiting for orders, and the Russians amusing themselves by shelling us from mortars. When we appeared, the Russians lined their parapets as thick as possible, and seemed to be expecting us to come on.

They flew two flags on the Malakoff Tower the whole time in defiance of us. About ten o'clock some of the regiments got orders to retire. We, the Royal Engineers, however, stayed until twelve o'clock, when we were told that the assault was not to be renewed, and that we could go. Thus ended our assault, of the result of which we felt so sure. The first plan made was that we should fire for three hours and go in at six o'clock, but the French changed it, and would not wait until we had silenced the enemy's artillery fire, and so we attacked at 3 a.m. My father can tell the effect of grape from twelve 68-pounders and 32-pounders at 200 yards upon a column; but whatever may be the effect, I am confident that if we had left the trenches in a mass, some of us would have survived and reached the Redan, which, once reached, the Highland Brigade and Guards would have carried all before them, and the place would have fallen. General Jones was struck by a stone in the forehead, but not much hurt. I believe it is said that the trenches were too high to get over. As the scaling-ladders were carried over them, this can hardly be sustained. So much for *our* assault.

Now for the assault which was made from the left attack. General Eyre had an order given him to make a feint at the head of the creek if we were successful at the Redan; however, at five o'clock, when we had failed at the Redan, we heard a very sharp attack on the head of the creek. The 44th and other regiments advanced, drove the Russians out of a rifle-pit they held near the cemetery, and entered some houses there. The Russians then opened a tremendous fire on the houses, and the men took shelter in line, being under no command, their own officers not knowing where they were to go, or anything about the place, and no Engineer officer being with them. The men sheltered themselves in the houses until they were knocked about their ears. They then remained in different places—in fact, wherever they could get any shelter, until dusk, as, if they had attempted to retire, they would have been all destroyed. The men of General Eyre's column found lots of drink in the houses. Our losses in the four columns are—1400 killed and wounded, 64 officers wounded, and 16 killed. The French lost 6000 killed and wounded, they say! Nothing has occurred since the assault, but it is determined to work forward by sap and mine!

In a subsequent letter he wrote:

Remember, in spite of all the absurd reports in the papers, that our troops never once passed the abattis in front of the Redan, which is sixty yards from it, and that we have never spiked a gun of the Russians....

And before closing his narrative account of the Redan, the passage in which Mr Kinglake refers to Gordon's evidence and action on this eventful day may well be quoted. It appears from his statement that Gordon lost his temper through excitement at the repulse, and even upbraided and used angry language to his old friend and comrade, Lieutenant, now General Sir Gerald, Graham, on his coming back to the trenches. Such language, it may be pointed out, could not have been used with less justice to any soldier taking part in the assault than to the man who had carried a ladder farther than anyone else, and twice endeavoured to place it against the Redan. It illustrates the perfervid zeal and energy of the young officer, who explained in his letters home how he thought the Russian fortress might have been carried at a rush, and appropriately introduces the passage in which Mr Kinglake records his opinion of Gordon:

This impassioned lieutenant of sappers was a soldier marked out for strange destinies, no other than Gordon—Charles Gordon—then ripening into a hero, sublimely careless of self, and a warrior saint of the kind that Moslems rather than Christians are fondly expecting from God.

I cannot refrain from quoting here a letter I received from Mr Kinglake when I sent him a copy of my edition of *General Gordon's Letters from the Crimea*, etc., as it records a somewhat more deliberate opinion on his character and career:

28 Hyde Park Place
Marble Arch
27th July 1884
Dear Sir,—I indeed feel greatly obliged to you for your kindness in sending me a copy of *General Gordon's Letters from the Crimea*.

Already I have read a great part of the volume, and I need hardly say that, apart from the reasons which link me to the Crimea, I have been greatly interested by seeing what was thought, and felt, and expressed in his early days by this really phenomenal man, whose romantic elevation above all that is base and common has made him, in even these days, a sort of warlike and heroic Redeemer.

Your Preface well and ably expresses an opinion that is widely entertained as to the conduct of our Government towards Gordon, and I don't know enough of the question to be able to gainsay your conclusion, but it would seem at first glance that, considering the imperative reasons, the vast distances, the changeful condition of things, and the consequent changes of mind, the task of doing justice between the Government and this heroic envoy would be one of some complexity. With my repeated thanks,—I remain, dear sir, very truly yours,
A. W. Kinglake

Ten days after the repulse at the Redan, Lord Raglan, the gallant soldier over whose bier Pelissier wept like a child, died "of wear and tear and general debility," as Gordon put it, and the siege again entered upon another dull and uninteresting stage. Nearly three months were to elapse before the capture of the fortress that had resisted so long, and the only incident of marked importance during that period was the battle of the Tchernaya, in which the officers in the trenches had no part. In that action the last effort of the Russian commanders to relieve the place and extricate Todleben from his peril was repulsed by the whole allied forces, for in this engagement both the Italians and Turks took part, with a loss of seven or eight thousand men. The only comment Gordon makes on the action is that "the Sardinians behaved very well." At last, on 8th September, a second general assault was delivered, the English again attacking the Redan, and, more fortunate in one sense than on the earlier occasion, effected a lodgement in the fortress, but were then driven out with heavy loss. But the French succeeded in storming and holding the Malakoff, which commanded the Redan, and the Russians retired to the northern side of the harbour during the night after blowing up their ships. The fall of Sebastopol, especially after the doubts held and expressed in July and August as to whether the siege would not have to be raised, caused the greatest excitement and widespread satisfaction. General Gordon sent home the following graphic description of this final and at last successful attack:

I must now endeavour to give you my idea of our operations from the eventful 8th of September to the present 16th. We knew on the 7th that it was intended that the French should assault the Malakoff Tower at twelve the next day, and that we and another column of the French should attack the Redan and central bastion. The next day proved windy and dusty, and at ten o'clock began one of the most tremendous bombardments ever seen or heard. We had kept up a tolerable fire for the last four days, quite warm enough; but for two hours this tremendous fire extending six miles was maintained. At twelve the French rushed at the Malakoff, took it with ease, having caught the defenders in their bomb-proof houses, where they had gone to escape from the shells, etc. They found it difficult work to get round to the Little Redan, as the Russians had by that time got out of their holes.

However, the Malakoff was won, and the tricolour was hoisted as a signal for our attack. Our men went forward well, losing apparently few, put the ladders in the ditch, and mounted on the salient of the Redan, but though they stayed there five minutes or more, they did not advance, and tremendous reserves coming up drove them out. They retired well and without disorder, losing in all 150 officers, 2400 men killed and wounded. We should have carried everything before us if the men had only advanced. The French got driven back with great loss at the central bastion, losing four general officers. They did not enter the work. Thus, after a day of intense excitement, we had only gained the Malakoff. It was determined that night that the Highlanders should storm the Redan the next morning.

I was detailed for the trenches, but during the night I heard terrible explosions, and going down to the trenches at 4 a.m. I saw a splendid sight—the whole town in flames, and every now and then a terrific explosion. The rising sun shining on the scene of destruction produced a beautiful effect. The last of the Russians were leaving the town over the bridge. All the three-deckers, etc., were sunk, the steamers alone remaining. Tons and tons of powder must have been blown up.

About eight o'clock I got an order to commence a plan of the works, for which purpose I went to the Redan, where a dreadful sight was presented. The dead were buried in the ditch—the Russians with the English—Mr Wright reading the Service over them. About ten o'clock Fort Paul was blown up—a beautiful sight. The town was not safe to be entered on account of the fire and the few Russians who still prowled about. The latter cut off the hands and feet of one Frenchman. They also caught and took away a sapper who would go *trying* to plunder—for as to plunder there was and is literally nothing but rubbish and fleas, the Russians having carried off everything else. I have got the lock and sight off a gun (which used to try and deposit its contents very often in my carcass, in which I am grateful to say it failed) for my father, and some other rubbish (a Russian cup, etc.) for you and my sisters. But you would be surprised at the extraordinary rarity of knick-knacks. They left their pictures in the churches, which form consequently the only spoil, and which I do not care about buying. I will do my best to get some better things if it is possible. On the 10th we got down to the docks, and a flag of truce came over to ask permission to take away their wounded from the hospital, which we had only found out that day contained 3000 wounded men. These unfortunate men had been for a day and a half without attendance. A fourth of them were dead, and the rest were in a bad way. I will not dwell any more on it, but could not imagine a more dreadful sight.

We have now got into the town, the conflagration being out, and it seems quite strange to hear no firing. It has been a splendid city, and the harbour is magnificent. We have taken more than 4000 guns, destroyed their fleet, immense stores of provisions, ammunition, etc. (for from the explosions they did not appear to be short of it), and shall destroy the dockyard, forts, quays, barracks, storehouses, etc. For guns, Woolwich is a joke to it. The town is strewn with our shell and shot, etc. We have traced voltaic wires to nearly every powder magazine in the place. What plucky troops they were! When you hear the details of the siege you will be astonished. The length of the siege is nothing in comparison with our gain in having destroyed the place.

We are not certain what the Russians are doing on the north side, and as yet do not know whether we shall follow them up or not. We ought to, I think. It is glorious going over their horrid batteries which used to bully us so much. Their dodges were infinite. Most of their artillerymen, being sailors, were necessarily handy men, and had devised several ingenious modes of riveting, which they found very necessary. There was a vineyard under our attack, a sort of neutral ground where no one dared to venture, either Russian or English. We found lots of ripe grapes there. The Russians used to fire another description of grape into it. One night I was working with a party at this very spot, and out of 200 men we lost 30 killed and wounded. We are engaged in clearing the roads, burning the rubbish, and deodorizing the town, taking account of the guns, etc. Nothing is stirring; the Russians fire a little into the town. We hear they are retreating, but do not believe it. The French, it seems, took the Malakoff by surprise. They had learnt from a deserter that the Russians used to march one relief of men out of the place before the other came in on account of the heavy fire; whilst this was being done the French rushed in and found the Malakoff empty. The Russians made three attempts to retake it, the last led by a large body of officers alone. Whenever the Russians commenced a battery they laid down first a line of wires to the magazine with which they could blow it up at any time.

With this final tribute to the courage of the Russian garrison, Charles Gordon's account of the siege and fall of Sebastopol closes. He took part in the expedition to Kimburn, when General Spencer commanded a joint force of 9000 men intended to dislodge the Russians from a fort they had built at that place, and also to attack a corps of 10,000 men supposed to be stationed at the important town of Kherson. The fort surrendered after four hours' bombardment by the fleet—the garrison not being "the same style of soldiers as the Sebastopol men"—but the Kherson force was never encountered, retiring as the allies advanced, who in their turn retired for fear of being drawn too far into the country. In one of several letters while on this expedition Gordon says that the Czar Alexander the Second was near Kimburn during the attack, and that he sent the Governor a telegram, "Remember Holy Russia," which the Russian General did by getting drunk. The expedition was then withdrawn after installing a French garrison in the fort, and Charles Gordon returned to his old quarters before Sebastopol. A fortnight after his arrival he was appointed to take part in the destruction of the docks, which was to signalise the downfall of Russia's power in the Black Sea. This closing episode is very well described in several of his letters written during the month of December 1855:

I am now, as you see, stationed in the dockyard preparing the shafts and galleries for the demolition of the docks. The French will destroy one half and ourselves the other. The quantity of powder we shall use is 45,000 lbs., in charges varying from 80 lbs. to 8000 lbs. The French do not sink their shafts so deep as we do, but use heavier charges. The docks are very well made, and the gates alone cost £23,000. We are taking one gate to London, and the French another to Paris. Our shafts are some of them very deep, and in others there are from eight to ten feet of water. There is not much prospect of the Russians leaving the north side. We can see them hutting themselves. . . . Our works at the docks approach completion, and we hope to blow up some portion of them on Saturday. The French blew up one last Saturday. The explosion presented a splendid appearance and succeeded admirably, not a stone being left standing. The powder for our demolition will be upwards of twenty-two tons. The Russians still (27th December) hold the north forts, and do not appear to be likely to leave this year as their huts are all built. We can see them quite distinctly on the other side. . . .

January 20, 1856.—We have blown up part of our docks, and are very busy with the remainder, which we hope to get over by the end of the month. I do not anticipate any movement of the army until March, when I suppose we shall go to Asia to relieve Kars, and make the Russians retire from the Turkish territory. . . .

February 3, 1856.—We all of us have been extremely busy in loading and firing our mines in the docks, which required all our time, as we were so very short of officers, having only three, while the French had twelve. Our force of sappers was only 150 and the French had 600. We have now finished the demolition, which is satisfactory as far as the effects produced are concerned; but having used the voltaic battery instead of the old-fashioned hose, we have found that electricity will not succeed in large operations like this, and I do not think that anyone will use it if there is a possibility of using hose. I am now engaged in making plans of the docks, and have not much time to myself. The French have done their work very well, using more powder than we, and firing all their mines with hose. I will try and get you a photograph of the docks as they *were* and as they *are*, which will tell you more than a dozen letters would. We had an alarm down here the other night about twelve o'clock. The Russians on the north side opened a tremendous fire throughout the whole line on us and on the French. We were all out under arms, expecting an attack by boats, but after being well shelled for an hour, the Russians left off, and all was again silent; but for the time it lasted the fire was terrific. I heard afterwards that it was caused by a French navy captain, who pulled over to the other side of the harbour, and tried to burn a steamer which was lying on its side. He and his companions arrived unperceived, found the steamer quite new, and were getting into it, when the Russian sentinel challenged. They answered 'Russe,' but the sentry called 'To arms,' and the Russians fired into the boat, and then continued the fire from all their guns, I suppose expecting a grand attack. Only one man, however, was hurt by a splinter on the arm. The French will blow up Fort Nicholas on Monday. They only got their order the night before last, and are obliged to make a hasty demolition of it. They will use 105,000 lbs. of powder in the demolition. The Russians had ruined this fort, but had not had time to put in the powder; the excavations were complete. It certainly is a splendid fort, mounting 128 guns, and capitally finished for barracks. It would hold 6000 men. The Russians evidently intended this to be an exceptionally strong place, and they appear to have been making a quay all the way round the dockyard creek. We have seen a great deal of the French engineers; they are older men than ours, and seem well educated. The non-commissioned officers are much more intelligent than our men. With us, although our men are not stupid, the officers have to do a good deal of work which the French sapper non-commissioned officer does. They all understand line of least resistance, etc., and what they are about. The Russians do not molest us much now. We can hear them call out and sing, especially on Sundays. We can see them drill, which they do every day. They even have the coolness to go out and fish in the harbour. We never fire, neither do the French. I do not think they purpose leaving the north side; in fact, it would not be at all wise of them to do so. We had some French engineers to dine with us the other day; they were very agreeable, and we learnt a great deal from them about their mining. They used to hear the Russians mining within ten feet of them, and when they did this they used to put in their powder as quick as possible and blow in the Russian mines. The Russians had two systems or layers of mines, one about ten feet below the surface of the ground and the other about forty feet. The French only knew of the higher one, and they found out after the place was taken that their advanced trenches were quite mined and loaded in the lower tier. In the Bastion du Mât there were no less than thirty-six mines loaded and tamped. I saw one myself in the upper tier when I was surveying it. They (the Russians) worked out a strata of clay between two layers of rock, so that no wood was required to keep the earth from falling in.

Soon after these letters a truce was concluded with the Russians in anticipation of the peace which was ultimately signed at Paris in

March 1856. The prospects of peace were not altogether agreeable to the English army, which had been raised to an effective strength of more than 40,000 men, and was never in a better condition for war than at the end of the two years since it first landed in the Chersonese. Gordon's correspondence contains two or three remarks, giving characteristic evidence to the strength and extent of this sentiment. In one passage he says:

> We do not, generally speaking, like the thought of peace until after another campaign. I shall not go to England, but expect I shall remain abroad for three or four years, which *individually* I would sooner spend in war than peace. There is something indescribably exciting in the former.

Another comment to the same effect is the following:

> Suders, the Russian General, reviewed us and the French army last week. He must have thought our making peace odd.

Gordon did not obtain any honour or promotion for his Crimean services. He was included in Sir Harry Jones's list of Engineer Subalterns who had specially distinguished themselves during the siege. The French Government, more discerning than his own, awarded him the Legion of Honour.

The letters from the Crimea are specially interesting for the light they throw on General Gordon's character. They illustrate better than anything else he wrote during his career the soldierly side of his character. The true professional spirit of the man of war peers forth in every sentence, and his devotion to the details of his work was a good preparatory course for that great campaign in China where his engineering skill, not less than his military genius, was so conspicuously shown. As a subaltern in the Crimea Gordon showed himself zealous, daring, vigilant, and with that profound national feeling that an army of Englishmen was the finest fighting force in the world, combined with an inner conviction that of that army his kindred Highlanders were the most intrepid and leading cohort. This was a far more attractive and comprehensible personality than the other revealed in later days, of the Biblical pedant seeking to reconcile passing events with ancient Jewish prophecies, and to see in the most ordinary occurrences the workings of a resistless and unalterable fate. That was not the true Gordon, but rather the grafting of a new character on the original stem of Spartan simplicity and heroism. But to the very end of his career, to the last message from Khartoum, the old Gordon—the real

Gordon, the one who will never be forgotten—revealed himself just as he was in the trenches before Sebastopol.

Gordon's connection with the Russian War and the Eastern Question did not terminate with the Treaty of Paris. On 10th May he received orders to join Colonel Stanton, for the purpose of assisting in the delimitation of the new frontier in Bessarabia. He imagined that the work would take six months; it really took a year. A not unimportant principle was involved in this question, and an error in a map was nearly securing for the Russians a material advantage. At the Paris Congress it was determined to eloin the Russians from the Danube and its tributary lakes and streams. The Powers therefore stated that the Russian frontier should pass south of Bolgrad, judging from the small scale-map supplied by the Russians that Bolgrad was north of Lake Yalpukh, which opens into the river Danube. When the Boundary Commission came on the ground, they found that Bolgrad was on Lake Yalpukh, and that if the frontier passed to the south of it the Russians would have access to the Danube; and therefore, knowing the spirit of the Treaty, the English Commissioners referred the question to the Paris Congress. A sketch was prepared by Gordon and his colleagues, to show the diplomatists its exact position, and led to the frontier being laid down north of Bolgrad and Lake Yalpukh. Austria, as well as France, Turkey, and Russia, was represented on this Commission, and Gordon's comrade was Lieutenant, afterward General Sir Henry, James, who had served with him in the trenches, and who had one day lost his way and walked into the Russian lines, as Gordon himself had so nearly done.

Gordon's letters give an interesting account of his work, and bring out with his usual clearness all the points at issue; but it is unnecessary to follow very closely the events of the year he passed in the lower Danube region. How excellent his work must have been can be judged from the fact that the Government sent him back some years later to act as British Consul at Galatz. The delimitation work commenced with a personal inspection of the frontier from Katamori on the Pruth to Boma Sola on the Black Sea, a distance of 200 miles. Then the frontier was defined on the map, and finally it had to be marked on the ground with the usual posts and distinctive marks. Thirty-two separate plans had to be prepared before the frontier could be adjusted, and the frequent bickerings and quarrels gave rise to many surmises that the negotiations might be broken off and hostilities ensue. The main point of dispute as to Bolgrad threatened to form a *casus belli* with even a new arrangement of the Powers, as

France gave up the case, and thus encouraged Russia to prove more obdurate. But England and the other Powers stood firm, and Bolgrad was included in Moldavia.

The following extracts give a tolerably complete account of what was done. Writing from Kichenief on 9th January 1857, Gordon said:

We are now settled as to the frontier question. Russia has given up Bolgrad and received a portion of territory in exchange equal to that surrendered, both as to number of inhabitants and also as to extent of land. This mode of compensation will give us more than half our work to do over again. I had almost finished my plans, and one-half of these will have to be redrawn. However, it is a consolation to know that the thing is settled. We heard all this by telegraph from Paris, and by the same message learnt that we are to proceed at once to work on the frontier in order to get it finished by 30th March, and thus allow of the ceded territory being handed over to the Moldavians on that day. You may imagine what a hurry they are in to get this finished. The Russians pretend to believe that they have got the best of the dispute, but it will be difficult to persuade the world to be of the same opinion. Although so cold, there is not much snow, and it is beautifully clear weather, capital for sledging. The new frontier leaves Tobak and Bolgrad in Moldavia, and gives a piece of land near the Pruth in exchange to Russia. . . . The territory will be given over in two parts. The southern consists of Ismail, Kilia, Reni, and Bolgrad, as well as the delta of the Danube. The northern part consists of the land between the Pruth and Yalpukh. . . . We have finished our work, everything has been signed, and the total number of the plans we have made is upwards of 100. For my part, I have had enough of them for my whole life.

This wish was not to be gratified, for before Colonel Stanton's Commission was dissolved orders came for him to hand over his officers and men to Colonel—now Field-Marshal Sir Lintorn—Simmons, for the purpose of settling the boundary in Armenia, where a dispute had arisen about the course of the river Aras, the ancient Araxes. Gordon, who had now had two and a half years of foreign service without a break, did not relish this task, and even went to the expense of telegraphing for permission to exchange; but this effort was in vain, for the laconic reply of the Commander-in-Chief was: "Lieutenant Gordon must go." If Gordon had under-estimated the time required for the Bessarabian delimitation, he slightly over-estimated that for the Armenian, as his anticipated two years was diminished in the result to twenty-one months.

He left Constantinople on 1st May 1857 on board a Turkish steamer, *Kars*, bound for Trebizonde. The ship was overcrowded with dirty passengers, and the voyage was disagreeable, and might have been dangerous if the weather had not proved exceptionally favourable. On arriving at Trebizonde horses had to be engaged for the ten days' journey across the 180 miles of difficult country separating that port from Erzeroum, the Armenian capital. The total caravan of the English and French Commissioners—the latter being Colonel Pelissier, a relative of the Marshal—numbered ninety-nine horses; and the Turkish Commissioner, being unable to obtain any money from his Government, seized the horses necessary for his journey in a manner that first opened Gordon's eyes to the ways of Pashas. He stopped on the road every caravan he met, threw off their goods, put on his own, and impounded the animals for his journey. After a brief stay at Erzeroum—which Gordon describes as a very pretty place at a distance, but horribly dirty when entered, and where there are eight or nine months of very hard winter—the Commission passed on to Kars, which became its headquarters. The heroic defence of that fortress was then recent, and it is still of sufficient interest as a military episode to justify the quotation of the evidence Gordon, with his characteristic desire to be well informed, collected on the spot while the events themselves were fresh. For convenience' sake, his remarks on Kars and the whole campaign are strung together here, although they appeared in several letters:

Kars is, as you can easily imagine, a ruined city, and may perhaps never recover its former strength and importance. As far as the works of defence are concerned, they are excessively badly traced. A little pamphlet published by Kmety, a Hungarian, gives a graphic description of the siege. One thing difficult if not impossible to realise without seeing it, is the large extent of the position. Kars has been twice in the hands of the Russians during the last thirty years, Paskievitch having taken it by assault in 1829. We passed the battlefield at Kuyukdere, where the Russians in very small force under Bebutoff were attacked by a very superior force of Turks, under the direction of General Guyon, the Hungarian. By some mistake the Turkish left lost its way during the night, and was eight miles distant from the field when the right came into action. The battle was very hotly contested, but the Turks had at last to retire with the loss of several guns. Had the affair gone off as Guyon[1] intended, the Russians would have been licked. This battle, I should add, was fought in August 1854, before any English officer had arrived in this country. The Russian loss was very severe: there were 3,200 wounded alone brought into Gumri for treatment. The first day from Gumri we passed Baiandoor, where the Turks and Russians had a small battle in 1853, and where the former lost a splendid opportunity of taking Gumri, which was nearly denuded of troops. My Turkish colleague, Osman Bey (I believe this officer to be identical with Ghazi Osman, the defender of Plevna), was present, and got into Gumri as a spy, disguised in the character of a servant. The Russian army avenged the slight check they received from the Turks by taking all their artillery of the right wing.

As illustrating his professional zeal and powers of scientific examination, the following description of the fortress of Alexandropol or Gumri is a striking production from so young an officer:

The fortress of Alexandropol (40° 47' N. lat., 43° long. 45' E., 4500 feet above the sea) is situated on the left bank of the river Arpatchai, which here forms the boundary between Russia and Turkey. It is distant thirty-five miles from Kars and eighty-four miles from Tiflis. The plain on which it is situated is perfectly level and very peculiar. It has a stratum of alluvial soil for the depth of one foot six inches on the surface, and then a substratum of fine uniform lava, ten to fifteen feet thick, supposed to have issued from Mount Alagos (13,450 feet), an extinct volcano thirty miles from Alexandropol. The depth of the earth allows the growth of grain, but entirely prevents that of trees, which with their roots cannot penetrate into the lava. The Russians have taken advantage of this bed of lava in the ditch of the fortress. The fortress is well constructed and in perfect repair. There are upwards of 200 guns (varying from 36-pounders to 12-pounders) mounted on the works, and about 100 in reserve, of which 30 are field-guns with their equipment wagons, etc. The garrison would be 5000 to 6000, including artillery. There are large supplies of ammunition and military stores. The ditch, twelve feet deep, of the two western fronts has not been exca-

---

1. Guyon was an Englishman, but one of the National Commanders in the Hungarian Rebellion of 1848. I have given a brief account of his adventurous career at pp. 148-49 of *General Gordon's Letters from the Crimea*, etc.

vated near the flanks on account of the expense. The Russians have constructed in the centres of the two curtains a *caponnière* with two guns in each flank to defend the dead angles caused by the non-excavation of the whole of the ditch. In the centre of these two fronts is a large *caponnière*, mounting ten guns in the upper tier and eight in the lower tier. This *caponnière* is on a lower level than the enceinte of the place. The counterscarp at the north-west and south-west angles of these two fronts is for the distance of twenty yards composed of a crenellated wall four feet six inches thick. This was caused by the irregularity of the ground. The bomb-proof barracks of the northern fronts mount in casemate two tiers of fourteen guns at the curtains. The flanks have five guns in casemates open to the rear, in addition to the guns on the parapet above. The lunette in the ditch is eight feet deep. The eastern front has an escarp fourteen feet high cut in the lava, and well flanked by the *caponnière* defending the entrances, mounting four guns. The bomb-proof barracks in the northern fronts have one tier of eight guns in casemate at the curtains, and three guns in each flank in casemates open to the rear. The two outworks are closed at the gorge with a loopholed wall, flanked by a small guard-house. They have no ditches, but an escarp of ten feet in the lava. The tower marked *A* in my plan is sixty yards in diameter, with a well in the centre. It has its gorge closed with a ditch and loopholed wall. It mounts fifteen guns on the top, and fifteen guns in casemate. It is proposed to connect it by a crenellated wall with the main work. The tower marked *B* has a ditch and small glacis. It mounts eight guns in casemate, and eight on the top. Its object is to flank the long ravine which runs southward from it. All the buildings in the interior of the fortress are bomb-proof. The great fault of the fortress as it is constructed at present is that it does not so much as see the town with its population of 9310. It is now proposed, however, to make a large work on the site marked *K* with a view of meeting this want. During the war in 1853, when the Turks were 35,000 strong at Baiandoor, six miles from Alexandropol, and the Russians had only two battalions in the fortress, the latter demolished all the houses which were on this ground. I think that should it ever be in our power to besiege this place (which is not likely, from the enormous difficulty of getting a siege train there), that batteries might be established on the hillocks between the fortress and the river, to breach the large *caponnière* and the tower *A* which, from the formation of the ground, would not be opposed by more fire than the direct fire of the works they were intended to breach, and which would be limited by their circular form to about seven guns. The soil is not unfavourable on these hills. The hill on which the cemetery of the officers killed at Kars and Kuyukdere is situated is also favourable for batteries. The principal well, which is sunk to a good depth, is in the north-eastern bastion.

General Gordon's letters contain two or three interesting descriptions that, in view of more recent events, deserve quotation. Of the Kurds he thus speaks, and the description stands good at the present day:

We met on our road a great number of Kurds, who live as their fathers did, by travelling about, robbing, etc., with their flocks. Their children are short of clothing. In spite of the Cossacks, etc., they are as lawless as ever, and go from Turkey to Russia and back again as they like. They are fine-looking people, armed to the teeth, but are decreasing in numbers. They never live in houses, but prefer tents and caves. On the mountains we fell in with the tribes of Kurds, who live at this height during the summer months, quite isolated from the rest of mankind. I paid a visit to the chief of a tribe of 2000, and he passed a great number of compliments on the English. This Bey is all powerful with his tribe; he settles all disputes, divides the pasture land among the families, etc. Although living in such a deserted spot, they read the Turkish papers, and they asked several questions about the English war with Persia. They are very fanatical, and are much encouraged in their religious fervour by the Sultan's agents. Their houses consist of stone walls covered with camel's-hair tents, which are quite waterproof, and lined inside with capital carpets made by themselves. We encamped near them and obtained our milk, etc., from them; but, in order to let us know their habits, they stole the horse of the Russian officer's interpreter during the night. I should not mind trusting them at all, for the Bey would not allow them to take our horses; perhaps this was only from his hatred to the Russians.

He gives some particulars of the Lazes, to one of whose villages he paid a visit, and as he believed that he was the only Englishman who had ever done so, his remarks were based on special local knowledge:

On one side of it was Lazistan, and this part of Lazistan is peopled by the fiercest tribe of Lazes, who scarcely acknowledge even the Sultan. We had an escort of forty infantry, and were not molested. This tribe and the Kabouletians supply the Constantinople Turks with slaves, whom they kidnap from the Gourelians, who are on the Russian side. The Adjars (the tribe referred to) are most daring, and even proposed to us to bring any person we might choose out to Batoum for £40 to £120. In consequence of these kidnappings, etc., a deadly enmity exists between the two peoples, and whenever they get a chance they kill one another. During the last eighteen months sixty-two people have been kidnapped, sixteen killed, and twenty or thirty wounded on the part of the Gourelians. The Russian guards of the frontier are helpless against these people, for the latter are armed with a capital rifle and are also splendid shots, while the Cossacks have only a trumpery smooth bore. The country of the Adjars is very mountainous indeed, and quite impracticable except on foot, being covered with dense forests.

Of Ani, the ancient, once famous, and now deserted capital of Armenia, he gives the following picture:

We passed through Ani, the ancient capital of Armenia. This city is completely deserted, and has splendid churches still standing in it. These churches are capitally built and preserved. Some coloured drawings on their walls are to be seen even now. The towers and walls are almost intact, but the most extraordinary thing about so large a place is the singular quietness. There are many ruined cities in the neighbourhood, and all dating from about the eleventh century. At that period Ani itself contained 100,000 inhabitants and 500 churches, which shows that more people went to church among them than with us. Before the end of that century it passed into the hands of the Greeks and Saracens. Afterwards the Mongols took it, and at last an earthquake drove out the remaining inhabitants in 1339, since which time it has been perfectly deserted. The churches of Ani were built with lava, and crosses of black lava were let in very curiously into the red lava. With the exception of the churches and the king's palace, the city is level with the ground, the foundations of the houses being alone discernible. These churches were covered with Armenian inscriptions cut on the walls.

The delimitation work in itself was uninteresting, being carried on in barren and solitary regions where there was nothing but rock, without either grass or inhabitants. Gordon said he would not take thirty square miles for a gift, and yet the Turks and Russians clung to it, bringing witnesses from among the tribes who would swear whatever they were paid for. The question at issue was where the old frontier between the Persian province of Erivan and the Pashalik of Baizeth was fixed. The Persians ceded the province of Erivan to Russia in 1828, and both the Turks and Russians had their own, and necessarily conflicting, views as to where the frontier was. General Gordon's own belief that there had never been any real frontier at all was no doubt the right one. The English officers, without any assistance from their Turkish colleagues, who merely looked on when they were not keeping up the supply of witnesses, had to effect the best arrangement they could with the Russians. In the course of his survey of the frontier, which he said he examined almost foot by foot, Gordon came to Mount Ararat, which he very nearly ascended, as he tells the reader in the following graphic narrative:

When we arrived at the foot of Mount Ararat we were unable to proceed along the frontier any further because the ground becomes extremely broken by the innumerable streams of lava which have run down from it. The ground is black with cinders. They look as if quite recently emitted, and no one would imagine from their appearance that Ararat had been extinct so long. Our road went along the northern or Russian slope of Ararat, and passed through a very old city called Kourgai, where there are still the remains of a church and part of an old castle. Even the Armenians do not pretend to know its history, but some of them say that Noah lived there. It is situated half-way up the mountain, and there is no living person within twelve miles of it. There used to be a populous village named Aralik, with 5000 inhabitants, a little above it, but in 1840 an earthquake shook Mount Ararat, and in four minutes an immense avalanche had buried this place so completely as to leave scarcely any vestige of its site. Not a single person escaped, which is not to be wondered at, considering the mass that fell. Stones of twenty or thirty tons were carried as far as fifteen to twenty miles into the plain. It has left a tremendous cleft in Ararat itself. Other villages were destroyed at the same time, but none so completely as this. The village immediately below Aralik was also destroyed, but the graveyard remained untouched, and the tombstones stand up intact in the midst of the ruins. The common people say that it was saved on account of a saint who was buried there. All these places have a very lonely look. Both the Kurds and the Armenians, if they can possibly help it, never pass near Mount Ararat, while they think it a great sin to ascend it.

I must now tell you of my ascent, or rather my near ascent, of Great Ararat.

I and my interpreter and three sappers went up to a Kurdish encampment where an old Kurd lived who assisted five of our countrymen to ascend about two years ago. The only assistance, however, that he appeared able to give us was to show us where these Englishmen had encamped the night before their ascent. We consequently pitched our tents there, and settled ourselves for the night. The night proved to be very stormy, with thunder and rain, which was a bad lookout for us. However, we started at 4 a.m. the next morning, and had some very hard work up to the line of perpetual snow. My interpreter and two of the sappers gave it up before this, but I and the other, Corporal Fisher, held on.

The whole of this time there was a thick fog, which now and then cleared away, though only for brief moments, and enabled us to get a splendid view of the country spread out as a map beneath us, with cumuli clouds floating about. The snow which I mounted was at a very steep slope, and quite hard, nearly ice, on the surface. It was so steep that we could not sit down without holding on tightly to our poles. Corporal Fisher was about half a mile to my left, and had a better ascent as it was not quite so steep. About two o'clock I began to get very tired, not able to get up more than two yards without resting. This was caused by the rarefication of the air. The mist cleared just at this time for a minute, and I was enabled to see the summit about 1000 feet above me, but still a further very steep ascent. Little Ararat was also visible 3000 feet below me. It began to snow soon after this, and became intensely cold. The two together settled me, and I turned round, although very reluctantly, and sitting down, slid over in a very few minutes the distance which had taken me so many hours to clamber up. Corporal Fisher managed to get up to the top, and describes the crater to be very shallow, although the top is very large. The Kurd told me afterwards that the road I took was very difficult, and that the other English explorers went up a road which was comparatively easy. I believe, however, that if the weather had been more favourable I should have succeeded.

This was not his only mountaineering experience. Some weeks later he ascended Mount Alagos—that is, the Motley Mount, from its various colours. It is 13,480 feet above the sea, or about 3000 feet lower than Ararat.

We started with some Kurdish guides to the mountain, and after a good deal of delay got to the place where the only path to the summit commences. Here we were obliged to dismount and take to our legs. After about two hours and a half we got to the summit, and were extremely glad of it, for although it is not to be compared to Mount Ararat, it is still rather difficult. Trusting to my Ararat experience, I thought of descending in the snow, and started. I was much astonished at finding the slope far steeper than I expected, and consequently went down like a shot, and reached the bottom one hour and a half before the others. A Russian doctor tried it after me, and in trying to change his direction was turned round, and went to the bottom sometimes head foremost. He was not a bit hurt. There was no danger, as we had only to keep ourselves straight. My trousers are the only sufferers! I was the first up. None of the Russians succeeded!

With one more quotation, Gordon's description of Etchmiazin, the celebrated monastery where the Armenian Catholicos resides, the extracts from these early letters may be concluded:

We passed through the oldest of the Armenian churches and monasteries, a place called Etchmiazin. It professes to be 1500 years old, and certainly has the appearance of great antiquity; it was existing during the time of the ruined city of Ani, and is built in a similar style. The relics there are greatly esteemed. People make pilgrimages to this monastery from all parts. There is, firstly, an arm of St Gregory, which is enclosed in a gold case covered with precious stones; next the piece of the ark, which is necessarily of great antiquity; a piece of the cross and of the spear, and a finger-nail of St Peter complete the relics. All these are enveloped in gold cases, and richly ornamented with every sort of precious stones. The monastery owns ten villages and a great deal of land. The monks gave us a grand dinner, and their feeding certainly was not bad. The monks' council chamber was splendidly got up, all the ceiling being carved and gilded.

The concluding stages of the delimitation work were rapidly concluded, and before the end of September 1857 Colonel Simmons and his staff had returned to Constantinople. The illness of all the English officers except Gordon detained them some weeks in the Turkish capital, and he wrote home that his surveying duties had been superseded by those of sick nurse. But before the end of October he was back again in England, and met his father and the other members of his family after a still longer interval. While engaged on the frontier commission, his comrade in the trenches, Lieutenant William Christian Anderson, of his own Corps, had married one of his sisters, but, after a very short period of wedded happiness, he died suddenly. After his death a son was born who bore the same name, is now an officer in the Royal Artillery, and served on General Graham's staff at Souakim. Charles Gordon summed up his comrade's character in these words:

> I am extremely distressed to hear of poor Willie Anderson's death, and every one who knew him will be so. He was a sterling good comrade and officer, greatly liked by both officers and men, and our Corps has sustained a great loss in him. I am so very sorry for poor dear ———. It is such a sudden blow to her, and I am sure they must have been so happy together during their short married life.

Gordon, therefore, found a certain amount of gloom in the family circle during the Christmas of 1857, and as his desire to join the staff of the army was not immediately attainable, the orders he suddenly received in April 1858 to again proceed to the Caucasus, in consequence of a slight frontier dispute with Russia, were not altogether disagreeable to him as a return to that active work which he loved. For some reason, which was probably the wish to save a little money by economy in travelling, with the view of carrying out his generous plans towards others, he took his passage to Constantinople in a slow steamer from the Thames, touching at Havre. He described his fellow-passengers as not very select, but amusing, and the voyage as "a yachting excursion, time being apparently no object." He only remained ten days at Constantinople, and reached Redout Kaleh in the Caucasus on 3rd June, visiting Sebastopol on the way. He described it as still an utter ruin; "the grass had so overgrown the place where the camps stood that it was with difficulty I found my hut."

On 12th June Gordon joined his Russian colleague, Ogranovitch, at Ozurgeth; but the Turkish representative did not arrive for a month later, which interval Gordon employed in recording his impressions of Russian and Georgian society in the Caucasus:

I dined with the Governor-General, Prince Eristaw, who left the next day for Swaneti to overawe the subjects of the late Prince (he was shot at Kutais for stabbing Prince Gagarin, the predecessor of Prince Eristaw), who do not seem to have realised his death. The Prince takes two battalions of infantry and two guns nominally as an escort. There are some very pretty ladies at Kutais who dance their national dances capitally. They dance alone, and all the gentlemen beat time with their hands. I was surprised at seeing the ladies wear a sort of bracelet of black beads, to which they attached great value. I am sure they are nothing more than bog oak. . . . I have since discovered they are *cannel coal, not bog oak.* The ladies are very pretty, but have not very cleanly habits in general; they prefer their nails tipped, and do not hesitate at taking a bone and gnawing it. They live in extremely dirty houses, or rather huts. They are generally all princesses, and the men all princes, who, however, do not hesitate to accept small donations. I am always in fear and trembling lest they should give me anything, as it is necessary to give in return. I, unfortunately, happened to notice a certain glass letterweight with the Queen on it, and observed that it was like Her Majesty. I was given it on the spot, and with deep regret had to part with my soda-water machine the next day. I admire nothing now, you may be sure. The servants of Prince Dimitri Gouriel have made a good thing out of my visit, for each time they bring anything—butter, fruit, etc.—orders are given that an equivalent be given them in money. My hands get quite sticky with shaking hands with so many princes, but I have hitherto borne up like a martyr under my trials. On being invited to the house of a prince, you would figure yourself invited to a palace; but it is not the case here, and you would find it out to your cost if you did not take something to eat in your pockets.

The work of this Commission proved exceedingly fatiguing—Gordon breaking in characteristically with the statement: "I do not complain when there is no occasion"—and consisted chiefly in replacing the pyramids carefully removed by the population during the twelve months since they were erected. The successful result of this Commission was entirely due to Gordon's energy and untiring labour. His Russian and Turkish colleagues were always quarrelling, and Gordon had to play the part of peacemaker—for which, he said, "I am naturally not well adapted"—an admission that may be commended to those who think that Gordon was a meek and colourless individual, with more affinity to a Methodist parson than the dauntless and resolute soldier he really was.

Early in October the whole delimitation was concluded, and without a hitch, much to Gordon's satisfaction. By 17th November he had reached Constantinople on his way home, but notwithstanding the special hardships of his work and his long absence from England, with one brief interval, he was still anxious for work and action. In the closing letter of his correspondence he said:

> I do not feel at all inclined to settle in England and be employed in any sedentary way, and shall try and get employed here (Constantinople) if it is possible.

While these letters contain a very vivid account of the striking and remarkable events that occurred during the long military and diplomatic struggle with Russia, they are not less interesting or important for the many unconscious glimpses Gordon gives into his own character. In them may be found references to habits and things which show that the young officer was a sportsman, and by no means indifferent to creature comforts; and as the most careful search through all his later writings of every kind will bring no similar discovery, these acquire a special importance as showing that the original Gordon only differed from his comrades in being more earnest, more active, and more enthusiastic. I take at random such statements as "Our feeding is pretty good, but the drinking is not," "The Russians gave a spread (vulgar) on Saturday, noisily and badly got up. Their wine was simply execrable," and "How I wish I could get some partridge shooting! My bag up to the present (on the Danube) is 200—not bad! eh?" Then again, on a more delicate subject, there are numerous references to ladies, and to his appreciation of beauty. In a chaffing passage in one of his letters, he wrote that one of his sisters "wants me to bring home a Russian wife, I think; but I am sure you would not admire the Russian ladies I have seen." Again, the ladies of the Caucasus are pronounced "very pretty," and "the Gourelians are beautiful—in fact, I never saw so many handsome women as the peasants among them." At this time Gordon was certainly not a misogynist, but I am assured that the rumours as to his having met with an early disappointment in love are quite baseless of truth. From a very early period of his life, certainly before the Crimea, Gordon had made up his mind not to marry, and was in the habit of going even further, and wishing himself dead. This sentiment led him to constantly refer to himself as "the dead man"; and some years later he wrote, "There is a Miss —— here, the nicest girl I ever met; but don't be afraid, the dead do not marry." His own secret opinion seems to have been that marriage spoilt both men and women, and it will be at least admitted that if he had married he could never have lived the disinterested, heroic life which remains a marvel for the world.

CHAPTER 3

The China War

Gordon was back in England in good time for the Christmas festivities of 1858, and a few months later—1st April 1859—he was gazetted to the rank of Captain. About the same time he also received the appointment of Field-Work Instructor and Adjutant at Chatham, where his practical knowledge gained in the Sebastopol trenches was turned to good account in the theoretical training of future officers of his Corps. He was thus employed when the conflict in China, which had been in progress for some years, assumed a graver character in consequence of the Chinese refusal to ratify the Treaty of Tientsin and Admiral Hope's repulse in front of the Taku forts. Gordon at once volunteered for active service, and on 22nd July 1860 he sailed for the Far East. He did not reach Tientsin until the following 26th September, being, as he said in his first letter home, "rather late for the amusement, which won't vex mother." Not only had he missed the capture of the Taku forts, but also the one battle of the war, that fought at Chan-chia-wan on 9th September. He was, however, in time for the sack of the Summer Palace, which he describes in the following letter:

On the 11th October we were sent down in a great hurry to throw up works and batteries against the town, as the Chinese refused to give up the gate we required them to surrender before we would treat with them. They were also required to give up all the prisoners. You will be sorry to hear that the treatment they have suffered is very bad. Poor De Norman, who was with me in Asia, is one of the victims. It appears that they were tied so tight by the wrists that the flesh mortified, and they died in the greatest torture. Up to the time that elapsed before they arrived at the Summer Palace they were well treated, but then the ill-treatment began. The Emperor is supposed to have been there at the time.

To go back to the work—the Chinese were given until twelve on the 13th to give up the gate. We made a lot of batteries, and everything was ready for the assault of the wall, which is battlemented and 40 feet high, but of inferior masonry. At 11.30 p.m. the gate was opened, and we took possession; so our work was of no avail. The Chinese had then until the 23rd to think over our terms of peace, and to pay up £10,000 for each Englishman and £500 for each native soldier who died during their captivity. This they did, and the money was paid, and the Treaty signed yesterday. I could not witness it, as all officers commanding companies were obliged to remain in camp.

Owing to the ill-treatment the prisoners experienced at the Summer Palace, the General ordered it to be destroyed, and stuck up proclamations to say why it was so ordered. We accordingly went out, and, after pillaging it, burned the whole place, destroying in a Vandal-like manner most valuable property which would not be replaced for four millions. We got upwards of £48 a-piece prize money before we went out here; and although I have not as much as many, I have done well. Imagine D—— giving sixteen shillings for a string of pearls, which he sold the next day for £500!

The people are civil, but I think the grandees hate us, as they must after what we did to the Palace. You can scarcely imagine the beauty and magnificence of the places we burnt. It made one's heart sore to burn them; in fact, these palaces were so large, and we were so pressed for time, that we could not plunder them carefully. Quantities of gold ornaments were burnt, considered as brass. It was wretchedly demoralising work for an army. Everybody was wild for plunder.

You would scarcely conceive the magnificence of this residence, or the tremendous devastation the French have committed. The throne-room was lined with ebony, carved in a marvellous way. There were huge mirrors of all shapes and kinds, clocks, watches, musical boxes with puppets on them, magnificent china of every description, heaps and heaps of silks of all colours, embroidery, and as much splendour and civilization as you would see at Windsor; carved ivory screens, coral screens, large amounts of treasure, etc. The French have smashed everything in the most wanton way. It was a scene of utter destruction which passes my description.

It may be of interest to state here that Gordon bought the throne referred to. Its supports are the Imperial Dragon's claws, and the cushions are of yellow Imperial silk. He presented it long afterwards to the headquarters of his Corps at Chatham, where it now stands.

On the exchange of the Treaty ratifications, which took place within the walls of the Imperial capital, the force under Sir Hope Grant was withdrawn to Tientsin, and after a brief space from China. But pending the payment of the instalments of the war indemnity, a garrison of 3000 men, under General Staveley, was left at Tientsin, and Captain Gordon was attached to this force. He had a very busy time of it at first, for suitable quarters had to be provided for our troops, and Gordon was fully employed in the construction of barracks and stables. Among the other tasks that engaged his attention at the time was the management of a fund for the benefit of the Chinese poor, and he was much distressed by an unfortunate accident that attended its distribution.

We had collected about nine hundred dollars for the poor, and had asked the mandarins to issue tickets to the most deserving. This they would not do, so a certain day was fixed upon which to distribute the funds. There were about 3000 beggars, and in the crush seven women and one boy were killed. The poor women on their little feet, on which they are never very safe, were thrown down and trampled upon.

During the eighteen months that Gordon resided at Tientsin he took every opportunity of seeing the country, and as often as he could he rode from that town along the banks of the Peiho river to the Taku forts at its mouth. The distance is about forty miles each way, and he computed that he accomplished it not fewer than twenty times. He also visited Peking in August 1861, and remained several days on a visit to Sir Frederick Bruce at the British Legation. At that date rumours were already current that the Emperor Hienfung, who never returned to Peking after our occupation, but made Yehol his capital and place of residence, was dead. These were true, but some time elapsed before it was officially announced that the Emperor had died on the 22nd of that month, the very day that Gordon reached Peking himself, and wrote the following letter:

The Emperor is reported to be dead, and his coffin has been sent for; but this is no proof, since it is the custom to send for a man's coffin when he is seriously ill, and it is kept for him even if he lives fifty years after.

Writing again some time after, he says on the grave event:

A great operation relating to the funeral of Hienfung is going on: a marble block, weighing sixty tons, is being removed from the quarries to the west of Peking to the cemetery in the east. It is drawn along upon a huge truck by six hundred ponies, and proceeds at the rate of four miles per day. When it arrives it is to be set up and carved into the shape of an elephant; several other large stones are also *en route*.

But the most interesting expedition Gordon undertook from Tientsin was that to the Great Wall, and here I must borrow Dr Birkbeck Hill's graphic description, which is based on a long letter from Gordon himself:

In December 1861, accompanied by Lieutenant Cardew of the 67th Regiment, he made a tour on horseback to the outer Wall of China at Kalgan. A Chinese lad of the age of fourteen who knew a little English acted as their servant and interpreter, while their baggage was carried in two carts. In the course of their journey they passed through districts which had never before been visited by Europeans. Against the northern side of the city of Siuen-hoa (*not* Sinen-hoa, as printed in Dr Hill's book) they found that the sand had drifted with the wind till it had formed a sloping bank so high that it reached to the top of the walls, though they were nearly twenty feet high. Nature had followed in the steps of the generals of old, and had cast up a bank against the town. At Kalgan the Great Wall was with its parapet about 22 feet high and 16 feet broad. Both of its faces were built of bricks, each of which was three times the size of one of our bricks. The space between was filled in with rubble. 'It is wonderful,' writes Colonel Gordon, 'to see the long line of wall stretching over the hills as far as the eye can reach.' From Kalgan they travelled westwards to Taitong, where the wall was not so high. There they saw huge caravans of camels laden with 'brick tea' going towards Russia. Here they were forced to have the axle-trees of their carts widened, for they had come into a part of the country where the wheels were always set wider apart than in the province whence they came. Their carts therefore no longer filled the deep ruts which had been worn in the roads.

The chief object of their journey had been to ascertain whether there was in the inner wall any pass besides the Tchatiaou, which on that side of the country led from the Russian territory to Peking. They pushed along southwards, in vain trying for a long time to find a way eastward over the mountains. It was not till they reached Taiyuen that they struck into the road that led to Peking or Tientsin.

In this town, for the first time on their journey, they got into any kind of trouble. When their bill was brought them for their night's lodging they found that the charge was enormous. Seeing that a dispute would arise, they sent on their carts, and waited at the inn till they felt sure that they had got well on their way. They then, like the three Quakers with whom Charles Lamb travelled to Exeter, offered what they thought a reasonable sum. It was refused. They tried to mount their horses, but the people of the inn stopped them. Major Gordon took out his revolver, for show more than for use, for he allowed them to take it from him. He thereupon said, 'Let us go to the Mandarin!'

To this they agreed, and at the same time they gave him back his revolver. They all walked towards the Mandarin's house—the two Englishmen alongside their horses. On the way Major Gordon said to his companion, 'Are you ready to mount?' 'Yes,' he answered. So they mounted quietly, and went on with the people. When they reached the Mandarin's they turned horses, and scampered after their carts as fast as they could. The people yelled and rushed after them, but it was too late.

Some way beyond Taiyuen they came upon the pass over the mountains which led down into the country drained by the Peiho. The descent was a terrible one. All along the cold had been intense—so much so that raw eggs were frozen hard as if they had been boiled. To add to their troubles, when they were on in front their carts were attacked by robbers; but the Chinese lad—an ugly imp—kept them off with his gun. When they drew near Paoting-fu they sent on with the lad the two carts and their tired horses, which had now carried them for three weeks without the break of a single day, and they hired a fresh cart in which they thought to ride to Tientsin. But with the boy gone they had no interpreter, and in their impatience, 'their new driver'—to quote our traveller's own words—'got rather crossly dealt with.' They stopped near Paoting-fu for the night. Early next morning as they were washing they heard the gates of the inn open and the rumble of cartwheels. They guessed what was happening. 'Half stripped as I was, I rushed out and saw our cart bolting away. I ran for a mile after it, but had to come back and hire another with which we got to Tientsin—more than fourteen days over our leave.'

From this pleasant but uneventful occupation Gordon was summoned to a scene where important events were in progress, and upon which he was destined to play what was perhaps, after all, the most brilliant part in the long course of his remarkable career. His brother puts the change into a single sentence:

On the 28th of April 1862 Captain Gordon left the Peiho and arrived at Shanghai on 3rd of May, and at once dropped into the command of a district with the charge of the engineer part of an expedition about to start, with the intention of driving the rebels out of a circuit of thirty miles from Shanghai.

By the end of March 1862 the Chinese Government had sufficiently carried out its obligations to admit of the withdrawal of the force at Tientsin, and General Staveley transferred the troops and his quarters from that place to Shanghai, where the Taeping rebels were causing the European settlement grave anxiety, and what seemed imminent peril. The Taepings, of whose rebellion some account will be given in the next chapter, were impelled to menace Shanghai by their own necessities. They wanted arms, ammunition, and money, and the only means of obtaining them was by the capture of the great emporium of foreign trade. But such an adventure not merely implied a want of prudence and knowledge, it could only be attempted by a breach of their own promises. When Admiral Hope had sailed up the Yangtsekiang and visited Nanking, he demanded and received from Tien Wang, the Taeping king or leader, a promise that the Taeping forces should not advance within a radius of thirty miles of Shanghai. That promise in its larger extent had soon been broken, and an attack on Shanghai itself, although unsuccessful, crowned the offences of the rebels, and entailed the chastisement a more prudent course would have averted. Without entering into the details here that will be supplied later on, it will suffice to say that in January 1862 the Taepings advanced against Shanghai, burning all the villages *en route*, and laid irregular siege to it during more than six weeks. Although they suffered several reverses, the European garrison was not in sufficient strength to drive them away, and a general anxiety prevailed among the European community when the arrival of General Staveley altered the posture of affairs.

Before Gordon arrived two affairs of some importance had taken place. At Wongkadza, a village twelve miles west of Shanghai, General Staveley obtained a considerable success, which was, however, turned into a disaster by the disobedience of his orders. The Taepings had retired to some stronger stockades, and General Staveley had ordered the postponement of the attack until the next day, when the trained Chinese troops, carried away by their leaders' impetuosity, renewed the assault. The result was a rude repulse, with the loss of nearly 100 men killed and wounded. The next day the stockades were evacuated, and within another week the fortified villages of Tsipu and Kahding were also taken. It was at this point that Gordon arrived from Tientsin, and reached the scene of action just as the arrangements for attacking the important village of Tsingpu were being completed.

That the Taepings were not contemptible adversaries, at least those under their redoubtable leader Chung Wang, was shown by their attempting to destroy Shanghai by fire, even while these operations were in progress. The plot nearly succeeded, but its promoters were severely punished by the summary execution of 200 of their number. The force assembled for the attack on Tsingpu assumed almost the dimensions of an army. General Staveley commanded 1,429 British troops with twenty guns and mortars, in addition to a naval brigade of 380 men and five guns. There was also a French contingent of 800 men and ten guns, under Admiral Protet. At Tsingpu Gordon specially distinguished himself by the manner in which he reconnoitred the place, and then placed and led the ladder parties after two breaches had been pronounced practical. The Taepings fought well, but the place was carried, and the Chinese auxiliaries killed every one they found with arms in their hands. Commenting on Gordon's part in this affair, General Staveley wrote in his official despatch:

> Captain Gordon was of the greatest use to me when the task of clearing the rebels from out of the country within a radius of thirty miles from Shanghai had to be undertaken. He reconnoitred the enemy's defences, and arranged for the ladder parties to cross the moats, and for the escalading of the works; for we had to attack and carry by storm several towns fortified with high walls and deep wet ditches. He was, however, at the same time a source of much anxiety to me from the daring manner he approached the enemy's works to acquire information. Previous to our attack upon Tsingpu, and when with me in a boat reconnoitring the place, he begged to be allowed to

65

land in order better to see the nature of the defences; presently, to my dismay, I saw him gradually going nearer and nearer, by rushes from cover to cover, until he got behind a small outlying pagoda within 100 yards of the wall, and here he was quietly making a sketch and taking notes. I, in the meantime, was shouting myself hoarse in trying to get him back, for not only were the rebels firing at him from the walls, but I saw a party stealing round to cut him off.

A letter from Gordon gives an interesting account of the two subsequent affairs at Nanjao, where Admiral Protet was killed, and at Cholin, where the Taepings suffered a severe but, as it proved, not a decisive defeat.

On going through the village a Chang-mow (rebel leader) came out of a house rubbing his eyes, evidently having been taking a siesta; he was horrified, and bolted, but was soon caught, and the sailors had much difficulty in saving his life from the villagers, who flew upon and would have killed him. Poor man! he had such a nice costume when taken, but in five minutes afterwards you would scarcely have known him; all his finery, and even more, had been taken from him. The small force encamped and entrenched themselves 900 yards from Cholin, much to the surprise and anger of the garrison. They came down in force on the next morning with no end of banners. Upon the principle that inquiring minds should not be balked, they were allowed to come pretty close, but then the poor things received a check, and the beautiful silk banners were furled up and carried back to the town.

The next day General Staveley sent us word to come back, since he would attack Nanjao first, but as there were nearly 1000 villagers depending upon our protection and crowding round our camp, I was sent back with an armed party, and Captain Willes remained in front of the town. I went back by a different road and came on the General four miles from Nanjao. We marched on, and halted near the town, which was reconnoitred during the night, and the guns placed in position by 5 p.m. On the 17th we opened fire at seven, and attacked the place. Here Admiral Protet was killed; he was among 500 men, and was the only one struck. The town was a wretched affair, and a good many Chang-mows escaped. These Chang-mows are very funny people; they always run when attacked. They are ruthlessly cruel, and have a system of carrying off small boys under the hope of training them up as rebels. We always found swarms of these boys who had been taken from their parents (whom the rebels had killed) in the provinces.

I saved one small creature who had fallen into the ditch in trying to escape, for which he rewarded me by destroying my coat with his muddy paws in clinging to me. I started soon after the attack for Cholin, and got there on the 18th. The rebels had made a sortie since my departure, and had got into a pretty mess. Willes let them come up and then advanced on them; over sixty were killed, and several taken prisoners. The General then came. We got our guns in position during the night, opened fire next morning, and assaulted at seven. The place was miserable and poor. The Armstrong guns, which enfiladed one face, did great execution.

The fruits of these successes were lost by the signal overthrow and practical annihilation of a large Chinese army at Taitsan. One of General Staveley's detachments was cut off, and with his communications threatened he found himself compelled to abandon Kahding, and to retire towards Shanghai. Tsingpu had also to be abandoned, and the garrison suffered some loss in effecting its retreat. Of the first results of General Staveley's campaign there thus remained very little, and it was only in the autumn that these places were retaken, and the campaign against the Taepings in the Shanghai districts continued with varying fortune throughout the remainder of the year 1862 and the early months of 1863.

While these military events were in progress Major Gordon, who was raised to the rank of Major in the army in December 1862 for his services in China, had been trusted with the congenial task, and one for which he was pre-eminently well suited, of surveying and mapping the whole of the region for thirty miles. This work, necessary in itself for many reasons, proved of incalculable value to him in the operations which he eventually undertook and carried out to a successful issue against the rebels. His own letters show how thoroughly he fulfilled his instructions, and how his surveys ended in his complete mastery of the topography of the region between the Grand Canal, the sea, and the Yangtsekiang:

I have been now in every town and village in the thirty miles' radius. The country is the same everywhere—a dead flat, with innumerable creeks and bad pathways. The people have now settled down quiet again, and I do not anticipate the rebels will ever come back. They are rapidly on the decline, and two years ought to bring about the utter suppression of the revolt. I do not write about what we saw, as it amounts to nothing. There is nothing of any interest in China; if you have seen one village you have seen all the country. I have really an immensity to do. It will be a good thing if the Government support the propositions which are made to the Chinese.

The weather here is delightful—a fine cold, clear air which is quite invigorating after the summer heats. There is very good pheasant-shooting in the half-populated districts, and some quail at uncertain times. It is extraordinary to see the quantities of fishing cormorants there are in the creeks. These cormorants are in flocks of forty and fifty, and the owner in a small canoe travels about with them. They fish three or four times a day, and are encouraged by the shouts of their owners to dive. I have scarcely ever seen them come up without a fish in their beaks, which they swallow, but not for any distance, for there is a ring to prevent it going down altogether. They get such dreadful attacks of mumps, their throats being distended by the fish, which are alive, when the birds seem as if they were pouter pigeons. They are hoisted into the boats and then are very sea-sick. Would you consider the fish a dainty?

And again he writes about the Taepings, who were not in his eyes "a people nobly struggling to be free," but a horde of ruthless marauders.

We had a visit from the marauding Taepings the other day. They came close down in small parties to the settlement and burnt several houses, driving in thousands of inhabitants. We went against them and drove them away, but did not kill many. They beat us into fits in getting over the country, which is intersected in every way with ditches, swamps, etc. You can scarcely conceive the crowds of peasants who come into Shanghai when the rebels are in the neighbourhood—upwards of 15,000, I should think, and of every size and age—many strapping fellows who could easily defend themselves come running in with old women and children.

The people on the confines are suffering very greatly, and are in fact dying of starvation. It is most sad this state of affairs, and our Government really ought to put the rebellion down. Words could not depict the horrors these people suffer from the rebels, or describe the utter desert they have made of this rich province. It is all very well to talk of non-intervention, and I am not particularly sensitive, nor are our soldiers generally so, but certainly we are all impressed with the utter misery and wretchedness of these poor people. . . . In the midst of those terrible times the British and foreign merchants behaved nobly and gave great relief, while the Chinese merchants did not lag behind in acts of charity. The hardest heart would have been touched at the utter misery of these poor harmless people, for whatever may be said of their rulers, no one can deny but that the Chinese peasantry are the most obedient, quiet, and industrious people in the world.

The propositions referred to in the former of these two letters were that the services of Major Gordon should be lent to the Chinese Government for the suppression of the Taeping rebellion, that he should assume the command of an Anglo-Chinese legion of which the nucleus already existed, and that he might enlist the services of a certain number of our own officers. Considerable delay took place in the execution of this project, as it was necessary to send to Europe for the necessary authority; and another explanation was given subsequently to the effect that Gordon insisted on finishing his survey first. But Sir Charles Staveley, who nominated Major Gordon for the work, has effectually disposed of this latter statement by declaring that the former was the true and only cause. At length these propositions were sanctioned, and on 26th March 1863 Major Gordon proceeded to Sungkiang, a town west of Shanghai and south of Tsingpu, to take over the command of the Chinese force, which had already been named the Ever Victorious Army, and which in his hands justified its name.

Before closing this chapter it will be well to give some account of the origin of this force, and of the more important events that preceded Gordon's appointment to the command. As far back as April 1860 the Viceroy of the Two Kiang provinces had begged the English and French representatives to lend him military assistance in dealing with the rebels. The request was not complied with, but when some of the richest native merchants of Shanghai, with one Takee at their head, formed themselves into a patriotic association, and bound themselves to provide the funds required to raise a European-led force, no impediments were placed in their way. In July 1860 the services of two American adventurers who had had some military experience in Central America and elsewhere were enlisted and taken into the pay of this merchants' guild. Their names were Ward and Burgevine, and they were both adventurers of an unscrupulous and unattractive type. In addition to excellent pay, they were promised handsome money rewards for the capture of specified places, and what spoil there was to take should be theirs. Such a prospect was very inviting to the bold spirits of a great port like Shanghai, with its trading ships from every quarter of the world, and they succeeded in recruiting about 100 Europeans and 200 Manilla men or Spanish half-breeds.

In order to test the quality of this force it was decided to attack Sungkiang; and in July, only a week or so after it was organised, Ward led his somewhat motley band against that place. The result was unfavourable, as his attack was repulsed with some loss. Nothing daunted, Ward collected some more Manilla men and renewed the attack. He succeeded in capturing one of the gates, and in holding it until an Imperial army of 10,000 men arrived, when the town was carried by storm. Having thus proved its mettle, Ward's force became very popular, and it was increased by many fresh recruits, chiefly Greeks and Italians. It also was strengthened by the addition of some artillery, two six-pounder and later two eighteen-pounder guns.

The Chinese merchants then offered Ward and his quarter-master Burgevine a large reward for the capture of Tsingpu; and their legion, accompanied by a Chinese force of 10,000 men, who were, however, only to look on while it did the fighting, accordingly marched on that place. The attack made during the night of 2nd August resulted in a most disastrous repulse, most of the Europeans being either killed or wounded, Ward himself receiving a severe wound in the jaw. He renewed the attack with fresh men and two eighteen-pounders three weeks later; but after bombarding the place for seven days, he was attacked by the Taeping hero Chung Wang, and routed, with the loss of his guns and military stores. It was on this occasion that Chung Wang, following up his success, and doubly anxious to capture Shanghai because this new and unexpected force was organised there, attacked that town, and was only repulsed by the English and French troops who lined its walls.

This reverse at Tsingpu destroyed the reputation of Ward's force, and for several months he remained discredited and unemployed. In March 1861 he reappeared at Sungkiang, at the head of sixty or seventy Europeans whom he had recruited for the Imperial cause; but at that moment the policy of the foreign Consuls had undergone a change in favour of the Taepings, and Ward was arrested as a disturber of the peace. Perhaps a more serious offence was that the high pay he offered and prospect of loot had induced nearly thirty British sailors to desert their ships. He was released on his claiming that he was a Chinese subject, and also on his sending orders to his colleague Burgevine to return the troops they had enlisted. Burgevine thought he saw in this a chance of personal distinction, and before disbanding the men he made with them another attack on Tsingpu. This attack, like its two predecessors, was repulsed with heavy loss, and the original Ward force was thus finally discredited. It should be borne in mind, to distinguish it from what followed, that it was a mercenary force of European and Spanish half-breeds, without a single Chinese in it.

In September 1861 these two men altered their proceedings, and gave a new turn to the whole question. As it was impossible for them to recruit foreigners, they induced Takee and his associates to provide the funds for a native Chinese force, which they undertook to train and organise. In this task they made considerable progress, and with a view to making it popular with the Chinese, and also to give the men confidence, this new force was named, probably by Takee, the Chun Chen Chün or Ever Victorious Army. This proud title was given long before the claim to it was justified, but its subsequent appropriateness has buried in oblivion the slender claim it possessed to it on its inception.

By the end of January 1862 Ward had succeeded in training two regiments of 1000 men each, and with these he captured Quanfuling and 200 boats in the rear of the Taeping force, which attacked Shanghai for a third time in that month. When the English and French forces assumed the offensive before the arrival of Sir Charles Staveley, part of Ward's Corps accompanied them in the attack on Kachiaou. It led the attack, and behaved extremely well, thus giving rise to very favourable anticipations as to what a properly-trained Chinese army might do.

In a second action at Tseedong the force maintained the reputation it had gained. The Chinese fought with great bravery, and the difficulty, in fact, was in keeping them back. The English general reviewed them after this encounter, and declared himself much impressed with their appearance. Representations were made at Peking, and on 16th March 1862 an Imperial decree gave the first public recognition of the Ever Victorious Army.

Although reverses followed, the Corps maintained the reputation it had gained for steadiness and discipline. Under General Staveley at Wongkadza it acted well and lost heavily, and in all the subsequent movements of that officer it took a prominent part. When Tsingpu was captured, as already described, one of Ward's regiments was left in it as a garrison, but on the evacuation of that place in consequence of the return of Chung

Wang with fresh and more numerous forces, it narrowly escaped annihilation. It was then that the Taeping general named them in scornful irony, "Cha-Yang-Kweitser," or "Sham Foreign Devils," the point of the sarcasm being that these troops wore an European costume.

During the summer of 1862, when the heat rendered active operations impossible, everything was done to increase both the numbers and the efficiency of the Ever Victorious Army. By the month of July its strength had been raised to 5000 men, the commissioned officers being all Europeans except one Chinese, named Wongepoo, who had been given a commission for special gallantry by Admiral Hope. Ward was in chief command, and Colonel Forrester and Burgevine were his first and second lieutenants. When the weather became a little cooler in August, it was determined to utilise this force for the recapture of Tsingpu, which was taken at the second assault on the 9th of that month, although not without heavy loss in officers and men. Six weeks later the important Taeping position at Tseki, across the Hangchow Bay and not far distant from Ningpo, was attacked by Ward and a party of English blue-jackets. The operation was perfectly successful, but Ward was shot in the stomach and died the next day. His loss was a very considerable one, for, as Gordon said, "he managed both the force and the mandarins very ably." Colonel Forrester should have succeeded to the command, but he declined the post, which then devolved upon Burgevine.

After a brief space the services of Captain Holland of the Royal Marine Light Infantry were lent to Burgevine in the capacity of Chief of the staff, and as this was done at the suggestion of the Futai Li—since famous to Europeans as Li Hung Chang—it did not conduce to greater harmony between him and Burgevine, for their antagonism had already become marked. An occasion soon offered to fan this feeling to a flame. A Chinese army under Li and General Ching advanced to attack a Taeping position near Tsingpu, at the same time that Burgevine at the head of his corps assailed it from the other side. The brunt of the fighting fell on the latter, but when Li issued his bulletin he claimed all the credit of the victory, and totally ignored Burgevine and his men. Burgevine did not accept this rebuff meekly, and his peremptory manner offended the Chinese. The breach was widened by the distrust many of the Chinese merchants as well as officials felt as to his loyalty, and soon it was seen that the funds so freely supplied to Ward would not be forthcoming in his case.

Burgevine's character has been described in the following sentence by Gordon himself:

He was a man of large promises and few works. His popularity was great among a certain class. He was extravagant in his generosity, and as long as he had anything would divide it with his so-called friends, but never was a man of any administrative or military talent, and latterly, through the irritation caused by his unhealed wound and other causes, he was subject to violent paroxysms of anger, which rendered precarious the safety of any man who tendered to him advice that might be distasteful. He was extremely sensitive of his dignity.

The situation between the Chinese authorities and Burgevine soon became so strained that the former presented a formal complaint to General Staveley, and begged him to remove Burgevine. This, as the English commander pointed out, was for obvious reasons beyond his power, but he made representations to his Government, and suggested that an English officer should be lent to the Chinese, and he nominated Gordon as the best qualified for the work. Pending the arrival of the required authority, the Chinese, assisted by Burgevine's own impetuosity, brought their relations with him to a climax. The merchant Takee withheld the pay of the force; Burgevine was first ordered to proceed with his troops to Nanking, and then, on consenting, the order was withdrawn; some weeks later a fresh order to the same effect was issued, and Burgevine demanded the payment of all arrears before he would move, and thus Li's object of exposing Burgevine as a disobedient officer to the Government that employed him was attained.

The ever victorious army, excited by the absence of its pay, and worked upon by the exhortations of its chief, was on the point of mutiny, and Burgevine hastened to Shanghai to obtain by force rather than persuasion the arrears. On 4th January 1863 he saw Takee, a violent scene ensued, and Burgevine used violence. Not only did he strike Takee, but he carried off the treasure necessary to pay his men. Such conduct could not be upheld or excused. Li Hung Chang made the strongest complaint. Burgevine was dismissed the Chinese service, and General Staveley forwarded the notice to him with a quiet intimation that it would be well to give up his command without making a disturbance. Burgevine complied with this advice, handed over the command to Captain Holland, and came back to Shanghai on 6th of January. He published a defence of his conduct, and expressed his regret for having struck Takee.

Captain Holland was thus the third commander of the Ever Victorious Army, and a set of regulations was drawn up between Li Hung

Chang and General Staveley as to the conduct and control of the force. It was understood that Captain Holland's appointment was only temporary until the decision of the Government as to Gordon's nomination arrived, but this arrangement allowed of the corps again taking the field, for although it cost the Chinese £30,000 a month, it had done nothing during the last three months of the year 1862. Early in February 1863, therefore, Captain Holland, at the head of 2,300 men, including a strong force of artillery—600 men and twenty-two guns and mortars—was directed to attack Taitsan, an important place about fifty miles north-east of Shanghai. An Imperialist army of nearly 10,000 men acted in conjunction with it. The affair was badly managed and proved most disastrous.

After a short bombardment a breach was declared to be practicable, and the ladder and storming parties were ordered to the assault. Unfortunately, the reconnoitring of the Taeping position had been very carelessly done, and the attacking parties were checked by a wet ditch, twenty feet wide and six feet deep, of which nothing had been seen. Situated only forty yards from the wall of the town, and without any means of crossing it, although some few did by throwing across a ladder, the storming party stood exposed to a terrific fire. Captain Holland ordered a retreat, but it was not managed any better than the attack. The light guns were removed too quickly, and the heavy ones were stuck so fast in the mud that they could not be removed at all. The Taepings attacked in their turn, and the greatest confusion prevailed, during which the survivors of the larger half of the Ever Victorious Army escaped in small detachments back to Sungkiang. Twenty European officers were killed or wounded, besides 300 Chinese privates. Captain Holland exposed himself freely, but this, his only action in independent command, resulted in complete and unqualified failure. Gordon himself summed up the causes of this serious and discouraging reverse:

> The causes of the failure were the too cheap rate at which the rebels were held. The force had hitherto fought with the allies with them (except at Tsingpu). They now had to bear the brunt of the fighting themselves, the mistake of not having provided bridges in spite of the mandarin's information, and the too close proximity of the heavy guns to the walls, and the want of cover they had, and finally the withdrawal of the lighter guns before the heavy guns, whose removal they should have covered. There is little doubt that the rebels had been warned

by persons in Shanghai of the intended attack, and that several foreigners, who had been dismissed by Captain Holland, were with the rebels defending the breach. As may be imagined, Burgevine's removal had caused considerable feeling among his acquaintances, who were not sorry to see the first expedition of the force under an English officer fail, being in hopes that the command would again revert to Burgevine.

This reverse occurred on 13th February, and no further steps of any consequence were taken until the appointment of Major Gordon, which at last was sanctioned in the latter portion of March, about a week before ill-health compelled General Staveley to resign his command in China. That officer was connected with the Gordon family, his sister, a most amiable and sympathetic lady, being Lady Gordon, widow of the late Sir Henry Gordon. As far back as May 1861—that is, prior to most of the events described in this chapter—Gordon's sensitiveness about his family connection with the commanding officer in China had impelled him to write this letter:

I was much put out in Henry's writing, and I think hinting he could do something for me, and I went to Staveley and told him so. It is the bother of one's life to be trying after the honours of the profession, and it has grown in late years into a regular trade—everyone uses private interest.

When Gordon gave this early manifestation of his independent spirit he was little more than twenty-eight years of age, but it should certainly be noted as showing that in one respect he was very little changed in his later years from what he was in his youth.

After these reverses in February nothing more was attempted until Major Gordon arrived at Sungkiang on 25th March 1863 to take over the command of the force. It is to be hoped that the last few pages have made clear what that force was like. In the first place, it had been one composed entirely of Europeans, a band somewhat resembling those that have set up and cast down the mushroom republics that separate the conquests of Pizarro from those of Cortes. That force achieved nothing and had an ignominious end. It was succeeded by the larger force of drilled Chinese, to which was given the name of the Ever Victorious Army. Although these Chinese showed far more courage than might have been expected of them, none of their leaders—Ward, Burgevine, or Holland—seemed able to turn their good qualities to any profitable purpose. They were as often defeated as successful, and at the very moment of Gordon's assuming the command the defeat of Captain Holland at Taitsan, and a subsidiary reverse of Major Tapp at Fushan, had reduced their morale to the lowest point, and even justified a belief that for military purposes this force was nearly, if not quite, worthless.

CHAPTER 4

The Taeping Rebellion

In order to bring before the reader the magnitude of Gordon's achievements in China it is necessary to describe briefly the course of the Taeping rebellion, and to show the kind of opponents over whom he was destined to obtain so glorious and decisive a victory. But as this would be to tell a thrice-told tale, I content myself with giving in an abridged form the account I prepared from the papers of General Gordon and other trustworthy sources, which appears in the last volume of my *History of China*.

As far back as the year 1830 there had been symptoms of disturbed popular feeling in Kwangsi, the most southern province of China adjacent to Tonquin. The difficulty of operating in a region which possessed few roads, and which was only rendered at all accessible by the West River or Sikiang, had led the Chinese authorities, much engaged as they were about the foreign question, to postpone those vigorous measures, which, if taken at the outset, might have speedily restored peace and stamped out the first promptings of revolt. The authorities were more concerned at the proceedings of the formidable secret Association, known as the "Triads," than at the occurrences in Kwangsi, probably because the Triads made no secret that their object was the expulsion of the Manchus and the restoration of the old Ming dynasty. The true origin of the Triads is not to be assigned, but there seems reasonable ground for the suspicion that they were connected with the discontented monks of a Buddhist monastery which had been suppressed by the Government. Between them they seem to have formed the inception of what became the famous Taeping rebellion.

The summer of 1850 witnessed a great accession of energy on the part of the rebels in Kwangsi, which may perhaps have been due to the death of the Emperor Taoukwang. The important town of Wuchow on the Sikiang, close to the western border of Kwantung, was besieged by a force reported to number 50,000 men. The governor was afraid to report the occurrence, knowing that it would carry his own condemnation and probable disgrace; and it was left for a minor official to reveal the extent to which the insurgents had carried their depredations. Two leaders named Chang assumed the style of royalty; other bands appeared in the province of Hoonan as well as in the southern parts of Kwantung, but they all collected by degrees on the Sikiang, where they placed an embargo on merchandise, and gradually crushed out such trade as there had been by that river. Their proceedings were not restricted to the fair operations of war. They plundered and massacred wherever they went. They claimed to act in the name of the Chinese people; yet they slew all they could lay hands upon, without discrimination of age or sex.

The confidence of the insurgents was raised by frequent success, and by the manifest inability of the Canton Viceroy to take any effectual military measures against them. Two hundred imperial troops were decoyed into a defile, and slaughtered by an overwhelming force in ambush. This reverse naturally caused considerable alarm in Canton itself, and defensive measures were taken. Governor Yeh was sent against them with 2000 men, and he succeeded in compelling, or as some say in inducing, them to retreat. Any satisfaction this success may have occasioned was soon dispelled, for at Lienchow, near the small port of Pakhoi, the rebels not merely gained a victory, but were joined by the troops sent to attack them. But these successes at several different points were of far less significance than the nomination of a single chief with the royal title of Tien Wang, or the Heavenly King.

The man on whom their choice fell was named Hung-tsiuen. He was the son of a small farmer, who lived in a village near the North River, about thirty miles from Canton. If he was not a Hakka himself, he lived in a district which was considered to belong exclusively to that strange race, which closely resembles our gipsies. He belonged to a degraded race, therefore, and it was held that he was not entitled to that free entry into the body of the civil service, which is the natural privilege of every true-born Chinese subject. His friends declared that he came out high at each of the periodical examinations, but their statements may have been false in this as in much else. The fact is clear that he failed to obtain his degrees, and that he was denied admission into the public service. Hung was therefore a disappointed candidate, the more deeply disappointed, perhaps, that his sense of injured merit and the ill-judging flattery of his admirers made his rejection appear unjust.

Hung was, at all events, a shrewd observer of the weakness of the Government, and of the popular discontent. He perceived the opportunity of making the Manchu dynasty the scapegoat of national weakness and apathy. He could not be the servant of the Government. Class contempt, the prejudices of his examiners, or it may even have been his own haughty presumption and self-sufficiency, effectually debarred him from the enjoyment of the wealth and privileges that fall to the lot of those in executive power in all countries, but in Asiatic above every other. To his revengeful but astute mind it was clear that if he could not be an official he might be the enemy of the Government and its possible subverter.

The details of his early career have been mainly recorded by those who sympathised with the supposed objects of his operations; and while they have been very anxious to discover his virtues, they were always blind to his failings. The steps of his imposture have therefore been described with an amount of implicit belief which reflected little credit on the judgment of those who were anxious to give their sanction to the miracles which preceded the appearance of this adventurer in the field. Absurd stories as to his dreams, allegorical coincidences showing how he was summoned by a just and all-powerful God to the supreme seat of power, were repeated with a degree of faith so emphatic in its mode of expression as to make the challenge of its sincerity appear extremely harsh. Hung, the defeated official candidate, the long-deaf listener to the entreaties of Christian missionaries, was thus in a brief time metamorphosed into Heaven's elect for the Dragon Throne, into the iconoclastic propagator of the worship of a single God, and the destroyer of the mass of idolatry stored in the hearts and venerated in the temples of the Chinese people for countless ages. Whether Hung was merely an intriguer or a fanatic, he could not help feeling some gratitude to those who so conveniently echoed his pretensions to the Throne at the same time that they pleaded extenuating circumstances for acts of cruelty and brigandage often unsurpassed in their infamy.

If he found the foreigners thus willing to accept him at his own estimate, it would have been very strange if he had not experienced still greater success in imposing upon the credulity of his own countrymen. To declare that he had dreamt dreams which showed that he was selected by a heavenly mandate for Royal honours was sufficient to gain a small body of adherents, provided only that he was prepared to accept the certain punishment of detection and failure. If Hung's audacity was shown by nothing else, it was demonstrated by the lengths to which he carried the supernatural agency that urged him to quit the ignominious life of a Kwantung peasant for the career of a pretender to Imperial honours. The course of training to which he subjected himself, the ascetic deprivations, the loud prayers and invocations, the supernatural counsels and meetings, was that adopted by every other religious devotee or fanatic as the proper novitiate for those honours based on the superstitious reverence of mankind, which are sometimes no inadequate substitute for temporal power and influence, even when they fail to pave the way to their attainment.

Yet when Hung proceeded to Kwangsi there was no room left to hope that the seditious movement would dissolve of its own accord, for the extent and character of his pretensions at once invested the rising with all the importance of open and unveiled rebellion. After the proclamation of Hung as Tien Wang, the success of the Kwangsi rebels increased. The whole of the country south of the Sikiang, with the strong military station of Nanning, fell into their hands, and they prepared in the early part of the year 1851 to attack the provincial capital Kweiling, which commanded one of the principal high roads into the interior of China. So urgent did the peril at this place appear that three Imperial Commissioners were sent there direct by land from Peking, and the significance of their appointment was increased by the fact that they were all Manchus. They were instructed to raise troops *en route*, and to reach Kweiling as soon as possible. Their movements were so dilatory that that place would have fallen if it had not been for the courage and military capacity shown by Wurantai, leader of the Canton Bannermen. This soldier fully realised the perils of the situation. In a memorial to the Throne he spoke plainly:

"The outer barbarians (Europeans) say that of literature China has more than enough, of the art of war not sufficient. The whole country swarms with the rebels. Our funds are nearly at an end, and our troops few; our officers disagree, and the power is not concentrated. The commander of the forces wants to extinguish a burning wagon-load of fagots with a cupful of water. I fear we shall hereafter have some serious affair—that the great body will rise against us, and our own people leave us."

The growth of the rebellion proved steady if slow. Although 30,000 troops were stated to be concentrated opposite the Taeping positions, fear or inexperience prevented action, and the numbers and courage of the Imperialists melted away. Had the Chinese authorities only pressed on, they must, by sheer weight, have swept the rebels into Tonquin, and there would thus have been an end of Tien Wang and his aspirations. They lacked the nerve, and their vacillation gave confidence and reputation to an enemy that need never have been allowed to become formidable.

While the Imperial authorities had been either discouraged or at the least lethargic, the pretender Tien Wang had been busily engaged in establishing his authority on a sound basis, and in assigning their respective ranks to his principal followers who saw in the conferring of titles and posts, at the moment of little meaning or value, the recognition of their past zeal and the promise of reward for future service. The men who rallied round Tien Wang were schoolmasters and labourers. To these some brigands of the mountain frontier supplied rude military knowledge, while the leaders of the Triads brought as their share towards the realisation of what they represented as a great cause skill in intrigue, and some knowledge of organisation. Neither enthusiasm nor the energy of desperation was wanting; but for those qualities which claim respect, if they cannot command success, we must look in vain. Yet the peasants of Kwangsi and the artisans of Kwantung assumed the title of "Wang" or prince, and divided in anticipation the prizes that should follow the establishment of some dynasty of their own making.

The war dragged on in the Sikiang valley during two years, but the tide of success had certainly set in the main against the Imperialists, as was shown by the scene of operations being transferred to the northern side of that river. The campaign might have continued indefinitely until one side or the other was exhausted had not the state of the province warned Tien Wang that he could not hope to feed much longer the numerous followers who had attached themselves to his cause. He saw that there would very soon remain for him no choice except to retire into Tonquin, and to settle down into the ignominious life of a border brigand. To Tien Wang the thought was intolerable, and in sheer desperation he came to the resolve to march northwards into the interior of China. It was not the inspiration of genius but the pressure of dire need that urged the Taeping leader to issue his orders for the invasion of Hoonan. He issued a proclamation on the eve of beginning this march, announcing that he had received "the divine commission to exterminate the Manchus and to possess the Empire as its true sovereign."

It was at this stage in the rebellion that the name "Taepings" came into general use, and various accounts are given as to its origin. Some say it was taken from the small town of that name in the south-west of Kwangsi, where the insurrection began; others that the characters mean "Universal Peace," and that it was the style assumed by the new dynasty. In seeming contradiction with this is the fact that some of the Taepings themselves declared that they never heard the name, and did not know what it meant. At this particular juncture the rebels were in the heart of Kwangsi, at the district capital of Woosuen. In May 1851 they moved to Siang, a little north of that place. They ravaged the country, making no long stay anywhere. In August they were at Yungan, where 16,000 men were ranged under the banner of the Heavenly King, and for a moment Tien Wang may have thought of making a dash on Canton. Respect for Wurantai's military capacity induced him to forego the adventure, and at Yungan, where he remained until April 1852, the Taeping leader made his final arrangements for his march northwards.

At Yungan a circumstance occurred which first promised to strengthen the Taepings, and then to lead to their disruption. Tien Wang was joined there by five influential chiefs and many members of the Triad Society. For a time it seemed as if these allies would necessarily bring with them a great accession of popular strength; but whether they disapproved of Tien Wang's plans, or were offended by the arrogant bearing of the Wangs, who, but the other day little better than the dregs of the people, had suddenly assumed the yellow dress and insignia of Chinese royalty, the Triad leaders took a secret and hurried departure from his camp, and hastened to make their peace with the Imperialists. The principal of these members of the most formidable secret society in China—Chang Kwoliang by name—was given a military command of some importance, and afterwards distinguished himself among the Imperial commanders. In April 1852 the Taeping army left its quarters at Yungan and marched direct on Kweiling, the principal city of the province, where the Imperial commissioners sent from Peking had long remained inactive. Tien Wang attacked them at the end of April or the beginning of May, but he was repulsed with some loss. Afraid of breaking his force against the walls of so strong a place, he abandoned the attack and marched into Hoonan. Had the Imperial generals only been as energetic in offensive measures as they had shown themselves obstinate in defence, they might have harassed his rear, delayed his progress, and eventually brought him to a decisive engagement under many disadvantages. But the Imperial Commissioners at Kweiling did nothing, being apparently well satisfied with having rid themselves of the presence of such troublesome neighbours.

On 12th of June the Taepings attacked the small town of Taou in Hoonan with better success. Some resistance was offered, and one of the Taeping Wangs, known as the "Southern King," was killed. This was a great loss, because he was a man of some education, and had taken the most prominent part in the organisation of the Taeping rebellion. General Gordon inclined to the opinion that he was the real originator of the whole rising. His loss was a severe blow to the Taepings, whose confidence in themselves and their cause was alike rudely shaken. They could not however turn back, for fear of the force at Kweiling, and to halt for any time was scarcely less dangerous. Necessity compelled them therefore to press on, and in August they captured the three small towns of Kiaho, Ching, and Kweyang. Their next march was both long and forced. Overrunning the whole adjacent country, they appeared early in the month of September before the strong and important town of Changsha, situated on the river Seang, and only fifty miles south of the large lake Tungting.

At this town, the capital of Hoonan, some vigorous preparations had been made to withstand them. Not merely was the usual garrison stationed there, but it so happened that Tseng Kwofan, a man of great ability and some considerable resolution, was residing near the town at the time. Tseng Kwofan had held several offices in the service, and as a member of the Hanlin enjoyed a high position and reputation; but he was absent from the capital on one of those frequent periods of retirement to their native province which the officials of China have to make on the occasion of any near relative's death.

When tidings of the approach of the Taepings reached him he threw himself with all the forces he could collect into Changsha. At the same time he ordered the local militia to assemble as rapidly as possible in the neighbourhood, in order to harass the movements of the enemy. He called upon all those who had the means to show their duty to the state and sovereign by raising recruits or by promising rewards to those volunteers who would serve in the army against the rebels. Had the example of Tseng Kwofan been followed generally, it is not too much to say that the Taepings would never have got to Nanking. As it was, he set the first example of true patriotism, and he had the immediate satisfaction of saving Changsha.

When the Taepings reached Changsha they found the gates closed and the walls manned. They proceeded to lay siege to it; they cut off its supplies, and they threatened the garrison with extermination. They even attempted to carry it by storm on three separate occasions. During eighty days the siege went on; but the Taepings were then compelled to admit that they were as far from success as ever. They had suffered very considerable losses, including another of their Wangs, the Western King, and although it was said that the loss of the

Imperialists was larger, they could better afford it. On the 1st December they accordingly abandoned the siege and resumed their march northwards. They crossed the Tungting Lake on boats and junks which they had seized, and secured the town of Yochow on the Yangtsekiang without meeting any resistance. Here they captured much war material, including a large supply of gunpowder left by the great Chinese Viceroy, Wou Sankwei, of the seventeenth century. From Yochow they hastened down the river. The important city of Hankow surrendered without a blow. The not less important town of Wouchang, on the opposite or southern bank of the river, was then attacked, and after a siege of a fortnight carried by storm. The third town of Hanyang, which completes the busy human hive where the Han joins the great river, did not attempt any resistance.

These successes raised the Taepings from the depths of despair to the heights of hope. The capture of such wealthy places dispelled all their doubt and discouragement. They were able to repay themselves for the losses and hardships they had undergone, and the prize they had thus secured furnished ground for hoping for more. But even now it was no part of their mission to stand still. They waited at Hankow only long enough to attach to their cause the many thousands attracted to Tien Wang's flag by these successes. The possibility of pursuit by Tseng Kwofan at the head of the warlike levies of Hoonan, where each brave is considered equal to two from another province, was still present to their minds. But he unfortunately rested content with his laurels, while the Taepings swept like an irresistible wave or torrent down the valley of the Yangtsekiang.

The capture of Kiukiang, a town situated on the river near the northern extremity of the lake Poyang, and of Ganking followed in quick succession, and on 8th March the Taepings sat down before Nanking, the old capital of the Mings. The siege lasted only sixteen days. Notwithstanding that there was a considerable Manchu force in the Tartar city, which might easily have been defended apart from the Chinese and much larger town, the resistance offered was singularly faint-hearted. The Taepings succeeded in blowing in one of the gates. The townspeople fraternised with the assailants, and the very Manchus, who had looked so valiant in face of Sir Hugh Gough's force ten years before, now surrendered their lives and their honour after a mere show of resistance to a force which was nothing better than an armed rabble. The Manchu colony of Nanking, to the number of some 4000 families, had evidently fallen off from its high renown. Instead of dying at their posts, they threw themselves on the pity of the Taeping leader. Their cowardice helped them not; of 20,000 Manchus not 100 escaped. The tale rests on irrefragable evidence. "We killed them all to the infant in arms; we left not a root to sprout from; and the bodies of the slain we cast into the Yangtse."

The capture of Nanking and this sweeping massacre of the dominant race seemed to point the inevitable finger of fate at the Tatsing dynasty. It was no longer possible to regard Tien Wang and his miscellaneous gathering as an enemy beneath contempt. Without achieving any remarkable success, having indeed been defeated whenever they were opposed with the least resolution, the Taepings found themselves in possession of the second city in the Empire. With that city they acquired the control of the navigation of the Great River, and they cut off the better part of the communications between the northern and southern halves of the Empire. They abandoned Hankow, and confined their occupation of the river banks to the part between Kiukiang and Nanking; but they determined to secure the Grand Canal, which enters the river east of the city. On 1st April 1853 they occupied Chinkiangfoo, on the southern side of the river, and they held it, but although they also captured Yangchow on the northern bank, they evacuated it in a few days. These successes were obtained without any loss, as all the garrisons fled at the mere approach of the dreaded Taepings.

The Imperialist authorities seemed paralysed by the rapidity and success of the rebels, who devoted all their efforts to strengthening the defences of Nanking and to provisioning it in view of all eventualities. But the thoughts of Tien Wang and his immediate advisers were still of offensive and forward measures, and when Nanking was equipped for defence a large part of the Taeping army was ordered to march against Peking. At this time it was computed that the total number of the Taepings did not fall short of 80,000 trustworthy fighting men, while there were perhaps more than 100,000 Chinese pressed into their service as hewers of wood and drawers of water. The lines of Nanking and the batteries along the Yangtsekiang were the creation of the forced labour of the population which had not fled before the Taepings.

On the 12th of May an army, stated to consist of 200,000 men, but probably consisting of less than half that number of combatants, crossed the Yangtse and marched northwards. It would be uninteresting to name the many small places they captured on their way, but on 19th June they reached Kaifong, the capital of Honan, and once of China itself. They had thus transferred in a few weeks their advanced posts from the Yangtsekiang to the Hwangho, or Yellow River.

The garrison of Kaifong made a resolute defence, and repulsed the

Taepings, who at once abandoned the siege in accordance with their usual custom, and resumed their march. They succeeded in crossing the Yellow River under the eyes of the Kaifong garrison, and they then attacked Hwaiking, an important prefectural town, where they encountered a stout resistance. They besieged it for two months, and then had to give up the attempt. Forces were gathering from different directions, and it became necessary to baffle their opponents. They marched westwards for some distance along the southern bank of the Hwangho, turned suddenly north at Yuenking, and on reaching Pingyang they again turned in an easterly direction, and secured the Lin Limming Pass which leads into the Metropolitan province of Pechihli. The whole of the autumn of 1853 was taken up with these manoeuvres, and it was on 30th September that the Taepings first appeared in the province containing the capital. They met with little or no opposition. They had mystified their pursuers, and surprised the inhabitants of the districts through which they passed. Having forced the Limming Pass, the Taepings found no difficulty in occupying the towns on the southwest border of Pechihli. The defeat of the Manchu garrison in a pass that was considered almost impregnable gave the Taepings the prestige of victory, and the towns opened their gates one after another. They crossed the Hootoo River on a bridge of boats which they constructed themselves, and then occupied the town of Shinchow; on 21st October they reached Tsing, about twenty miles south of Tientsin and only one hundred from Peking; but beyond this point neither then nor at any other time did the rebels succeed in getting.

The forcing of the Limming Pass produced great confusion at Peking. It was no longer a question of suffering subjects and disturbed provinces. The capital of the Empire, the very person of the Emperor, was in imminent danger of destruction at the hands of a ruthless foe. The city was denuded of troops. Levies were hastily summoned from Manchuria in order to defend the line of the Peiho and the approaches to the capital. Had the Taepings shown better generalship there is no saying but that they would have succeeded in capturing it, as the Imperialists had left quite unguarded the approach by Chingting and Paoting, and the capture of Peking would have sounded the knell of the Manchu dynasty. But the Taepings did not seize the chance—if it were one—and they were far from being in the best of spirits. They had advanced far, but it looked as if it was into the lion's mouth. Their march had been a remarkable one, but it had been attended with no striking success. In their front was the Tientsin militia, strengthened by a large if nondescript force, led by the Mongol chief Sankolinsin.

In their rear the levies of Hoonan, of the vast district that had suffered from their exactions, were closing up, and soon they were closely beleaguered in a hastily-fortified camp at Tsinghai. In this they were besieged from the end of October to the beginning of March 1854. The Imperial generals, afraid to risk an assault, hoped to starve them out, and so they might have done had not Tien Wang sent a fresh army to extricate this force from its peril. Then the retreat began, but, beset by assailants from every side, it was slow and disastrous. The struggle went on until March 1855, when Sankolinsin was able to declare that not a Taeping remained north of the Yellow River. Only a very small portion of the two armies sent to capture Peking ever returned to the headquarters of Tien Wang.

While these events, and others that do not call for description as being of minor importance, were in progress, symptoms of disintegration were already beginning to reveal themselves in the camp at Nanking. After its capture Tien Wang himself retired into the interior of his palace and never afterwards appeared in public. All his time was passed in the harem, and the opportunity was thus given his more ambitious lieutenants to assert themselves. Tung Wang, the "Eastern King," became principal Minister. He, too, claimed to have communion with Heaven, and on celestial advice he began to get rid of those of his comrades who opposed his schemes. He even summoned Tien Wang to his presence and reproved him for his proceedings. A plot was then formed against Tung Wang, and he was slain with three of his brothers, in the presence of Tien Wang, by another of the Taeping chiefs. Nor did the slaughter stop there, for it is alleged, although the numbers must not be accepted literally, that 200,000 of his partisans—men, women, and children—were massacred. These internal dissensions threatened to break up the Taeping confederacy, and no doubt they would have done so but for the appearance of the most remarkable man associated with the movement, and one of the most heroic figures in China's history.

A young officer, rejoicing in the innumerable Chinese name of Li, had attracted Tung Wang's favourable notice, and was by him entrusted with a small command. It will be more convenient to speak of him by his subsequent title of Chung Wang, or the "Faithful King." He distinguished himself in his first enterprise by defeating a large Imperial army besieging Chinkiang, and in relieving the garrison when on the point of surrender. But while engaged on this task the Imperialists closed in on his rear and cut off his retreat back to Nanking, whither Tien Wang hastily summoned him to return. He endeavoured to make his way along the northern bank, but was checked at Loohoo by the ex-Triad Chang Kwoliang, the same who deserted the Taepings in Kwangsi. Chang had crossed the river to oppose him, and Chung Wang, hastily conveying his army over the river, fell upon and destroyed the weakened force that the Imperial general had left there, under General Chi, who committed suicide. Chang Kwoliang crossed after him, but only to suffer defeat, and Chung Wang made his way into Nanking. He then attacked the main Imperial army before its walls, under the Emperor's generalissimo Heang Yung, and drove it out of its entrenchments. Heang took his defeat so much to heart that he also committed suicide, but Chang Kwoliang made a supreme effort to retrieve the day, and succeeded in retaking all the lost positions, with the exception of the Yashua Gate of Nanking.

While these events were in progress in the Taeping capital, some events that must be briefly referred to happened on a different scene. The Triads, aided by the mob, rose in Shanghai, overcame the Emperor's officers and garrison, and on 7th September 1853 obtained complete mastery of the native city. The foreign settlement was placed in a state of siege, the men-of-war covered the approaches to the factories, and a volunteer corps was carefully organised and constantly employed. Then an Imperial army re-appeared on the scene, and laid siege to Shanghai, but it was conducted with no skill, and the situation remained unchanged. After twelve months' delay the French Admiral, Laguerre, decided to help the Imperialists, and he began to bombard the walls in December 1854. He combined with them in an assault, and 400 French sailors and the Imperialists attacked the walls which had been breached. The assault ended disastrously, for the rebels defended the houses, and at last drove back the assailants with much loss. The pressure of famine compelled the besieged some months later to make a sortie, when the Imperialists recovered the town. A similar rising, with a similar result, occurred at Amoy. The insurgents caused a great loss of life and property, but in the end the authorities gained the upper hand. These events compelled the foreign consuls and their Governments to reconsider their policy, which had been one of sympathy towards the Taepings, and gradually the conviction became universal that it would be well for civilization and trade if a speedy end were put to the Taeping rebellion. But for our own quarrel and war with the central Government these views would have borne fruit in acts at an earlier date than they did.

During the campaign of 1858 the Taepings more than held their own through the courage and activity shown by Chung Wang. He relieved the town of Ganking when closely pressed by Tseng Kwofan, and although he could not prevent a fresh beleaguerment of Nanking, it caused him no apprehension because the Emperor's generals were well known to have no intention of attacking. Notwithstanding this, it was clearly foreseen that in time Nanking must fall by starvation. In these straits Chung Wang proved the saviour of his party. The city was invested on three sides; only one remained open for any one to carry out the news of Tien Wang's necessities. In this moment of peril there was a general reluctance to quit the besieged town, but unless someone did, and that quickly, the place was doomed. In this supreme moment Chung Wang offered to go himself. At first the proposal was received with a chorus of disapproval, but at last, when he went to the door of Tien Wang's palace and beat the gong which lay there for those who claimed justice, he succeeded in overcoming the opposition to his plan, and in impressing upon his audience the real gravity of the situation. His request was granted, and having nominated trusty men to the command during his absence, he left by the southern gate. A few days later and Tseng's last levies constructed their fortified camp in front of it. The Emperor's generals unfortunately reverted to their old dilatory measures, because they failed to realise the importance with which the possession of Nanking still invested the Taepings. Without that city they would have been nothing but a band of brigands, who could easily have been dispersed. With it they could claim the status of a separate dynasty. Yet the capture of Nanking was put off until the last act of all. These sapient leaders, whose military knowledge was antiquated, acted with an indifference to the most obvious considerations, that would have been ludicrous if it had not been a further injury to a suffering people. In 1858 their apathy was such that it not merely saved Nanking but played the whole game into the hands of Chung Wang.

That chief succeeded in collecting a small force, with which he at once began to harass Tseng's army. By transferring his army rapidly from one side of the river to the other, he succeeded in supplying his deficiency in numbers; but with all his activity he could make no impression on the mass of his opponents. He even got the worst of it in several skirmishes, but by a supreme effort he succeeded in overpowering the Imperial force north of the river at Poukou, and thus relieved the pressure on Nanking. But this was only momentary, and after a doubtful and wearisome campaign throughout the year 1859, the situation again became one of great gravity for the besieged Taepings who were now confined to Nanking and a few other towns in the Yangtse valley.

In this extremity Chung Wang conceived a fresh plan for extricating his cause from the difficulties that beset it. By January 1860 all Chung Wang's arrangements were completed. He distributed considerable sums of money among his men to put them in good humour, and then set forth. His first movements were directed to misleading his enemy as to his real object, and having succeeded in this he marched as rapidly as possible towards the important harbour of Hangchow, in the bay of the same name, south of Shanghai. On 19th March he succeeded in capturing the Chinese city, but the Tartar portion held out, and a relieving army compelled Chung Wang to retire. What seemed an unredeemed calamity proved a stroke of good fortune, for the Imperialists had sent their best troops to pursue him, and thus materially weakened the force before Nanking. Chung Wang saw his chance, and while the Imperialists were rejoicing in Hangchow at its recovery, he hastened back by forced marches, and fell upon the besieging army. In the desperate engagement that followed 5000 Imperialists were slain, and the remainder were driven ignominiously from the field. Thus, at the blackest moment of their fortunes, did Chung Wang succeed in delivering his kinsmen who had so long been shut up in Nanking. This siege had then continued with more or less interruption for seven years.

Nor did Chung Wang's success stop here. He fought a battle at Tayan with his old adversary Chang Kwoliang, and defeated him with a loss of 10,000 men. At the height of the engagement Chang Kwoliang was drowned while crossing a canal, and this decided the battle. Encouraged by these successes, and with increased forces—for most of the prisoners he took were incorporated in his army—Chung Wang assumed the offensive, and after winning no fewer than three regular engagements, he succeeded in capturing the important city of Soochow, on the Grand Canal, and this became his chief quarters during the remainder of this long struggle. By these successes he obtained fresh supplies, and commanded the great and hitherto little touched resources of the wealthy province of Kiangsu. It was thus that he was brought into the neighbourhood of Shanghai, and made those attempts to acquire possession of the Chinese city which were set forth in the last chapter, and which were the true cause of the inception of the foreign, or foreign-trained force, that began with Ward.

After his repulse at Shanghai, Chung Wang was recalled to Nanking. He went reluctantly, leaving Hoo Wang, "the Protecting King," as his deputy at Soochow. He found there everything in confusion, and that Tien Wang, instead of laying in rice for a fresh siege, was absorbed in his devotion and amusements, while the other chiefs were engaged in plundering their own subjects. Dissatisfied with what he saw at Nanking, Chung Wang again took the field, and transferred the scene of hostilities to the province of Kiangsi, but although he showed great activity, and marched 800 miles, he gained little, and, indeed, was defeated on one or two occasions. Nor could he save Ganking, which, after being besieged for three years, surrendered to Tseng Kwotsiuen, and thus all hope of succour from the west, or of retreat there, in the last resort, was removed from the hard-beset garrison of Nanking. As some set-off to this reverse, Chung Wang captured the ports of Ningpo and Hangchow, after a gallant defence by a small Manchu garrison. The Taepings could scarcely now hope for durable success, but their capacity for inflicting an enormous amount of injury was evidently not destroyed. Chung Wang's energy and military skill alone sustained their cause, but the lovers of rapine and turbulence flocked in their thousands to his standard.

In the Yangtse valley—in fact, wherever Chung Wang was not—the Taepings met with many reverses that counterbalanced these successes. Several Chinese armies approached Nanking from different sides, and Tien Wang in a state of panic summoned Chung Wang, his only champion, back to his side. That warrior obeyed the summons, leaving Mow Wang in charge of Soochow, but he could do no good. He found nothing but disorder at the Taeping capital, and no troops with which he could venture to assume the offensive against the powerful army, in numbers at all events, that the two Tsengs had drawn round Nanking. In this position his troubles were increased by the suspicion of Tien Wang, who deprived him of all his honours, and banished him to the province of Anhui, adjacent to both Kiangsi and Kiangsu, and joined with them in the same viceroyalty. This order to depart was a relief to Chung Wang, who was thus able to complete his own measures for the defence of Soochow and the other places along the Canal that had fallen to his arms. He saw clearly that the success of the foreigners in keeping him back at a distance of thirty miles from Shanghai, and in expelling him from Ningpo, signified his being shut in just as effectively on the east, as he already was on the west by the fall of every place except Nanking, and by the miserable inefficiency of the garrison in that place. He may have really despaired, but this Chinese Frederick was resolved, if he could, to break his chains. Unfortunately for him, a new and more formidable antagonist than any he had met appeared on the scene at this juncture, in the person of Gordon.

This summary of the progress and nature of the Taeping rebellion up to the 25th March 1863 when Gordon assumed the command will make clear what follows to the general reader. It would be as great a mistake to minimise the fighting military strength of the Taepings as it would be to exaggerate it. There was a moment, years before Gordon came on the scene, when the Imperial commanders by a little energy and promptitude might have stamped out the rebellion; but having missed the opportunity the military skill and daring of Chung Wang had revived the Taeping cause, and made it more formidable than ever from a military point of view. The blunders of the Imperial commanders precluded any confidence as to their superior numbers and resources effecting their natural result, and although Gordon himself declared that the Taeping cause was a lost one before he assumed the command, no cause could be pronounced irretrievable with a leader so expert and resolute as Chung Wang, and opponents so incapable and craven as his were. But another thing was certainly incontestable, and that was that the Taepings could not in any sense be regarded as patriots. Their regular mode of conduct stamped them at once as undiscriminating plunderers of all, whether Chinese or Manchu, who had the misfortune to fall into their hands, and their acts of cruelty surpassed description and even belief. Some instances of the massacres they perpetrated have been mentioned, but these were only a few out of the many that stained, or rather characterised, their usual proceedings. It will suffice to say that their ordinary way of dealing with their prisoners was to crucify them, and there will then be no difficulty in accepting the conclusion that the Chinese population thoroughly detested them, and regarded them as a scourge rather than as deliverers.

Nor does a closer examination of the system of administration set up at Nanking by the leader Tien Wang raise one's opinion of the cause or its promoters. The foreign missionaries long thought that the Taepings were the agents of Christianity, and that their success would lead to the conversion of China. That faith died hard, but at last in 1860 a missionary had to confess that after visiting Nanking "he could find nothing of Christianity but its name falsely applied to a system of revolting idolatry," and out of that and other irresistible testimony resulted the conclusion that the conversion of China by the agency of the Taepings was a delusion. The missionaries were not alone in their belief among foreigners. The Consuls and their Governments entertained a hope that the Taepings might establish an administration which would be less difficult to deal with than they had found the existing one at Peking. They attempted to, and did in an informal manner, establish some relations with Tien Wang. They acquainted him with the articles of the Treaty of Tientsin, and they requested him to conform with its conditions. On a second occasion Sir George Bonham, our head representative in China, even honoured him with a visit; but closer acquaintance in the case of our diplomatists, as of the missionaries, stripped the Taepings of the character with which interested persons would wish they had been invested. From the first feeling of friendship and sympathy there consequently ensued a slow but steady revulsion, until at last the general feeling was that the Taepings were little more than marauders, and as such a scourge to the country and a standing injury to the trade and interests of Europeans. Then came the desire to see the rising suppressed, and finally the disillusionment culminated in active measures being taken to assist the Imperial Government in suppressing a rebellion which had defied all its efforts for more than ten years. Of these measures the appointment of Major Gordon to the command of the Ever Victorious Army was both the last and the most effectual in producing the desired result.

CHAPTER 5

The Ever Victorious Army

The appointment of any English officer would have led to some improvement in the direction of the Chinese Imperial forces assembled for the suppression of the Taeping rebellion; but the nature of the operations to be carried out, which were exclusively the capture of a number of towns strongly stockaded and protected by rivers and canals, rendered it specially necessary that that officer should be an engineer. In addition to the advantages of his scientific training, Major Gordon enjoyed the benefit of the preliminary course he had gone through under General Staveley. He had seen the Taepings fight, and something also of the defence and capture of their positions. He had also thoroughly mastered the topographical features of the region in and beyond which he was about to conduct military operations. There is little doubt that he assumed the command with a plan of campaign already decided upon in his brain. The Taepings with whom he had to deal derived their power and importance from the possession of Soochow, and from their access to several ports whence they obtained arms and ammunition. Therefore the capture of that city and the cutting off of their supplies represented his principal objects. Very much had to be accomplished before Soochow could be even approached, and the main object of Gordon's first campaign was the capture of Quinsan, which he saw would be far more suitable as headquarters for him and his force than the existing one at Sungkiang. Even before that could be attempted many matters had to be arranged. Not only had Major Gordon to relieve more than one beleaguered loyal garrison, but he had to establish his authority over his own force, which was on the verge of mutiny and clamouring for the return of Burgevine. His own opinion of that force was given in the following letter to a military friend:

I hope you do not think that I have a magnificent army. You never did see such a rabble as it was; and although I think I have improved it, it is still sadly wanting. Now both officers and men, although ragged and perhaps slightly disreputable, are in capital order and well disposed."

Before entering on these matters the following letter to his mother will be read with interest, as showing what was in Gordon's mind at the time he assumed the command. The letter was written on 24th March 1863, the day before he rode over to Sungkiang to take up his command.

I am afraid you will be much vexed at my having taken the command of the Sungkiang force, and that I am now a mandarin. I have taken the step on consideration. I think that anyone who contributes to putting down this rebellion fulfils a humane task, and I also think tends a great deal to open China to civilization. I will not act rashly, and I trust to be able soon to return to England; at the same time, I will remember your and my father's wishes, and endeavour to remain as short a time as possible. I can say that, if I had not accepted the command, I believe the force would have been broken up and the rebellion gone on in its misery for years. I trust this will not now be the case, and that I may soon be able to comfort you on this subject. You must not fret on this matter. I think I am doing a good service. . . . I keep your likeness before me, and can assure you and my father that I will not be rash, and that as soon as I can conveniently, and with due regard to the object I have in view, I will return home.

Major Gordon rode over to Sungkiang, situated on the line of the thirty-mile radius from Shanghai, on 25th March, and the following morning he inspected his force. He delivered a brief address, stating that there was no intention to dismiss any of them, and that so long as they behaved well he would carefully uphold their rights and interests. These words had a tranquillising effect, and Major Gordon's assumption of the command might be described as being then ratified by the Ever Victorious Army. The good he effected was very nearly undone two days later by the civil magistrate hanging some soldiers for marauding. After the affair looked like becoming serious, Gordon succeeded in pacifying his men and restoring order. In this state of affairs it was most desirable that no time should be lost in resuming active operations, and the Taeping successes at Taitsan and Fushan rendered them doubly necessary.

The first task entrusted to Major Gordon was the relief of Chanzu, which was closely assailed by the Taepings and believed to be on the point of surrendering. Chanzu lies some distance south of Fushan and west of Taitsan, and its garrison at this time was composed of Taepings who had deserted their comrades and joined the Imperial forces. Several attempts had been made to relieve it, but without success, and Gordon was urged by his Chinese colleagues to signalise his assumption of the command by carrying out this most desirable and necessary task. The best means of approaching it was by the river, and on 31st March Gordon accordingly sailed from Shanghai to the mouth of the Fushan Creek. His force numbered about 1200 men, and included 200 artillery with four 12-pounders and one 32-pounder. The enemy had constructed some stockades at Fushan, outside the ruined city of that name, and Gordon attacked these on the 4th April. He began with a heavy bombardment, and when he ordered the advance the Taepings, disheartened by his fire, evacuated their positions and retired with very little loss to either side. Gordon then marched on Chanzu, ten miles south of Fushan, and reached it without further fighting. The relief of Chanzu being thus effected, Gordon hastened back to Sungkiang, where he arrived little more than a week after he left it. The success and swiftness of this movement greatly impressed Li Hung Chang, who publicly recorded his great satisfaction at the very different manner in which the new commander transacted business from Burgevine.

In a letter to the British Consul at Shanghai, Mr Markham, Li wrote:

The officer Gordon having received command of the Ever Victorious Army, having immediately on doing so proceeded to Fushan, working day and night, having worked harmoniously with the other generals there, having exerted himself and attacked with success the walled city of Fushan and relieved Chanzu, and at once returned to Sungkiang and organised his force for further operations to sweep out the rebels, having proved himself valiant, able, and honest, I have congratulated myself and memorialised his Imperial Majesty to confer on him the dignity and office of Tsung-ping (Brigadier-General), to enable me to consider him as part of my command. Again, since Gordon has taken the command, he has exerted himself to organise the force, and though he has had but one month he has got the force into shape. As the people and place are charmed with him, as he has already given me returns of the organisation of the force, the formation of each regiment, and the expenses ordinary and extraordinary in the clearest manner, wishing to drill our troops and save our money, it is evident that he fully comprehends the state of affairs.

On his return to Sungkiang, Major Gordon devoted himself to the thorough reorganisation of his force. He began by abolishing the system of rewards for the capture of towns, and he forbade plundering on pain of death. These were strong steps to take with a force such as that he had under him, but he succeeded in making them acceptable by increasing the pay of the men, and by substituting on his staff English officers—the services of a few being lent him by the commanding officer at Shanghai—for the adventurers who had followed Ward and Burgevine. The total strength of the force was fixed at 4000 men, and his artillery consisted of four siege and two field batteries. The men were paid regularly by a Chinese official appointed by Li Hung Chang, and the cost to the Chinese Government averaged £20,000 a month. At the same time, Gordon collected a pontoon train and practised his men in all the work of attacking fortified places before he ventured to assume the offensive. He also organised a flotilla of small steamers and Chinese gunboats capable of navigating the canals and creeks which traversed the province of Kiangsu in all directions. Of these the principal was the steamer *Hyson*—a paddle-wheel vessel drawing 3½ feet of water, armed with a 32-pounder in her bow, and a 12-pounder at her stern, and possessing the faculty of moving over the bed of a creek on her wheels—and it took a very active and prominent part in the subsequent operations.

The strategy on which Major Gordon at once decided, and from which he never deviated, was to cut off the Taeping communications with the sea and the river Yangtsekiang, whence they were able to obtain supplies of ammunition and arms from little-scrupulous foreign traders. The expulsion of the Taepings from the Shanghai district and from Ningpo had done something towards the success of this project, but they still held Hangchow and the line of the Yangtsekiang to within ten miles of the entrance of the Woosung River on which Shanghai stands. The loss of Fushan and Chanzu had made an indent in this territory, and in order to complete this breach in the Taeping position, Gordon had decided and made all his plans to attack Quinsan, when he was compelled to defer it in consequence of the following incident.

The rude repulse at Taitsan had been, it will be recollected, the culminating misfortune of the force before Gordon's assumption of the command, but a Chinese army under Li Hung Chang's brother, San Tajin, continued to remain in the neighbourhood of the place. The Taeping commander laid a trap for him, into which he fell in what was, for a Chinese officer fully acquainted with the fact that treachery formed part of the usages of war in China, a very credulous manner. He expressed a desire to come over, presents and vows were exchanged, and at a certain hour he was to surrender one of the gates. The Imperial troops went to take possession, and were even admitted within the walls, when they were suddenly attacked on both flanks by the treacherous Taepings. Fifteen hundred of San Tajin's men were killed or captured, and he himself was severely wounded. In consequence of this reverse, the main Chinese army, under General Ching, a brave but inexperienced officer, could not co-operate with Gordon against Quinsan, and it was then decided that Gordon himself should proceed against Taitsan, and read the triumphant foe at that place a lesson. It was computed that its garrison numbered 10,000 men, and that it had several European deserters and renegades among its leaders, while the total force under Gordon did not exceed 3000 men. Their recent successes had also inspired the Taepings with confidence, and, judging by the previous encounters, there seemed little reason to anticipate a satisfactory, or at least a speedy issue of the affair for the Imperialists. That the result was more favourable was entirely due to Gordon's military capacity and genius.

Major Gordon acted with remarkable and characteristic promptitude. He only heard of the catastrophe to San Tajin on 27th April; on 29th April, after two forced marches across country, he appeared before Taitsan, and captured a stockade in front of one of its gates. Bad weather prevented operations the next day, but on 1st May, Gordon having satisfied himself by personal examination that the western gate offered the best point of attack, began the bombardment soon after daybreak. Two stone stockades in front of the gate had first to be carried, and these, after twenty minutes' firing, were evacuated on part of Gordon's force threatening the retreat of their garrison back to the town. The capture of these stockades began and ended the operations on that day. The next morning Gordon stationed one regiment in front of the north gate to cut off the retreat of the garrison in that direction, and then resumed his main attack on the west gate. By this time he had been joined by some of his gunboats, and their fire, aided by the artillery he had with him, gradually made a good impression on the wall, especially after the guns had been drawn as near as 200 yards to it. The breach was then deemed sufficiently practicable; the gunboats went up the creek as near the walls as possible, and the two regiments advanced to the assault. The Taepings fought desperately in the breach itself, and no progress was made. It is probable that a reverse would have followed had not the howitzers continued to throw shells over the wall, thus inflicting heavy losses on the Taepings, who swarmed in their thousands behind. At that critical moment Gordon directed another regiment to escalade the wall at a point which the Taepings had left unguarded, and the appearance of these fresh troops on their flank at once decided the day, and induced the Taeping leaders to order a retreat. The Taepings lost heavily, but the loss of the Ever Victorious Army was in proportion equally great. The latter had twenty men killed and 142 wounded, one European officer killed and six wounded. But the capture of Taitsan under all the circumstances was an exceptionally brilliant and decisive affair. With it may be said to have begun the military reputation of the young commander, whose admirable dispositions had retrieved a great disaster and inflicted a rude blow on the confidence of a daring enemy.

From Taitsan he marched to Quinsan; but his force was not yet thoroughly in hand, and wished to return to Sungkiang, in accordance with their practice under Ward of spending their pay and prize-money after any successful affair before attempting another. Gordon yielded on this occasion the more easily because he was impressed by the strength of Quinsan, and also because his ammunition had run short. But his trouble with his men was not yet over, and he had to face a serious mutiny on the part of his officers. For improved economy and efficiency Gordon appointed an English commissariat officer, named Cookesley, to control all the stores, and he gave him the rank of lieutenant-colonel. This gave umbrage to the majors in command of regiments, who presented a request that they should be allowed the higher rank and pay of lieutenant-colonel; and when this was refused they sent in their resignations, which were accepted. The affair was nearly taking a serious turn, as the troops refused to march; but Gordon's firmness overcame the difficulty. Two of the majors were reinstated, and the others dismissed, but this incident finally decided Gordon to change his headquarters from Sungkiang to some place where the bad traditions of Ward and Burgevine were not in force. The active operations now undertaken against Quinsan served to distract the attention of the men, and to strengthen their commander's influence over them. General Gordon's own description of this affair is well worth quoting:

The force arrived at their old camping ground near the east gate of Quinsan on the evening of 27th of May. General Ching had established some five or six very strong stockades at this place, and, thanks to the steamer *Hyson*, had been able to hold them against the repeated attacks of the rebels. The line of rebel stockades was not more than 800 yards from his position. The force encamped near the stockades; and at daybreak of the 28th the 4th and 5th Regiments, with the field artillery, moved to attack them. The right stockade was attacked in front, and its right flank turned, on seeing which the rebels retreated. They were in large force, and had it not been for the numerous bridges they had constructed in their rear, they would have suffered much, as the pursuit was pressed beyond the north gate close up to a stockade they held at the north-east angle of the city. Captain Clayton, 99th Regiment, a very gallant officer who had gained the goodwill and admiration of every one of the force, was unfortunately wounded in the attack, and died some months afterwards of his wounds. Our loss was two killed and sixteen wounded.

General Ching was now most anxious to get me to attack the east gate on the following day. His object was that he had written to the Futai Li, who had in turn passed the statement on to Peking, to say that he had his stockades on the edge of the ditch, and merely wanted a boat to get into the city. This he showed by a plan. The east gate looked, if possible, more unpromising than it did before, and I declined to attack it without reconnoitring the other side of the city. Accordingly, the next day, 29th May, I went in the *Hyson* with General Ching and Li Hung Chang to reconnoitre the west side, and after three hours' steaming came within 1000 yards of the main canal, which runs from the west gate of Quinsan to Soochow. At the junction of the creek we came up with this main canal at the village of Chunye. This place is eight miles from Quinsan, and twelve from Soochow. The only road between these two places runs along the bank of the creek. The rebels had here on its bank two stockades of no great strength, and about 500 yards inland, they had, near the village of Chunye, a very strong stone fort. About 1000 yards from the stockades the creek was staked across. At the time of our arrival large numbers of troops were passing towards and from Soochow with horsemen, etc. We opened fire on them and on their boats. The rebels seemed perfectly amazed at seeing us, and were ready for a run. General Ching was as sulky as a bear when he was informed that I thought it advisable to take these stockades the next day, and to attack on this side of the city.

At dawn on 30th May the 4th Regiment, 350 strong, with field artillery, all in boats and *Hyson*, accompanied by some fifty Imperial gunboats, started for Chunye. The Imperial gunboats started some hours previous, but had contented themselves with halting one and a half miles from the stockades. The whole flotilla—some eighty boats, with their large white sails and decorated with the usual amount of various-coloured flags, with the *Hyson* in the middle—presented a very picturesque sight, and must have made the garrison of Quinsan feel uncomfortable, as they could see the smallest move from the high hill inside the city, and knew, of course, more than we did of the importance of the stockades about to be attacked.

At noon we came up to the stakes before alluded to, and landed the infantry. The Imperial gunboats, now very brave, pulled up the stakes, and a general advance with the steamer and troops was made. The rebels stood for a minute, and then vacated the stockades and ran. The reason of the rebels defending these stockades so badly was on account of the ill-feeling between the chiefs in charge of Quinsan and Chunye, and the neglect of the former to furnish rice to the latter.

The *Hyson* (with Gordon on board) now steamed up towards Soochow at a slow pace, owing to the innumerable boats that crowded the creek, which, vacated by their owners, were drifting about with their sails up in every direction. The rebels were in clusters along the bank, marching in an orderly way towards Soochow. The *Hyson* opened fire on them and hurried their progress, and, hanging on their rear, kept up a steady fire till they reached Ta Edin, where a large arch bridge spanned the creek, and where the rebels had constructed a splendid stone fort. We expected that the rebels would make a stand here, but they merely fired one shot, which was answered by a shell from the *Hyson*, which went into the embrasure, and the rebels continued their flight. It became rather hazardous to pass this fort and leave it unoccupied, with the number of armed rebels who were between Chunye and Ta Edin. The *Hyson*, moreover, had no force on board of any importance. There were with me five or six Europeans and some thirty Chinamen—gunners, etc. However, six of us landed, and held the fort somehow till more Imperialists came up, while the *Hyson* pushed on towards Soochow.

The *Hyson* continued the pursuit, threading her way through the boats of all descriptions which crowded the creek, and harassing the rear of the rebel columns which extended along the road for over a mile. About two miles from Ta Edin another stone fort was passed without a shot being fired; this was Siaon Edin. Everything was left in the forts by the rebels. Soon after passing this place the steamer headed some 400 rebels, and Captain Davidson ran her into the bank, and took 150 of them prisoners on board the *Hyson*—rather a risk, considering the crew of that vessel and her size. Soon after this four horsemen were descried riding at full speed about a mile in rear of the steamer. They came up, passed the steamer amid a storm of bullets, and joined the rebel column. One of them was struck off his horse, but the others coolly waited for him, and one of them stopped and took him up behind him. They deserved to get off. About three miles further on another stockade of stone was passed at a broken bridge called Waiquaidong, and the pursuit was carried on to about three-quarters of a mile from Soochow. It was now getting late (6 p.m.), and we did not know if the rebels in our rear might not have occupied the stockades, in which case we should have had to find another route back. On our return we met crowds of villagers, who burnt at our suggestion the houses in the forts at Waiquaidong and Siaon Edin, and took the boats that were in the creek.

We met many boats that had appeared deserted on our passing up sailing merrily towards Soochow, but which, when they saw the red and green of the steamer and heard her whistle, were immediately run into the bank and were deserted. Just before Siaon Edin was reached we came on a large body of rebels, who opened a sharp fire of rifles on us striking the gun twice. They had got under cover of a bridge, which, however, after a short delay, we managed to enfilade with a charge of grape and thus cleared them out. We then steamed into the bank and took in more prisoners. Four chiefs, one a Wang, galloped past on horseback; and although not two yards from the steamer, they got away. The Wang got shoved into the water and lost his pony. A party of rebels were encamped in Siaon Edin, not dreaming of any further annoyance for that night, and were accordingly astonished to hear the steamer's whistle, and rushed out in amazement, to meet a shell at the entrance, which killed two of them. The steamer now pushed on to Ta Edin, and found it unoccupied; while waiting there to collect some of the prisoners, about 200 rebels came so suddenly on the steamer that we were obliged to whistle to keep them off till the gun could be got ready.

It was now 10.30 p.m., and the night was not very clear. At this moment the most tremendous firing and cheering was heard from Chunye, and hurried our progress to that place. Just before we reached it a gunboat disarranged the rudder, and then we were dodging about from side to side for some ten minutes, the firing and cheering going on as before. At last we got up to the junction of the creek, and steaming through the Imperial, and other boats, we came on the scene of action. The gunboats were drawn up in line, and were firing as fast as they could. The stone fort at the village was sparkling with musketry, and at times astounding yells burst forth from it. The *Hyson* blew her whistle, and was received with deafening cheers from the gunboats, which were on the eve of bolting. She steamed up the creek towards Quinsan, and at the distance of 200 yards we saw a confused mass near a high bridge. It was too dark to distinguish very clearly, but on the steamer blowing the whistle the mass wavered, yelled, and turned back. It was the garrison of Quinsan attempting to escape to Soochow, some seven or eight thousand men.

Matters were in too critical a state to hesitate, as the mass of the rebels, goaded into desperation, would have swept our small force away. We were therefore forced to fire into them, and pursue them towards Quinsan, firing, however, very rarely, and only when the rebels looked as if they would make a stand. The steamer went up to about a mile from Quinsan, and then returned. Several officers landed and took charge of the prisoners who were extended along the bank, and at 4 a.m., 31st May, everything was quiet. The *Hyson* had fired some eighty or ninety rounds during the day and night; and although humanity might have desired a smaller destruction, it was indispensably necessary to inflict such a blow on the garrison of Soochow as would cause them not to risk another such engagement, and thus enable us to live in peace during the summer—which it indeed did, for the rebels never came on this road again. Their loss must have been from three to four thousand killed, drowned, and prisoners. We took 800, most of whom entered our ranks. They lost all their arms and a very large number of boats. At 5 a.m. on 31st May the troops at Chunye and the *Hyson* moved towards Quinsan, and found the remainder of the force who had been left at the east gate already in the city. The possession of Quinsan was of immense importance in a strategical point of view. The circumference of its walls is some five miles, but they are very inferior. Its ditch is over forty yards wide, and from the nature of the creeks around it would prove very difficult to take. The high hill enclosed within its walls would enable the slightest move to be seen, and if two or three guns were placed on the spurs of this hill it would form a very formidable citadel. The rebels did not know its importance till they lost it.

Such was the capture of Quinsan, told in the simple words of its captor. It confirmed the reputation gained by the fall of Taitsan, and proved that the new commander was a man of extraordinary military intuition as well as energy. There is scarcely room to doubt that if Gordon had attacked Quinsan where the Chinese commander wished him to do, at its very strongest point, he would have met with a rude repulse. By attacking them on the side of Soochow, and by threatening their communication with that place, he terrified the large garrison so much that in the end they evacuated the place without resistance. Gordon himself believed that if the mandarins at the head of the Imperial army would have consented to support him in immediate measures for an assault on Soochow, that city would have fallen in the panic that ensued after the loss of Quinsan. The opportunity being lost, it will be seen that many months of arduous fighting followed before the same result was achieved.

The reasons which rendered a change in the headquarters of the force desirable have already been mentioned, and Major Gordon at once decided to remove them to Quinsan, a strong and advantageously-placed position embarrassing to the Taepings, and equally encouraging to the Imperialists. But if this removal was necessary on grounds of discipline and policy, it was very unpopular with the men themselves, who were attached to Sungkiang, where they could easily dispose of their plunder. They determined to make an effort to get the offensive order withdrawn, and a proclamation was drawn up by the most disaffected, who were the non-commissioned officers, and sent to Major Gordon with an intimation that the artillery would blow all the officers to pieces unless their demands were complied with. Major Gordon at once sent for all the non-commissioned officers, who paraded before him. When he demanded the name of the writer of the proclamation they were silent. At this Major Gordon announced that unless the name was given up, he would shoot one out of every five of them. At this statement the men groaned, when Gordon, noticing the man who groaned loudest, and shrewdly conceiving him to be a ringleader, seized him with his own hands, dragged him from the ranks, and ordered two of his bodyguard to shoot the man on the spot. The order was at once carried out, and then Gordon, turning to the rest, gave them one hour to reflect whether they would obey orders, or compel him to shoot one in every five. Within this time they gave way, and discipline was restored. Gordon in his official despatch expressed regret for the man's death, but, as he truly said, "it saved many others which must have been lost if a stop had not been put to the independent way of the men." But the matter did not quite end here, for more than 2000 men deserted, but Gordon found no difficulty in filling their places from his prisoners and the villages round Quinsan. It is worthy of note that his own bodyguard was mainly composed of Taeping prisoners, and some of the most faithful of them had been the bearers of the Snake banners of the rebel Wangs.

Having thus settled the differences within his own force, and having fully established his own authority, Major Gordon would have prosecuted the attack on Soochow with vigour, if other difficulties had not occurred which occupied his time and attention. In the first place, there was a serious quarrel with General Ching, who was sore because he had not gained the credit for the capture of Quinsan, and who did everything he could to hamper and humiliate the force. At last he went to the length of firing on a column of Gordon's force, and as he refused all satisfaction, that officer was on the point of marching to attack him, when Dr—now Sir Halliday—Macartney arrived in his camp, being sent in a fully accredited manner, and escorted by the Futai's bodyguard, as a peace messenger from Li Hung Chang. On this occasion Sir Halliday Macartney first gave evidence of the exceptional diplomatic tact which he has since evinced in so many important negotiations, when China derived much advantage from his energy, ability, and devotion to her cause. The storm then blew over, but the second affair was more serious. Li Hung Chang became remiss in his payment of the force, and on 25th July Gordon sent in his formal resignation. There is every reason to believe that at this moment Gordon was thoroughly sick of his command, and would willingly have returned to Europe. The difficulties with his own men, the want of co-operation, to say nothing of appreciation on the part of the Chinese authorities, had damped even his zeal in what he reiterated was the good cause of restoring peace and security to a suffering people; and in addition to these troubles he had to carry on a correspondence with anonymous writers, who made many baseless charges in the Shanghai and Hongkong papers of cruelty against the men under his command. The English General at Shanghai used all his influence, however, with the Chinese Governor to pay up the arrears, and with Gordon to retain the command, because, as he said, there was "no other officer who combined so many dashing qualities, let alone skill and judgment."

But the event that really decided Gordon to withdraw his resignation was the unexpected return of Burgevine. That adventurer had proceeded to Peking after his dismissal from the command, and obtained some support from the American minister in pressing his claims on the Chinese. He had been sent back to Shanghai with letters which, although they left some loophole of escape, might be interpreted as ordering Li Hung Chang to reinstate him in the command. This Li, supported by the English commanding officer at Shanghai, had resolutely refused to do, and the feud between the men became more bitter than ever. Burgevine remained in Shanghai and employed his time in selling the Taepings arms and ammunition. In this way he established secret relations with their chiefs, and seeing no chance of Imperial employment he was not unwilling to join his fortunes to theirs. This inclination was increased by the belief that he might be able to form a force of his own which would give a decisive turn to the struggle, and his vanity led him to think that he might pose on the rebel side as no unequal adversary of Gordon, to whom all the time he professed the greatest friendship. These feelings arose from or were certainly strengthened by the representations made by several of the officers and men whom Gordon had dismissed from his army. They easily led Burgevine to think that he was not forgotten, and that he had only to raise his standard to be joined by many of his old men.

A fortnight before Gordon's resignation Dr Macartney—who had some time before begun his remarkable career in the Chinese service, and of whom Gordon himself said: "He drilled troops, supervised the manufacture of shells, gave advice, brightened the Futai's intellect about foreigners, and made peace, in which last accomplishment his *forte* lay"—wrote to him, stating that he had positive information that Burgevine was enlisting men for some enterprise, that he had already enrolled 300, and that he had even chosen a special flag for his force. A few days later Burgevine, probably hearing of this communication, wrote to Gordon, begging him not to believe any rumours about him, and stating that he was coming up to see him. Gordon unfortunately believed in this statement, and as he wished to exhibit special lenience towards the man whom he had displaced in the command, he went bail for him, so that he retained his personal liberty when the Chinese arrested Burgevine's agent Beechy, and wished to arrest Burgevine himself. On 2nd August Burgevine threw off the mask. At the head of a band of thirty-two rowdies, he seized the new steamer *Kajow* at Sungkiang, and with that vessel hastened to join the Taepings. The very day that this happened Gordon reached Shanghai for the purpose of resigning his command, but on the receipt of this intelligence he at once withdrew his resignation and hastened back to Quinsan. Apart from public considerations, he felt doubly bound to do this because Burgevine had not been arrested on his pledged word.

The position was undoubtedly critical, for the prospect of plunder offered by Burgevine was very attractive to mercenaries like the Ever Victorious Army, and there was a very real risk that the force at Quinsan, deprived of its commander, might be induced to desert *en masse* under the persuasive promises of Burgevine. When Gordon reached Quinsan he was so apprehensive as to what might occur that he removed his heavy artillery and most of his munitions of war to Taitsan, where General Brown, in command at Shanghai, undertook to see that they were protected. The situation at Quinsan was full of peril, for although Burgevine had thrown away a chance, by taking a roundabout instead of a direct route to Soochow, of striking a decisive blow before Gordon could get back, the Taeping leader, Mow Wang, had not been so negligent, and his operations for the recovery of several places taken by Gordon in the last few days of his command were on the point of success, when that officer's return arrested the course of his plans. It must be pointed out that after this date the Taepings fought with far more skill than before. They had a very considerable European contingent, probably nearly 300 men, and these served not only as leaders, but as trainers of the rebel Chinese forces. They had also obtained some good cannon, and the steamer *Kajow* proved of material value on water. Gordon found on his return, therefore, that the difficulties of the campaign were materially increased. His opponents were far stronger and more confident, while his own resources remained unchanged. Gordon tersely summed up the situation in an official despatch:

There is no knowing what an immense amount of damage might have been done if the rebels had had a more energetic man than Burgevine, and it would be as well not to point out the line which might have been taken.

The first engagements of this more difficult and keenly-contested phase of the campaign took place at Kahpoo, a place on the canal some miles south of Soochow. Gordon had taken it a week before he left for Shanghai, as a sort of parting gift to the Chinese, but when he arrived there on 9th August he found the garrison hard pressed, although the *Hyson* was stationed there—and indeed nothing but his arrival with a third steamer, the *Cricket*, averted its recapture. After five days' operations, that do not require description, the neighbourhood of Kahpoo was cleared of rebels, and Gordon returned to Quinsan, where the most essential task had to be accomplished of restoring the discipline of his own force. As some assistance in this difficult task General Brown lent him the services of 200 Beluches, whose admirable conduct and splendid appearance went far to restore a healthy spirit among his own men. At the same time these troops ensured the safety of Quinsan and also of Gordon himself, at least against the treachery of Burgevine's sympathisers.

The season of the year, the hottest and most trying of the long Chinese summer, compelled inaction, and Gordon felt doubly the need of caution now that he was brought face to face with the most arduous undertaking of the whole war, viz. the siege and capture of Soochow. General Ching's headquarters were at Ta Edin, and he had also occupied in force Waiquaidong, only two miles from the eastern gate of Soochow. Before the end of September he had pushed on still further, and erected his stockades within half a mile of that position. At this moment Gordon, anxious as to what might happen to his too-adventurous colleague, advanced with his force to his aid, and took up the supreme direction of the attack on Soochow. As usual, Gordon began by making a careful examination of the extensive rebel positions at and round Soochow, and the result of it was that he decided to capture the stockades and village of Patachiaou, one mile distant from the south wall of that city. His plan met with easy success, for the Taepings were not expecting an attack in that quarter, and offered little resistance.

Easily as they had been driven out of it, the Taepings made a very determined effort to retake it a few days later, and it was only by desperate exertions that Gordon succeeded in holding what he had won. This was the first occasion on which Burgevine and the *Kajow* steamer, commanded by Captain Jones, "a daring and capable officer," to use Gordon's words, came into action. The rebels were extremely confident for this reason, and also because they had some heavy artillery. Gordon had to keep to his stockades, and to send the *Hyson* out of action from fear of its being damaged by the enemy's shell, but the Taepings were afraid to come to close quarters, and eventually retreated before a well-timed sortie. In this engagement Gordon had the co-operation of a French-trained Chinese regiment, under the command of a gallant officer, Captain Bonnefoy. After this there was a lull, but Gordon felt too weak to attempt anything serious against Soochow, and he deprecated all operations until he could strike an effective blow. In this respect he differed materially from his Chinese colleague, General Ching, who was most restless and enterprising, but his ill-directed energy produced no result, and even assisted the enemy's plans.

At this juncture the Taeping hero Chung Wang arrived from Nanking with reinforcements, and imparted a new vigour to the defence. But whether on account of jealousy, or of disappointment at the poor services he had rendered, it also resulted in the dismissal of Burgevine, an incident of which some brief account may be given before following the main course of the campaign. More than one ground of dispute led up to this conclusion. In the first place, Burgevine was disappointed at finding several of the rebel Wangs as clever and ambitious as he was, and they were disappointed at the amount of service and help he could give them. This feeling culminated in angry scenes, when, on being sent into Shanghai in disguise to purchase arms with a large sum of money, he returned to Soochow without either money or weapons. He was apparently given, as a last chance, the opportunity of regaining his reputation by entrapping Gordon into the rebel power, and he thoroughly entered into the scheme, although he failed to carry it out. On 3rd October—that is to say, two days after the failure to retake Patachiaou—Burgevine made the first step in this plot by addressing a letter to Gordon, thanking him for the offer of medicines he had sent, and offering to meet him whenever he liked to discuss matters. On the 6th he met Gordon at the stockades, and declared his willingness to abandon the Taepings and come over with all his force, including the *Kajow*. He and his companions were guaranteed their lives, and the arrangement seemed complete. Two days later he had a second interview with the English officer, when he made the extraordinary proposition that he and Gordon should join bands, attack both Taepings and Imperialists, and fight for their own hand. This mad and unprincipled proposal excited Gordon's anger, but it was only Burgevine's old filibustering idea revived under unfavourable conditions. It was while smarting under this rebuff that Burgevine proposed to Captain Jones a fresh plot for entrapping Gordon, while he, unsuspecting evil, was engaged in conferences for their surrender; but to Jones's credit, let it be stated that he refused to have any part in such black treachery. Thereupon Burgevine attempted to take Jones's life, either to conceal his own treachery or to enable him to carry out his interrupted plans. Much delay occurred in carrying out the project of Burgevine's desertion, and Gordon, rendered specially anxious to save his and the other foreigners' lives, because one party had escaped without Burgevine, wrote a strong letter on the subject to Mow Wang, Chung Wang's chief lieutenant. He also sent him a present of a pony, at which the rebel chief was so much pleased that he agreed to release Burgevine, and on 18th October that person appeared at the outworks of Gordon's position. His personal safety was entirely due to Gordon's humane efforts, and to the impression that officer had made on the Taepings as a chivalrous opponent. The American Consul at Shanghai, Mr Seward, officially thanked Major Gordon for his "great kindness to misguided General Burgevine and his men." Nearly two years later this adventurer met the fate he so narrowly escaped on several occasions. He had been forbidden by his own Consul as well as the Chinese Government ever to return to China, but in June 1865 he broke his parole. Before he could be arrested he met with his death by accident, being drowned when crossing a Chinese river, but rumours were prevalent that his death was an act of vengeance instigated by his old enemy the Futai, Li Hung Chang.

The assumption of the supreme command by Chung Wang was soon followed by those offensive operations which had made that dashing leader the most famous of all the rebel generals. Gordon and the bulk of his corps were at Patachiaou, south of Soochow—only General Ching and the Chinese army were north of that place—and he resolved to attack them and force his way through to Chanzu, which he wished to recover as opening a road to the river and the outer world. Gordon divined his intention, and for some time prevented him carrying it out by making threatening demonstrations with his gunboats on the western side of Soochow; but his own attention was soon diverted to another part of the country where a new and unexpected danger threatened his own position and communications. A large rebel force, computed to number 20,000 men, had suddenly appeared behind Major Gordon's position and attacked the Imperial garrison stationed at Wokong, a place on the canal twelve or thirteen miles south of Soochow. The news that reached Gordon on 12th October from this quarter was that the garrison, having been repulsed in a sortie with a loss of several hundred men, could not hold out many hours. Gordon at once hastened to the rescue at the head of one of his regiments, and with the invaluable *Hyson* steamer. He found his allies quite cowed, afraid even to open the gates of their stockades to admit him and his men, and the enemy drawn up in imposing lines at a distance of about 1500 yards. He at once ordered the attack, and during three hours the engagement was contested in the most obstinate and spirited manner. The rebels, having their line of retreat secure, fought bravely. Gordon had to bring up his heavy guns to within forty yards of the wall before they would gave way, and even then they stood at the second and third inner stockades. Gordon never gave them a chance of recovering, but having got them on the run, kept them at it for a distance of ten miles. This was one of Gordon's greatest victories in the open field. The Taepings never fought better, yet with 1000 good Chinese troops Gordon routed more than 20,000 of them.

Chung Wang had begun his march towards Chanzu, but after some slight successes met with a rude repulse at Monding, where he also lost the steamer *Kajow*, which was sunk by an accidental explosion. He then established his headquarters at Wusieh, a place on the Grand Canal, about twenty-five miles north of Soochow. Here he hoped to effect some diversion that might relieve the increasing pressure on Soochow itself.

In the meantime that pressure had greatly increased, owing to the bolder measures to which Gordon resorted after the European contingent abandoned the Taeping side. His first step was to attack and capture the stockades at Wuliungchow, a village two miles west of Patachiaou, which commanded a passage leading from the Taiho Lake to the south gate of Soochow. Gordon managed to conceal the real object of his attack from the Taepings, and to capture the stockades with little loss. The wet weather and the unexpected nature of the attack explained this easy success, for the stockades were strong and well placed. Chung Wang returned from Wusieh with the special object of retaking them, but he was repulsed with some loss, and then hurried back to that place. A few days later part of Gordon's force, under Major Kirkham, was sent to Wokong, which was again being threatened by the Taepings, and obtained a brilliant success, capturing 1300 prisoners and not fewer than 1600 boats, including sixteen gunboats.

Having achieved this success on the south, Gordon proceeded with

111

his plans to secure an equally advantageous position on the north side. He left two regiments at Wuliungchow, which he greatly strengthened, and with the remainder he went to Waiquaidong, where he proposed to deliver his attack on the Leeku stockades, only a short distance in front of the north gate of Soochow. This operation was carried out with complete success, and it was promptly followed up by the capture of the rebel positions at Wanti, which enabled the forces round Soochow to join hands with the other considerable Imperial army that had been placed in the field by the energy of Li Hung Chang, and entrusted to the command of his brother, San Tajin. This last force was opposed to Chung Wang, but although numerically the stronger, the want of the most rudimentary military knowledge in its commander reduced this army of 20,000 men to inglorious inaction. At this stage of the struggle it will be well to sum up in Gordon's own words the different positions held by the contending forces:

> We held the Taiho Lake with the steamers the *Hyson*, the *Tsatlee*, *Firefly*, and 200 men (Imperialists), which cruised off Moodow, and prevented supplies coming to Soochow up the creek which leads from that village to the small West Gate, or Shih-mün, of Soochow, and where they had many actions with the rebel gunboats. The next great water outlet was closed to the rebels by our possession with 1000 men (Imperialists) of Wuliungchow. Off the Pon-mün, or South Gate, the next main water and road communication to the south was closed to them by our occupation by 1500 men (Imperialists) of the Patachiaou stockades on the Grand Canal, south of the south-east angle of Soochow. The next, which led from the east gate of Soochow to Quinsan, was closed by Ching's force of 3000 or 4000 men, nearly two miles from the gate. These men were well posted in strong and well-constructed stockades. The next position held was Leeku, where I had one regiment, and at Wanti there was another regiment. The total force in the stockades was about 8500 men, leaving for field operation 2500 Imperialists, 2100 of the Quinsan Corps, and 400 Franco-Chinese. San Tajin had 20,000 to 30,000, in three separate camps. He was utterly incapable for command of any sort.
>
> The rebels held Soochow with some 40,000 men in and around the city. The city of Wusieh held some 20,000 men, and Chung Wang had at Mahtanchow some 18,000 more. Chung Wang's position was central between Wusieh and Soo-

chow, some ten miles in advance of the Grand Canal, so as to be able to give help to either city, and to attack on the flank any advance made by us on their grand line of communications by that canal.

The city of Soochow, now so closely beleaguered, was of imposing appearance. An English traveller who saw it at this time thus describes it:

Further than the eye could penetrate in the misty morning stretched the grizzled walls of Soochow, a city celebrated for ages in the history of China for its size, population, wealth, and luxury, but now stripped of its magnificence, and held by an army of Taeping banditti against the Imperial forces. To the right and left, mile after mile, rose the line of lofty wall and grey turret, while above all appeared not only the graceful pagodas, which have been for ages the boast of Soochow and the dense foliage of secular trees—the invariable glory of Chinese cities—but also the shimmering roofs of newly decorated palaces confidently occupied by the vainglorious leaders of the rebellion. The proximity of the rebel line became apparent with surprising suddenness, for, following their usual custom, they greeted the rising sun with a simultaneous display of gaudy banners above the line of their entrenchments. The mud walls they had thrown up in advance, scarcely distinguishable before, were now marked out by thousands of flags of every colour from black to crimson, whilst behind them rose the jangling roll of gongs, and the murmurs of an invisible multitude.

Had Gordon been free to act, or even if he had possessed authority over the two Chinese commanders, his plan of campaign would have been simple and decisive. He would have effected a junction of his forces with San Tajin; and having overwhelmed Chung Wang and his 18,000 men with his combined army of double that strength, he would have appeared at the head of his victorious troops before the bewildered garrison of Wusieh. He would probably have thus terminated the campaign at a stroke. Even the decisive defeat of Chung Wang alone might have entailed the collapse of the cause now tottering to its fall. But Major Gordon had to consider not merely the military quality of his allies, but also their jealousies and differences. General Ching hated San Tajin on private as well as on public grounds. He desired a monopoly of the profit and honour of the campaign. His own reputation would be made by the capture of Soochow. It would be diminished and cast into the shade were another Imperial commander to defeat Chung Wang and close the line of the Grand Canal. If Gordon detached himself from General Ching, he could not feel sure what folly that jealous and impulsive commander might not commit. He would certainly not pursue the vigilant defence before Soochow necessary to guard the extensive line of stockades, and to prevent its large garrison sallying out and assailing his own rear. Gordon had consequently for these considerations to abandon the tempting idea of crushing Chung Wang and capturing the towns in the rear of Nanking, and to have recourse to safer if slower methods.

But if he had to abandon the larger plan, he still stuck tenaciously to his main idea that the way to capture Soochow was to isolate it, and above all to sever Chung Wang's communication with it. Several weeks passed before Gordon could complete the necessary arrangements, but at last, on 19th November, he left Leeku at the head of the greater part of his own force and a large contingent of Ching's braves to attack the stockades at Fusaiquan on the Grand Canal, about four miles north of Leeku. The Taeping position was a strong one, including eight separate earthworks, a stone fort, and several stockades. Gordon said "it was far the best built and strongest position he had yet seen," but the rebels evacuated it in the most cowardly manner without attempting the least resistance. Gordon goes on to say: "Our loss was none killed, and none wounded! We had expected a most desperate defence. If ever men deserved beheading, the Taeping leaders did on this occasion." The immediate consequence of this success was that Chung Wang quitted his camp in face of San Tajin, and, joining the Wusieh corps, concentrated his whole force for the defence of the Grand Canal.

Having thus strengthened his position towards the north, Gordon, very much to Ching's satisfaction, fell in with his views to begin a direct attack on Soochow itself. For good reasons it was decided that the north-east angle of Soochow was the weakest, but before it could be attacked it was necessary to capture the strong stockades which the rebels had erected in front of the East and North Gates. The East Gate, or Low Mun, stockades were selected for the first attack, and as the scene of a reverse to Ching's force on 14th October, the Chinese commander was specially anxious to capture them. They were exceedingly formidable, consisting of a line of breastwork, defended at intervals with circular stockades, and the position was well chosen and strongly fortified. After reconnoitring it, and obtaining all the information he could from deserters, Gordon determined on a night attack; but unfortunately not only were his plans revealed to the Taepings by traitors in his own camp, but his arrangements miscarried. As is often the case with night attacks, the plan of attack was not adhered to, and much confusion followed. The breastwork was carried by a small part of his troops, but the stockades in its rear were never reached. Encouraged by Gordon's example, who seemed to be at every point at the same moment, his men held on to the breastwork, but the supports would not move up, and when he hastened to the rear to encourage them, the Taepings under Mow Wang attacked in their turn and manned the breastwork. There was nothing now to be done but to draw off the troops, which was executed with comparatively slight loss; but 165 officers and men were killed or wounded—the majority being killed or missing. This loss would have been much greater if the Taepings had only had the courage to leave their position, but fortunately they showed themselves unable to follow up their success. This was Gordon's first defeat, but it was so obviously due to special causes that it did not much dishearten his men, or diminish the high reputation he and his force had gained by thirteen previous victories.

But the necessity to retrieve such a reverse was obvious, and Gordon collected the whole of his corps for the purpose of capturing the Low Mun stockades. He also placed his siege guns in position, and began a heavy bombardment in the morning of 29th November as the preliminary to attack. On his side, Mow Wang made all his preparations for defence, which had been rendered the more necessary because there were dissensions among the Taeping leaders themselves, one of whom, named Lar Wang, had offered to surrender with his followers to General Ching on terms. Partly on this account Chung Wang rode into Soochow with a bodyguard of a few hundred men by the only bridle-path available, and his presence composed for the moment the quarrels of the Taeping leaders. But the result depended on the successful defence of the stockades in front of the East Gate, and Gordon was equally intent on capturing them. After a short bombardment the breastwork seemed so knocked about that Gordon ordered a column to advance to the assault, but it was met by a tremendous fire and compelled to turn back. Then the bombardment was renewed, and the field-pieces were pushed forward as far as possible. A second assault was then delivered, but the creek—fourteen yards across—was too wide for the bridge, and things again looked black, when the officers boldly jumped into the water, and their men following, the whole position was captured at a rush. Once this success was gained, the defence of the Taepings, who had fought well, collapsed, and stockade after stockade was carried with little or no loss. Gordon himself, with a mere handful of men, captured three more stockades and a stone fort that he said could have held out after all the other positions had fallen. The loss of the corps in this severe but decisive engagement was heavy, amounting to 6 officers killed, and 3 wounded; 50 men killed, and 128 wounded, besides 5 Europeans of the Bodyguard. But this assault was decisive, inasmuch as it was the last that had to be made on the defences of Soochow before the fall of that place.

At this point it will be appropriate to say something about Gordon's relations with his own officers, many of whom contemplated, whenever dissatisfied with their treatment or at prolonged inaction, selling their cause and services to the Taepings. During the siege he discovered that Captain Perry had written a letter giving the enemy information, but Gordon agreed to look over the offence on the condition that Perry led the next forlorn hope, which happened to be the affair at the Leeku stockades. Gordon had forgotten the condition, but Perry remembered it, and led the assault. He was shot in the mouth, and fell into the arms of his commander, ever at the point of danger. Perry was the first man killed, and Gordon's epitaph was that he was "a very good officer." Although Gordon was a strict and even severe disciplinarian, he was always solicitous of the interests of the officers who worked under him, and he set apart the greater portion of his pay in the Chinese service, which had been fixed at £1,200 a year, for their benefit, more especially for the purchase of medicine and comforts for the ill or wounded. There was no exaggeration at all in the statement that he left China without any savings and as poor as when he reached it.

From the gallant deeds of Gordon and his corps the course of the siege passes to the intrigues and negotiations between General Ching and Lar Wang. These had made so much progress that Lar Wang's troops abandoned the formidable stockades in front of the North Gate, which were occupied without the least attempt at resistance. Several interviews took place with the Taeping leaders, and Gordon was present at some of these, but Li Hung Chang asserts that he was not present at the most important of them; and that he was not a signatory of the convention of surrender. He was strongly in favour of good terms being granted to the rebels, and impressed his views on both Li Hung Chang, who had come up to the camp to be present at the fall of Soochow, and General Ching. From both he received the most positive assurances that the lives of all the Wangs would be spared, and such was no doubt their intention, but events were too strong for them. The most interesting of these leaders, with, of course, the exception of Chung Wang, was Mow Wang, who would have nothing to say to a surrender, and wished to fight to the death. He was the man who had sent back Burgevine, and Gordon admired his courage so much that he resolved to spare no effort to save his life. He asked Li to assign Mow Wang to him, and this request was granted. Unfortunately all these efforts were thrown away, for on the 4th December, during a banquet given at Mow Wang's palace, the other Wangs had fallen upon and murdered that chief, who would have resisted with all his force their projected surrender of the place. The next day Lar Wang, who had taken an oath of brotherhood with General Ching, gave up one of the gates, and his numerous followers undertook to shave their heads in token of surrender. The Imperialist troops occupied the gate, and prepared to take possession of the city, but Gordon would not allow any of his men to leave the stockades as he foresaw the impossibility of preventing them from plundering if they were permitted to advance into the city. But he went and represented the case to Li Hung Chang, and demanded two months' pay for his men as a reward for their good service, and as some compensation for the loss of loot. Li replied that he could not grant the request, and Gordon at once resigned for the second time during his connection with the Chinese Government. There was serious risk of an outbreak on the part of the discontented soldiers of the Ever Victorious Army, but on General Ching providing one month's pay Gordon used his influence with his men to march quietly back to Quinsan. The men at first received this order with shouts of dissatisfaction, and even threatened to attack the Futai Li, but Gordon succeeded in overcoming their objections, and the worst that happened was a noisy demonstration as the troops passed Li Hung Chang's tent, where Gordon and another officer stood on guard.

The Chinese officials were delighted to thus get rid of the Ever Victorious Army, without which they would never have seen the inside of Soochow. Its presence diminished their credit and interfered with the execution of the plans which they had no doubt held throughout all the negotiations with Lar Wang. Neither Li nor Ching wished Lar Wang and his colleagues to be saved, and thus allowed to become rivals to themselves in the race of official honour and wealth. There was nothing surprising in this, and the only matter for astonishment is that Lar Wang, well acquainted with the Punic faith of his countrymen, and with such a black record from the Government point of view, should have so easily placed faith in the word of his enemies. This was the more extraordinary because Gordon himself went into the city and saw Lar Wang at his own house before he left for Li Hung

Chang's quarters, where a banquet had been arranged, and asked him very pressingly whether he was quite satisfied. Gordon himself seems to have had suspicions or apprehensions, for he even offered to take him on board his own steamer with which he was going to cruise in the Taiho Lake. Lar Wang, however, was quite confident, and said that all was well. This confidence was doubly unfortunate, for Gordon had excused himself from the Futai's banquet on the ground that his presence might seem humiliating to the Taeping leaders, whereas it was the only thing that could have averted their fate. As Gordon was leaving the city the Wangs passed him, laughing and talking, and riding apparently unarmed to the Futai's quarters. The next time Gordon saw them was when he beheld their headless bodies lying on the river bank near their host's camp.

Gordon after this walked through the city, as some hours would elapse before the steamer could get round to the south-west side, where he intended to embark. While on his way he was joined by Dr Macartney. They both proceeded to the walls near the Eastern Gate, and on looking towards the Futai's quarters Gordon noticed a large crowd, but he did not attach any significance to it. About half an hour later a large number of Imperial soldiers entered the city, and set up a yell, as was their custom, and fired off guns. Gordon represented to their officers that this conduct was against the agreement, and might lead to disturbance, as the city was still crowded with Taepings. At this juncture General Ching appeared. As Gordon was supposed to be on his steamer on his way to the lake, he seemed taken aback, and turned pale. To Gordon's repeated inquiries as to whether all was well, he made a rambling statement that Lar Wang had made unreasonable demands, that he had refused to carry out the exact terms of the surrender, and finally, that he had run away. Gordon then asked Dr Macartney, as he knew Chinese, to go to Lar Wang's house, and reassure him if he found him there, but this statement must be taken in conjunction with the important narrative I give two pages further on. Gordon went a little way with General Ching, and then decided to wait at the North Gate for further intelligence, while the Chinese commander continued his round. Gordon then began to question his own interpreter as to what he thought, and on receiving the reply that "there was something improper," he determined to proceed himself with all speed to Lar Wang's house. On his way he passed through crowds of excited Taeping soldiers, and he also met a band of Imperialists laden with plunder. Lar Wang's palace had been pillaged and gutted, but an uncle of his, named Wangchi, was there, and he begged Gordon to help him to escort the females of Lar Wang's family to his own house. Gordon agreed to do this, but when he reached Wangchi's house, he found five or six hundred armed men in the courtyard. The doors were closed, and Wangchi refused to allow either Gordon or his interpreter to leave. During the night large bodies of excited Taepings, who knew that their chiefs had been entrapped, although, fortunately, not aware of their murder, rallied on this spot, and Gordon was thus placed in a position of the greatest personal peril.

At length leave was given him to send his interpreter, escorted by two Taepings, to summon his own bodyguard, and to take an order to another part of his force to seize the Futai and hold him as a hostage for the safety of the Wangs. The interpreter was attacked on the way by Imperialists, who wounded him, and tore up Gordon's letters. When one of the Taeping guides brought back this news Gordon was allowed to leave himself for the same purpose; but he was arrested on the way by some Imperialists, detained for several hours, and the morning was far advanced before he was able to send back his bodyguard for the protection of Wangchi's house and family. He then moved a further force into the city, to prevent the massacre that the Imperialists seemed to be contemplating, and in this task he was gallantly seconded by Captain Bonnefoy and the Franco-Chinese contingent. Having taken these steps, Gordon waited near the Eastern Gate for all his steamers, with which he intended to seize the Futai, and make him give up the Wangs. At this moment General Ching approached him, but before he could begin his excuses, "he met with such a storm that he made a precipitate retreat into the city." Ching then sent an English officer, one of Gordon's own force, to explain matters, but he did not know whether the chiefs were alive or dead. He went on to say, however, that Lar Wang's son was in his tent, and on the boy being sent for, he said that his father had been executed on the opposite side of the creek. The steamers had still not arrived, and Gordon asked one of his lieutenants, Prince F. von Wittgenstein, to cross the creek in his boat and report what he saw. He returned with the intelligence that there were nine headless bodies. Gordon then crossed himself, and identified Lar Wang and several of his companions. There was consequently no further doubt as to what had happened, or anything left for Gordon to do than to secure them decent burial. Having done this he abandoned his trip to the Taiho Lake, and hastened to Quinsan.

The exact mode of this assassination seems to have been as follows: when the Wangs came out of the city they were met by General Ching, who did not, however, accompany them to the Futai Li Hung Chang. That official received them in a stockade near his boat, some conversation ensued, and then Li left the stockade. Here again reference should be made to the authoritative narrative that follows. A party of Imperial troops closed the gates, seized the Wangs, and at once beheaded them. Li Hung Chang very soon afterwards left his quarters for a different and remote part of the Imperial camp.

This treacherous act, although quite in accordance with Chinese traditions, was generally denounced at the time, and has excited much discussion since. Major Gordon certainly felt it very keenly, for he considered that his word had been pledged as much as the Chinese commander's for the safety of the leaders who surrendered. It has been shown how energetically he acted once he suspected that anything was wrong, but it seems as if it were going too far to say that he thought for a moment of exacting a summary revenge on the person of Li Hung Chang. Sir Henry Gordon, writing with at least a sense of responsibility, says on this point:

> It is not the fact that Major Gordon sought the Futai with the intention of shooting him. It is a complete misrepresentation to say he did so. It is true he endeavoured unsuccessfully to have an explanation with him, but not of the nature asserted.

But it must also be reaffirmed that as long as Gordon thought he could save the Wangs' lives he was prepared to secure the person of Li Hung Chang and hold him as a hostage for their safety. Of that, at least, there can be no question.

I must now ask the reader to return to the point when Gordon and Dr Macartney were standing on the wall near the Low Mun Gate, in order that the following important and authoritative narrative may be understood. General Ching entered by this gate at the head of a party of his troops, and Gordon, somewhat uneasy at the signs of commotion he thought he had detected across the creek, at once addressed him, asking—"Well, how did it go off? Have the Wangs seen the Futai?"

Taken off his guard, or confused between the sudden question and his own knowledge of what had occurred, Ching quickly replied, "They have not seen the Futai."

"What!" replied Gordon, equally hastily; "that must be nonsense. I saw the Wangs myself ride out of the city to the rendezvous, and spoke to them."

Ching then corrected himself by saying, "Oh, yes, that is all right, but they have not shaved their heads, and they want to retain half the city," the western half, that nearest to the relieving force, still at a considerable distance from Soochow, under the heroic Chung Wang.

To which Gordon at once responded, "That won't do. They must conform with what has been agreed upon," and turning to Macartney, he said, "Will you go to the Lar Wang's palace and tell him that this cannot be, and meet me afterwards at Wuliungchow, where I am to join the steamer *Hyson* to go on the Taiho Lake?"

Macartney at once accepted the mission, and proceeded to the Lar Wang's palace, but before following him thither it is necessary to refer to two earlier passages, one known and the other up to this moment unknown, in the relations of General Gordon and Sir Halliday Macartney.

The passage which is known is that where Macartney, sent as the representative of the Futai Li Hung Chang, and escorted by that Governor's own bodyguard, healed the breach caused between Gordon and General Ching by the latter firing on some of Gordon's troops and treating the matter with marked levity, which so enraged Gordon that he was on the point of attacking the Imperialist troops when Sir Halliday Macartney arrived as peacemaker, and with equal tact and energy averted the catastrophe. This incident has already been referred to, and need not further detain us. I come now to the second and more interesting matter.

Some weeks before the fall of Soochow, but at a moment when it had become clear that the place could not hold out much longer, Gordon approached Macartney and said:

"I want to speak to you very privately, and as I do not wish any one to hear our conversation, will you come on board my boat?"

When they were both on board, Gordon ordered his Chinese sailors to pull out to the centre of the lake before he would say a word. Having thus rendered secrecy assured, Gordon spoke as follows:

"McCartney, I have brought you out here so that nobody should know of our conversation, and that we might speak out as man to man. I must tell you, in the first place, that as soon as Soochow falls I intend to resign the command and return home. With that intention in my mind, I have been anxiously considering who was the best man to name as my successor in the command of the Ever Victorious Army, and, after the most careful consideration, I have come to the conclusion that you are the best man. Will you take the command?"

This unexpected question was the more embarrassing to Macartney, because, long before Gordon was appointed, rumour had freely credited him with coveting the command of the Ever Victorious

Army in succession to Burgevine, and, as a matter of fact, the Chinese authorities had wished him to have the command. However, nothing had come of the project, and Macartney, after his post as Burgevine's military secretary had ceased to exist with the dismissal and treason of that adventurer, was appointed to a separate command of a portion of the Imperialist forces. The course of events had now, in an unexpected but highly complimentary manner, brought the realisation of any hopes he may have entertained on the subject within his reach. He replied to Gordon as follows:

"As you speak so frankly to me, I will speak equally frankly to you, and tell you something I have never told a living person. Rumour has credited me with having aspired to the command of this force, but erroneously so. My ambition was to work myself up at Court, and only to take the command if forced on me as a provisional matter, and as a stepping-stone to my real object, which was, when my knowledge of the language was perfected, to acquire at Peking some such influence as that possessed by Verbiest and the other French missionaries in the seventeenth and eighteenth centuries. I should never have mentioned this to you lest you should not have believed it, but now that the command is at my feet I may make this avowal without any hesitation as to your accepting it. As you really think I can best succeed to the command of the force when you resign it, I am perfectly willing to accept the task."

To which Gordon replied: "Very well, then. That is settled."

With this private understanding, as to which nothing has been published until this moment, the conversation closed with a final injunction from Gordon of profound secrecy, as, should it become known, he might be unable to get certain of his more ambitious officers to take part in capturing the city. When Gordon therefore turned to Macartney, and asked him to proceed to the Lar Wang's palace and inform him that the terms of the convention must be carried out, it is necessary in order to throw light on what follows to state what their relations were at that moment. Gordon had selected Macartney as his successor in preference to all his own officers.

Macartney hastened to the Lar Wang's palace, but as he had lent Gordon his horse, his movements were slightly retarded. On reaching the building he noticed some signs of confusion, and when he asked one of the attendants to take him at once to his master, he received the reply that the Lar Wang was out. Sir Halliday Macartney is not a man to be lightly turned from his purpose, and to this vague response he spoke in peremptory terms:

"The matter is of the first importance. I *must* see the Lar Wang. Take me to him."

Then the servant of the Taeping leader did a strange thing.

"You *cannot* see my master," he said, and turning his face to the wall, so that no one else might see, he drew his open hand in a cutting position backwards and forwards. This is the recognised Chinese mode of showing that a man's head has been cut off.

Being thus apprised that something tragic had happened, Macartney hastened away to Wuliungchow to keep his appointment with Gordon, and to acquaint him with what had taken place at the Lar Wang's palace. But no Gordon came, and more than a day elapsed before Macartney and he met again under dramatic circumstances at Quinsan. After waiting at Wuliungchow some hours, Sir Halliday resolved to proceed to the Futai's camp, and learn there what had happened. But on arriving he was informed that the Futai was not in the camp, that no one knew where he was, and that Gordon was in a state of furious wrath at the massacre of the Wangs, which was no longer concealed. Macartney then endeavoured to find Gordon, but did not succeed, which is explained by the fact that Gordon was then hastening to Quinsan to collect his own troops. Baffled in these attempts, Macartney returned, after a great many hours, to his own camp near the Paotichiaou Bridge, there to await events, and on his arrival there he at last found the Futai Li who had come to him for security. Li put into his hands a letter, saying, "I have received that letter from Gordon. Translate its contents."

After perusing it, Macartney said: "This letter is written in a fit of indignation. You and Gordon are and have been friends, and I am also the friend of you both. The most friendly act I can do both of you is to decline to translate it. Let me therefore return you the letter unread."

"Very well," replied Li; "do as you think best, but as I am not to know the contents, I do not wish to have the letter. Please keep it."

Sir Halliday Macartney kept the letter, which remained in his possession for some time, until, in fact, he handed it, with an explanatory account of the whole affair, to Sir Harry Parkes, as will be explained further on.

After this point had been settled, Li Hung Chang went on to say that he wished Macartney to go and see Gordon at Quinsan, and speak to him as follows:—

"Tell Gordon that he is in no way, direct or indirect, responsible in this matter, and that, if he considers his honour involved, I will sign any proclamation he likes to draft, and publish it far and wide that he had no part in or knowledge of it. I accept myself the full and sole responsibility for what has been done. But also tell Gordon that this is China, not Europe. I wished to save the lives of the Wangs, and at first thought that I could do so, but they came with their heads unshaved, they used defiant language, and proposed a deviation from the convention, and I saw that it would not be safe to show mercy to these rebels. Therefore what was done was inevitable. But Gordon had no part in it, and whatever he demands to clear himself shall be done."

I do not gather that Sir Halliday Macartney had any serious misgivings about this mission when he undertook it. His relations with Gordon were, as has been shown, of a specially cordial and confidential character, and even if he failed to induce Gordon to abandon the threatening plans he had described in his letter to Li Hung Chang, which was in his pocket, there was no reason to apprehend any personal unpleasantness with one who had given the clearest proof of friendship and esteem. As I cannot give the full text of the original letter from General Gordon, I content myself by stating that its two principal passages were that Li Hung Chang should at once resign his post of Governor of Kiangsu, and give up the seals of office to Gordon, so that he might put them in commission until the Emperor's pleasure should be ascertained; or that, failing that step, Gordon would forthwith proceed to attack the Imperialists, and to retake from them all the places captured by the Ever Victorious Army, for the purpose of handing them back again to the Taepings. When Gordon went so far as to write a letter of that character, which, it must be admitted, was far in excess of any authority he possessed, it must be clear that the envoy, who came to put forward counsels that were intended to restore harmony, but that by so doing might assume the aspect of palliating the Futai's conduct, could not count on a very cordial reception from a man of Gordon's temperament, whose sense of honour and good faith had been deeply injured by the murder of the rebel leaders.

Still, Sir Halliday accepted the mission without hesitation, and hastened to carry it out without delay. It was late in the day when he saw Li Hung Chang, but having procured a native boat with several rowers, he set off in the evening, and reached Quinsan in the middle of the night. Gordon was then in bed and could not be disturbed, and while Macartney waited he drank some coffee Gordon's servant made for him, which he much needed, as he had left Soochow without having broken his fast during the whole day. After a short time, and before day had really broken, Gordon sent down word that he would see him, and Macartney went upstairs to an ill-lighted room, where he found

Gordon sitting on his bedstead. He found Gordon sobbing, and before a word was exchanged, Gordon stooped down, and taking something from under the bedstead, held it up in the air, exclaiming:

"Do you see that? Do you see that?"

The light through the small Chinese windows was so faint that Macartney had at first some difficulty in recognising what it was, when Gordon again exclaimed:

"It is the head of the Lar Wang, foully murdered!" and with that burst into hysterical tears.

At once perceiving that any conversation under these circumstances would do no good, Macartney said he would retire and see Gordon later. Some hours afterwards breakfast was served in a large room downstairs, where there were present not only many of the officers, but also several European merchants and traders of Shanghai, who had been in the habit of supplying the force with its commissariat requirements. Gordon came in, and Macartney took a seat beside him. After a few minutes' silence Gordon turned to Macartney, and said abruptly:

"You have not come for yourself. You have come on a mission from the Futai. What is it?"

When Macartney suggested that so public a place might not be the most suitable, Gordon said: "There are only friends here. I have no secrets. Speak out."

There was no longer any honourable way of avoiding the challenge, and Macartney described exactly what has been already recorded as to Li Hung Chang having come to him with Gordon's letter, which from friendly motives he had declined to translate, and stating that Li took the whole responsibility on himself, and would exonerate Gordon from the least complicity in the affair, with which the Chinese statesman averred Gordon had had nothing to do. He went on to urge with regard to the measures threatened by Gordon in expiation of the massacre that they were not justifiable, and would not in the end redound to Gordon's own credit. In conclusion, he said he felt sure that "a little reflection would show Gordon that to carry on a personal war with the Futai would be to undo all the good that had been done. Moreover, you must recollect that although you, no doubt, have at this moment the military force to carry out your threats, it will no longer be paid by the Chinese authorities. You will only be able to keep your men at your back by allowing them to plunder, and how long will that prove successful, and what credit will you get by it?"

Gordon here stamped his foot, saying he would have none of Macartney's mild counsels. To which Macartney replied, "Mild or not, they are the only ones your Minister at Peking and our Queen will approve. Nay, what I advise you to do is even that you would yourself do if you would but reflect, and not let yourself be influenced by those men sitting at your table."

To these undoubtedly prudent representations, supported as they were by at least one of those present, Mr Henry Dent, who got up and said that, in his opinion, Dr Macartney's advice ought to be followed, while the others who wished the war to go on from interested motives remained silent, Gordon did and would not listen. The hot fit of rage and horror at the treacherous murder of the Wangs, kept at fever-point by the terrible memorial in his possession, was still strong upon him, and his angry retort was—"I will have none of your tame counsels," and there and then ordered the *Hyson*, with a party of infantry, to be got ready to attack the Futai, at the same time offering Macartney a passage in the steamer.

On hearing this decisive declaration Macartney left the table, and hastening to one of Gordon's officers, who was a personal friend, he begged the loan of a horse and a pair of spurs. Having obtained what he wanted, he set off riding as hard as he could by the road, which was somewhat shorter than the canal, so that he might warn Li Hung Chang as to what was going to happen, and also bring up his own troops to oppose the advance of Gordon, who actually did move out of Quinsan with the intention of carrying out his threats, but returned there when his flotilla had proceeded half way.

By that time he had fortunately reflected on the situation, and a sanguinary struggle was averted. Gordon came to see that his honour was not in the slightest or most remote degree involved, and that China was not a country to which the laws of chivalry could be applied; but before he had reached this stage of mental equilibrium he had penned a most regrettable and cruelly unjust despatch, not about Li Hung Chang or any one involved in the massacre, but about Dr, now Sir Halliday Macartney, whose sole fault had been that he wished to make peace, and to advise Gordon to act in the very sense which he afterwards himself adopted.

In a despatch to General Brown, commanding at Shanghai, which appears in the *Blue Book* (China, No. 3, 1864, p. 198), Gordon wrote:

I then went to his (Li's) boat and left him a note in English, informing him of what my intention had been, and also my opinion of his treachery. I regret to say that Mr Macartney did not think fit to have this translated to him. . . . On 8th December the Futai sent Mr

Macartney to persuade me that he could not have done otherwise, and I blush to think that he could have got an Englishman, late an officer in Her Majesty's army, to undertake a mission of such a nature.

This statement, appearing in an official publication, has been largely quoted, especially in Mr Egmont Hake's *Story of Chinese Gordon*, and the original injury done by Gordon, for which at the time he atoned, was thus repeated in an offensive and altogether unjustifiable form twenty years after Gordon had stated publicly that he was sorry for having written this passage, and believed that Sir Halliday Macartney was actuated by just as noble sentiments as himself.

It is not an agreeable task for any biographer to record that his hero was in the wrong, but as General Gordon frankly and fully admitted that in this matter he was altogether to blame, and as Mr Hake's error shows that his retractation never obtained that publicity which he himself desired, I conceive myself to be carrying out his wishes in placing the following facts prominently before the reader.

When the Blue Book was published with the despatch referred to, Dr Macartney took no notice of it. Some time afterwards he met the late Sir Harry Parkes, then Consul-General at Shanghai, and he described what I have set forth in the same language. Sir Harry Parkes, than whom England never had a finer representative in the Far East, at once said: "This is very interesting. Sir Frederick Bruce is coming down shortly. I wish you would write out what you have told me, so that I might show it to him." Dr Macartney wrote out his narrative, and with it he sent Gordon's original letter to Li Hung Chang. Those documents have never been published, but they should still exist in the Shanghai Consulate. Sir Frederick Bruce's (brother of the ambassador Lord Elgin, and himself the First British Minister at Peking) comment after perusing them was: "Dr Macartney showed very great judgment and good sense, and no blame attaches to him in this matter."

A considerable period intervened between the breakfast scene at Quinsan and Gordon's next meeting with Macartney. In that period much had happened. Gordon had forgiven Li Hung Chang, done everything that Macartney had recommended as the right course in the memorable scene at Quinsan, and by some of the most remarkable of his military exploits had crushed the Taeping rebellion, but the two principal actors in this affair had not crossed each other's path.

Six weeks after Gordon brought his operations in the field to an end at Chanchufu in May he returned to Soochow, and Li Hung Chang, wishing to do him honour, asked him to an official breakfast at his *yamen*. At the same time Li Hung Chang said to Macartney: "I have asked Gordon to breakfast. I know you and he have had some difference. How would you meet him if you came too?"

To this question Macartney replied: "I would meet Gordon exactly as Gordon met me. It is true that Gordon did me an injustice, but I am quite ready to blot it out from my memory if Gordon will admit it. Gordon acted under a strong feeling of excitement when he was not master of himself, and I have no more thought of holding him strictly responsible for what he wrote at such a moment than I would a madman."

Li Hung Chang said: "Very well, then. I ask you to come to breakfast to meet him." On Macartney's return to his house he found a letter from Gordon waiting for him. In this letter Gordon admitted that he had done him a wrong, and was prepared to sign any paper to that effect that Macartney might prepare.

Macartney thereupon replied to Gordon, pointing out that the mere publication of a letter of retractation was not an adequate reparation for an injurious statement which had been given a wide circulation, and to a certain extent placed beyond recall by appearing in an official publication, but that if he might publish Gordon's own letter offering to do this in the *North China Herald*, he would be satisfied, and the matter, as far as he was concerned, might be considered at an end. To this course Gordon at once acquiesced, subject to the omission of one paragraph affecting a third person, and in no respect relating to Sir Halliday or his conduct. This letter, which the Editor of that paper stated he "published at Colonel Gordon's request," on 23rd July 1864, read as follows:

Shanghai
July 5, 1864
My Dear Macartney,—It is with much regret that I perceive in the last Blue Book issued on China affairs a Report from me to General Brown on the occurrences at Soochow, which report contains an injurious remark on your conduct.

I am extremely sorry that I ever penned that remark, as I believe you went out of your way on this occasion wholly on the same public grounds which led eventually to my taking the field myself, and I can only excuse my having done so by recollecting the angry feelings with which I was actuated at that time.

It will be my duty to rectify this error in other quarters, and in the meantime I beg you to make what use you may think fit of this letter.—Yours truly,
C. G. Gordon

On the next day Gordon and Macartney met at breakfast at the *yamen* of the Futai Li Hung Chang, and Gordon at once came up to Macartney and said:

"Do not let us talk of the past, but of the future. I am one of those who hold that when a man has wronged another he should seek opportunities through his life of making him redress. Now you are founding an Arsenal at Soochow, and I am going back to England, where I have a brother in the Arsenal at Woolwich. From him I can get you books, plans, and useful information. I will do so."

Gordon was as good as his word. He sent Macartney expensive plans and books, besides most valuable information. He also promised to write to the Duke of Cambridge as Commander-in-Chief, admitting that he was not justified in his criticism of Dr Macartney, who had acted in every way becoming an English gentleman and officer. Thus ended the misunderstanding between the two Englishmen who rendered China the best service she has ever obtained from foreigners; and knowing both these distinguished men intimately, I have much pleasure in testifying from my own knowledge to the accuracy of the following statement of Sir Halliday Macartney to myself that "after this, Gordon and I remained firm friends evermore."

Gordon's indignation at this outrage did not soon subside, and three weeks after it happened an opportunity presented itself for showing and perhaps relieving his mind. A high Chinese officer presented himself at his quarters at Quinsan to announce the receipt of an Imperial decree and presents from Peking as a reward for his share in the capture of Soochow. Gordon at once said that he would not accept the presents, and that they were not to be brought to him. The Chinese officer replied that they should not be brought, but that the emissary of the Emperor ought to be received. To this Gordon assented, and on 1st January 1864 he went down to receive him at the West Gate. On arriving there he met a procession carrying a number of open boxes, containing 10,000 *taels* (then about £3000 of our money) in Sycee shoes, laid on red cloth, also four Snake flags taken from the Taepings—two sent by Li Hung Chang, and two by another mandarin who had had no part in the Soochow affair. Gordon made the procession turn about and take the whole lot back again. He wrote his reply stating his reason on the back of the Imperial rescript itself; he rejected Li Hung Chang's flags, but he accepted the other two as being in no sense associated with the disgrace of the Taeping massacre. In this manner did Gordon show the Chinese what he thought of their conduct. His characteristic reply to the Imperial rescript read as follows:

Major Gordon receives the approbation of His Majesty the Emperor with every gratification, but regrets most sincerely that, owing to the circumstance which occurred since the capture of Soochow, he is unable to receive any mark of H.M. the Emperor's recognition, and therefore respectfully begs His Majesty to receive his thanks for his intended kindness, and to allow him to decline the same.

At this moment it will be recollected that Gordon was, strictly speaking, no longer in command. He had resigned, because his very reasonable demand for a gratuity to his troops had not been complied with. But circumstances were too strong for him, and a number of considerations, all highly creditable to his judgment and single-mindedness, induced him to sink his private grievances, and to resume the command on grounds of public policy and safety. The internal condition of the Ever Victorious Army itself, which inaction had brought to the verge of mutiny, was the determining fact that induced Gordon to resume the command, even at the price of meeting Li Hung Chang and sinking his differences with him. There had been much intrigue among the officers of the force as to who should succeed Gordon in the command, if he persisted in his resolve to give it up, and before tranquillity was restored sixteen of the agitating officers had to be dismissed. The force itself welcomed the formal resumption of the command by Gordon, and not the less because it signified a return to active operations after more than two months' inaction. The murder of the Wangs took place on 7th December 1863; it was on 18th February 1864 that Gordon marched out of Quinsan at the head of the bulk of his force.

In a letter written at the time, Sir Robert Hart, whose services to the Chinese Government, spread over the long period of forty years, have been of the highest order and importance, said:

The destiny of China is at the present moment in the hands of Gordon more than of any other man, and if he be encouraged to act vigorously, the knotty question of Taepingdom versus 'union in the cause of law and order' will be solved before the end of May, and quiet will at length be restored to this unfortunate and sorely-tried country. Personally, Gordon's wish is to leave the force as soon as he can. Now that Soochow has fallen, there is nothing more that he can do, whether to add to his own reputation or to retrieve that of British officers generally, tarnished by Holland's defeat at Taitsan. He has little or nothing personally to gain from future successes, and as he has himself to lead in all critical moments, and is constantly exposed to danger, he has before him the not very improbable contingency of being hit sooner or later. But he lays aside his personal feelings, and seeing well that if he were now to leave the force it would in all probability go at once to the rebels or cause some other disaster, he consents to remain with it for a time.

During that interval some minor successes had been obtained by the Imperialists. Several towns surrendered to Li Hung Chang, and Chung Wang evacuated Wusieh and retired to Chanchufu, also on the Grand Canal. At the same time he hastened himself to Nanking, in the vain hope of arousing Tien Wang to the gravity of the situation, and inducing him to make some special effort to turn the fortune of the war. General Ching succeeded in capturing Pingwang, and with it another entrance into the Taiho Lake. San Tajin moved his camp close up to Changchufu and engaged the Taepings in almost daily encounters, during one of which the *Firefly* steamer was retaken, and its English captain killed. In consequence of this all the Europeans left the service of the Taepings, and as their fleet had been almost entirely destroyed, they were now hemmed in within a small compass, and Gordon himself estimated that they ought to be finally overcome within two months. In this hope he resumed the command, and his decision was officially approved of and confirmed by the British Minister at Peking.

The Taepings still retained possession of Hangchow and some other towns in the province of Chekiang, but all communication between them and Nanking had been severed by the fall of Soochow, so far at least as the routes east of the Taiho Lake were concerned. West of that lake they still held Yesing and Liyang, which enabled them to maintain communication, although by a roundabout route. Gordon determined to begin his campaign by attacking these two places, when the severance would be complete.

Yesing, on the north-west corner of the lake, was the first object of attack. Liyang is about fifty miles further inland than that town. The Taepings at Yesing were not dreaming of an attack when Gordon, at the head of his force, suddenly appeared before its walls. He found the surrounding villages in a most appalling state of distress, the inhabitants living on human food. The town was well surrounded by ditches and stockades, and Gordon felt compelled to reconnoitre it most carefully before deciding on his plan of attack. While engaged in this work his ardour carried him away, and he was nearly captured by the enemy. It was one of the narrowest of his many escapes during the war, and went far to justify the reputation he had gained of having a charmed life. A very striking instance of his narrowly escaping a premature end had occurred during the siege of Soochow itself, when the marvellous fifty-three-arch bridge at Patachiaou was destroyed. One evening Gordon was seated smoking a cigar on one of the damaged parapets of the bridge, when two shots fired by his own men struck the stone-work close by him. He got down at the second shot, and entered his boat. Hardly had he done so when the bridge collapsed with a tremendous crash, nearly smashing his boat and killing two men. In all the engagements, except when confined to his boat, Gordon always led the attack, carrying no weapons, except a revolver which he wore concealed in his breast, and never used except once, against one of his own mutineers, but only a little rattan cane, which his men called his magic wand of Victory. A graphic picture was drawn by one of his own officers of this unarmed leader in the breach of an assaulted position urging on his men by catching them by the sleeve of their coats, and by standing indifferent and unresisting in the midst of the thickest fire. Gordon long afterwards admitted that during the whole of these scenes he was continuously praying to the Almighty that his men should not turn tail. In the varied and voluminous annals of war there is no more striking figure than this of human heroism combined with spiritual fervour.

The attack on Yesing lasted several days, as, owing to the manner in which the country was cut up by canals, all the operations had to be conducted with great caution. The capture of the southern stockades was followed after a day's interval by the evacuation of the latter and the flight of the garrison, who however pillaged the town as far as they could before leaving. Gordon would not let his men enter the town, as he knew they would pillage, and thus get out of hand. They were so disappointed that several cases of insubordination occurred, and one mutineer had to be shot. The Imperialists were left to garrison Yesing, but under strict injunctions that they were on no account to take life; and under the threats of Li Hung Chang, who did not wish a repetition of the Soochow affair, these were strictly obeyed. All these arrangements having been made, Gordon resumed his march towards Liyang on 4th March, the infantry proceeding overland, and the artillery in the boats and *Hyson* steamer.

At Liyang the rebels had collected a large force, and made every preparation for a vigorous defence. But Gordon was quite confident of success, although he was now operating in the heart of a hostile country, and at a distance from his base. The sound flotilla which mounted formidable artillery, and which co-operated with him on the creek that led to the walls of Liyang, gave him sound reasons for confidence, and additional ground of security in the event of any accident. But his military skill and careful arrangements were not subjected to any severe test, as a mutiny broke out among the Taepings themselves, and the half in favour of surrender got possession of the city, and closed the gates on those of their comrades who wished to hold out. Major Gordon promptly accepted their surrender, and guaranteed their personal safety to all, thus obtaining a signal success without any loss. This was the more satisfactory because Liyang was found to be an admirable position for defence, strongly fortified with numerous stockades, well supplied with provisions for several months' siege, and garrisoned by 15,000 well-armed and well-clothed rebels. These men were disarmed, and allowed to go where they liked after they had shaved their heads in token of surrender. The provisions they had stored up for their own use were distributed among the starving peasants of the surrounding country. Gordon himself saved the lives of the female relatives of the Taeping Wang, who had wished to hold out, not however, it should in fairness be stated, from the official Chinese, but from the Taepings who had surrendered. After the capitulation was over, Gordon took 1000 of the Taepings into his own force, and he also engaged the services of another 1500 as a new contingent, to fight under their own officers. In this unusual manner he nearly doubled the effective strength of his own corps, and then advanced north to attack the town of Kintang, rather more than forty miles north of Liyang. At this point Gordon experienced his first serious rebuff at the hands of Fortune, for the earlier reverse at the Soochow stockades was so clearly due to a miscarriage in the attack, and so ephemeral in its issue, that it can scarcely be counted.

Unlike the other Taeping towns, all of which were stockaded positions, Kintang had no outer defences. It presented the appearance of a small compact city with a stone wall. No flags were shown; the place might have been deserted, but the complete silence seemed ominous. Gordon selected his point of attack, and began a bombardment, which continued during three hours, and then he ordered the assault. As the bugles sounded the advance, the Taepings appeared for the first time on the walls, and received the assailants with a heavy fire. At this critical moment Gordon received a severe wound below the knee, and had to be carried to his boat. His place was taken by Major Brown, brother of the General commanding at Shanghai, who advanced waving Gordon's own flag, but he too received a severe wound, and was carried off the field. The rebels fought with great desperation, and Gordon, who remained conscious, sent orders from his boat for the discontinuance of the attack. The loss was heavy—two officers killed, eleven wounded, and 115 rank and file killed and wounded. Gordon, notwithstanding his wound, would have renewed the attack, but for the receipt of alarming intelligence from his rear. Li Hung Chang wrote that the Taepings had turned the flank of his brother's army, and captured Fushan. They were at that moment besieging Chanzu, and had carried terror into the very heart of the Imperial position. Gordon's wound—the only one of any severity he ever received—excited much sympathy among the Chinese, and was made the subject of an Imperial edict ordering Li Hung Chang to call on him daily, and "requesting Gordon to wait until he shall be perfectly restored to health and strength."

In the extremity to which he was reduced, the brilliant idea had occurred to Chung Wang to assume the offensive at a point most remote from the scene where Gordon was acting in person. Hence the sudden and successful attack on Fushan, and his strategy was rewarded by the paralysis it produced in the Imperial plans. Gordon at once hastened back to Liyang, where he left a strong garrison, and taking only 1000 men, half of whom were the irregular Taeping contingent raised at Liyang itself, proceeded by forced marches to Wusieh. As the late Sir George Chesney well said, it is impossible to decide whether the temerity or the confidence of the young wounded commander was the more calculated to excite wonder. On arriving here, he found that nothing worse had happened than what had been already reported, while in the south, beyond his sphere of operations, the important city of Hangchow had been evacuated by the Taepings; and with this loss another avenue for obtaining arms and ammunition was closed to them.

The relief of Kongyin, which was hard pressed, was the first task Gordon set himself; and as he could not leave his boat on account of his wound, the conduct of operations was attended with much difficulty. After obtaining several minor successes, and approaching to within a few miles of Kongyin, Gordon found it necessary to completely alter his plans, and to attack the Taepings in their headquarters at Waisso, before relieving the former place. He accordingly proceeded to Waisso with his artillery on board the flotilla, and his infantry marching by land. The latter, carried away by some trifling successes, attacked the Waisso stockades without his orders, and even without his knowledge; and having invited a reverse by their rashness and disobedience, rendered it complete by an inexcusable panic, during which the Taeping cavalry, not more than 100 strong, rode through the best regiment of the force; the rebels, carrying a sword in each hand, cut down the fugitives right and left. The pursuit lasted for three miles, and 7 European officers killed, 1 wounded, 252 men killed, and 62 wounded, represented the heavy loss in this disastrous affair. The survivors, many of whom had thrown away their arms, were so panic-stricken that Gordon had to retire, and to summon up fresh troops.

For this disaster Gordon held the officers, and not the men, to be blameworthy. They led the men into a false position, and then did not make the proper movements. If the men had only formed square, Gordon wrote, it would have been all right with them. After this Gordon waited to allow of his wound being thoroughly cured, and on 6th April he again appeared before Waisso. A large Imperial force also enveloped the place on all sides but one, which had been left apparently open and unguarded in the hope that the garrison would use it as a means of reaching a place of safety. The Imperialists had, however, broken all the bridges along this route, so that the Taepings would soon encounter serious difficulties to their progress, and admit of their being taken at a great disadvantage. Gordon approached the place with much caution, and he found it so strongly fortified on the south side, opposite his line of approach, that he moved round to the north in search of a more favourable point of attack. This simple manoeuvre so disconcerted the Taepings that they abandoned several of their stockades, which Gordon promptly seized; and finding that these in turn commanded others, he succeeded in carrying the whole of a most formidable position with little or no loss. The Taeping garrison fled in confusion and suffered heavily at the hands of the Imperial troops. It rallied on the camp before Kongyin, and the day after this success Gordon marched from Waisso to attack them. The Taepings were thoroughly disorganised, and apparently amazed at the number of their opponents, for the whole of the population rose against them in revenge for the outrages they had perpetrated. There was only one action, and that of an insignificant description, when the whole Taeping force before Kongyin broke into a rout. The Imperialist plan for retarding their retreat succeeded to admiration, and of more than 10,000 men not a tenth escaped from the sword of their pursuers.

In a letter written at this time to his mother, Gordon, who, at the end of February had been raised to the rank of Lieutenant-Colonel in the army for distinguished conduct in the field, gave a graphic account of the condition of the region in which he was operating:

The rebels are very much pressed, and three months should finish them. During the pursuit from Kongyin the Imperialists and villagers killed in one village 3000. I will say this much—the Imperialists did not kill the coolies and boys. The villagers followed up and stripped the fugitives stark naked, so that all over the country there were naked men lying down in the grass. The cruelties these rebels had committed during their raid were frightful; in every village there were from ten to sixty dead, either women—frightfully mutilated—old men, or small children. I do not regret the fate of these rebels. I have no talent for description, but the scenes I have witnessed of misery are something dreadful, and I must say that your wish for me to return with the work incomplete would not be expressed if you saw the state of these poor people. The horrible furtive looks of the wretched inhabitants hovering around one's boat haunts me, and the knowledge of their want of nourishment would sicken anyone. They are like wolves. The dead lie where they fall, and are in some cases trodden quite flat by the passers-by. I hope to get the Shanghai people to assist, but they do not *see* these things, and to *read* that there are human beings eating human flesh produces less effect than if they saw the corpses from which that flesh is cut. There is one thing I promise you, and that is, that as soon as I can leave this service, I will do so; but I will not be led to do what may cause great disasters for the sake of getting out of the dangers, which, in my opinion, are no greater in action than in barracks. My leg is all right; the eleventh day after I received the wound I was up, and by the fifteenth day I could walk well. The ball went through the thick part of the leg, just below the knee.

Having thus cleared the district due north of Wusieh, Gordon proceeded against the main Taeping position at Chanchufu, north-west of that place, and on the Grand Canal. Here Chung Wang had fortified thirty stockades, and commanded in person. On inspecting it, Gordon found it so strong that he summoned up his troops from Liyang, and it was not until 22nd April, ten days after Waisso, that he had collected all his force of 4000 men for the attack. On the very day he accomplished this the Imperialists alone attacked some stockades outside the West Gate, and carried them by a heavy and unnecessary loss of life. Their defenders, instead of retreating into Chanchufu, fled northwards to their next possession, at Tayan. The same night part of the garrison left behind made a sortie, but Gordon was apprised of it, and it was easily repulsed. The next day he captured all the stockades on the southern, or, more correctly, the western side of the Canal, but the Taepings still held a strong stone fort on the opposite side, which defied all the efforts of the Imperialists. Two hundred of the Liyang corps gallantly crossed the Canal in boats, forced open the back door of the fort, and carried it at a rush. With this success all the outworks of Chanchufu were taken, and the town itself closely besieged. Gordon then proceeded to plant his batteries opposite the point he had selected for attack, but a regrettable affair happened in the night, when the picket on guard fired into the party working at the battery, and killed Colonel Tapp, an excellent officer who commanded the artillery of the force. This mishap was quickly followed by others. The Imperialists under their own generals wished to get all the credit of the capture, and attacked several times on their own side, but always without obtaining any advantage. Nor was Gordon himself more fortunate. After a severe bombardment, to which the Taepings made no reply, Gordon assaulted on 27th April. His men succeeded in throwing two pontoons across the ditch, twenty yards wide, and some of his officers reached the wall; but the Taepings met them boldly with a terrific storm of fire-balls, bags of powder, stink-pots, and even showers of bricks. Twice did Gordon lead his men to the assault, but he had to admit his repulse with the loss of his pontoons, and a great number of his best officers and men. Ten officers killed and 19 wounded, 40 men killed and 260 wounded, represented the cost of this disastrous failure.

Undaunted by this defeat, Gordon proceeded to lay siege in regular form, and Li Hung Chang lent him the services of his own troops in order to dig the necessary trenches. Working only at night, and with equal celerity and secrecy, a succession of trenches were made right up to the edge of the ditch. At the same time, proclamations in large characters were exhibited, offering terms to all who came over, except the Wang in command; and many desertions took place. At last, on 11th May, the place was again assaulted, this time at mid-day; and owing to the short distance from the advance trench to the breach, the Chinese troops of all kinds were able to come to close fighting with the Taepings without any preliminary loss. The Taepings fought with great courage, even although their chief Hoo Wang was taken prisoner early in the fight, but at last they were overwhelmed by numbers. Hoo Wang and all the Canton and Kwangsi men—that is to say, the original Taeping band—were executed, and the completeness of the triumph was demonstrated by the surrender, two days later, of Tayan, the last of the Taeping possessions on the Grand Canal. On the spur of the moment, two hours after the successful assault, Gordon wrote a hurried few lines to his mother, stating, to relieve her anxiety, that he would "not again take the field," and that he was happy to say he had "got off safe."

The capture of Chanchufu was the last achievement of the Ever Victorious Army, which marched back to Quinsan, its headquarters, in preparation for its disbandment, which had been decided on by the joint conclusion of the Chinese and European authorities. It had done its work, and the Chinese naturally regarded the presence of this formidable and somewhat unruly force with no little apprehension. The Taepings were now confined to Nanking, and the Viceroy, Tseng Kwofan, felt confident that before long he would be able to capture that city. The British Government had decided that the service of Major Gordon under the Chinese should terminate on 1st June 1864, and some weeks before that order was put in force the army was quietly disbanded, without any disturbance or display. The troops themselves would have given their commander a demonstration, but he evaded them, and escaped quietly into Shanghai, passing without regret from the position of the arbiter of an Empire's destiny to the routine of an English officer's existence. At the same time a considerable part of his force was taken into the service of Li Hung Chang. Gordon's own opinion of his work was given in the following letter:

I have the satisfaction of knowing that the end of this rebellion is at hand, while, had I continued inactive, it might have lingered on for years. I do not care a jot about my promotion or what people may say. I know I shall leave China as poor as I entered it, but with the knowledge that, through my weak instrumentality, upwards of eighty to one hundred thousand lives have been spared. I want no further satisfaction than this.

Having retired from the active direction of the campaign, Gordon still retained sufficient interest in the work he had had in hand so long to incline him to accept an invitation to visit the lines of Tseng Kwofan before Nanking. On 26th June he visited that Viceroy's camp, and found that his position extended over from twenty-four to thirty miles, and that he commanded 80,000 troops, who were, however, badly armed. The troops were well fed, but ill paid, and at last confident of success. While Gordon was there, or only a few hours after he left, Tien Wang, the leader of the moribund Taeping cause, seeing no chance of escape, swallowed gold leaf in the approved regal fashion, and died. On the 19th July the Imperialists succeeded in running a gallery under the wall of Nanking, and in charging it with 40,000 lbs. of powder. The explosion destroyed fifty yards of the wall, and the Imperialists at once stormed the breach. Chung Wang made a valiant defence in his own palace, and then cut his way out, at the head of 1000 men. Very few of these escaped, but Chung Wang and the young Tien Wang, son of the defunct leader, were among the fortunate few. Chung Wang was soon captured, and beheaded on 7th August, after being allowed a week's respite to write the history of the Taeping rebellion. At least it may be claimed for him that he was the only true hero of the rebel movement. Gordon's own estimation of this leader is given in these words:

> He was the bravest, most talented, and enterprising leader the rebels had. He had been in more engagements than any other rebel leader, and could always be distinguished. His presence with the Taepings was equal to a reinforcement of 5000 men, and was always felt by the superior way in which the rebels resisted. He was the only rebel chief whose death was to be regretted; the others, his followers, were a ruthless set of bandit chiefs.

The young Tien Wang was eventually captured and executed. Thus terminated, in the blood of its authors and leaders, the great rebellion, which had inflicted an incalculable amount of misery and loss on the Chinese people in a vain attempt to subvert the existing dynasty. Six hundred cities were stated to have been destroyed during its course, and sixteen out of the eighteen provinces to have witnessed the ravages of civil war.

Having thus concluded his work as commander of the Ever Victorious Army, it might have been thought that Gordon would be allowed to carry out his own wish of returning home as quickly as possible, but the English, as well as the Chinese, authorities were desirous of organising a purely Chinese force, with the object of supplying the Government with the means of asserting its authority over any internal enemies. Sir Frederick Bruce came specially from Pekin to Shanghai on the subject, and Gordon undertook to give the necessary organisation his personal supervision until it was in fair working order. From the end of June until the middle of November Colonel Gordon was engaged in the Chinese camp, which was formed at a place near Sungkiang, drilling recruits, and endeavouring to inspire the officers with the military spirit. He describes his work in the following short note, which is also interesting as expressing his impressions about the Chinese people:

I have the manual, and platoon, and company drill in full swing, also part of the battalion drill, and one or two men know their gun drill very fairly. This is so far satisfactory, and I think, if the whole country was not corrupt, they might go on well and quickly, but really it is most irritating to see the jealousies of the mandarins of one another. The people are first-rate, hard-working, and fairly honest; but it seems as soon as they rise in office they become corrupt. There is lots of vitality in the country, and there are some good men; but these are kept down by the leaden apathy of their equals, who hate to see reform, knowing their own deficiencies.

By the end of November Gordon was able to think of returning home, as he had given a start to military reform in China; but before he sailed he had to receive a congratulatory address from the most prominent citizens and merchants of Shanghai, expressing their "appreciation and admiration of his conduct." They had not always been so discriminating, and at the beginning their sympathies had been for the Taepings, or at least for strict non-intervention. The Chinese Government also gave exceptional signs of its gratitude to the noble-minded soldier, who had rendered it such invaluable aid. It again offered him a large sum of money, which was declined with as much firmness, although less emphasis, as on the earlier occasion. But he could not reject the promotion offered him to the high rank of Ti-Tu, or Field Marshal in the Chinese army, or churlishly refuse to receive the rare and high dignity of the Yellow Jacket. The English reader has been inclined on occasion to smile and sneer at that honour, but its origin was noble, and the very conditions on which it was based ensured that the holders should be very few in number.

The story of its origin will admit of being retold. When the Manchus conquered China, in the middle of the seventeenth century, they received material aid from a Chinese soldier named Wou Sankwei. He was rewarded with the Viceroyalty of the whole of south-western China, in which region he became supreme. After many years the Manchus thought he posed with too great an air of independence, and he was summoned to Peking to give an account of his stewardship. But Wou Sankwei was too old to be caught by so simple a ruse. He defied the Manchus, and established his authority throughout the larger part of the country south of the Great River. The young and afterwards illustrious Emperor Kanghi threw himself into the struggle with ardour, and it continued for many years, and devastated almost as large an area as did the Taeping rebellion. Kanghi did not obtain a decisive triumph until after the death of Wou Sankwei, when he bestowed a yellow riding jacket and an ornament of peacock's feathers for the cap on his principal lieutenants. He also decreed that this decoration should be made a regular order, to be conferred only on generals who had led victorious armies against rebel forces. Gordon was thus perfectly qualified to receive the order founded by the famous Manchu contemporary of the Grand Monarque.

The Chinese Government also sent him six mandarin dresses in the correct fashion for a commanding officer of the rank of Ti-Tu, and a book explaining how they should be worn. Gordon said very little about it, his only comment being: "Some of the buttons on the mandarin hats are worth thirty or forty pounds. I am sorry for it, as they cannot afford it over well; it is, at any rate, very civil of them." The two Empress Regents also struck a heavy gold medal in his honour, the destination of which will be told hereafter, and Li Hung Chang did everything possible to demonstrate the respect and regard he entertained for his European colleague. That that was no transitory feeling was well shown thirty-two years later, when the famous Chinese statesman seized the occasion of his visit to London to place wreaths on the statue and cenotaph of his old comrade in arms. General Gordon valued the Yellow Jacket and the Gold Medal very highly. When he gave up the medal for the cause of charity he felt its loss keenly, and it became a phrase with him to signify the height of self-sacrifice to say, "You must give up your medal." Prince Kung, in a special and remarkable despatch to the British Minister, narrated in detail the achievements of Gordon, and declared in graceful language that "not only has he shown himself throughout both brave and energetic, but his thorough appreciation of that important question, a friendly understanding between China and foreign nations, is also deserving of the highest praise." The Minister was requested to bring these facts to the notice of the British Government, and it was even suggested by the Chinese Prince that some reward that Gordon would appreciate at the hands of his own Sovereign should be conferred on him, and would be hailed with satisfaction in China. If I add to this list the sword of Chung Wang, captured from one of his lieutenants, and presented afterwards by Gordon to the Duke of Cambridge, the rewards of Gordon from the Chinese are fully catalogued. At the hands of his own Government he received for his magnificent service a brevet lieutenant-colonelcy, and somewhat later the Companionship of the Bath.

Gordon had kept a journal, which he sent home; but subsequently, on finding that it was being circulated, he destroyed it. Of this fact there is no doubt, and it is of course impossible to say whether it contained more than the manuscript history of the Taeping war, which he lent me in 1881 as "a trustworthy narrative" for the purposes of my "History of China," and which was published many years later as a separate volume. The authorship of that history is a matter of speculation, but there seems little or no doubt that it was at least compiled under Gordon's own direction, from the reports of his lieutenants in China, and completed during his residence at Gravesend.

Of the true personal journal Gordon wrote in 1864:

> I do not want the same published, as I think, if my proceedings sink into oblivion, it would be better for every one; and my reason for this is that it is a very contested point whether we ought to have interfered or not, on which point I am perfectly satisfied that it was the proper and humane course to pursue, but I still do not expect people who do not know much about it to concur in the same. . . . I never want anything published. I am sure it does no good, and makes people chary of writing.

The same feeling came out in his last letter to his mother from China, 17th November 1864:

> The individual is coming home, but does not wish it known, for it would be a signal for the disbanded to come to Southampton, and although the waits at Christmas are bad, these others are worse.

Such a wish as this was impossible of gratification. The public press could not be silenced by the modesty of this retiring commander whose deeds had been so heroic and devoid of selfish purpose. The papers became so filled with accounts of his achievements that he gave up reading them, but *The Times* had at least crystallised the opinion of the day into a single sentence:

> Never did soldier of fortune deport himself with a nicer sense of military honour, with more gallantry against the resisting, and with more mercy towards the vanquished, with more disinterested neglect of opportunities of personal advantage, or with more entire devotion to the objects and desires of his own Government, than this officer who, after all his victories, has just laid down his sword.

The more calmly and critically the deeds of the Ever Victorious Army and Gordon's conduct during the campaign against the Taepings are considered, the greater will be the credit awarded to the high-minded, brave, and unselfish man who then gained the sobriquet of "Chinese" Gordon. Among all the deeds of his varied and remarkable career he never succeeded in quite the same degree in winning fame and in commanding success. At Khartoum the eyes of the world were on him, but the Mahdi was allowed to remain victorious, and the Soudan still awaits fresh conquest. But during the two Taeping campaigns he was completely successful, and closed his work with an unqualified triumph. It was also the only occasion when he led an army in the field, and proved his claims to be considered a great commander. Of serious warfare it may be said to have been his last experience, for his own Government was very careful to give him no active military employment—garrison, and even consular duties being deemed more suitable for this victorious leader than the conduct of any of those little expeditions commencing with the Red River and Ashanti for which he was pre-eminently qualified—and under the Khedive he controlled an army without finding a real foe. Gordon's title to rank among skilful military commanders rests on his conduct at the head of the Ever Victorious Army during the Taeping war. It has earned the praise of many competent military authorities as well as the general admiration of the public, and Lord Wolseley must have had it in his mind when, in vindicating his sanity, he exclaimed that he "wished other English generals had been bitten with his madness."

Those who have thought that Gordon won his victories in China by sheer personal gallantry, and nothing else, have taken a very shallow view of the case, and not condescended to study the details. In his general conception of the best way to overcome the Taepings he was necessarily hampered by the views, wishes, jealousies, and self-seeking purposes of his Chinese colleagues. But for them, his strategy would have been of a very different character, as he himself often said. He had to adjust his means to the best attainable end, and it must be allowed that he did this with remarkable tact and patience—the very qualities in which he was naturally most deficient. If we consider his strategy as being thus fettered by the Chinese officials Li Hung Chang and General Ching, whose first object was not so much the overthrow of the Taeping Government as the expulsion of the Taepings from the province for which they were responsible, it will be admitted that nothing could be better than his conception of what had to be done, and how it was to be effected. The campaign resolved itself into the cutting off of all their sources of supply from the sea and Treaty ports, and the shutting up of their principal force within the walls of Soochow. How well and successfully that was accomplished has been narrated, but a vainglorious commander could not have been held back after the fall of Chanchufu from leading his victorious force to achieve a crowning triumph at Nanking, which Gordon could easily have carried by assault before the order in council withdrawing his services came into effect.

More frequent opportunity was afforded for Gordon to reveal his tactical skill than his strategical insight, and in this respect the only trammels he experienced were from the military value and efficiency of his force, which had its own limitations. But still it would be unjust to form too poor an estimate of the fighting efficiency and courage of either Gordon's force or his Taeping opponents from the miserable exhibition the Chinese recently made of themselves during the war with Japan. The heavy losses incurred, the several repulses Gordon himself experienced, would alone tell a different tale, if there were not the obstinate resistance offered to General Staveley and the French by the Taepings to show that they were not altogether contemptible adversaries. Gordon himself thought that his force could fight very well, and that his officers, if somewhat lacking in polish, were not to be surpassed in dash and devilry. For the Taepings, especially behind walls, and when it was impossible to out-manoeuvre them, he had also the highest opinion, and his first object on every occasion was to discover a weak point in their position, and his patience and perspicuity were generally rewarded. The very first step he took on approaching any place that he had to attack was to reconnoitre it himself, either on foot or in one of his steamers, and he wrote a powerful despatch pointing out the general neglect of this precaution in the conduct of our Eastern campaigns, with its inevitable heavy attendant loss of precious lives. As he truly said, a careful reconnaissance generally revealed points of weakness in the enemy's position, and the Taepings, like all Asiatics, were easily demoralised when their line of retreat was threatened, or when attacked at some point where their preparations had not been perfected. Among his own personal qualifications, his untiring energy and his exceptional promptitude in coming to a decision were the most remarkable. No exertion relaxed his effort or diminished his ardour, and in face of fresh perils and disappointments he was always ready with a new plan, or prepared with some scheme for converting defeat into victory. One of his chief characteristics was his quickness in seeing an alternative course of action when his original plan had either failed or been thwarted by others. Of his personal courage and daring sufficient instances have been given to justify the assertion that in those qualities he was unsurpassable; and if he had never done anything else than lead the Ever Victorious Army, it would be sufficient to secure him a place among the most remarkable of English soldiers. In China he will be remembered for his rare self-abnegation, for his noble disdain of money, and for the spirit of tolerance with which he reconciled the incompatible parts of "a British officer and a Chinese mandarin."

CHAPTER 6

Gravesend and Galatz

After the exciting and eventful ten years which began in the Crimea and ended in China, the most tranquil period in Gordon's career follows, until he was once again launched on the stormy sea of public affairs in Africa. He used to speak of the six years following his return from the Far East as the happiest of his life, and by a fortunate although unusual coincidence the details of his existence during the tranquil and uneventful period have been preserved with great amplitude and fidelity by several witnesses associated with him in his beneficent as well as his official work. It would be easy to fill a small volume with these particulars, which have been already given to the world, but here it will suffice to furnish a summary sufficient to bring out the philanthropic side of his character, and to explain how and why it came to be thought that Gordon was the man to solve that ever-pressing but ever-put-off problem of diminishing the pressure of excessive population and poverty in the eastern districts of London.

General Gordon arrived in England early in 1865, and proceeded to join his family at Rockstone Place, Southampton, where he was then doubly welcomed, as his father was in declining health, and died soon afterwards. Here Gordon passed a quiet six months, refusing all invitations with extreme modesty, and in every way baffling the attempts of relations, friends, and admirers to make a lion of him. He would not permit anyone to say that his suppression of the Taeping rebellion was a marvellous feat, and he evaded and resented all the attempts made by those in power to bring him into prominence as a national hero. Modesty is becoming as an abstract principle of human conduct, but Gordon carried it to an excess that made it difficult not so much for his fellow-men to understand him, as for them to hold ordinary workaday relations with him. This was due mainly to two causes—a habitual shyness, and his own perception that he could not restrain his tongue from uttering unpalatable and unconventional truths. He was so unworldly and self-sacrificing in his own actions that he could not let himself become even in a passive sense subservient to the very worldly means by which all men more or less advance in public and private life. The desire of Ministers and War Office authorities to bring him forward, to eulogise his Chinese exploits, and in the end to give him worthy employment, was regarded by him as that secret favouritism that he abhorred. He retired into his shell at every effort made to bring him into prominence. He tore up his diary sooner than that it should be the means of giving him notoriety. He even refused special employment and promotion, because it would put him over the heads of his old comrades at the Woolwich Academy. The inevitable result followed. Those in power came to regard him as eccentric, and when occasions arose that would have provided him with congenial and much-desired employment on active service for his own country, his name was passed over, and the best soldier in England was left in inglorious and uncongenial inactivity. This was regrettable, but natural. The most heroic cannot pose as being too elevated above their fellows, or they will be left like Achilles sulking in his tent.

There were moments, we have been told, when in the bosom of the family circle he threw off the reserve in which he habitually wrapped himself, and narrated in stirring if simple language the course of his campaigns in China. These outbursts were few and far between. They became still less frequent when he found that the effect of his description was to increase the admiration his relatives never concealed from him. His mother, whose feelings towards him were of a specially tender nature, and whose solicitude for his personal safety had been more than once evinced, took the greatest pride in his achievements, and a special pleasure at their recital. But even her admiration caused Charles Gordon as much pain as pleasure, and it is recorded that while she was exhibiting to a circle of friends a map drawn by him during his old term days at the Academy, he came into the room, and seeing that it was being made a subject of admiration, took it from his mother, tore it in half, and threw it into the fire grate. Some little time after he repented of this act of rudeness, collected the fragments, pasted them together, and begged his mother's forgiveness. This damaged plan or map is still in existence. His extraordinary diffidence and shrinking from all forms of praise or exaltation was thus revealed at a comparatively early stage of his career, and in connection with the first deeds that made him famous. The incident just described shows that his way of asserting his individuality was not always unattended with unkindness to those who were nearest and dearest to him. His distrust of his own temper, and of his capacity to speak and act conventionally, urged him towards a solitary life; and when his fate took him into places and forms of employment where solitude was the essential condition of the service, it is not surprising that his natural shyness and humility, as well as that habit of speaking his own mind, not only without fear or favour, but also, it must be admitted, with considerable disregard for the feelings of others, became intensified, and the most noticeable of his superficial characteristics.

But although Gordon was averse to praise and any special promotion, he was most anxious to resume the work of his profession, in which he took a peculiar pride, and for which he felt himself so thoroughly well suited. His temperament was naturally energetic and impulsive. The independent command he had exercised in China had strengthened these tendencies, and made a dull routine doubly irksome to one whose eager spirit sought action in any form that offered. The quiet domestic life of the family circle at Southampton soon became intolerable to his restless spirit, and although he was entitled to two years' leave after his long foreign service, he took steps to return to active service as an engineer officer within a very few months of his return to England.

On 1st September 1865 he was appointed Commanding Royal Engineer officer at Gravesend, to superintend the erection of the new forts to be constructed in that locality for the defence of the Thames. For such a post his active military service, as well as his technical training, eminently suited him; and although there was little promise of excitement about it, the work was distinctly congenial, and offered him a field for showing practical judgment and skill as an engineer. He threw himself into his task with his characteristic energy and enthusiasm. But how far the latter was damped by his prompt discovery that the whole project of the Thames defences was faulty and unsound it is impossible to say, but his attention to his work in all its details certainly showed no diminution or falling off. There were five forts in all to be constructed—three on the south or Kent side of the river, *viz.*, New Tavern, Shornmead, and Cliffe; and two, Coalhouse and Tilbury, on the north or Essex side. An immense sum had been voted by Parliament for their construction, and Gordon was as loud as an officer dare be in his denunciation of this extravagant waste of money as soon as he discovered by personal examination that the three southern forts could be turned into islands, and severed from all communication by

an enemy cutting the river bank at Cooling; and also that the northern forts were not merely unprotected in the rear, like those of the
Chinese, but completely commanded from the Essex range of hills.
Notwithstanding this important discovery, made at the very beginning, the original scheme was prosecuted to the end, with enormous
outlay and useless result, for an entirely new system of river defences
had to be formed and carried out at a later period. But for these errors
Gordon was in no sense responsible, and they would not have been
committed if his advice and representations had been heeded.

Mr Arthur Stannard, who was assistant to the manager of the firm
which had been entrusted with the contract for the building of these
forts, gave in the *Nineteenth Century* for April 1885 the best account
we possess of the manner in which Colonel Gordon discharged his
official duties at Gravesend.

Colonel Gordon's headquarters were at a quaint-looking, old-fashioned house with a good-sized garden, close to the site on which the
New Tavern fort was to be erected. He considered himself to be on
official duty from eight o'clock in the morning until two o'clock in
the afternoon; and during these six hours he not only worked himself
without intermission, but expected all those under him to work in the
same untiring spirit. He was a severe and unsparing taskmaster, and
allowed no shirking. No other officer could have got half the work
out of his men that he did. He used to keep them up to the mark by
exclaiming, whenever he saw them flag: "Another five minutes gone,
and this not done yet, my men! We shall never have them again."

Another instance of his unflagging energy and extreme activity
was furnished in connection with the boat in which he had to visit
the different parts of the defences. A two-oared, slow-moving boat
was provided for the purpose, but Gordon soon grew tired of this
slow means of locomotion, and he started a four-oared gig. He trained
these men according to his own ideas, and expected them to row with
all their might and main, and to lose not a minute in casting off their
boat on his arrival. So fond was he of rapid motion, or so impressed
with the value of time, that he would continue to urge them on,
whenever any signs of slackening appeared, with exclamations: "A little faster, boys, a little faster!" and Mr Stannard states that he has seen
the boatmen land after such a row as this in as limp a condition as four
strong men could be. All his own movements were carried on at the
run, and his activity was such that few younger and taller men were
able to keep up with him. I well recollect myself my first interview
with General Gordon in 1881, when he roused me up by a surprise

morning visit at eight o'clock—I had not returned from a newspaper office till four o'clock—and carried me off, walking in a light, springy way which was half a run up to the top of Campden Hill, to interview the late Sir Harry Parkes.

While many incidents and the general tenor of his conduct show the natural gentleness of Gordon and his softness of heart, he was a strict disciplinarian, and even a martinet in some of his ways. As has been said, he came on duty at eight every morning punctually, but he would not allow himself to be intruded upon before that hour. Mr Stannard tells one story that furnishes striking evidence to this effect. Early in the morning the men were brought to a standstill in their work until Colonel Gordon arrived to decide some doubtful or disputed matter. It was noticed that his bedroom window was wide open, and the contractor's manager was induced to go up and knock at his door for instructions. Gordon opened his door a little way, and exclaimed in a testy and irritable tone, "Presently, presently." He made his regular appearance at eight o'clock, and no one ventured to again disturb him before the regulation hour.

With regard to his meals he was most abstemious, and at the same time irregular. His brother describes an arrangement by which he was able to take, at all events, his midday meal, and at the same time to carry on his official work, especially in the matter of receiving visitors. He had a deep drawer in his table, in which the food was deposited. When anyone came to see him, the drawer was closed, and all signs of a meal were concealed. At all periods of his career he was a small and frugal eater, partly because he deprecated extravagance in living, and partly because he considered that the *angina pectoris* from which he thought he suffered could be best coped with by abstention from a sumptuous or heavy diet. Some days he would almost starve himself, and then in the night Nature would assert herself, and he would have to come downstairs and take whatever he found in the larder. It is recorded that on one occasion he sucked ten or a dozen raw eggs. But if he denied himself the luxuries and even the necessaries of a decent table, he possessed the true spirit of hospitality, and never expected his guests to follow any different practice than their own. For them he was always at pains to provide dainty fare and good wine. Nor must undue stress be laid on the isolated cases cited of his indifference to his personal comfort. Gordon was always attentive to his dress and appearance, never forgetting that he was a gentleman and an English officer.

While quartered at Gravesend he received a visit from Sir William Gordon, who had just been appointed to the command of the troops in Scotland. Sir William was no relation, only a member of the same great clan, and he had served with Gordon in the trenches of the Crimea. He had a great admiration and affection for the younger officer, and begged him to accept the post of his *aide-de-camp* in the North. The idea was not a pleasant one to our Gordon, but his good-nature led him to yield to the pressing invitations of his friend; and after he had given his assent, he was ill with nervousness and regret at having tied himself down to an uncongenial post. In some way or other Sir William heard of his distress, and promptly released him from his promise, only exacting from him the condition that he should pay him a visit at his home in Scotland. Soon afterwards Sir William Gordon became seriously ill, and Charles Gordon hastened to the North, where he remained some time employed in cheering up his friend, who was suffering from hypochondria. Some time afterwards Sir William died under sad circumstances. He had wished to benefit General Gordon by his will, but the latter absolutely refused to have anything except a silver tea service, which he had promised Sir William, while alive, to accept, because "it would pay for his funeral," and save any one being put to expense over that inevitable ceremony. The fate of this tea service, valued at £70, cannot be traced. It had disappeared long before Gordon's departure for Khartoum, and was probably sold for some beneficent work.

The Sir William Gordon incident was not the only external affair that distracted his attention from the monotonous routine work of building forts on a set, but faulty and mistaken, plan. Glad as he was of any work, in preference to the dull existence of a prolonged holiday in the domestic circle, Gravesend was not, after all, the ideal of active service to a man who had found the excitement of warfare so very congenial to his own temperament. When, in the course of 1867 it became evident that an expedition would have to be sent to Abyssinia to release the prisoners, and to bring the Negus Theodore to his senses, Gordon solicited the Horse Guards to include him in any force despatched with this object. There is no reason to think that his wish would not have been complied with if the expedition had been fitted out from England, but it was very wisely decided that the task should be entrusted to the Anglo-Indian Army. The late Lord Napier of Magdala, then Commander-in-Chief of the Bombay Army, was appointed to the command. The officers of his staff, as well as the troops under him, were all drawn from the Bombay Army, and although his connection by marriage, Sir Charles Staveley, held a command under Napier, and would willingly have assisted towards the gratification of his wish, an exception in Gordon's case could not be made without that favouritism which he most deprecated. Still, it was a great disappointment to him, and he shut himself up for a whole day, and would see no one.

If the six years at Gravesend, "the most peaceful and happy of any portion of my life," as he truly said, had left no other trace than his official work, of which the details must necessarily be meagre, there would have been a great blank in his life, and the reader would necessarily possess no clue to the marked change between the Gordon of China and the Gordon of the Soudan. Not that there was any loss of power or activity, but in the transition period philanthropy had come to occupy the foremost place in Gordon's brain, where formerly had reigned supreme professional zeal and a keen appreciation—I will not say love—of warlike glory. His private life and work at Gravesend explain and justify what was said of him at that time by one of his brother officers: "He is the nearest approach to Jesus Christ of any man who ever lived."

It has been written of him that his house at Gravesend bore more resemblance to the home of a missionary than the quarters of an English officer. His efforts to improve and soften the hard lot of the poor in a place like Gravesend began in a small way, and developed gradually into an extensive system of beneficence, which was only limited by his small resources and the leisure left him by official duty. At first he took into his house two or three boys who attracted his attention in a more or less accidental manner. He taught them in the evening, fed and clothed them, and in due course procured for them employment, principally as sailors or in the colonies. For a naturally bad sailor, he was very fond of the sea; and perhaps in his heart of hearts he cherished the thought that he was performing a national work in directing promising recruits to the first line of our defence, and the main prop of this Empire. Soon his few special pupils swelled into a class, not all boarders, but of outsiders who came in to learn geography and hear the Colonel explain the Bible; and not only that, but to be told of stirring deeds beyond the sea by one who had himself contributed to the making of history. We can well believe that before this uncritical but appreciative audience, from whose favour he had nothing to hope, or, as he would say, to fear, Gordon threw off the restraint and shyness habitual to him. It was very typical of the man that, where others thought only of instructing the poor and the ignorant, his chief wish was to amuse them and make them laugh.

By this simple means his class increased, and grew too large for his room. Sooner than break it up or discourage new-comers, he consented to teach in the ragged schools, where he held evening classes almost every night. Where he had clothed two or three boys, he now distributed several hundred suits in the year; and it is said that his pupils became so numerous that he had to buy pairs of boots by the gross. All this was done out of his pay. His personal expenses were reduced to the lowest point, so that the surplus might suffice to carry on the good work. It very often left him nearly penniless until his next pay became due—and this was not very surprising, as he could never turn a deaf ear to any tale of distress, and often emptied his pockets at the recital of any specially touching misfortune. When any outside subject of national suffering appealed to his heart or touched his fancy, he would consequently have no means available of sending any help, and this was specially the case during the suffering of the Lancashire operatives after the close of the American Civil War. On that occasion he defaced the gold medal given him by the Chinese Empresses, and sent it anonymously to the fund, which benefited from it to the extent of £10; but, as has been already stated, he made this sacrifice with the greatest pain and reluctance.

Gordon's love of children, and especially of boys, was quite re-markable. He could enter into their feelings far better than he could into those of grown men, and the irritability which he could scarcely suppress even among his friends was never displayed towards them. He was always at their service, anxious to amuse them, and to minister to their rather selfish whims. Some accidental remark led his class to ex-press a wish to visit the Zoo. Gordon at once seized the idea, and said they should do so. He made all the arrangements as carefully as if he were organising a campaign. His duties prevented his going himself, but he saw them off at the station, under the charge of his assistant, and well provided with baskets of food for their dinner and refresh-ment on their journey. Of course he defrayed the whole expense, and on their return he gave them a treat of tea and strawberries. He also thought of their future, being most energetic in procuring them em-ployment, and anxious in watching their after-career.

For some reason that is not clear he called these boys his "kings." He probably used it in the sense that they were his lieutenants, and he borrowed his imagery from the "Wangs," or kings of the Taeping ruler. I am told, however, that he really used the word in a spiritual sense, testifying that these boys were as kings in the sight of God. He followed the course of the first voyage of those who went to sea, stick-ing pins in a map to show the whereabouts of their respective vessels. It is not astonishing that his pupils should have felt for him a special admiration and affection. He not merely supplied all their wants, but he endeavoured to make them self-reliant, and to raise them above the sordid and narrow conditions of the life to which they were either born or reduced by the improvidence or misfortune of their parents. Of course Gordon was often deceived, and his confidence and charity abused; but these cases were, after all, the smaller proportion of the great number that passed through his hands. He sometimes met with gross ingratitude, like that of the boy whom he found starving, in rags, and ill with disease, and whom he restored to health, and perhaps to self-respect, and then sent back to his parents in Norfolk. But neither from him nor from them did he ever receive the briefest line of acknowledgment. Such experiences would have disheartened or deterred other philanthropists, but they failed to ruffle Gordon's serenity, or to discourage him in his work.

Perhaps the following incident is as characteristic as anything that took place between Gordon and his "kings." A boy whom he had twice fitted out for the world, but who always came to grief after a few months' trial, returned for a third time in the evening. Gordon met him at the gate, a mass of rags, in a deplorable condition, and covered with vermin. Gordon could not turn him away, neither could he admit him into his house, where there were several boys being brought up for a respectable existence. After a moment's hesitation, he led him in silence to the stable, where, after giving him some bread and a mug of milk, he told him to sleep on a heap of clean straw, and that he would come for him at six in the morning. At that hour Gordon appeared with a piece of soap, some towels, and a fresh suit of clothes, and, ordering the boy to strip, gave him a thorough washing with his own hands from head to foot at the horse-trough. It is to be regretted that there is no record of the after-fate of this young prodigal, although it would be pleasant to think that he was the unknown man who called at Sir Henry Gordon's house in 1885, after the news of Gordon's death, and wished to contribute £25 towards a memorial, because he was one of the youths saved by General Gordon, to whom all his success and prosperity in life were due.

But it must not be supposed that Gordon's acts of benevolence were restricted to boys. He was not less solicitous of the welfare of the sick and the aged. His garden was a rather pretty and shaded one. He had a certain number of keys made for the entrance, and distributed them among deserving persons, chiefly elderly. They were allowed to walk about, in the evening especially, and see the flowers, vegetables, and fruit which Gordon's gardener carefully cultivated. Gordon himself declared that he derived no special pleasure from the sight of flowers, for the simple reason that he preferred to look at the human face; and the same reason is the only one I can find he ever gave for his somewhat remarkable reticence about dogs and other domestic animals. It was said of him that he always had handy "a bit o' baccy for the old men, and a screw o' tea for the old women." He would hurry off at a moment's notice to attend to a dying person or to read the Bible by a sick-bed. In the hospital or the workhouse he was as well known as the visiting chaplain, and often he was requested by the parish clergyman to take his place in visiting the sick. His special invention for the benefit of his large number of clients was a system of pensions, which varied from a shilling to as much as a pound a week. Many of these payments he continued long after he left Gravesend, and a few were even paid until the day of his death. It is not surprising, in view of these facts, that Gordon remained a poor man, and generally had no money at all. As he wrote very truly of himself to his assistant Mr Lilley, "You and I will never learn wisdom in money matters."

Many stories have been told of his tenderness of heart, and of his reluctance to see punishment inflicted, but perhaps the following is the most typical. A woman called on him one day with a piteous tale. Gordon went to his bedroom to get half a sovereign for her, and while he was away she took a fancy to a brown overcoat, which she hastened to conceal under her skirt. Gordon returned, gave her the money, and she left with a profusion of thanks. While on her road home the coat slipped down, and attracted the notice of a policeman, who demanded an explanation.

She said, "I took it from the Colonel," and was marched back for him to identify his property, and charge her with the theft.

When Gordon heard the story, he was far more distressed than the culprit, and refused to comply with the constable's repeated requests to charge her. At last a happy thought came to his relief. Turning to the woman, he said, with a twinkle in his eye, "You wanted it, I suppose?"

"Yes," replied the astonished woman.

Then turning to the equally astonished policeman he said, "There, there, take her away, and send her about her business."

Among the various economies he practised in order to indulge his philanthropy was that of not keeping a horse, and he consequently took a great deal of walking exercise. During his walks along the Kentish lanes and foot-paths he distributed tracts, and at every stile he crossed he would leave one having such an exhortation as "Take heed that thou stumbleth not." Yet all this was done in an honest, and, as I believe, a secretly humorous spirit of a serious nature, for Gordon was as opposed to cant and idle protestations as any man. There is a strikingly characteristic story preserved somewhere of what he did when a hypocritical, canting humbug of a local religious secretary of some Society Fund or other paid a visit to a house while he was present. Gordon remained silent during the whole of the interview. But when he was gone, and Gordon was asked what he thought of him, he replied by waving his hand and drawing it across his throat, which he explained signified in China that his head ought to be cut off as a humbugging impostor.

Although buried, as it were, at Gravesend, Gordon could not be altogether forgotten. The authorities at the Horse Guards could not comply with his request to be attached to the Abyssinian expedition, but they were willing enough to do him what in official circles was thought to be a very good turn when they could. The English membership of the Danubian Commission became vacant, and it was remembered that in his early days Gordon had taken part in the delimitation negotiations which had resulted in the formation of that body. The post carried with it the good pay of £2000 a year, as some compensation for the social and sanitary drawbacks and disadvantages of life in that region, and it was offered to Gordon, who accepted it. It cut short his philanthropical labours, but it drew him back into that current of active work for which he was already pining. He therefore accepted it, and having presented some of the Snake flags of the old Taeping Wangs to the local school in which he had toiled as a simple teacher, he left Gravesend quietly, and without any manifestation that it had lost its principal resident. Having mentioned the Snake flags, it is proper to add that the principal of these, including some of his own which were shot to ribbons, were left by General Gordon to his sister, the late Miss Gordon, who in her turn presented them, with the Yellow Jacket and its appendages, the chief mandarin dress, etc., to the Royal Engineers at Chatham. The Gravesend life closed with a notice in the local journal, from which the following extract may be made; but once a year the old flags that led the advance or retreat of the Chinese rebels are brought out from their cases and flaunted before the Gravesend scholars as the memorial of a brave and unselfish leader and teacher.

The farewell article in the local paper read as follows:

> Our readers, without exception, will learn with regret of the departure of Lieut.-Colonel Gordon, R.E., C.B., from the town

in which he has resided for six years, gaining a name by the most exquisite charity that will long be remembered. Nor will he be less missed than remembered in the lowly walks of life, by the bestowal of gifts, by attendance and administration on the sick and dying, by the kindly giving of advice, by attendance at the Ragged School, Workhouse, and Infirmary—in fact, by general and continued beneficence to the poor, he has been so unwearied in well-doing that his departure will be felt by many as a personal calamity. There are those who even now are reaping the rewards of his kindness. His charity was essentially charity, and had its root in deep philanthropic feeling and goodness of heart, shunning the light of publicity, but coming even as the rain in the night-time, that in the morning is noted not, but only the flowers bloom, and give a greater fragrance. . . . All will wish him well in his new sphere, and we have less hesitation in penning these lines from the fact that laudatory notice will confer but little pleasure upon him who gave with the heart and cared not for commendation.

Gordon left for Galatz on 1st October 1871. He had visited and described it fourteen or fifteen years before, and he found little or no change there. The special task entrusted to the Commission of which he was a member was to keep open by constant and vigilant dredging the mouth of the Sulina branch of the Danube. He discovered very soon that the duties were light and monotonous, and in the depressing atmosphere—social and political as well as climatic—of the Lower Danube, he pined more than ever for bracing work, and for some task about which he could feel in earnest. The same conclusion seems to have forced itself upon his mind at the beginning and at the end of his stay at Galatz. In one of his first letters he exclaims: "How I like England when I am out of it! There is no place in the world like it!" In another letter, written on the very day of his departure home, he wrote: "Tell S. to thank God that he was born an Englishman." Gordon was always intensely patriotic. His patriotism partook of the same deep and fervid character as his religion, and these and many other little messages in his private correspondence furnish striking evidence to the fact.

The mention of Galatz recalls an incident, showing how long was his memory, and how much he clung to old friendships. During the Commune—that is to say, when he was still at Gravesend—the papers stated that a General Bisson had been killed at the Bridge of Neuilly on 9th April 1871. He wrote to Marshal Macmahon to inquire if he was the same officer as his old colleague on the Danube, and received, to his regret, an affirmative answer. General Bisson and Gordon had kept up a correspondence, in which the former always signed himself Bisson, C.B., being very proud of that honour, which was conferred on him for the Crimea. He was taken prisoner early in the Franco-Prussian war, and was shot by the Communists almost immediately on his return from the Prussian prison. Gordon's stay at Galatz was varied by an agreeable trip in 1872 to the Crimea, where he was sent to inspect the cemeteries with Sir John Adye. They travelled in an English gunboat, which proved a comfortable sea-boat, and Gordon wrote, "General Adye is a very agreeable companion." The cemeteries were found much neglected, and in a sad state of disrepair. The Russian officers were pronounced civil, but nothing more. But Gordon saw clearly that, having torn up the Black Sea Treaty, they were ready to recover Bessarabia, and to restore Sebastopol to the rank of a first-class naval fortress. After the Crimean tour he came to England on leave. His time was short, but he managed to pay a flying visit to Gravesend. He also could not resist the temptation of attending the funeral of the Emperor Napoleon in January 1873, and he expressed his opinion of that ill-starred ruler in his usual terse manner—"a kind-hearted, unprincipled man." His youngest brother, to whom he was much attached, and who had shared in the Woolwich frolics, died about this time, and his mother was seized with paralysis, and no longer recognised him. He felt this change most acutely, for between him and his mother there had been a peculiar attachment, and when he was at home she would hardly ever let him out of her sight. He used to call his home visits doing duty as his mother's *aide-de-camp*. When he left England for Galatz she was unconscious, and passed away some months later while he was abroad.

It was while General Gordon was on the Danube that preparations were made for the expedition against the Ashantees, and many persons suggested General Gordon for the command. It would have been an excellent occasion for intrusting him with an independent command in his country's service; but Sir Garnet, now Lord, Wolseley had recently gained much credit by his conduct of the Red River Expedition, and was appointed to the command of this force. General Gordon was no doubt disappointed at the result, but not so much as he had been in the case of Abyssinia, and loyalty to an old Crimean colleague tempered his own loss with satisfaction at another's success. Still, on public grounds, it must be pronounced unfortunate that the last occasion which was offered of employing for a national cause the services of a soldier who added the fervour and modesty of Wolfe to the genius of Clive should have been allowed to pass by unutilised.

A casual meeting with Nubar Pasha at Constantinople, on his way back from the Crimea in 1872, was destined to exercise what may be styled a determining influence on the rest of Gordon's life. At that meeting Nubar Pasha sounded him as to his willingness to take service under the Khedive, and Gordon, attracted by the prospect of doing good work on a larger sphere, expressed his own readiness to take up the task of establishing authority, and suppressing slavery in the Soudan, provided that the permission of his own Government were granted. He heard nothing more of the matter for twelve months, but at the end of September 1873 he received a communication to the effect that the Khedive wished to appoint him to succeed Sir Samuel Baker, and that the British Government were quite willing to grant him the necessary permission. In a letter of 8th November 1873 to the Adjutant-General he said:

> I have written an account of what I know of the Khedive's having asked me to take Baker's place. It came about from a conversation I had with Nubar Pasha at our Embassy at Constantinople. This was twelve months ago. The next thing was a telegram a month ago. I have not determined what to do, but the Government have no objection.

He was not long, however, in making up his mind, and early in 1874 he was *en route* for Alexandria. One characteristic act in connection with his appointment deserves mention. The Khedive fixed his salary at £10,000 a year, but Gordon absolutely refused to accept more than £2000 a year—the same sum as he received for his post on the Danube. Various reasons have been given for this decision, but there is no ground for supposing that it was due to such a very narrow-minded prejudice as "that he would take nothing from a heathen." If he ever used these words, they must have been intended as a joke, and are not to be accepted seriously. A sufficient explanation of his decision is, that he had a supreme disdain for money, and the sum offered seemed far in excess of the post and work he had to perform. To have received £10,000 a year would have added immensely to his worries. He would not have known what to do with it, and the voluntary cutting of his salary relieved him of a weight of responsibility. Perhaps also he was far-seeing enough to realise that he would be less the mere creature of the Egyptian ruler with the smaller than with the larger salary, while he could gratify his own inner pride that no one should say that any sordid motive had a part in his working for semi-civilized potentates, whether Chinese or Mussulmen.

I am able to describe Gordon's exact feelings on this point in his own words:

> My object is to show the Khedive and his people that gold and silver idols are not worshipped by all the world. They are very powerful gods, but not so powerful as *our* God. From whom does all this money come? from poor miserable creatures who are ground down to produce it. Of course these ideas are outrageous. Pillage the Egyptians is still the cry.

CHAPTER 7

The First Nile Mission

A brief description of the conquest by Mehemet Ali and his successors of the Soudan—a name signifying nothing more than "the land of the blacks"—and of the events which immediately preceded the appointment of Gordon, is necessary to show the extent of the work entrusted to him, and the special difficulties with which he had to contend.

It was in 1819 that the great Pasha or Viceroy Mehemet Ali, still in name the lieutenant of the Sultan, ordered his sons Ismail and the more famous Ibrahim to extend his authority up the Nile, and conquer the Soudan. They do not seem to have experienced any difficulty in carrying out their instructions. Nobody was interested in defending the arid wastes of that region. The Egyptian yoke promised to be as light as any other, and a few whiffs of grape-shot dispersed the only adversaries who showed themselves. Ibrahim, who soon took the lead, selected Khartoum as the capital of the new province, in preference to Shendy, which had formerly been regarded as the principal place in the country. In this he showed excellent judgment, for Khartoum occupies an admirable position in the fork of the two branches of the Nile; and whatever fate may yet befall the region in which the Mahdi and his successor the Khalifa have set up their ephemeral authority, it is destined by Nature to be the central point and capital of the vast region between the Delta and the Equatorial Lakes.

Khartoum lies on the left bank of the Blue Nile—Bahr-el-Azrak—rather more than three miles south of its confluence with the White Nile—Bahr-el-Abiad—at the northern point of the Isle of Tuti. The channel south of that island affords a slightly nearer approach to the White Nile, coming out immediately opposite the fortified camp of Omdurman, which the Mahdi made his headquarters and capital after the famous siege of 1884. There was nothing attractive or imposing about Khartoum. It contained 3000 mud houses, and one more pre-tentious building in the Governor's official residence or palace, known as the Hukumdariaha. It is surrounded by a wall and ditch, except where the Blue Nile supplies the need; and its western wall is not more than half a mile from the banks of the White Nile, so that with proper artillery it commands both rivers. The Nilometer at this place used to give the first and early intimation to the cultivators in Lower Egypt of the quantity of water being brought down from the rivers of Abyssinia. There seems no other conclusion possible than that sooner or later this practical service will compel Egypt, whenever she feels strong enough, to re-establish her power at Khartoum; already there is evidence that the time has arrived.

Having conquered the Soudan easily, the rulers of Egypt experi-enced no difficulty in retaining it for sixty years; and if other forces, partly created by the moral pressure of England and civilized opinion generally, had not come into action, there is every reason to sup-pose that their authority would never have been assailed. Nor did the Egyptians stand still. By the year 1853 they had conquered Darfur on the one side, and pushed their outposts on the other 120 miles south of Khartoum. In the rear of the Egyptian garrison came the European trader, who took into his service bands of Arab mercenaries, so that he pushed his way beyond the Egyptian stations into the region of the Bahr Gazelle, where the writ of the Cairo ruler did not run. These traders came to deal in ivory, but they soon found that, profitable as it was, there was a greater profit in, and a far greater supply of, "black ivory." Thus an iniquitous trade in human beings sprang up, and the real originators of it were not black men and Mahommedans, but white men, and in many instances Englishmen. From slave buying they took to slave hunting, and in this way there is no exaggeration in declaring that villages and districts were depopulated. Such scandal-ous proceedings could not be carried on in the dark, and at last the Europeans involved felt compelled, by the weight of adverse opinion, or more probably from a sense of their own peril, to withdraw from the business. This touch of conscience or alarm did not improve the situation. They sold their stations to their Arab agents, who in turn purchased immunity from the Egyptian officers. The slave trade, by the pursuit and capture of any tribe rash enough to come within the spring of the Arab raiders, flourished as much as ever. The only change was that after 1860 Europeans were clear of the stigma that attached to any direct participation in it.

The condition of the Soudan during this period has been graphically described by Captain Speke, Dr Schweinfurth, and Sir Samuel Baker. They all agree in their facts and their conclusions. The people were miserably unhappy, because the dread and the reality of compulsory slavery hung over their daily life. Those who were not already slaves realised their impending fate. Villages were abandoned, districts passed out of cultivation, and a large part of the population literally vanished. Sir Samuel Baker, speaking of the difference between a region he knew well in 1864 and in 1872, wrote in the latter year: "It is impossible to describe the change that has taken place since I last visited this country. It was then a perfect garden, thickly populated, and producing all that man could desire. The villages were numerous, groves of plantains fringed the steep cliffs on the river's bank, and the natives were neatly dressed in the bark cloth of the country. The scene has changed! All is wilderness. The population has fled! Not a village is to be seen! This is the certain result of the settlement of Khartoum traders. They kidnap the women and children for slaves, and plunder and destroy wherever they set their foot." How true all this was will be seen in the course of Gordon's own experiences.

It has been stated that the Arab slave-dealers made terms with the Egyptian officials, and they were even not without influence and the means of gaining favourable consideration at Cairo itself. But as they increased in numbers, wealth, and confidence in themselves and their organisation, the Khedive began to see in them a possible danger to his own authority. This feeling was strengthened when the slavers, under the leadership of the since notorious Zebehr Rahama, the most ambitious and capable of them all, refused to pay their usual tribute. Dr Schweinfurth has given a vivid picture of this man in the heyday of his power. Chained lions formed part of his escort, and it is recorded that he had 25,000 dollars' worth of silver cast into bullets in order to foil the magic of any enemy who was said to be proof against lead. Strong as this truculent leader was in men and money, the Khedive Ismail did not believe that he would dare to resist his power. He therefore decided to have recourse to force, and in 1869 he sent a small military expedition, under the command of Bellal Bey, to bring the Bahr Gazelle into submission. Zebehr had made all his arrangements for defence, and on the Egyptian army making its appearance he promptly attacked and annihilated it. This success fully established the power and reputation of Zebehr, who became the real dictator of the Soudan south of Khartoum. The Khedive, having no available means of bringing his rebellious dependent to reason, had to acquiesce in the defeat of his army. Zebehr offered some lame excuse for his boldness and success, and Ismail had to accept it, and bide the hour of revenge.

Zebehr, encouraged by this military triumph, turned his arms against the Sultans of Darfour, who had incurred his resentment by placing an embargo on wheat during the course of his brief campaign with Bellal. This offensive action still further alarmed the Khedive Ismail, who was fully alive to the danger that might arise to his own position if a powerful military confederacy, under a capable chief, were ever organised in the Soudan. Instead of allying himself with the Darfourians, as would probably have been the more politic course, Ismail decided to invade their territory simultaneously with Zebehr. Several battles were fought, and one after another the Sultans of Darfour, whose dynasty had reigned for 400 years, were overthrown and slain. Zebehr received in succession the Turkish titles of Bey and Pasha, but he was not satisfied, for he said that as he had done all the fighting, he ought to receive the Governor-Generalship of Darfour. If he failed to win that title from the Khedive, he succeeded in gratifying a more profitable desire, by leading off into slavery the larger half of the population of Darfour. He was still engaged in this pursuit at the time of Gordon's appearance on the scene, and the force at his disposal was thus described by that officer: "Smart, dapper-looking fellows, like antelopes, fierce, unsparing, the terror of Central Africa, having a prestige far beyond that of the Government—these are the slave-dealers' tools," and afterwards they no doubt became the main phalanx of the Mahdi's military system.

The financial position of the Egyptian Government in the Soudan was as bad as the military and political. The Khedive's Governor-General at Khartoum, Ismail Yakoob Pasha, was nominally responsible for the administration of Darfour, although Zebehr reaped all the gain. This arrangement resulted in a drain on the Khedive's exchequer of £50,000 a year. The revenue failed to meet the expenditure in the other departments, and this was mainly due to the fact that the slavers no longer paid toll or tithe in the only trade that they had allowed to exist in the Soudan. What share of the human traffic they parted with was given in the way of bribes, and found no place in the official returns. All the time that this drain continued the Khedive was in a constant state of apprehension as to the danger which might arise to him in the south. He was also in receipt of frequent remonstrances from the English and other Governments as to the iniquities of the slave-trade, for which he was primarily in no sense to blame. On the other hand, he derived no benefit from the Soudan; and if he thought he could have obtained a secure frontier at Abou Hamid, or even at Wadi Halfa, he would have resigned all the rest without a sigh. But it was his strong conviction that no such frontier was attainable, and Ismail clung to his nominal and costly authority over the Soudan in the hope that some improvement might be effected, or that, in the chapter of accidents, the unexpected might come to his aid.

Alarmed as to his own position, in view of the ambition of Zebehr, and harassed by the importunities of England, Ismail, acting on the advice of his able and dexterous Minister, Nubar Pasha, one of the most skilful diplomatists the East has ever produced, came to the decision to relieve himself from at least the latter annoyance, by the appointment of Gordon. This was the main object the Khedive and his advisers had in view when they invited Gordon to accept the post of Governor of the Equatorial Provinces in succession to Sir Samuel Baker, who resigned what he found after many years' experience was a hopeless and thankless task. The post was in one sense peculiar. It was quite distinct from that of the Egyptian Governor-General at Khartoum, who retained his separate and really superior position in the administration of the Upper Nile region. Moreover, the finances of the Equatorial districts were included in the general Soudan Budget, which always showed an alarming deficit. These arrangements imparted a special difficulty into the situation with which Gordon had to deal, and his manner of coping with it will reveal how shrewd he was in detecting the root-cause of any trouble, and how prompt were his measures to eradicate the mischief. From the first he fully realised why he was appointed, viz. "to catch the attention of the English people"; but he also appreciated the Khedive's "terrible anxiety to put down the slave-trade, which threatens his supremacy." With these introductory remarks, the main thread of Gordon's career may be resumed.

After the brief hesitation referred to in the last chapter, and the reduction of his salary to what he deemed reasonable dimensions, Gordon proceeded to Cairo, where he arrived early in the year 1874. As in everything else he undertook, Gordon was in earnest about the work he had to attempt, and no doubt he had already formed in his mind a general plan of action, which would enable him to suppress the slave-trade. Here it will suffice to say that his project was based on the holding of the White Nile by a line of fortified posts, and with the river steamers, which would result in cutting off the slave hunters from their best source of supply. The expression of his plans in his earnest manner showed up by contrast the hollowness of the views and policy of those who had obtained his services. In his own graphic and emphatic way he wrote: "I thought the thing real and found it a sham, and felt like a Gordon who has been humbugged." He found Cairo "a regular hot-bed of intrigues," and among not only the Egyptian, but also the European officials. With a prophetic grasp of the situation he wrote, "Things cannot last long like this." Had Gordon been long detained at Cairo, where the etiquette and the advice offered him by every one in an official position exasperated him beyond endurance, there is no doubt that he would have thrown up his task in disgust. He was animated by the desire to make the sham a reality, and to convert the project with which he had been entrusted into a beneficial scheme for the suffering population of the Soudan. There, at least, he would be removed from the intrigues of the capital, and at liberty to speak his own thoughts without giving umbrage to one person and receiving worldly counsel from another.

One of the chief bones of contention during the few weeks he passed at Cairo was the dispute as to how he should travel to the scene of his government. He wished to go by ordinary steamer, with one servant. The Minister insisted that he should travel by a special steamer, and accompanied by a retinue. Gordon's plan would have saved the Khedive's Government £400, but he had to give way to the proprieties. The affair had an amusing issue. His special train to Suez met with an accident, and he and the Egyptian officials sent to see him off were compelled, after two hours' delay, to change into another train, and continue their journey in an ordinary passenger carriage, much to the amusement of Gordon, who wrote: "We began in glory and ended in shame!" On arrival at Souakim, Gordon was put into quarantine for a night, in order, as he said, that the Governor might have time to put on his official clothes.

Soon his attention was drawn from such frivolities as these to more serious matters. He left Cairo on 21st February, reached Souakim on 26th, left Souakim on 1st March, Berber on 9th March, and entered Khartoum 13th March. He brought with him 200 fresh troops, and was welcomed with considerable display and many hollow protestations of friendship by the Governor-General, Ismail Yakoob.

A few weeks before his arrival at Khartoum an important event had taken place, which greatly simplified his ulterior operations. The *sudd*, an accumulation of mould and aquatic plants which had formed into a solid mass and obstructed all navigation, had suddenly given way, and restored communication with Gondokoro and the lakes. The importance of this event may be measured by the fact that whereas the journey to Gondokoro, with the *sudd* in existence, took twenty months and even two years to perform, it was reduced by its dispersal to twenty-one days. General Gordon wrote the following very pretty description of this grassy barrier and its origin:

A curious little cabbage-like aquatic plant comes floating down, having a little root ready to attach itself to anything; he meets a friend, and they go together, and soon join roots and so on. When they get to a lake, the current is too strong, and so, no longer constrained to move on, they go off to the sides; others do the same—idle and loitering, like everything up here. After a time winds drive a whole fleet of them against the narrow outlet of the lake and stop it up. Then no more passenger plants can pass through the outlet, while plenty come in at the upper end of the lake; these eventually fill up all the passages which may have been made.

Gordon had the control of seven steamers, and in one of these he left Khartoum on 22nd March for the Upper Nile. He had already issued his first decree as Governor of the Equator, in which he declared the sale of ivory to be a Government monopoly, and forbade the importation of firearms and ammunition. It was while he was on this journey that he heard some birds—a kind of stork—laughing on the banks of the river. In his letters to his sister, which were to stand in the place of a diary, he facetiously remarks that he supposes they were amused at the idea of anyone being so foolish as to go up the Nile in "the hope of doing anything." But Gordon was not to be discouraged. Already he liked his work, amid the heat and mosquitoes day and night all the year round, and already he was convinced that he could do a good deal to ameliorate the lot of the unfortunate people. He reached Gondokoro on 16th April, where not only was he not expected, but he found them ignorant even of his appointment. He remained there only a few days, as he perceived he could do nothing without his stores, still *en route* from Cairo, and returned to Khartoum, which he reached in eleven days.

This brief trip satisfied him of several simple facts bearing on the situation in the Equatorial Province which the Khedive had sent him with such a flourish of trumpets to govern. He found very easily that the Egyptian Government possessed no practical authority in that region. Beyond the two forts at Gondokoro—garrison 300 men—and Fatiko—garrison 200 men—the Khedive had no possessions, and there was not even safety for his representatives half a mile from their guns.

As Gordon said: "The Khedive gave me a Firman as Governor-General of the Equator, and left me to work out the rest." He began the practical part of his task on the occasion of this return to Khartoum by insisting that the accounts of the Equatorial Province should be kept distinct from those of the Soudan, and also that Ragouf Pasha, sent nominally to assist but really to hinder him, should be withdrawn.

Having asserted his individuality after several rows with Ismail Yakoob, he became impatient at the delayed arrival of his stores and staff, and hastened off to Berber to hurry their progress. As he was fond of saying, "Self is the best officer," and his visit to Berber hastened the arrival of the supplies which were necessary for his subsequent operations. His staff consisted of Colonel Long, of the United States Army, who had accompanied him to Gondokoro and been left there; Major Campbell, Egyptian Staff; Mr Kemp, an engineer; M. Linant, a Frenchman; Mr Anson, Mr Russell, and the Italian Romulus Gessi. Two Royal Engineer officers, Lieutenants Chippendall and Charles Watson, joined him before the end of the year. He worked very hard himself, and he expected those under him to do the same. The astonished Egyptian officials looked on in amazement at one in high rank, who examined into every detail himself, and who took his turn of the hard work. One of Gordon's forms of recreation was to get out and help to pull his *dahabeah*. Tucking up his trousers, he would wade through the river fearlessly, having learnt from the natives that crocodiles never attack a person moving.

At first Ismail Yakoob and his colleagues were filled with curiosity and amusement at this phenomenal Englishman—so different, not merely from themselves, but from other Europeans—then apprehension seized them as to what he would do next in the way of exposing their neglect of duty, and finally only the capacity for one sentiment was left—relief whenever he turned his back on Khartoum.

Having collected his staff and supplies, he started up the Nile once more, to begin the establishment of the line of fortified posts, which he had resolved on as the best means of maintaining and extending his own authority, and at the same time of curtailing the raids of the slave-dealers. The first of these forts or stations he established at the entrance of the Saubat river, and while there he made a discovery which showed how the slave-trade flourished with such impunity. He seized some letters from a slave-dealer to the Egyptian commander at Fashoda, stating that he was bringing him the slaves he wanted for himself and many others, besides 2000 cows. By several skilful manoeuvres Gordon succeeded in rescuing all of them, restoring the cows to their owners, and compelling the soldiers of the slave hunters to return to their homes, generally in or near Khartoum. Nor was this his only success during the first two months of his government, for he detected one of his lieutenants in the act of letting a slave convoy pass in return for a bribe of £70. On this occasion he had the satisfaction of delivering 1600 human beings from slavery. This will show that one of his principal difficulties was caused by his own subordinates, who were hand-in-glove with the leading slave hunters. Another of Gordon's troubles arose from the collapse of his staff under the terrible heat. Of those enumerated as having gone up with or to him in May, all were dead or invalided in September; and the duties of sick-nurse at last became so excessive that Gordon had to order, in his own quaint manner, that no one who was sick should be allowed to come to headquarters. Only in this way was he able to obtain the time necessary for the accomplishment, single handed, of his various duties. Such was the strain on him that he gave positive injunctions that no more Europeans, and especially young English officers, were to be sent up to him.

As soon as it was realised that the new Governor was in earnest, that he was bent on crushing the slave-trade, and that he would not permit corruption or extortion in any form, he became the mark of general hostility. The intrigues to mislead and discredit him were incessant. Abou Saoud, who had been formerly banished by Sir Samuel Baker from the Soudan, and then taken into high favour by Gordon, turned out a fraud and a failure, while Raouf Bey, the nominee of the Khartoum Governor-General, was sent back in disgrace. With regard to Abou Saoud it may be said that Gordon never really trusted him, that is to say he was not taken in by him, but believed he would be less able to do injury in his service than at a distance. It was precisely the same principle as led him to solicit the co-operation of Zebehr in 1884.

Gordon's method of dealing with those who caused him trouble was short and simple. It consisted in a brief but unchallengeable order to go back to the base. As the officials would have been murdered by the people they had so long and so often injured if they attempted to seek shelter among them, they had no alternative save to obey; and thus, one after another, Gordon brushed the chief obstructionists from his path. He served the old troublesome soldiers who would not work or change their ways after the same fashion, by sending them to his Botany Bay at Khartoum. In the midst of all these troubles he kept well, although "a mere shadow," and he still retained the conviction that he would be able to do much good work in this unpromising region.

In dealing with the natives, he endeavoured first to induce them to cultivate the ground, providing them with seed and *dhoora (sorghum)*, and then to accustom them to the use of money. He bought their ivory and paid for it in coin, so that in a little time he found that the inhabitants, who had held aloof from all previous Egyptian officials, freely brought him their ivory and produce for sale. At the same time, he made it a point to pay scrupulously for any service the natives rendered, and he even endeavoured, as far as he could, to put employment in their way. The practice of the Egyptian officials had been to lay hands on any natives that came across their path, and compel them by force to perform any work they might deem necessary, and then to dismiss them without reward or thanks. The result was a deep-rooted execration of the whole Egyptian system, which found voice in the most popular war-cry of the region: "We want no Turks here! Let us drive them away!" But Gordon's mode was widely different. It was based on justice and reason, and in the long-run constituted sound policy. He paid for what he took, and when he used the natives to drag his boats, or to clear tracks through the grassy zone fringing the Nile, he always carefully handed over to them cows, *dhoora*, or money, as an equivalent for their work. On the other hand, he was not less prompt to punish hostile tribes by imposing taxes on them, and, when unavoidable, inflicting punishment as well. But the system averted, as far as possible, the necessity of extreme measures, and in this the first period of his rule in the Soudan he had few hostile collisions with the natives of the country. Indeed, with the exception of the Bari tribe, who entrapped Linant, Gordon's best lieutenant after Gessi, and slew him with a small detachment, Gordon's enemies in the field proved few and insignificant. Even the Baris would not have ventured to attack him but for the acquaintance with, and contempt of, firearms they had obtained during an earlier success over an Egyptian corps.

There is no doubt that this absence of any organised opposition was fortunate, for the so-called troops at the disposal of the Governor of the Equator were as miserably inefficient and contemptible, from a fighting point of view, as any General Gordon ever commanded; and at a later stage of his career he plaintively remarked that it had fallen to his lot to lead a greater number of cowardly and unwarlike races than anyone else. But it was not merely that they were such poor fighters that Gordon declared that three natives would put a company to flight, but they were so disinclined for any work, and so encumbered by their women and children, that their ability to make any military show might be as safely challenged as their combative spirit. Well might Gordon write: "I never had less confidence in any troops in my life." But even these shortcomings were not the worst. The Arab soldiers provided by the Egyptian Government, and sent up over and over again, in spite of Gordon's protests and entreaties, could not stand the climate. They died like flies. Of one detachment of 250, half were dead in three months, 100 of the others were invalided, and only 25 remained fit for duty. From a further body of 150 men sent as a reinforcement, half were reported on the sick list the day after their arrival. The main buttress of the Khedive's authority in this region was therefore hollow and erected on an insecure foundation. The Egyptian soldiers possessed firearms, and the natives, in their ignorance that they could not shoot straight, were afraid of them; but the natural progress of knowledge would inevitably prove fatal to that unreal supremacy, and eventually entail the collapse of the Cairo administration in the Soudan and the remoter districts on the Equator.

Realising the inefficiency of the Egyptian force, General Gordon set himself to the task of providing a better; and mindful of the contingent danger of creating a corps that might in the end prove a peril to the system it was meant to protect, he resolved that, if individually brave and efficient, it should be exceedingly limited in numbers, and incapable of casting aside its allegiance to the Khedive. He began in a small way by engaging the services of any stalwart Soudanese native whom chance placed in his path, and thus he organised in the first year of his rule a corps of about forty men as a sort of bodyguard. An accident brought him into contact with a party of the Niam Niam, a tribe of cannibals from the interior of Africa, but possessing a martial spirit and athletic frames. Gordon looked at them with the eye of a soldier, and on the spot enrolled fifty of them into the small force he was organising. He armed them with spears as well as guns, and as these spears were cutting ones, with a blade two feet long, they were the more formidable weapon of the two. Gordon describes the Niam Niam warriors as looking very fierce, and brave, and fearless. They were also thick-set and sturdy, and, above all, so indifferent to the tropical heat that they might be relied on not to break down from the climate like the Egyptian soldiers. Before the end of the year 1876 he had increased the numbers of these two contingents to 500 men. It was with these black troops that Gordon humbled the pride of the Baris, elated by their two successes, and provided for the security of the long Nile route to the lakes.

There was another advantage besides the military in this practical measure, one of those numerous administrative acts, in every clime and under innumerable conditions, that established the fame and the sound sense and judgment of General Gordon. It promoted economy, and contributed to the sound finance which Gordon always set himself to establish wherever he was responsible. One of Gordon's first resolutions had been that his part of the Soudan should cease to be a drain, like the rest, on the Cairo Exchequer. He determined that he at least would pay his way, and on the threshold of his undertaking he had insisted, and carried in the teeth of powerful opposition his resolution, that the accounts of the Equatorial Province should be kept distinct from those of the Soudan. The employment of black soldiers was very economical as well as efficient, and contributed to the satisfactory result which was shown in the balance-sheet of the Equatorial Province as described by General Gordon for the year 1875. In that year the Khedive received £48,000 from the Province which Gordon ruled at a total cost of only £20,000, while he had also formed a surplus or reserve fund of £60,000 more.

Having thus accomplished as much as possible towards the strengthening of the administration and tranquillisation of the people, some further particulars may be recorded of his measures and success in dealing with that slave-trade, the existence of which was the primary cause of his own appearance in the Soudan. Allusion has already been made to the considerable number of slaves rescued by a few grand coups at the expense of his own subordinates, but during the whole of these three years Gordon was in close contact with slaves, and the rescue of individuals was of frequent occurrence. Several touching incidents are recorded in the letters published from Central Africa as to his kindness towards women and infants, to some of whom he even gave the shelter of his own tent; and nothing could be more effective in the way of illustration than his simple description of the following passage with the child-wife of one of his own soldiers:

> The night before I left this place a girl of twelve years, in one of those leather strap girdles, came up to the fire where I was sitting, and warmed herself. I sent for the interpreter, and asked what she wanted. She said the soldier who owned her beat her, and she would not stay with him; so I put her on board the steamer. The soldier was very angry, so I said: 'If the girl likes to stay with you, she may; if she does not, she is free.' The girl would not go back, so she stays on the steamer.

Nor was this the only incident of the kind to show not merely the tenderness of his heart, but the extraordinary reputation Gordon had acquired by his high-minded action among these primitive and down-trodden races. Here are some others that have been selected almost at random out of his daily acts of gentleness and true charity:

I took a poor old bag of bones into my camp a month ago, and have been feeding her up, but yesterday she was quietly taken off, and now knows all things. She had her tobacco up to the last, and died quite quietly. . . . A wretched *sister* of yours (addressed to the late Miss Gordon) is struggling up the road, but she is such a wisp of bones that the wind threatens to over-throw her; so she has halted, preferring the rain to being cast down. I have sent her some *dhoora*, which will produce a spark of joy in her black and withered carcass. I told my man to see her into one of the huts, and thought he had done so. The night was stormy and rainy, and when I awoke I heard often a crying of a child near my hut within the enclosure. When I got up I went out to see what it was, and passing through the gateway, I saw your and my sister lying dead in a pool of mud—her black brothers had been passing and passing, and had taken no notice of her—so I ordered her to be buried, and went on. In the midst of the high grass was a baby, about a year or so old, left by itself. It had been out all night in the rain, and had been left by its mother. I carried it in, and seeing the corpse was not moved, I sent again about it, and went with the men to have it buried. To my surprise and astonishment, she was alive. After considerable trouble I got the black brothers to lift her out of the mud, poured some brandy down her throat, and got her into a hut with a fire, having the mud washed out of her eyes. She was not more than sixteen years of age. There she now lies. I cannot help hoping she is floating down with the tide to the haven of rest. The next day she was still alive, and the babe, not a year old, seized a gourd of milk, and drank it off like a man, and is apparently in for the pilgrimage of life. It does not seem the worse for its night out, depraved little wretch!...The black sister departed this life at 4 p.m., deeply lamented by me, not so by her black brothers, who thought her a nuisance. When I went to see her this morning I heard the 'lamentations' of something on the other side of the hut. I went round, and found another of our species, a visitor of ten or twelve months to this globe, lying in a pool of mud. I said, 'Here is another foundling!' and had it taken up. Its mother came up afterwards, and I mildly expostulated with her, remarking, however good it might be for the spawn of frogs, it was not good for our species. The creature drank milk after this with avidity.

Such incidents explain the hold Gordon obtained over the indigenous population of the Upper Nile. He made friends right and left, as he said, and the trust of the poor people, who had never received kindness, and whose ignorance of the first principles of justice was so complete that he said it would take three generations of sound and paternal government to accustom them to it, in General Gordon was complete and touching. A chapter might be filled with evidence to this effect, but it is unnecessary, as the facts are fully set forth in the "Letters" from Central Africa. The result alone need be dwelt on here. For only too brief a period, and as the outcome of his personal effort, these primitive races saw and experienced the beneficial results of a sound and well-balanced administration. The light was all too quickly withdrawn; but while it lasted, General Gordon stood out as a kind of redeemer for the Soudanese. The poor slaves, from whose limbs the chains of their oppressors had only just been struck, would come round him when anxious about his health, and gently touch him with their fingers. The hostile chiefs, hearing, as Bedden did, that he restored his cattle to and recompensed in other ways a friendly chief who had been attacked in mistake, would lie in wait for him, and lay their views and grievances before him. He could walk fearlessly and unarmed through their midst, and along the river banks for miles, when an Egyptian official would have required a regiment to guard him, and detached soldiers would have been enticed into the long grass and murdered. Even the hostile tribes like the Bari, who, from a mistaken view of their own military power, would not come to terms, showed their recognition of his merit by avoiding in their attacks the posts in which he happened to be. Thus there grew up round Gordon in the Soudan a sublime reputation for nobleness and goodness that will linger on as a tradition, and that, when these remote regions along the Equator fall under civilized authority, will simplify the task of government, provided it be of the same pattern as that dispensed by General Gordon.

As the subject has a permanent practical value, the following passage embodying General Gordon's views is well worth repetition:

I feel sure that a series of bad governments have ruined the people. Three generations of good government would scarcely regenerate them. Their secretiveness is the result of the fear that if they give, it may chance that they may want. Their indolence is the result of experience that if they do well, or if they do badly, the result will be *nil* to them, therefore why should they exert themselves? Their cowardice is the result of the fear of responsibility. They are fallen on so heavily if anything goes wrong. Their deceit is the result of fear and want of moral courage, as they have no independence in their characters. For a foreign power to take this country would be most easy. The mass are far from fanatical. They would rejoice in a good government, let its religion be what it might. A just administration of law, and security of person against arbitrary conduct, would do a great deal. It is the Government that needs civilizing far more than the people. Mehemet Ali and his descendants have always gone on the principle of enriching themselves by monopolies of all sorts. None, not even the present Khedive (Ismail), have brought in civilizing habits or customs with any desire to benefit the country, or, at any rate, they have subordinated this desire to that of obtaining an increased revenue.

But while Gordon brought kindness and conciliation into play, the settlement of the region entrusted to his care called for sterner measures, and he was not the man, with all his nobility of character and overflowing supply of the milk of human kindness, to refrain from those vigorous and decisive measures that keep turbulent races in subjection, and advance the cause of civilization, which in so many quarters of the world must be synonymous with British supremacy. The student of his voluminous writings will find many passages that express philosophical doubts as to our right to coerce black races, and to bind peoples who in their rude and primitive fashion are free to the car of our wide-world Empire. But I am under no obligation to save them the trouble of discovery by citing them, more especially because I believe that they give a false impression of the man. I have affirmed, and shall adduce copious and, as I think, convincing evidence, at every turn of his varied experiences, that the true Gordon was not the meek, colourless, milk-and-water, text-expounding, theological disputant many would have us accept as a kind of Bunyan's hero, but in action an uncompromising and resistless leader, who, when he smote, at once struck his hardest. Gordon has supplied the answer to his own misgivings as to our moral right to coerce and subject tribes who advanced their natural claims to be left undisturbed: "We cannot have them on our flank, and it is indispensable that they shall be subjected."

Having organised his new forces, equipped all his steamers—one of which was fitted out with machinery that had been left in Baker's time to rust in the Korosko Desert—General Gordon set himself to the task of systematically organising the line of posts which he had conceived and begun to construct in the first stages of his administration. The object of these posts was twofold. By them he would cut the slave routes in two, and also open a road to the great Lakes of the Equator. In the first few months of his residence he had transferred the principal station from Gondokoro to Lardo, twelve miles lower down the stream, and on the left instead of the right bank of the river. These places lie a little on each side of the fifth degree of north latitude, and Gordon fixed upon Lardo as his capital, because it was far the healthier. Above Lardo he established at comparatively short stages further posts at, in their order, Rageef, Beddem, Kerri, Moogie, and Laboré, immediately beyond the last of which occur the Fola Falls, the only obstruction to navigation between Khartoum and the Lakes. Above those Falls Gordon established a strong post at Duffli, and dragged some of his steamers overland, and floated them on the short link of the Nile between that place and Lake Albert, establishing a final post north of that lake, at Wadelai. When his fleet commanded that lake, he despatched his lieutenant, Gessi, across it up the Victoria Nile, connecting the two great lakes, and continued his chain of posts along it by Magungo, Anfina, Foweira, and Mrooli, to the very borders of Mtesa's dominion in Uganda. By means of these twelve posts General Gordon established the security of his communications, and he also inspired his men with fresh confidence, for, owing to the short distances between them, they always felt sure of a near place of refuge in the event of any sudden attack. Thus it came to pass that whereas formerly Egyptian troops could only move about in bodies of 100 strong, General Gordon was able to send his boats and despatches with only two soldiers in charge of them; and having entirely suppressed the slave-trade within his own jurisdiction, he was left free to accomplish the two ulterior objects of his mission, viz. the installation of the Khedive's flag on the Lakes, and the establishment of definite relations with Mtesa, whose truculent vassal, Kaba Rega, of Unyoro, showed open hostility and resentment at the threatened encroachment on his preserves.

It was neither a reprehensible nor an unintelligible vanity for the Egyptian ruler to desire the control of the whole of the great river, whose source had been traced south of the Equator, and 2000 miles beyond the limits of the Pharaohs' dominions. Nor was the desire diminished when, without sharing the gratification of the Prince in whose name he acted, General Gordon advanced cogent reasons for establishing a line of communication from Gondokoro, across the territory of Mtesa, with the port of Mombasa on the Indian Ocean. As Gordon pointed out, that place was nearly 1,100 miles from Khartoum, and only 900 from Mombasa, while the advance to the Lakes increased the distance from the one place by nearly 300 miles, and reduced that to the other in the same measure. This short and advantageous line of communication with the Equatorial Province and Upper Nile was beyond both the power and the sphere of the Khedive; but in the task of winning one of the most important of African zones formally recognised as lying within the British sphere of influence, the route advocated by General Gordon in 1875 has now become of the most undoubted value and importance.

The aversion to all forms of notoriety except that which was inseparable from his duty led Gordon to shrink from the publicity and congratulations sure to follow if he were the first to navigate those inland seas on the Equator. Having made all the arrangements, and provided for the complete security of the task, he decided to baffle the plans in his honour of the Royal Geographical Society, by delegating the duty of first unfurling the Khedive's flag on their waters to his able and much-trusted lieutenant, Gessi. Although he sometimes took hasty resolutions, in flat opposition to his declared intentions, he would probably have adhered to this determination but for reading in one of Dr Schweinfurth's published lectures that "it may be that Lake Albert belongs to the Nile basin, but it is not a settled fact, for there are seventy miles between Foweira and Lake Albert never explored, and one is not authorised in making the Nile leave Lake Albert. The question is very doubtful." The accidental perusal of this passage changed General Gordon's views. He felt that this task devolved on him as the responsible administrator of the whole region, and that his natural shrinking from trumpery and too often easily-earned geographical honours, which he has bluntly asserted should only be granted by the Sovereign, did not justify his evading a piece of work that came within his day's duty. Therefore he resolved to ascertain the fact by personal examination, and to set at rest the doubts expressed by the German traveller.

Expanding Dr Schweinfurth's remarks, he explained that "it was contended that the Nile did not flow out of Lake Victoria, and thence through Lake Albert, and so northward, but that one river flowed out of Lake Victoria and another out of Lake Albert, and that these two rivers united and formed the Nile. This statement could not be positively denied, inasmuch as no one had actually gone along the river from Foweira to Magungo. So I went along it with much suffering, and settled the question. I also found that from Foweira or Karuma Falls there was a series of rapids to Murchison Falls, thus *by degrees* getting rid of the 1000-feet difference of level between Foweira and Magungo." While mapping this region, Gordon one day marched eighteen miles through jungle and in pouring rain, and on each of the four following days he also walked fifteen miles—and the month was August, only a few miles north of the Equator, or, in other words, the very hottest period of the year. Having established the course of the Nile and its navigability to the Murchison Falls close to the Victoria Nyanza, General Gordon gave what he thought was a finishing touch to this exploring expedition by effecting an arrangement with King Mtesa.

But in order to explain the exact significance of this step, and the consequent disappointment when it was found that the arrangement was illusory and destitute of practical value, it is necessary to go back a little, and trace the course of events in the Uganda region.

The Egyptian advance towards the south brought in its train two questions of external policy. One was with Abyssinia, of which we shall hear much in the next chapter; and the other was with the kingdom of Uganda and the kinglets who regarded Mtesa as their chief. Of these the principal was Kaba Rega, chief of Unyoro, and the recognised ruler of the territory lying between the two Lakes. He was a man of capacity and spirit, and had raised himself to the position he occupied by ousting kinsmen who had superior claims to the privileges of supreme authority. In the time of Gordon's predecessor, Sir Samuel Baker, Kaba Rega had come to the front as a native champion, resolved to defy the Egyptians and their white leaders to do their worst. In a spirited attack on Baker's camp at Masindi, he endeavoured to settle the pretensions of his invaders at a blow, but he found that numbers were no match for the superior arms of his opponent. But defeat did not diminish his spirit. Baker decreed his deposition as King of Unyoro, proclaiming in his stead a cousin named Rionga, but the order had no practical effect. Kaba Rega retired a little from the vicinity of the Egyptian forces; he retained "the magic stool" of authority over the lands and peoples of Unyoro, and his cousin Rionga possessed nothing beyond the empty title contained in an Egyptian official decree. This was the position when Gordon appeared on the scene, and his first obligation was to give something like force and reality to the pretensions of Rionga.

If Kaba Rega had been satisfied to retain the practical marks of authority, it is probable that Gordon would have been well content to leave him alone, but irritated by the slight placed upon him by Sir Samuel Baker, he assumed the offensive on every possible occasion. He attacked Colonel Long, one of Gordon's lieutenants, on his way back from Mtesa, just as he had Baker; he threatened the Egyptian station at Foweira; and above all, he welcomed the thwarted slave-dealers, who were not averse to taking their revenge in any form at Gordon's expense. In these circumstances an active policy was forced on General Gordon, who promptly decided that Kaba Rega was "too treacherous" to be allowed to retain his kingdom, and that measures must be taken to set up Rionga in his place. It was at this moment, unfortunately, that General Gordon discovered the worthlessness of his troops, and when, in 1876, he had organised his new force, and was ready to carry out the policy he had decided on in 1874, he was thinking mostly of his departure from the Soudan, and had no time to proceed to extremities against these southern adversaries, for behind Kaba Rega stood Mtesa.

When Gordon, in January 1876, entered the territory of Unyoro, belonging to Kaba Rega, he found it desirable to take up the cause of Anfina, in preference to that of Rionga, as the more influential chief; but neither proved in popularity or expertness a match for Kaba Rega. The possession of "the magic stool," the ancestral throne or copper seat of the family of Unyoro, believed to be identified with the fortunes of the little kingdom, alone compensated for the few losses in the open field, as Kaba Rega was always careful to retreat on the approach of his most dangerous adversary. Neither of his kinsmen was likely to prove a formidable foe. Rionga passed his hours in native excesses, in the joy of receiving the titular rank of *Vakil* to the Khedive. Anfina alienated Gordon's friendly feeling by suggesting the wholesale assassination of Kaba Rega's officers and followers when they came on a mission to his camp. Kaba Rega carried off the stool to the south, or rather the west, of Victoria Nyanza, and bided his time, while Mtesa wrote a half-defiant and half-entreating letter to Gordon, asking him to spare Unyoro. Mtesa had his own views of gain, and when Gordon proposed to establish a fortified post with a garrison of 160 men at Urundogani, the Uganda ruler begged that it might be stationed at his own capital, Dubaga, with the view of either winning over the troops to his service or employing them against his own enemies. Gordon saw through this proposal and withheld his consent, but his lieutenant, Nuehr Agha, acted on his own responsibility, and moved with his force to Dubaga. In a few weeks Gordon learnt that they were all, practically speaking, prisoners, and that his already heavy enough task had been increased by the necessity of rescuing them.

Gordon accordingly advanced in person to Mrooli, the nearest point to Mtesa's capital without actually crossing his frontier, and as he had with him a strong force of his newly-raised black contingent, he felt confident of his capacity to punish Mtesa for any act of treachery, and to annex, if necessary, his kingdom. But Gordon did not wish to force a war on Mtesa, or to increase the burdens of the Nile dominion. All he wanted was the restoration of the men detained at Dubaga, and he soon received assurances that his presence, and the moral effect of the force he had brought with him, would attain this result without any necessity for fighting. As Gordon worded his complaint, it was a case not of his wishing to annex Mtesa, but of Mtesa annexing his soldiers.

Having satisfied himself that Mtesa was not willing to risk a quarrel, General Gordon sent Nuehr Agha with ninety men to bring back the 140 men detained at Dubaga, and the task was accomplished without any hitch or delay. This was due partly to the military demonstrations, and partly also to a clever diplomatic move by Gordon, who wrote to Mtesa expressing his readiness to recognise by treaty the independence of Uganda, and to provide a safe-conduct for the King's ambassadors to Cairo. At this time the late Dr Emin, who claimed to be an Arab and a Mahommedan, was at Dubaga, but his influence on the course of events was *nil*, and he and Gordon never met. After the return of the troops Gordon commenced his retirement to the Nile, and after an arduous and dangerous march of eighty miles through a swampy jungle beset by Kaba Rega's tribesmen, who were able to throw their spears with accurate aim for fifty yards, he succeeded in reaching Masindi without loss. Then Gordon drew up a plan of campaign for the effectual subjugation of Kaba Rega, but he did not wait to see it carried out, as the first move could not be made until the grass was dry enough to burn. As soon as that season arrived three columns were to march against the chief of Unyoro in the following order—one consisting of 150 black soldiers, and 3000 of the Lango tribe, under Rionga, moving from Mrooli to Kisoga; another of about the same strength from Keroto to Masindi; and the third operating from the Albert Lake with the steamer. The plan was a good one, but Kaba Rega, by having recourse to his old Fabian tactics, again baffled it.

Although these events happened when Gordon had reached Cairo, it will be appropriate to give here the result of this campaign. The Unyoro chieftain retired before the Egyptians, who carried off much cattle, and when they in turn retired, he advanced and reoccupied his country. After a brief period the Egyptians definitely gave up their stations at Mrooli, Foweira, and Masindi, on the left bank of the Victoria

Nile, and confined themselves to those on its right bank, and thus finally were Mtesa and Kaba Rega left to enjoy their own rude ideas of independence and regal power.

So far as General Gordon was concerned, the Uganda question was then, both for this period and for his subsequent and more important command, definitely closed. But one personal incident remains to be chronicled. When Gordon received Mtesa's request to garrison Dubaga, and had actually planted a station on the Victoria Lake, he telegraphed the facts to the Khedive, who promptly replied by conferring on him the Medjidieh Order. At the moment that Gordon received this intimation he had decided that it would not be politic to comply with Mtesa's request to garrison Dubaga, and he had only just succeeded in rescuing an Egyptian force from a position of danger in the manner described. He felt that he had obtained this decoration "under false pretences," but the recollection of the hard and honourable work he had performed must have soon salved his conscience.

At an early stage of his work Gordon felt disposed to throw it up, and during the whole three years a constant struggle went on within himself as to whether he should stay or return to England. Many causes produced this feeling. There was, in the first place, disillusionment on discovering that the whole thing, from the Egyptian Government point of view, was a sham, and that his name was being made use of to impose on Europe. But then he thought he saw an opportunity of doing some useful and beneficial work, and, stifling his disappointment, he went on. Arrived on the scene, he found himself thwarted by his Egyptian colleagues, and treated with indifference by the Cairene Government. He also discovered that his troops were worthless, and that not one of his officers, civil and military, cared a fig for the task in hand. Their one thought was how to do nothing at all, and Gordon's patience and energy were monopolised, and in the end exhausted, by attempts to extract work from his unwilling subordinates. Even the effort to educate them up to the simple recognition that a certain amount of work had to be done, and that unless it were well done, it had to be done over again, resulted in failure. To the plain instructions he gave, they would give an interpretation of their own; and while fully admitting on explanation that this was not the proper way of executing any task, they would invariably repeat it after their own fashion, until at length Gordon could see no alternative to performing the task himself. Thus were his labours indefinitely multiplied, and only his exceptional health and energy enabled him to cope with them at all. How much they affected him in his own despite may be judged from the exclamation which escaped him, after he had obtained a considerable success that would have elated any other leader—"But the worry and trouble have taken all the syrup out of the affair!"

The personal glimpses obtainable of Gordon during these depressing years, while engaged on a task he foresaw would be undone by the weakness and indifference of the Egyptian authorities as soon as he gave it up, are very illustrative of his energy and inherent capacity for command. The world at large was quite indifferent to the heroism and the self-denial, amounting to self-sacrifice, which alone enabled him to carry on his own shoulders, like a modern Atlas, the whole administration of a scarcely conquered region, which covered ten degrees of latitude. But we who have to consider his career in all its bearings, and to discover, as it were, behind his public and private acts, the true man, cannot afford to pass over so lightly passages that are in a very special degree indicative of the man's character and temperament. In no other period of his career did he devote himself more strenuously to the details, in themselves monotonous and uninteresting, of a task that brought him neither present nor prospective satisfaction. When the tools with which he was supplied failed him, as they did at every turn, he threw himself into the struggle, and supplied the shortcomings of all the rest. When it was a matter of pulling the boats up the river, he was the first at the ropes, and the last to leave them, wading through the water with his trousers up. If it was his steamer that had run aground, all the active labour, as well as the organisation, fell on him. Sooner than add to the work of those in attendance on him, he would be seen preparing and cooking his own food; and because he could do it better than his native servant, he would clean his duck-gun, with the whole camp agape, until his ways were realised, at an Excellency doing his own work. Nor did he spare himself physically. His average day's walk, which satisfied him that he was in good health, was fourteen miles; but he often exceeded twenty miles, and on one occasion he even walked thirty-five miles under a tropical sun. Of the conduct of his soldiers against an enemy, or in coping with the difficulties of river navigation, he was always nervous, and whether for work or for fighting he used, he said, "to pray them up as he did his men in China;" but without his knowledge, one of his own soldiers was vigilantly observant of his conduct, and has recorded, through the instrumentality of Slatin Pasha, his recollections of Gordon as a fighter and leader of soldiers:

Gordon was indeed a brave man. I was one of his chiefs in the fight against the Mima and Khawabir Arabs; it was in the plain of Fafa, and a very hot day. The enemy had charged us, and had forced back the first line, and their spears were falling thick around us; one came within a hair's-breadth of Gordon, but he did not seem to mind it at all, and the victory we won was entirely due to him and his reserve of 100 men. When the fight was at its worst he found time to light a cigarette. Never in my life did I see such a thing; and then the following day, when he divided the spoil, no one was forgotten, and he kept nothing for himself. He was very tender-hearted about women and children, and never allowed them to be distributed, as is our custom in war, but he fed and clothed them at his own expense, and had them sent to their homes as soon as the war was over.

This picture of Gordon lighting a cigarette in the press of a doubtful battle may well be coupled with that already given during the Taeping rebellion, of his standing unarmed in the breach of an assaulted stockade, while around him pressed on or wavered the individuals of a forlorn hope. It will be difficult for anyone to find in all the annals of war another instance of human courage more nearly approaching the sublime.

In November 1875 General Gordon had fully made up his mind to resign and return to Cairo, in consequence of the indifference with which he was treated by the Khedive's Government, and he had actually written the telegrams announcing this intention, and given orders to pack up the stores for the passage down the Nile, when the receipt of a long letter full of praise and encouragement from the Khedive Ismail induced him to alter his plans, to tear up the telegrams, and to continue his work. General Gordon gives his reason for changing his mind very briefly: "The man had gone to all this expense under the belief that I would stick to him; I could not therefore leave him." So he stayed on for another year. In July 1876 he formally and more deliberately resigned, but the execution of this decision had to be postponed by the necessity he felt under, as already explained, of solving the geographical questions connected with the Nile and the Lakes, and also of securing the southern frontier against Kaba Rega and Mtesa.

These tasks accomplished, or placed in the way of accomplishment, there remained no let or hindrance to his departure; and by the end of October he was in Khartoum. But even then he felt uncertain as to his ultimate plans, and merely telegraphed to the Cairo authorities that he intended to come down for a time. With his back turned on the scene of his labours, the old desire not to leave his work half done came over him, and all the personal inconvenience and incessant hardship and worry of the task were forgotten in the belief that he was called on by God "to open the country thoroughly to both Lakes." He saw very clearly that what he had accomplished in the three years of his stay did not provide a permanent or complete cure of the evils arising out of the slave-trade and the other accompaniments of misgovernment, and he did not like to be beaten, which he admitted he was if he retired without remedying anything. These reflections explain why, even when leaving, his thoughts were still of returning and resuming the work, little more than commenced, in those Mussulman countries, where he foresaw a crisis that must come about soon.

But these thoughts and considerations did not affect his desire for a change to Lower Egypt, or even to visit home; and leaving Khartoum on 12th November he reached Cairo on 2nd December. He then formally placed his resignation in the Khedive's hands, but it was neither accepted nor declined; and the Khedive, in some mysterious manner, seems to have arrived at the sound conclusion that after a brief rest General Gordon would sicken of inaction, and that it would be no difficult manner to lure him back to that work in the Soudan which had already established its spell over him. Of that work, considerable as it was as the feat of a single man, it need only be said that it would have remained transitory in its effect and inconclusive in its results if General Gordon had finally turned his back on it at the close of his tenure of the post of Governor of the Equatorial Province at the end of the year 1876. When he left Cairo in the middle of December for England there was really very little reason to doubt that at the right moment he would be ready to take up the work again.

CHAPTER 8

Governor-General of the Soudan

When General Gordon left Egypt for England in December 1876 it was with the expressed determination not to return; but the real state of his mind was not bitterness at any personal grievance, or even desire for rest, although he avowed his intention of taking six months' leave, so much as disinclination to leave half done a piece of work in which he had felt much interest, and with which he had identified himself. Another consideration presented itself to him, and several of his friends pressed the view on him with all the weight they possessed, that no signal success could be achieved unless he were placed in a position of supreme authority, not merely at the Equator, but throughout the vast province of the Soudan. Such was the decision Gordon himself, influenced no doubt by the views of two friends whose names need not be mentioned, but who were well known for their zeal in the anti-slavery cause, had come to a few weeks after his arrival in England; and not thinking that there was any reasonable probability of the Khedive appointing him to any such post, he telegraphed to the British Consul-General, Mr Vivian, his determination not to return to Egypt. This communication was placed before the Khedive Ismail, who had a genuine admiration for Gordon, and who appreciated the value of his services. He at once took the matter into his own hands, and wrote the following letter, which shows that he thoroughly understood the arguments that would carry weight with the person to whom they were addressed:

My Dear Gordon,—I was astonished yesterday to learn of the despatch you had sent to Mr Vivian, in which you inform me that you will not return; all the more so when I recall your interview at Abdin, during which you promised me to return, and complete the work we had commenced together. I must

therefore attribute your telegram to the very natural feelings which influenced you on finding yourself at home and among your friends. But I cannot, my dear Gordon Pasha, think that a gentleman like Gordon can be found wanting with regard to his solemn promise, and thus, my dear Gordon, I await your return according to that promise.—Your affectionate
Ismail

To such a letter as this a negative reply was difficult, if not impossible; and when General Gordon placed the matter in the hands of the Duke of Cambridge, as head of the army, he was told that he was bound to return. He accordingly telegraphed to the Khedive that he was willing to go back to the Soudan if appointed Governor-General, and also that he would leave at once for Cairo to discuss the matter. On his arrival there, early in February 1877, the discussion of the terms and conditions on which Gordon would consent to return to the Upper Nile was resumed. He explained his views at length to the Minister, Cherif Pasha, who had succeeded Nubar as responsible adviser to the Khedive, concluding with the ultimatum: "Either give me the Soudan, or I will not go." The only compromise that Gordon would listen to was that the Khedive's eldest son should be sent as Viceroy to Khartoum, when he, for his part, would be willing to resume his old post at the Equator. The Egyptian Ministers and high officials were not in favour of any European being entrusted with such a high post, and they were especially averse to the delegation of powers to a Christian, which would leave him independent of everyone except the Khedive. But for the personal intervention of the Khedive, Gordon would not have revisited Cairo; and but for the same intervention he would never have been made Governor-General, as, after a week's negotiation with Cherif, an agreement was farther off than ever, and Gordon's patience was nearly exhausted. The Khedive, really solicitous for Gordon's help, and suspecting that there was something he did not know, asked Mr Vivian to explain the matter fully to him. On hearing the cause of the difficulty, Ismail at once said: "I will give Gordon the Soudan," and two days later he saw and told General Gordon the same thing, which found formal expression in the following letter, written on 17th February 1877, the day before Gordon left for Massowah:

My Dear Gordon Pasha,—Appreciating your honourable character, your energy, and the great services that you have already rendered to my Government, I have decided to unite in one great Governor-Generalship the whole of the Soudan, Darfour, and the Equatorial Provinces, and to entrust to you the important mission of directing it. I am about to issue a Decree to this effect.

The territories to be included in this Government being very vast, it is necessary for good administration that you should have under your orders three Vakils—one for the Soudan properly so called and the Provinces of the Equator, another for Darfour, and the third for the Red Sea coast and the Eastern Soudan.

In the event of your deeming any changes necessary, you will make your observations to me.

The Governor-Generalship of the Soudan is completely independent of the Ministry of Finance.

I direct your attention to two points, viz.—the suppression of slavery, and the improvement of the means of communication.

Abyssinia extends along a great part of the frontiers of the Soudan. I beg of you, when you are on the spot, to carefully examine into the situation of affairs, and I authorise you, if you deem it expedient, to enter into negotiations with the Abyssinian authorities with the view of arriving at a settlement of pending questions.

I end by thanking you, my dear Gordon Pasha, for your kindness in continuing to Egypt your precious services, and I am fully persuaded that, with the aid of your great experience and your devotion, we shall bring to a happy end the work we are pursuing together.

Believe, my dear Gordon Pasha, in my sentiments of high esteem and sincere friendship.—Your affectionate
Ismail

Nothing could be more gracious than this letter, which made General Gordon independent of the men who he feared would thwart him, and responsible to the Khedive alone. It was followed up a few weeks later—that is to say, after the new Governor-General had left for his destination—by the conferring of the military rank of Muchir or Marshal. At the same time the Khedive sent him a handsome uniform, with £150 worth of gold lace on the coat, and the Grand Cordon of the Medjidieh Order, which, it may be worth noting here, General Gordon only wore when in Egyptian uniform. These acts on the part of the Khedive Ismail show that, whatever may have been his reasons for taking up the slavery question, he was really sincere in his desire to support Gordon, who fully realised and appreciated the good-will and friendly intentions of this Egyptian ruler. When an unfavourable judgment is passed on Ismail Pasha, his consistent support of General Gordon may be cited to show that neither his judgment nor his heart was as bad as his numerous detractors would have the world believe.

Having settled the character of the administration he was to conduct, General Gordon did not waste a day at Cairo. The holiday and rest to which he was fully entitled, and of which there can be no doubt that he stood greatly in need, were reduced to the smallest limits. Only two months intervened between his departure from Cairo for London on coming down from the Equator, and his second departure from Cairo to the Soudan. Much of that period had been passed in travelling, much more in exhausting and uncongenial negotiation in the Egyptian capital. All the brief space over enabled him to do was to pass the Christmas with several members of his family, to which he was so deeply attached, to visit his sisters in the old home at Southampton, and to run down for a day to Gravesend, the scene of his philanthropic labours a few years before. Yet, with his extraordinary recuperative force, he hastened with fresh strength and spirit to take up a more arduous and more responsible task than that he had felt compelled to relinquish so short a period before. With almost boyish energy, tempered by a profound belief in the workings of the Divine will, he turned his face once more to that torrid region, where at that time and since scenes of cruelty and human suffering have been enacted rarely surpassed in the history of the world.

Having thus described the circumstances and conditions under which General Gordon consented to take up the Soudan question, it is desirable to explain clearly what were the objects he had in his own mind, and what was the practical task he set himself to accomplish. Fortunately, this description need not be based on surmise or individual conjecture. General Gordon set forth his task in the plainest language, and he held the clearest, and, as the result showed, the most correct views as to what had to be done, and the difficulties that stood in the way of its accomplishment. He wrote on the very threshold of his undertaking these memorable sentences:

> I have to contend with many vested interests, with fanaticism, with the abolition of hundreds of Arnauts, Turks, etc., now acting as Bashi-Bazouks, with inefficient governors, with wild independent tribes of Bedouins, and with a large semi-independent province lately under Zebehr Pasha at Bahr Ga-

zelle. . . . With terrific exertion, in two or three years' time I may, with God's administration, make a good province, with a good army, and a fair revenue and peace, and an increased trade, and also have suppressed slave raids.

No one can dispute either the Titanic magnitude of the task to be accomplished or the benefit its accomplishment would confer on a miserably unhappy population. How completely the project was carried out by one man, where powerful Governments and large armies have failed both before and since, has now to be demonstrated.

General Gordon proceeded direct from Cairo to Massowah, which route he selected because he hoped to settle the Abyssinian dispute before he commenced operations in the Soudan. Both the Khedive and the British Government wished a termination to be put to the troubles that had for some time prevailed in the border lands of Abyssinia and the Eastern Soudan, and it was hoped that Gordon's reputation and energy would facilitate the removal of all difficulties with King John, who, after the death of Theodore, had succeeded in obtaining the coveted title of "Negus."

In order to understand the position, a few historical facts must be recorded. By the year 1874 King John's authority was established over every province except in the south, Shoa, where Menelik retained his independence, and in the north, Bogos, which was seized in the year stated by Munzinger Bey, a Swiss holding the post of Governor of Massowah under the Khedive. In seizing Bogos, Munzinger had dispossessed its hereditary chief, Walad el Michael, who retired to Hamaçem, also part of his patrimony, where he raised forces in self-defence. Munzinger proposed to annex Hamaçem, and the Khedive assented; but he entrusted the command of the expedition to Arokol Bey, and a Danish officer named Arendrup as military adviser, and Munzinger was forced to be content with a minor command at Tajoura, where he was killed some months later. The Egyptian expedition meantime advanced with equal confidence and carelessness upon Hamaçem, Michael attacked it in several detachments, and had the double satisfaction of destroying the troops and capturing their arms and ammunition. Such was the disastrous commencement of those pending questions to which the Khedive Ismail referred in his letter to General Gordon.

The Khedive decided to retrieve this reverse, and to continue his original design. With this object a considerable number of troops were sent to Massowah, and the conduct of the affair was entrusted to Ratib

Pasha and an American soldier of fortune, Colonel Loring Pasha. By this time—1876—Michael had quarrelled with King John, who had compelled him to give up the weapons he had captured from the Egyptians, and, anxious for revenge, he threw in his lot with his recent adversaries. The Egyptian leaders showed they had not profited by the experience of their predecessors. They advanced in the same bold and incautious manner, and after they had built two strong forts on the Gura plateau they were induced, by jealousy of each other or contempt for their enemy when he appeared, to leave the shelter of their forts, and to fight in the open. The Egyptian Ratib had the good sense to advise, "Stay in the forts," but Loring exclaimed: "No! march out of them. You are afraid!" and thus a taunt once again sufficed to banish prudence. The result of this action, which lasted only an hour, was the loss of over 10,000 Egyptian troops, of 25 cannon, and 10,000 Remington rifles. The survivors took refuge in the forts, and succeeded in holding them. Negotiations then followed, and King John showed an unexpected moderation and desire for peace with Egypt, but only on the condition of the surrender of his recalcitrant vassal Michael. Michael retaliated by carrying raids into King John's territory, thus keeping the whole border in a state of disorder, which precluded all idea of a stable peace.

Such was the position with which General Gordon had to deal. He had to encourage the weakened and disheartened Egyptian garrison, to muzzle Michael without exposing the Khedive to the charge of deserting his ally, and to conclude a peace with Abyssinia without surrendering either Bogos or Michael. At this stage we are only called upon to describe the first brief phase of this delicate question, which at recurring intervals occupied Gordon's attention during the whole of his stay in the Soudan. His first step was to inform Michael that the subsidy of money and provisions would only be paid him on condition that he abstained from attacking the Abyssinian frontier; his next to write a letter to King John, offering him fair terms, and enclosing the draft of a treaty of amity. There was good reason to think that these overtures would have produced a favourable result if it had been possible for General Gordon to have seen King John at that time, but unfortunately a fresh war had just broken out with Menelik, and King John had to proceed in all haste to Shoa. He did not reply to Gordon's letter for six months, and by that time Gordon was too thoroughly engaged in the Soudan to take up the Abyssinian question until the force of events, as will be seen, again compelled him to do so.

Having decided that the Abyssinian dispute must wait, General

Gordon proceeded by Kassala on his journey to Khartoum. Travelling not less than thirty miles a day, in great heat, organising the administration on his way, and granting personal audience to everyone who wished to see him, from the lowest miserable and naked peasant to the highest official or religious personage, like the Shereef Said Hakim, he reached Khartoum on the 3rd May. He did not delay an hour in the commencement of his task. His first public announcement was to abolish the *courbash*, to remit arrears of taxation, and to sanction a scheme for pumping the river water into the town. The *Kadi* or mayor read this address in the public square; the people hailed it with manifestations of pleasure, and Gordon himself, carried away by his enthusiasm for his work, compresses the long harangue into a brief text: "With the help of God, I will hold the balance level."

But the measures named were not attended by any great difficulty in their inception or execution. They were merely the preliminaries to the serious and risky disbandment of the Bashi-Bazouks, and the steps necessary to restrict and control, not merely the trade in, but the possession of, slaves. As General Gordon repeatedly pointed out, his policy and proceedings were a direct attack on the only property that existed in the Soudan, and justice to the slave could not be equitably dispensed by injustice to the slave-owner. The third class of slave raider stood in a separate category, and in dealing with him Gordon never felt a trace of compunction. He had terminated the career of those ruthless scourges of the African races at the Equator, and with God's help he was determined to end it throughout the Soudan. But the slave question in Egypt was many-sided, and bristled with difficulties to anyone who understood it, and wished to mete out a fair and equable treatment to all concerned.

It was with the special object of maintaining the rights of the owners as well as of the slaves that Gordon proposed a set of regulations, making the immediate registration of slaves compulsory, and thus paving the way for the promulgation of the Slave Convention already under negotiation. His propositions were only four in number, and read as follows:

1. Enforce the law compelling runaway slaves to return to their masters, except when cruelly treated.
2. Require masters to register their slaves before 1st January 1878.
3. If the masters neglect to register them, then Regulation 1 not to be enforced in their favour.
4. No registration to be allowed after 1st January 1878.

By these simple but practical arrangements General Gordon would have upheld the rights of the slave-owners, and thus disarmed their hostility, at the same time that he stopped the imposition of servitude on any fresh persons. In the course of time, and without imposing on the Exchequer the burden of the compensation, which he saw the owners were in equity entitled to, he would thus have put an end to the slave trade throughout the Soudan.

The Anglo-Egyptian Convention on the subject of the slave trade, signed on 4th August 1877, was neither so simple nor so practical, while there was a glaring inconsistency between its provisions and the Khedivial Decree that accompanied it.

The second article of the Convention reads:"Any person engaged in traffic of slaves, either directly or indirectly, shall be considered guilty of stealing with murder (*vol avec meurtre*)," and consequently punishable, as General Gordon assumed, with death. But the first and second clauses of the Khedive's Decree were to a different effect. They ran as follows:

> The sale of slaves from family to family will be prohibited. This prohibition will take effect in seven years in Cairo, and in twelve years in the Soudan.
>
> After the lapse of this term of years any infraction of this prohibition will be punished by an imprisonment of from five months to five years.

The literal interpretation of this decree would have left Gordon helpless to do anything for the curtailment of the slave trade until the year 1889, and then only permitted to inflict a quite insufficient punishment on those who broke the law. General Gordon pointed out the contradiction between the Convention and the Decree, and the impossibility of carrying out his original instructions if he were deprived of the power of allotting adequate punishment for offences; and he reverted to his original proposition of registration, for which the Slave Convention made no provision, although the negotiators at Cairo were fully aware of his views and recommendations expressed in an official despatch three months before that Convention was signed. To these representations Gordon never received any reply. He was left to work out the problem for himself, to carry on the suppression of the slave trade as best he could, and to take the risk of official censure and repudiation for following one set of instructions in the Convention in preference to those recorded in the Decree. The outside public blamed the Khedive, and Gordon himself blamed Nubar Pasha and the Egyptian Ministry; but the real fault lay at the doors of the British Government, which knew of Gordon's representations and the discrepancy between the orders of the Khedive and the Convention they had signed together, and yet did nothing to enforce the precise fulfilment of the provisions it had thought it worth while to resort to diplomacy to obtain. The same hesitation and inability to grasp the real issues has characterised British policy in Egypt down to the present hour.

If Gordon had not been a man fearless of responsibility, and resolved that some result should ensue from his labours, he would no doubt have expended his patience and strength in futile efforts to obtain clearer and more consistent instructions from Cairo, and, harassed by official tergiversation and delay, he would have been driven to give up his task in disgust if not despair. But being what he was—a man of the greatest determination and the highest spirit—he abandoned any useless effort to negotiate with either the English or the Egyptian authorities in the Delta, and he turned to the work in hand with the resolve to govern the Soudan in the name of the Khedive, but as a practical Dictator. It was then that broke from him the characteristic and courageous phrase: "I will carry things with a high hand to the last."

The first and most pressing task to which Gordon had to address himself was the supersession of the Turkish and Arab irregulars, who, under the name of "Bashi-Bazouks," constituted a large part of the provincial garrison. Not merely were they inefficient from a military point of view, but their practice, confirmed by long immunity, had been to prey on the unoffending population. They thus brought the Government into disrepute, at the same time that they were an element of weakness in its position. Gordon saw that if the Khedive had no better support than their services, his authority in the Soudan was liable at any moment to be overthrown. It had been the practice of the Cairo authorities to send up, whenever reinforcements were asked for, Arnaut and Arab loafers in that city, and these men were expected to pay themselves without troubling the Government. This they did to their own satisfaction, until Gordon resolved to put an end to their misdeeds at all cost, for he found that not merely did they pillage the people, but that they were active abettors of the slave trade. Yet as he possessed no military force, while there were not fewer than 6000 Bashi-Bazouks scattered throughout the provinces, he had to proceed with caution. His method of breaking up this body is a striking illustration of his thorough grasp of detail, and of the prudence, as well as daring, with which he applied what he conceived to be the most sensible means of removing a grave difficulty. This considerable force was scattered in numerous small garrisons throughout the province. From a military point of view this arrangement was bad, but it enabled each separate garrison to do a little surreptitious slave-hunting on its own account. General Gordon called in these garrisons, confined the Bashi-Bazouks to three or four places, peremptorily stopped the arrival of recruits, and gradually replaced them with trustworthy black Soudanese soldiers. Before he laid down the reins of power, at the end of 1879, he had completely broken up this body, and as effectually relieved the Soudanese from their military tyrants as he had freed them from the whip.

Having put all these matters in trim, Gordon left Khartoum in the middle of the summer of 1877 for the western province of Darfour, where a number of matters claimed his pressing attention. In that province there were several large Egyptian garrisons confined in two or three towns, and unable—through fear, as it proved, but on account of formidable enemies, as was alleged—to move outside them. The reports of trouble and hostility were no doubt exaggerated, but still there was a simmering of disturbance below the surface that portended peril in the future; and read by the light of after events, it seems little short of miraculous that General Gordon was able to keep it under by his own personal energy and the magic of his name. When on the point of starting to relieve these garrisons, he found himself compelled to disband a regiment of 500 Bashi-Bazouks, who constituted the only force at his immediate disposal. He had then to organise a nondescript body, after the same fashion as he had adopted at the Equator, and with 500 followers of this kind—of whom he said only 150 were any good—he started on his march for the districts which lie several hundred miles west of the White Nile, and approach most nearly of the Khedive's possessions to Lake Tchad.

The enemies with whom General Gordon had to deal were two. There was first Haroun, who claimed, as the principal survivor after Zebehr's invasion of Darfour, already described, to be the true Sultan of that State; and secondly, Suleiman, the son of Zebehr, and the nominal leader of the slave-dealers. While the former was in open revolt, the latter's covert hostility was the more to be dreaded, although Suleiman might naturally hesitate to throw off the mask lest his revolt might be the signal for his father's execution at Cairo—Zebehr having been detained there after his too confiding visit a few years before. It was therefore both prudent and necessary to ignore Suleiman until Haroun had been brought into subjection, or in some other way compelled to desist from acts of hostility.

General Gordon's plan was simple in the extreme. Leaving the Nile with 500 men, he determined to collect *en route* the efficient part of the scattered garrisons, sending those who were not efficient to the river for transport to Khartoum, and with this force to relieve the garrison at Fascher, the most distant of the large towns or stations in Darfour. It will be understood that these garrisons numbered several thousand men each, while Gordon's relieving body was only a few hundreds; but their morale had sunk so low that they dared not take the field against an enemy whom their own terror, and not the reality, painted as formidable. Even before he began his advance, Gordon had taken a fair measure of the revolt, which he expressed himself confident of suppressing without firing a shot. At Dara, the place which in the Mahdist war was well defended by Slatin Pasha, he released 1800 troops; but he was kept in inactivity for some weeks owing to the necessity of organising his force and of ascertaining how far Suleiman, with his robber confederacy of 10,000 fighting men at Shaka—only 150 miles south-east of Dara—might be counted on to remain quiet. During this period of suspense he was compelled to take the field against a formidable tribe called by the name of the Leopard, which threatened his rear. It is unnecessary to enter upon the details of this expedition, which was completely successful, notwithstanding the cowardice of his troops, and which ended with the abject submission of the offending clan.

Having assembled a force of a kind of 3,500 men, he resolved to make a forced march to Fascher, and then with the same promptitude to descend on Shaka, and settle the pending dispute with Suleiman. These plans he kept locked in his own bosom, for his camp was full of spies, and his own surroundings were not to be trusted.

Leaving the main portion of his troops at Dara, he advanced on Fascher at the head of less than 1000 men, taking the lead himself with the small bodyguard he had organised of 150 picked Soudanese. With these he entered Fascher, where there were 3000 troops, and the Pasha, Hassan Helmi, had 10,000 more at Kolkol, three days' journey away. Gordon found the garrison quite demoralised, and afraid to move outside the walls. He at once ordered Hassan Pasha to come to him, with the intention of punishing him by dismissal for his negligence and cowardice in commanding a force that, properly led, might have coerced the whole province, when the alarming news reached the Governor-General that Suleiman and his band had quitted Shaka, and were plundering in the neighbourhood of Dara itself. The gravity of this danger admitted of no delay. Not a moment could be spared to either punish an incapable lieutenant or to crush the foe Haroun, whose proceedings were the alleged main cause of trouble in Darfour.

Gordon returned with his bodyguard as fast as possible, and, leaving even it behind, traversed the last eighty-five miles alone on his camel in a day and a half. Here may be introduced what he wrote himself on the subject of these rapid and often solitary camel journeys:

> I have a splendid camel—none like it; it flies along, and quite astonishes even the Arabs. I came flying into this station in Marshal's uniform, and before the men had had time to unpile their arms, I had arrived, with only one man with me. I could not help it; the escort did not come in for an hour and a half afterwards. The Arab chief who came with me said it was the telegraph. The Gordons and the camels are of the same race— let them take an idea into their heads, and nothing will take it out.... It is fearful to see the Governor-General arrayed in gold clothes, flying along like a madman, with only a guide, as if he were pursued.... If I were fastidious, I should be as many weeks as I now am days on the road; I gain a great deal of prestige by these unheard-of marches. It makes the people fear me much more than if I were slow.

The situation was in every way as serious as was represented. The Dara garrison as a fighting force was valueless, and with the exception of his small bodyguard, still on the road from Fascher, Gordon had not a man on whom he could count. Suleiman and his whole force were encamped not three miles from the town. Gordon quite realised the position; he saw that his own life, and, what he valued more, the whole work on which he had been so long engaged, were at stake, and that a moment's hesitation would mean ruin. He rose to the crisis. At daybreak, attired in his official costume, with the Medjidieh gleaming on his breast, he mounted his horse and rode off to Suleiman's camp. Suleiman meditated treachery, and a trifle would have decided him to take the step of seizing Gordon, and holding him as hostage for his father. Had Gordon delayed even a few hours, there is no doubt that the slave-hunters would have executed their original design; but his extraordinary promptitude and self-confidence disconcerted them, and probably saved his own life. Gordon rode down the brigand lines; Suleiman, described as "a nice-looking lad of twenty-two," received him with marks of respect, and the Governor-General, without giving them a moment to think, at once summoned him and his chief lieutenants to an audience in the tent placed at his disposal. Here Gordon went straight to the point, accusing them of meditated rebellion, and telling them that he meant to break up their confederacy. After listening to this indictment, they all made him submission very abjectly; but Gordon saw that Suleiman had not forgiven him, and when the truth came afterwards to be known, it was found that he did not carry out his project only because his principal lieutenants had deserted him. When the negotiations were over, Suleiman retired with 1500 men to Shaka, where we shall hear of him again, and Gordon took into his pay the other half of the brigand force. In this remarkable manner did he stave off the greatest peril which had yet threatened him in the Soudan.

The following corroborative account of this incident was furnished long afterwards by Slatin Pasha:

> In the midst of all this discussion and difference of opinion, Gordon, travelling by Keriut and Shieria, had halted at a spot about four hours' march from Dara; and having instructed his escort to follow him as usual, he and his two secretaries started in advance on camels. Hearing of his approach, Suleiman had given orders to his troops to deploy in three lines between the camp and the fort, and while this operation was being carried out, Gordon, coming from the rear of the troops, passed rapidly through the lines, riding at a smart trot, and, saluting the troops right and left, reached the fort. The suddenness of Gordon's arrival left the leaders no time to make their plans. They therefore ordered the general salute; but even before the thunder of the guns was heard, Gordon had already sent orders to Suleiman and his chiefs to appear instantly before him. . . . Thus had Gordon, by his amazing rapidity and quick grasp of the situation, arrived in two days at the settlement of a question which literally bristled with dangers and difficulties. Had Suleiman offered resistance at a time when Darfour was in a disturbed state, Gordon's position and the maintenance of Egyptian authority in these districts would have been precarious in the extreme.

What Gordon's own opinion of this affair was is revealed in the following extremely characteristic letter written to one of those anti-slavery enthusiasts, who seemed to think that the whole difficulty could be settled by a proclamation or two, and a rigid enforcement of a strict law sentencing every one connected with the slave trade without discrimination to death:

> There are some 6000 more slave-dealers in the interior who will obey me now they have heard that Zebehr's son and the other chiefs have given in. You can imagine what a difficulty

there is in dealing with all these armed men. I have separated them here and there, and in course of time will rid myself of the mass. Would you shoot them all? Have they no rights? Are they not to be considered? Had the planters no rights? Did not our Government once allow slave-trading? Do you know that cargoes of slaves came into Bristol Harbour in the time of our fathers? I would have given £500 to have had you and the Anti-Slavery Society in Dara during the three days of doubt whether the slave-dealers would fight or not. A bad fort, a coward garrison, and not one who did not tremble—on the other side a strong, determined set of men accustomed to war, good shots, with two field-pieces. I would have liked to hear what you would all have said then. I do not say this in brag, for God knows what my anxiety was.

The drama, of which the first act took place in Suleiman's camp outside Dara, was not then ended. Gordon knew that to leave a thing half done was only to invite the danger to reappear. Suleiman had retired with his 1500 men to Shaka, the followers of Zebehr from all sides throughout the province would flock to his standard, and in a little time he would be more formidable and hostile than before. Four days after Suleiman left Dara, Gordon set out for the same place, at the head of four companies, and after a six days' march through terrible heat he reached Shaka. The slave-hunters had had no time to recover their spirits, they were all completely cowed and very submissive; and Suleiman craved favour at the hands of the man against whose life he had only a few days before been plotting. Unfortunately Gordon could not remain at Shaka, to attend in person to the dispersion of Suleiman's band, and after his departure that young leader regained his confidence, and resorted to his hostile and ambitious designs; but the success of General Gordon's plans in the summer of 1877 was complete, and sufficed to greatly diminish the gravity of the peril when, twelve months later, Suleiman broke out afresh, and fell by the hands of Gessi.

While General Gordon was facing these personal dangers, and coping with difficulties in a manner that has never been surpassed, and that will stand as an example to all time of how the energy, courage, and attention to detail of an individual will compensate for bad troops and deficient resources, he was experiencing the bitter truth that no one can escape calumny. The arm-chair reformers of London were not at all pleased with his methods, and they were quite shocked when they heard that General Gordon, whom they affected to regard as the nominee of the Anti-Slavery Society, and not as the responsible lieutenant of a foreign potentate, was in the habit, not merely of restoring fugitive slaves to their lawful owners, but even of purchasing slaves with his own and the Government money, in order to convert them into soldiers. From their narrow point of view, it seemed to them that these steps were a direct encouragement of the slave-trade, and they denounced Gordon's action with an extraordinary, but none the less bitter, ignorance of the fact that he was employing the only practical means of carrying out the mission which, in addition to his administrative duties, had been practically imposed on him as the representative of civilization. These good but misinformed persons must have believed that the Egyptian garrison in the Soudan was efficient, that communications were easy, and the climate not unpleasant, and that Gordon, supported by zealous lieutenants, had only to hold up his hand or pass a resolution, in the fashion of Exeter Hall, for the chains, real and metaphysical, to fall from the limbs of the negro population of Inner Africa. That was their dream. The reality was a worthless and craven army, a climate that killed most Europeans, and which the vigour and abstemiousness of Gordon scarcely enabled him to endure, communications only maintained and represented by the wearying flight of the camel across the desert, treachery and hostility to his plans, if not his person, among his colleagues—all these difficulties and dangers overcome and rendered nugatory by the earnestness and energy of one man alone. Well might his indignation find vent in such a grand outburst as this:

> I do not believe in you all. You say this and that, and you do not do it; you give your money, and you have done your duty; you praise one another, etc. I do not wonder at it. God has given you ties and anchors to this earth; you have wives and families. I, thank God, have none of them, and am free. Now understand me. If it suit me, I will buy slaves. I will let captured slaves go down to Egypt and not molest them, and I will do what I like, and what God, in His mercy, may direct me to do about domestic slaves; but I will break the neck of slave raids, even if it cost me my life. I will buy slaves for my army; for this purpose I will make soldiers against their will, to enable me to prevent raids. I will do this in the light of day, and defy your resolutions and your actions. Would my heart be broken if I was ousted from this command? Should I regret the eternal camel-riding, the heat, the misery I am forced to witness, the discom-

forts of everything around my domestic life? Look at my travels in seven months. Thousands of miles on camels, and no hope of rest for another year. You are only called on at intervals to rely on your God; with me I am obliged continually to do so. Find me the man and I will take him as my help who utterly despises money, name, glory, honour; one who never wishes to see his home again; one who looks to God as the Source of good and Controller of evil; one who has a healthy body and energetic spirit, and one who looks on death as a release from misery; and if you cannot find him, then leave me alone. To carry myself is enough for me; I want no other baggage.

Gordon's troubles were not only with English visionaries. The Egyptian officials had always regarded the delegation of supreme powers to him with dislike, and this sentiment became unqualified apprehension when they saw how resolute he was in exercising them. Ismail Pasha was disposed to place unlimited trust in his energetic Governor-General, but he could not but be somewhat influenced by those around him while Gordon was far away. When, therefore, Gordon took into his own hands the power of life and death, and sentenced men to be hanged and shot, he roused that opposition to the highest point of activity, and received repeated remonstrances by telegraph from Cairo. To these he replied firmly, but quietly, that on no other condition could the administration be carried on, and that his authority as Viceroy would be undermined if he could not dispense prompt justice. Notwithstanding all his representations, he never obtained the ratification of his right to pass death sentences; but with that strong will that he showed in every crisis, he announced his determination to act on his own responsibility. On at least two occasions he expresses a feeling of gratification at having caused murderers to be hung.

This is a suitable moment to lay stress on the true views Gordon held on the subject of bloodshed. While averse to all warfare by disposition, and without the smallest trace of what might be called the military spirit, General Gordon had none of that timid and unreasoning shrinking from taking life, which is often cruel and always cowardly. He punished the guilty without the least false compunction, even with a death sentence, and if necessity left no choice, he would have executed that sentence himself, provided he was quite convinced of its justice. As a rule, he went unarmed in the Soudan, as in China; but there were exceptions, and on at least one occasion he took an active and decisive part in a conflict. He was being attacked by one of the tribes, and his men were firing wildly and without result. Then Gordon snatched a rifle from one of his men, and firing at the hostile leader, killed him. There are at least two other incidents that will show him in a light that many of his admirers would keep suppressed, but that bring out his human nature. A clumsy servant fired off his heavy duck-gun close to his head, and Gordon very naturally gave him a smart box on the ears which the fellow would remember for a week. Excited by the misery of a slave-gang, he asked the boy in charge of them to whom they belonged, and as he hesitated, he struck him across the face with his whip. Gordon's comment on this act is that it was "cruel and cowardly, but he was enraged, and could not help it." One feels on reading this that one would have done so oneself, and that, after all, Gordon was a man, and not a spiritual abstraction.

Thus ended the first eventful year of General Gordon's tenure of the post of Governor-General of the Soudan. Some idea of the magnitude of the task he had performed may be gathered from the fact that during this period he rode nearly 4000 miles on his camel through the desert. He put before himself the solution of eight burning questions, and by the end of 1877 he had settled five of them more or less permanently. He had also effected many reforms in the military and civil branches of the administration, and had formed the nucleus of a force in which he could put some confidence. By the people he was respected and feared, and far more liked than he imagined. "Send us another Governor like Gordon" was the burden of the Soudanese cry to Slatin when the shadow of the Mahdi's power had already fallen over the land. He had respected their religion and prejudices. When their Mahommedan co-religionists had ground them down to the dust, even desecrating their mosques by turning them into powder magazines, General Gordon showed them justice and merciful consideration, restored and endowed their mosques, and exhorted them in every way to be faithful to the observance of their religion. He was always most exact in payment for services rendered. This became known; and when some of the Egyptian officials—a Pasha among others—seized camels for his service without paying for them, the owners threw themselves on the ground, kissing Gordon's camel's feet, told their tale, and obtained prompt redress. What more striking testimony to his thoughtfulness for others could be given than in the following anecdote? One of his native lieutenants, a confirmed drunkard, but of which Gordon was ignorant, became ill, and the Governor-General went to see and sit by him in his tent. All the man asked for was brandy, and General Gordon, somewhat shocked at the repeated request, expostulated with him that he, a believer in the Koran, should drink the strong waters so expressly forbidden by that holy book. But the man readily replied, "This is as medicine, and the Prophet does not forbid us to save life." Gordon said nothing, but left the tent, and some hours later he sent the man two bottles of brandy from his own small store. Even the Soudanese, who were afraid of him in his terrible mood, knew the many soft corners he kept in his heart, and easily learnt the way to them. For misfortune and suffering of every kind his sympathy was quickly won, and with his sympathy went his support, to the utmost limit of his power.

After the campaign in Darfour, Gordon returned to Khartoum, where he was preparing for fresh exertions, as well as for a settlement of the Abyssinian difficulty, when a sudden and unexpected summons reached him to come down to Cairo and help the Khedive to arrange his financial affairs. The Khedive's telegram stated that the Egyptian creditors were trying to interfere with his sovereign prerogative, and that His Highness knew no one but Gordon who could assist him out of this position. The precise date on which this telegram reached Gordon was 25th January 1878, when he was passing Shendy—the place on the Nile opposite Metammeh, where the British Expedition encamped in January 1885—but as he had to return to Khartoum to arrange for the conduct of the administration during his absence, he did not arrive at Dongola on his way to the capital until the 20th of the following month. He reached Cairo on 7th March, was at once carried off to dine with the Khedive, who had waited more than an hour over the appointed time for him because his train was late, and, when it was over, was conveyed to one of the finest palaces, which had been specially prepared in his honour. The meaning of this extraordinary reception was that the Khedive Ismail thought he had found a deliverer from his own troubles in the man who had done such wonders in the Soudan. That ruler had reached a stage in his affairs when extrication was impossible, if the creditors of Egypt were to receive their dues. He was very astute, and he probably saw that the only chance of saving himself was for some high authority to declare that the interests of himself and his people must be pronounced paramount to those of the foreign investors. There was only one man in the world likely to come to that conclusion, with a spotless reputation and a voice to which public opinion might be expected to pay heed. That man was Gordon. Therefore he was sent for in post haste, and found the post of President of "An Inquiry into the State of the Finances of the Country" thrust upon him before he had shaken off the dust of his long journey to Cairo.

The motives which induced the Khedive to send for General Gordon cannot be mistaken; nor is there any obscurity as to those which led General Gordon to accept a task in which he was bound to run counter to the views of every other European authority, and still more to the fixed policy of his and other Governments. In the first place, Gordon being the servant of the Khedive, it would have been impossible for him to have said no to a request which was entitled to be regarded as a command. In the second place, Gordon did not know all the currents of intrigue working between Cairo and the capitals of Europe, and he convinced himself that a sound workable plan for the benefit of Egypt and her people would command such general approval that "the financial cormorants," as he termed the bondholders, or rather their leaders, would have to retire beaten from the field. He had no doubt that he could draw up such a plan, based on a suspension and permanent reduction of interest, and the result will convince any disinterested person of the fact, but Gordon was destined to find that all persons cannot be guided by such disinterestedness as his, of which the way he treated his Egyptian salary furnished such a striking instance. When sent to the Equator, he was offered £10,000 a year, and accepted £2000; as Governor-General, he was nominated at £12,000 a year, and cut it down to a half; and when, during this very Cairo visit, a new and unnecessary official was appointed under the Soudan Administration, he insisted that his own salary should be further reduced to £3000, to compensate for this further charge. Such an example as this did not arouse enthusiasm or inspire emulation in the Delta. General Gordon never dealt with a question in which abstract justice was deemed more out of place, or had less chance of carrying the day.

As the matter was very important, and interested persons might easily have misrepresented his part in it, General Gordon drew up a memorandum explaining every incident in the course of the affair. This document was published by his brother, Sir Henry Gordon, in 1886, and the following description merely summarises its contents.

As far back as the year 1875 the Khedive Ismail began to discover that the financial position of his Government was bad, and that it would be impossible to keep up the payment of the interest on the debt at the high rate of seven per cent., which Egypt had bound itself to pay. He therefore applied to the British Government for advice and assistance. In response to his representations, a Financial Commission, composed of three members—Mr Cave, Colonel Stokes, and Mr Rivers Wilson—was sent to Egypt for the purpose of inquiring into the financial position of that country. They had no difficulty in coming to the conclusion that it was unsound, and that the uneasiness of Ismail Pasha had not been expressed a day too soon. They recommended that an arrangement should be come to with the bondholders by which all the loans were to be placed on the same footing, and the rate of interest reduced to some figure that might be agreed upon. It then became necessary to negotiate with the bondholders, who appointed Mr Goschen for the English section, and M. Joubert for the French, to look after their rights. The result of their efforts in 1876 was that they united the loans into one, bearing a uniform rate of six per cent, instead of seven, and that four Commissioners were appointed to look after the debt in the interests of the bondholders, while two other European officials were nominated—one to control the receipts, the other the expenditure. In less than two years Ismail Pasha discovered that this arrangement had not remedied the evil, and that the Government was again on the verge of bankruptcy. It was at this juncture that the Khedive applied to General Gordon, in the hope that his ability and reputation would provide an easy escape from his dilemma.

General Gordon agreed to accept the post of President of this Commission of Inquiry, and he also fell in with the Khedive's own wish and suggestion that the Commissioners of the Debt should not be members of the Commission. This point must be carefully borne in mind, as the whole negotiation failed because of the Khedive's weakness in waiving the very point he rightly deemed vital for success. Having laid down the only principle to which he attached importance, the Khedive went on to say that M. de Lesseps would act in conjunction with General Gordon, and that these two, with some vague assistance from financial experts, were to form the Commission. It soon became evident that M. de Lesseps had no serious views on the subject, and that he was only too much disposed to yield to external influences.

On the very threshold of his task, which he took up with his usual thoroughness and honest desire to get at the truth, General Gordon received a warning that the greatest difficulties were not those inherent to the subject, but those arising from the selfish designs of interested persons. As soon as it became known that General Gordon had accepted this task, and that he had agreed to the Khedive's suggestion that the Debt Commissioners were not to sit on the Commission, there was a loud outburst of disapproval and dismay in diplomatic and financial circles. This part of the story must be given in his own words:

> Mr Vivian, the English Consul-General, said to me, 'I wonder you could accept the Presidency of the Commission of Inquiry without the Commissioners of the Debt.' I said, 'I was free to accept or refuse.'
>
> I then called on the German Consul-General, and when there the French and Austrian Consuls-General, and also Vivian, came in, and attacked me for having accepted the post of President. I said 'I was free.' And then they said, 'I was risking his Highness his throne; that he ran a very serious risk personally, if he formed the Commission of Inquiry without the creditors' representatives, *viz.* the Commissioners of the Debt.' I said, 'Why do you not tell him so?' They said, 'You ought to do so.' I said, 'Well, will you commission me to do so, from you, with any remarks I like to make as to the futility of your words?' They all said, 'Yes, we authorise you to do so—in our names.'

General Gordon went that evening to the Abdin Palace, where he was engaged to dine with the Khedive; and having asked permission to make an important communication, saw Ismail before dinner, when words to this effect were exchanged:

Gordon said: "I have seen the four Consuls-General today, and they told me to tell your Highness from them that you run a serious personal risk if you have a Commission of Inquiry without the Commissioners of Debt being upon it."

The Khedive replied as follows: "I do not care a bit. I am only afraid of England, and I feel sure she will not move. You will see Lesseps tomorrow, and arrange the *enquête* with him." Encouraged by the Khedive's firmness, and fully convinced that no good result would follow if the Debt Commissioners, who only considered the bondholders' interests, were on this inquiry, Gordon met Lesseps the next morning in the full expectation that business would now be begun. The further ramifications of the intrigue, for it soon became one, for the discomfiture and discrediting of Gordon, must be told in his own words:

> The next day Lesseps came to my Palace with Stanton (Stokes's old Danube Secretary, now Resident-Commissioner for the British Government Suez Canal Shares at Paris, an old friend of mine). Lesseps began, 'We must have the Commissioners of the Debt on the *enquête*.'

I said, 'It is a *sine quâ non* that they are not to be upon it.' Lesseps replied, 'They must be upon it.'

Then in came Cherif Pasha (the Premier), and said, 'Are you agreed?' I left Lesseps to speak, and he said, 'Yes,' at which I stared and said, 'I fear not.' Then Lesseps and Cherif discussed it, and Lesseps gave in, and agreed to serve on the Commission without the Commissioners of the Debt, but with the proviso that he would ask permission to do so from Paris. Cherif Pasha was pleased.

But I instinctively felt old Lesseps was ratting, so I asked Cherif to stop a moment, and said to Stanton, 'Now, see that Lesseps does not make a mess of it. Let him say at once, Will he act without the Commissioners of Debt or not? Do this for my sake; take him into that corner and speak to him.' Stanton did so, while I took Cherif into the other corner, much against his will, for he thought I was a bore, raising obstacles. I told him that Lesseps had declared before he came that he would not act unless with the Commissioners of the Debt. Cherif was huffed with me, and turned to Lesseps, whom Stanton had already dosed in his corner of the room, and he and Lesseps had a close conversation again for some time; and then Cherif came to me and said, 'Lesseps has accepted without the Commissioners of the Debt.'

I disgusted Cherif as I went downstairs with him by saying, 'He will never stick to it.'

If Gordon was not a diplomatist, he was at least very clear-sighted. He saw clearly through M. de Lesseps, who had no views on the subject, and who was quite content to play the part his Government assigned him. A few minutes after the interview described he obtained further evidence of the hostility the projected inquiry without the Commissioners had aroused. He met Major Evelyn Baring, then beginning the Egyptian career which he still pursues as Lord Cromer, who was desirous of knowing what decision had been arrived at. On hearing that the Commissioners were to be excluded, Major Baring remarked, "It was unfair to the creditors," which seems to have drawn from Gordon some angry retort. There is no doubt that at this moment Gordon lost all control over himself, and employed personalities that left a sore feeling behind them. That they did so in this case was, as I am compelled to show later on, amply demonstrated in December 1883 and January 1884. The direct and immediate significance of the occurrence lay in its furnishing fresh evidence of the unanimity of hostility with which all the European officials in the Delta regarded the Khedive's proposal, and his attempt to make use of General Gordon's exceptional character and reputation. It is a reflection on no particular individual to assert that they were all resolved that General Gordon's appeal to the abstract sense of justice of the world should never be promulgated.

The first practical proposal made was to telegraph for Mr Samuel Laing, a trained financier, who had acted in India at the head of the finances of that country; but General Gordon refused to do this, because he knew that he would be held responsible for the terms he came on; and instead he drew up several propositions, one of them being that the services of Mr Laing should be secured on conditions to be fixed by the Khedive. During this discussion, it should be noted, Lesseps paid no attention to business, talking of trivial and extraneous matters. Then Gordon, with the view of clinching the matter, said:

"There are two questions to decide:

"*First*, how to alleviate the present sufferings of the unpaid civil employees and of the army, as well as the pressing claims of the floating debt.

"*Second*, and afterwards to inquire into the real state of the revenue by a Commission."

This was the exact opposite of the bondholders' view, for the settlement of the grievances of the public and military service and of the floating debt would *then* have left nothing for the payment of the coupons on the permanent external debt of a hundred millions. In fact, General Gordon boldly suggested that the funds immediately wanted must be provided by the non-payment of the next coupon due.

It is impossible to resist the conclusion that if General Gordon had had his way, the Arabi revolt would have been averted; the Khedive Ismail, the ablest member of his house, would not have been deposed; and an English occupation of Egypt, hampered by financial and diplomatic shackles that neutralise the value of its temporary possession, need never have been undertaken. But *dis aliter visum*. It is equally impossible to resist the conclusion that the forces arrayed against Gordon on this occasion were such as he could not expect to conquer.

The concluding scenes of the affair need only be briefly described. M. de Lesseps had never swerved from his original purpose to refer the matter to Paris, but even Gordon was not prepared for the duplicity he showed in the matter, and in which he was no doubt encouraged by the prevalent feeling among the foreigners at Cairo. The first point in all tortuous diplomacy, Eastern or Western, is to gain time;

and when General Gordon, intent on business, called on Lesseps the next day—that is to say, two days after his arrival from Khartoum—the French engineer met him with the smiling observation that he was off for a day in the country, and that he had just sent a telegram to Paris. He handed Gordon a copy, which was to this effect:

> His Highness the Khedive has begged me to join with M. Gordon and *the Commissioners of the Debt* in making an inquiry into the finances of Egypt; I ask permission.

Gordon's astonished ejaculation "This will never do" was met with the light-hearted Frenchman's remark, "I must go, and it must go."

Then General Gordon hastened with the news and the draft of the telegram to the Khedive. The copy was sent in to Ismail Pasha in his private apartments. On mastering its contents, he rushed out, threw himself on a sofa, and exclaimed, "I am quite upset by this telegram of Lesseps; some one must go after him and tell him not to send it." Then turning to Gordon, he said, "I put the whole affair into your hands." Gordon, anxious to help the Khedive, and also hoping to find an ally out of Egypt, telegraphed at great length to Mr Goschen, in accordance with the Khedive's suggestion. Unfortunately, Mr Goschen replied with equal brevity and authority, "I will not look at you; the matter is in the hands of Her Majesty's Government." When we remember that Gordon was the properly-appointed representative of an independent Prince, or at least of a Prince independent of England, we cannot wonder at his terming this a "rude answer." Mr Goschen may have had some after-qualms himself, for he telegraphed some days later in a milder tone, but Gordon would not take an affront from any man, and left it unanswered.

At this crisis Gordon, nothing daunted, made a proposal which, if the Khedive had had the courage to carry it out, might have left the victory with them. He proposed to the Khedive to issue a decree suspending the payment of the coupon, paying all pressing claims, and stating that he did all this on the advice of Gordon. Failing that, Gordon offered to telegraph himself to Lord Derby, the Foreign Secretary, and accept the full responsibility for the measure. Ismail was not equal to the occasion. He shut himself up in his harem for two days, and, as Gordon said, "the game was lost."

General Gordon was now to experience the illimitable extent of human ingratitude. Even those who disagreed with the views he expressed on this subject cannot deny his loyalty to the Khedive, or the magnitude of the efforts he made on his behalf. To carry out the wishes of the Prince in whose service he was for the time being, he was prepared to accept every responsibility, and to show an unswerving devotion in a way that excited the opposition and hostility even of those whom he might otherwise have termed his friends and well-wishers. By an extreme expedient, which would either have ruined himself or thwarted the plans of powerful statesmen, and financiers not less powerful, he would have sealed his devotion to Ismail Pasha; but the moral or physical weakness of the Oriental prevented the attempt being made. The delay mentioned allowed of fresh pressure being brought to bear on the Khedive; and while Gordon emphatically declared, partly from a sense of consistency, and partly because he hoped to stiffen the Khedive's resolution that he would not act with the Debt Commissioners on the Inquiry, Ismail Pasha was coerced or induced into surrendering all he had been fighting for. He gave his assent to the Commissioners being on the Inquiry, and he turned his back on the man who had come from the heart of Africa to his assistance. When Gordon learnt these facts, he resolved to return to the Soudan, and he was allowed to do so without the least mark of honour or word of thanks from the Khedive. His financial episode cost him £800 out of his own pocket, and even if we consider that the financial situation in the Delta, with all its cross-currents of shady intrigue and selfish designs, was one that he was not quite qualified to deal with, we cannot dispute that his propositions were full of all his habitual nobility of purpose, and that they were practical, if they could ever have been put into effect.

This incident serves to bring out some of the limitations of Gordon's ability. His own convictions, strengthened by the solitary life he had led for years in the Soudan, did not make him well adapted for any form of diplomacy. His methods were too simple, and his remedies too exclusively based on a radical treatment, to suit every complaint in a complicated state of society; nor is it possible for the majority of men to be influenced by his extraordinary self-abnegation and disregard for money. During this very mission he boasted that he was able to get to bed at eight o'clock, because he never dined out, and that he did not care at everyone laughing at him, and saying he was in the sulks. This mode of living was due, not to any peculiarity about General Gordon—although I trace to this period the opinion that he was mad—but mainly to his honest wish not to be biased by any European's judgment, and to be able to give the Khedive absolutely independent advice, as if he himself were an Egyptian, speaking and acting for Egypt. Enough has been said to explain why he failed to accomplish a really impossible task.

Nor is it necessary to assume that because they differed from him and strenuously opposed his project, the other Englishmen in authority in the Delta were influenced by any unworthy motives or pursued a policy that was either reprehensible or unsound.

From this uncongenial task General Gordon returned to the work which he thoroughly understood, and with regard to which he had to apprehend no serious outside interference, for the attraction of the flesh-pots of Egypt did not extend into the Soudan. Still, he felt that his "outspokenness," as he termed it, had not strengthened his position. He travelled on this occasion by the Red Sea route to Aden, thence to Zeila, with the view of inspecting Harrar, which formed part of his extensive Government. During this tour Gordon saw much that disquieted him—a large strip of country held by fanatical Mahommedans, the slave trade in unchecked progress where he had not thought it to exist—and he wrote these memorable words:

> Our English Government lives on a hand-to-mouth policy. They are very ignorant of these lands, yet some day or other they or some other Government will have to know them, for things at Cairo cannot stay as they are. His Highness will be curbed in, and will no longer be absolute sovereign; then will come the question of these countries.

At Harrar, Gordon dismissed the Governor Raouf, whom he describes as a regular tyrant, but who, none the less for his misdeeds, was proclaimed Governor-General of the Soudan when Gordon left it less than two years after this visit to Harrar. When this affair was settled, General Gordon proceeded *via* Massowah and Souakim to Khartoum, where he arrived about the middle of June. On his way he had felt bound to remove eight high military officers from their commands for various offences, from which may be gathered some idea of the colleagues on whom he had to depend. He reached Khartoum not a moment too soon, for the first news that greeted him was that Suleiman had broken out in open revolt, and was practically master of the Province of Bahr Gazelle, which lies between Darfour and the Equatorial Province.

But before describing the steps he took to suppress this formidable revolt, which resembled the rising under the Mahdi in every point except its non-religious character, some notice may be given of the financial difficulties with which he had to cope, and which were much increased by the Khedive's practice of giving appointments in a promiscuous manner that were to be chargeable on the scanty and inadequate revenues of the Soudan.

In the year 1877 the expenditure of the Soudan exceeded the revenue by over a quarter of a million sterling; in 1878 Gordon had reduced this deficit to £70,000. In the return given by the Khedive of his resources when foreign intervention first took place, it was stated that the Soudan furnished a tribute of £143,000. This was untrue; it had always been a drain on the Cairo exchequer until in 1879 General Gordon had the satisfaction, by reducing expenditure in every possible direction and abolishing sinecures, of securing an exact balance. The most formidable adversary Gordon had to meet in the course of this financial struggle was the Khedive himself, and it was only by sustained effort that he succeeded in averting the imposition of various expenses on his shoulders which would have rendered success impossible. First it was two steamers, which would have cost £20,000; then it was the so-called Soudan railway, with a liability of not less than three quarters of a million with which the Khedive wished to saddle the Soudan, but Gordon would have neither, and his firmness carried the day. When the Cairo authorities, in want of money, claimed that the Soudan owed £30,000, he went into the items, and showed that, instead, Cairo owed it £9000. He never got it, but by this he proved that, while he was the servant of the Khedive, he would not be subservient to him in matters that affected the successful discharge of his task as that Prince's deputy in the Soudan.

We must now return to the revolt of Suleiman, the most serious military peril Gordon had to deal with in Africa, which was in its main features similar to the later uprising under the Mahdi. At the first collision with that young leader of the slave-dealers, Gordon had triumphed by his quickness and daring; but he had seen that Suleiman was not thoroughly cowed, and he had warned him that if he revolted again the result would inevitably be his ruin. Suleiman had not taken the warning to heart, and was now in open revolt. His most powerful supporters were the Arab colonies, long settled in interior Africa, who, proud of their descent, were always willing to take part against the Turko-Egyptian Government. These men rallied to a certain extent to Suleiman, just as some years later they attached themselves to the Mahdi. As General Gordon wrote in 1878: "They were ready, and are still ready, to seize the first chance of shaking off the yoke of Egypt." It was during Gordon's absence at Cairo that Suleiman's plans matured, and he began the campaign by seizing the province of Bahr Gazelle. Immediately on receiving this intelligence, General Gordon fitted out an expedition; and as he could not take the command himself, he entrusted it to his best lieutenant, Romolo Gessi, an Italian of proved merit.

Natural difficulties retarded the advance of the expedition. Heavy floods kept Gessi confined in his camp during three months, and the lukewarm supporters of the Government regarded this inaction as proof of inferiority. They consequently rallied to Suleiman, who soon found himself at the head of a force of 6000 men, while Gessi had only 300 regulars, two cannon, and 700 almost useless irregulars. It was as difficult for him to let the Governor-General know that he needed reinforcements as it was for General Gordon to send them. Some of his subordinates, in command of outlying detachments, refused to obey his summons, preferring to carry on a little slave-hunting on their own account. His troops were on the verge of mutiny: he had to shoot one ringleader with his own hand.

At last the floods fell, and he began his forward movement, fighting his way against detached bodies of slave-hunters, but after each success receiving the welcome of the unfortunate natives, of whom Suleiman had consigned not fewer than 10,000 in the six previous months to slavery. At last Gessi was himself compelled to halt at a place called Dem Idris, fifty miles north of the fort which Suleiman had constructed for his final stand, and named after himself. These places are about 200 miles south of both Dara and Shaka, while between them runs the considerable stream called Bahr Arab. Gessi was now in close proximity to the main force under Suleiman, but he had to halt for five months before he felt in any way equal to the task of attacking it. During that period he had to stand on the defensive, and sustain several attacks from Suleiman, who had made all his plans for invading Darfour, and adding that province to the Bahr Gazelle.

The first of these engagements was that fought on 28th December 1878, when Suleiman, at the head of 10,000 men, attacked Gessi's camp at Dem Idris. Fortunately, he had neglected no precaution, and his regulars, supported by a strong force of friendly natives, nobly seconded his efforts. Suleiman's force was repulsed in four assaults, and had to retire with a loss of 1000 men. But Gessi's difficulties were far from removed by this victory. Suleiman's losses were easily repaired, while those of Gessi could not be replaced. His men were also suffering from fever, and the strain on himself, through the absence of any subordinates to assist him, was terrible. It was a relief to him when Suleiman delivered his second attack, fifteen days after the first. On this occasion Suleiman appealed to the religious fanaticism of his followers, and made them swear on the Koran to conquer or die; and the black troops, as the less trustworthy, were placed in the van of battle and driven to the assault by the Arabs. Gessi made an excellent disposition of his troops, repulsing the two main attacks with heavy loss; and when the attack was resumed the next day, his success was equally complete. Unfortunately, Gessi was unable to follow up this advantage, because his powder was almost exhausted, and his men were reduced to pick up bullets from the field of combat. Tidings of his position reached Suleiman, who made a final attack on the 28th of January 1879, but owing to the fortunate arrival of a small supply of powder, Gessi was able to fight and win another battle.

It was not until the 11th March, however, that Gessi received a sufficient supply of ammunition to enable him to assume the offensive. Suleiman's camp or fort was a strongly barricaded enclosure, surrounded by a double row of trunks of trees. The centre of the enclosure was occupied by an inner fort, which was Suleiman's own residence. On Gessi attacking it, his first shell set fire to one of the huts, and as the wood was dry, the whole encampment was soon in a blaze. Driven to desperation, the brigands sallied forth, only to be driven back by the steady fire of Gessi's troops, who by this time were full of confidence in their leader. Then the former broke into flight, escaping wherever they could. Suleiman was among those who escaped, although eleven of his chiefs were slain, and the unfortunate exhaustion of Gessi's powder again provided him with the respite to rally his followers and make another bid for power.

This further period of enforced inaction terminated at the end of April, when the arrival of a full supply of powder and cartridges enabled Gessi to take the field for the last time. On the 1st May the Egyptian commander started to attack the slave robber in his last stronghold, Dem Suleiman. Three days later he fought the first of these final battles outside that fort, and succeeded in cutting off the retreat of the vanquished Arabs into that place of shelter. He then broke into the fort itself, where there were only a few men, and he almost succeeded in capturing Suleiman, who fled through one gate as Gessi entered by another. Thanks to the fleetness of his horse, Suleiman succeeded in making good his escape. Before his hurried flight Suleiman murdered four prisoners sooner than allow of their recapture, and throughout the long pursuit that now began all slaves or black troops who could not keep up were killed. These were not the only crimes perpetrated by these brigands. Superstition, or the mere pleasure of cruelty, had induced them when their fortunes were getting low to consecrate a new banner by bathing it in the blood of a murdered child. For these iniquities the hour of expiation had now arrived.

After the capture of Dem Suleiman, Gessi began a pursuit which, considering the difficulties of the route owing to heavy rain, topo-graphical ignorance, and the deficiency of supplies, may be character-ised as remarkable. Gessi took with him only 600 men, armed with Remington rifles; but they could carry no more than three or four days' provisions, which were exhausted before he came up with even the rearmost of the fugitive Arabs. There the troops turned sulky, and it was only by promising them as spoil everything taken that he re-stored them to something like good temper. Six days after the start Gessi overwhelmed one band under Abou Sammat, one of the most active of the slave-hunters, and learnt that Suleiman himself was only twenty-four hours ahead. But the difficulties were such that Gessi was almost reduced to despair of the capture of that leader, and as long as he remained at large the rebellion could not be considered suppressed.

Fortune played the game into his hand at the very moment that the result seemed hopeless. In the middle of the night several men came to his camp from Sultan Idris, one of the Arab chiefs, thinking it was that of Rabi, the chief of Suleiman's lieutenants. Gessi sent one of them back to invite him to approach, and at once laid his own plans. He resolved to destroy Rabi's force, which lay encamped close by, before the other band could come up; and by a sudden assault at daybreak he succeeded in his object. The whole band was exterminated, with the exception of Rabi himself, who escaped on a fast horse. Then Gessi laid his ambuscade for Sultan Idris, who marched into the trap pre-pared for him. This band also was nearly annihilated, but Sultan Idris escaped, leaving, however, an immense spoil, which put the Egyptian soldiers in good humour. For the disposal of this booty, and for other reasons, Gessi resolved to return to Dem Suleiman.

At this point it was alone possible to criticise the action of the en-ergetic Gessi during the whole course of the campaign, and General Gordon no doubt thought that if he had paid no attention to the spoil captured from Rabi and Sultan Idris, but pressed the pursuit against Suleiman, he might then and there have concluded the campaign. On the other hand, it is only fair to state that Gessi had to consider the sentiment of his own troops, while he was also ill from the mental strain and physical exertion of conducting the campaign virtually by himself. The spoil, moreover, did not benefit him in the least. It went into the coffers of the Government, or the pockets of the soldiers, not into his. So little reward did he receive that Gordon intended at first to give him £1000 out of his own pocket, and eventually found himself able to increase it to a sum of £2000 out of the Soudan exchequer.

But Suleiman was still at large, and the slave-dealers were fully determined to preserve their profitable monopoly, if by any means they could baffle the Government. The Egyptian officials were also inclined to assist their efforts, and while Gessi was recovering his strength, he had the mortification of seeing the fruits of his earlier success lost by the inaction or more culpable proceedings of his lieutenants. It was not until July 1879 that Gessi felt able to take the field in person, and then with less than 300 men, while Suleiman's band alone numbered 900. But there was no time to wait for reinforcements if Suleiman, who had advanced to within a short distance of Gessi's camp, was to be captured. Owing to the promptitude of his measures, Gessi came up with Suleiman in three days' time at the village of Gara, which he reached at daybreak on 16th of July. His measures were prompt and decisive. Concealing his troops in a wood, so that the smallness of their numbers might not be detected, he sent in a summons to Suleiman to surrender within ten minutes. Surprised, and ignorant of the strength of the Egyptian force, he and his followers agreed to lay down their arms: but when Suleiman saw the mere handful of men to whom he had yielded, he burst out crying. The situation suggested to him the hope of escape. Gessi learnt that when night came Suleiman and his men had arranged to break their way through. He therefore resolved to anticipate them. He held in his hands the ringleaders of the rebellion. If they escaped, all his work was lost; a summary act of justice would conclude the affair, and secure the Government against fresh attacks for a long time. To use his own words, Gessi "saw that the time had come to have done with these people once for all."

He divided the captives into three bands. The first, composed of the black soldiers, little better than slaves, he released on the condition that they left at once and promised to settle down to a peaceful life. This they agreed to joyfully. Having got rid of these, the larger number of Suleiman's band, he seized the smaller body of slave-dealers—157 in number—and having chained them, sent them under a guard as prisoners to his own camp. Then he seized Suleiman and ten of his chief supporters, and shot them on the spot. Thus perished Suleiman, the son of Zebehr, in whose name and for whose safety he had gone into revolt, in the very way that Gordon had predicted two years before in the midst of his brigand power at Shaka; and thus, with a remarkable combination of skill and courage, did Gessi bring his arduous campaign of twelve months' duration to a victorious conclusion.

Although the credit of these successful operations was entirely due to Gessi, it must not be supposed that General Gordon took no part in controlling them; but, for the sake of clearness, it seemed advisable to narrate the history of the campaign against Suleiman without a break. Early in 1879, when Gessi, after obtaining some successes, had been reduced to inaction from the want of ammunition, Gordon's anxiety became so great on his account that he determined to assume the command in person. His main object was to afford relief to Gessi by taking the field in Darfour, and putting down the rebels in that province, who were on the point of throwing in their lot with Suleiman. Gordon determined therefore to march on Shaka, the old headquarters of Zebehr and his son. On his march he rescued several slave caravans, but he saw that the suppression of the slave trade was not popular, and the contradictory character of the law and his instructions placed him in much embarrassment. Still, he saw clearly that Darfour was the true heart of the slave trade, as the supply from Inner Africa had to pass through it to Egypt, and he thought that a solution might be found for the difficulty by requiring every one of the inhabitants to have a permission of residence, and every traveller a passport for himself and his followers. But neither time nor the conditions of his post allowed of his carrying out this suggestion. It remains, however, a simple practical measure to be borne in mind when the solution of the slave difficulty is taken finally in hand by a Government in earnest on the subject, and powerful enough to see its orders enforced.

General Gordon reached Shaka on 7th April, and at once issued a notice to the slave-dealers to quit that advantageous station. He also sent forward reinforcements of men and stores to Gessi, but in a few days they returned, with a message from Gessi that he had received enough powder from his own base on the Nile to renew the attack on Suleiman. Within one week of Gordon's arrival not a slave-dealer remained in Shaka, and when envoys arrived from Suleiman, bearing protestations that he had never been hostile to the Egyptian Government, he promptly arrested them and sent them for trial by court-martial. Their guilt as conspirers against the Khedive was easily proved, and they were shot. Their fate was fully deserved, but Gordon would have spared their lives if Suleiman had not himself slain so many hostages and helpless captives.

Gordon's final operations for the suppression of the slave trade in Darfour, carried on while Gessi was engaged in his last struggle with Suleiman, resulted in the release of several thousand slaves, and the dispersal and disarmament of nearly 500 slave-dealers. In one week he rescued as many as 500 slaves, and he began to feel, as he said, that he had at last reached the heart of the evil.

But while these final successes were being achieved, he was recalled by telegraph to Cairo, where events had reached a crisis, and the days of Ismail as Khedive were numbered. It may have been the instinct of despair that led that Prince to appeal again to Gordon, but the Darfour rebellion was too grave to allow of his departure before it had been suppressed; and on the 1st July he received a telegram from the Minister Cherif, calling on him to proclaim throughout the Soudan Tewfik Pasha as Khedive. The change did not affect him in the least, he wrote, for not merely had his personal feelings towards Ismail changed after he threw him over at Cairo, but he had found out the futility of writing to him on any subject connected with the Soudan, and with this knowledge had come a feeling of personal indifference.

On his return to Khartoum, he received tidings of the execution of Suleiman, and also of the death of the Darfourian Sultan, Haroun, so that he felt justified in assuming that complete tranquillity had settled down on the scene of war. The subsequent capture and execution of Abdulgassin proved this view to be well founded, for, with the exception of Rabi, who escaped to Borgu, he was the last of Zebehr's chief lieutenants. The shot that killed that brigand, the very man who shed the child's blood to consecrate the standard, was the last fired under Gordon's orders in the Soudan. If the slave trade was then not absolutely dead, it was doomed so long as the Egyptian authorities pursued an active repressive policy such as their great English representative had enforced. The military confederacy of Zebehr, which had at one time alarmed the Khedive in his palace at Cairo, had been broken up. The authority of the Khartoum Governor-General had been made supreme. As Gordon said, on travelling down from Khartoum in August 1879, "Not a man could lift his hand without my leave throughout the whole extent of the Soudan."

General Gordon reached Cairo on 23rd August, with the full intention of retiring from the Egyptian service; but before he could do so there remained the still unsolved Abyssinian difficulty, which had formed part of his original mission. He therefore yielded to the request of the Khedive to proceed on a special mission to the Court of King John, then ruling that inaccessible and mysterious kingdom, and one week after his arrival at Cairo he was steaming down the Red Sea to Massowah. His instructions were contained in a letter from Tewfik Pasha to himself. After proclaiming his pacific intentions, the Khedive exhorted him "to maintain the rights of Egypt, to preserve intact the frontiers of the State, without being compelled to make any restitution to Abyssinia, and to prevent henceforth every encroachment or other act of aggression in the interests of both countries."

In order to explain the exact position of affairs in Abyssinia at this period, a brief summary must be given of events between Gordon's first overtures to King John in March 1877, and his taking up the matter finally in August 1879. As explained at the beginning of this chapter, those overtures came to nothing, because King John was called away to engage in hostilities with Menelik, King of Shoa, and now himself Negus, or Emperor of Abyssinia. In the autumn of the earlier year King John wrote Gordon a very civil letter, calling him a Christian and a brother, but containing nothing definite, and ending with the assertion that "all the world knows the Abyssinian frontier." Soon after this Walad el Michael recommenced his raids on the border, and when he obtained some success, which he owed to the assistance of one of Gordon's own subordinates, given while Gordon was making himself responsible for his good conduct, he was congratulated by the Egyptian War Minister, and urged to prosecute the conquest of Abyssinia. Instead of attempting the impossible, he very wisely came to terms with King John, who, influenced perhaps by Gordon's advice, or more probably by his own necessities through the war with Menelik, accepted Michael's promises to respect the frontier. Michael went to the King's camp to make his submission in due form, and in the spring of 1879 it became known that he and the Abyssinian General (Ras Alula) were planning an invasion of Egyptian territory. Fortunately King John was more peacefully disposed, and still seemed anxious to come to an arrangement with General Gordon.

In January 1879 the King wrote Gordon a letter, saying that he hoped to see him soon, and he also sent an envoy to discuss matters. The Abyssinian stated very clearly that his master would not treat with the Khedive, on account of the way he had subjected his envoys at Cairo to insult and injury; but that he would negotiate with Gordon, whom he persisted in styling the "Sultan of the Soudan." King John wanted a port, the restoration of Bogos, and an Abouna or Coptic Archbishop from Alexandria, to crown him in full accordance with Abyssinian ritual. Gordon replied a port was impossible, but that he should have a Consul and facilities for traffic at Massowah; that the territory claimed was of no value, and that he certainly should have an Abouna. He also undertook to do his best to induce the British Government to restore to King John the crown of King Theodore, which had been carried off after the fall of Magdala. The envoy then returned to Abyssinia, and nothing further took place until Gordon's departure for Massowah in August, when the rumoured plans of Michael and Ras Alula were causing some alarm.

On reaching Massowah on 6th September, Gordon found that the Abyssinians were in virtual possession of Bogos, and that if the Egyptian claims were to be asserted, it would be necessary to retake it. The situation had, however, been slightly improved by the downfall of Michael, whose treachery and covert hostility towards General Gordon would probably have led to an act of violence. But he and Ras Alula had had some quarrel, and the Abyssinian General had seized the occasion to send Michael and his officers as prisoners to the camp of King John. The chief obstacle to a satisfactory arrangement being thus removed, General Gordon hastened to have an interview with Ras Alula, and with this intention crossed the Abyssinian frontier, and proceeded to his camp at Gura. After an interview and the presentation of the Khedive's letter and his credentials, Gordon found that he was practically a prisoner, and that nothing could be accomplished save by direct negotiation with King John. He therefore offered to go to his capital at Debra Tabor, near Gondar, if Ras Alula would promise to refrain from attacking Egypt during his absence. This promise was promptly given, and in a few days it was expanded into an armistice for four months.

After six weeks' journey accomplished on mules, and by the worst roads in the country, as Ras Alula had expressly ordered, so that the inaccessibility of the country might be made more evident, General Gordon reached Debra Tabor on 27th October. He was at once received by King John, but this first reception was of only a brief and formal character. Two days later the chief audience was given at daybreak, King John reciting his wrongs, and Gordon referring him to the Khedive's letters, which had not been read. After looking at them, the King burst out with a list of demands, culminating in the sum of £2,000,000 or the port of Massowah. When he had finished, Gordon asked him to put these demands on paper, to sign them with his seal, and to give the Khedive six months to consider them and make a reply. This King John promised to do on his return from some baths, whither he was proceeding for the sake of his health.

After a week's absence the King returned, and the negotiations were resumed. But the King would not draw up his demands, which he realised were excessive, and when he found that Gordon remained firm in his intention to uphold the rights of the Khedive, the Abyssinian became offended and rude, and told Gordon to go. Gordon did not require to be told this twice, and an hour afterwards had begun his march, intending to proceed by Galabat to Khartoum. A messenger was sent after him with a letter from the King to the Khedive, which on translating read as follows: "I have received the letters you sent me by *that man* (a term of contempt). I will not make a secret peace with you. If you want peace, ask the Sultans of Europe."With a potentate so vague and so exacting it was impossible to attain any satisfactory result, and therefore Gordon was not sorry to depart. After nearly a fortnight's travelling, he and his small party had reached the very borders of the Soudan, their Abyssinian escort having returned, when a band of Abyssinians, owning allegiance to Ras Arya, swooped down on them, and carried them off to the village of that chief, who was the King's uncle.

The motive of this step is not clear, for Ras Arya declared that he was at feud with the King, and that he would willingly help the Egyptians to conquer the country. He however went on to explain that the seizure of Gordon's party was due to the King's order that it should not be allowed to return to Egypt by any other route than that through Massowah.

Unfortunately, the step seemed so full of menace that as a precaution Gordon felt compelled to destroy the private journal he had kept during his visit, as well as some valuable maps and plans. After leaving the district of this prince, Gordon and his small party had to make their way as best they could to get out of the country, only making their way at all by a lavish payment of money—this journey alone costing £1400—and by submitting to be bullied and insulted by every one with the least shadow of authority. At last Massowah was reached in safety, and every one was glad, because reports had become rife as to King John's changed attitude towards Gordon, and the danger to which he was exposed. But the Khedive was too much occupied to attend to these matters, or to comply with Gordon's request to send a regiment and a man-of-war to Massowah, as soon as the Abyssinian despot made him to all intents and purposes a prisoner. The neglect to make that demonstration not only increased the very considerable personal danger in which Gordon was placed during the whole of his mission, but it also exposed Massowah to the risk of capture if the Abyssinians had resolved to attack it.

The impressions General Gordon formed of the country were extremely unfavourable. The King was cruel and avaricious beyond all belief, and in his opinion fast going mad. The country was far less advanced than he had thought. The people were greedy, unattractive, and quarrelsome. But he detected their military qualities, and some of the merits of their organisation. "They are," he wrote, "a race of warriors, hardy, and, though utterly undisciplined, religious fanatics. I have seen many peoples, but I never met with a more fierce, savage set than these. The King said he could beat united Europe, except Russia."

The closing incidents of Gordon's tenure of the post of Governor-

General of the Soudan have now to be given, and they were not characterised by that spirit of justice, to say nothing of generosity, which his splendid services and complete loyalty to the Khedive's Government demanded. During his mission into Abyssinia his natural demands for support were completely ignored, and he was left to whatever fate might befall him. When he succeeded in extricating himself from that perilous position, he found that the Khedive was so annoyed at his inability to exact from his truculent neighbour a treaty without any accompanying concessions, that he paid no attention to him, and seized the opportunity to hasten the close of his appointment by wilfully perverting the sense of several confidential suggestions made to his Government. The plain explanation of these miserable intrigues was that the official class at Cairo, seeing that Gordon had alienated the sympathy and support of the British Foreign Office and its representatives by his staunch and outspoken defence of Ismail in 1878, realised that the moment had come to terminate his, to them, always hateful Dictatorship in the Soudan. While the Cairo papers were allowed to couple the term "mad" with his name, the Ministers went so far as to denounce his propositions as inconsistent. One of these Ministers had been Gordon's enemy for years; another had been banished by him from Khartoum for cruelty; they were one and all sympathetic to the very order of things which Gordon had destroyed, and which, as long as he retained power, would never be revived. What wonder that they should snatch the favourable opportunity of precipitating the downfall of the man they had so long feared! But it was neither creditable nor politic for the representatives of England to stand by while these schemes were executed to the detraction of the man who had then given six years' disinterested and laborious effort to the regeneration of the Soudan and the suppression of the slave trade.

When Gordon discovered that his secret representations, sent in cipher for the information of the Government, were given to the Press with a perverted meaning and hostile criticism, he hastened to Cairo. He requested an immediate interview with Tewfik, who excused himself for what had been done by his Ministers on the ground of his youth; but General Gordon read the whole situation at a glance, and at once sent in his resignation, which was accepted. It is not probable that, under any circumstances, he would have been induced to return to the Soudan, where his work seemed done, but he certainly was willing to make another attempt to settle the Abyssinian difficulty. Without the Khedive's support, and looked at askance by his own countrymen in the Delta, called mad on this side and denounced as inconsistent on the other, no good result could have ensued, and therefore he turned his back on the scene of his long labours without a sigh, and this time even without regret.

The state of his health was such that rest, change of scene, and the discontinuance of all mental effort were imperatively necessary, in the opinion of his doctor, if a complete collapse of mental and physical power was to be avoided. He was quite a wreck, and was showing all the effects of protracted labour, the climate, and improper food. Humanly speaking, his departure from Egypt was only made in time to save his life, and therefore there was some compensation in the fact that it was hastened by official jealousy and animosity.

But it seems very extraordinary that, considering the magnitude of the task he had performed single-handed in the Soudan, and the way he had done it with a complete disregard of all selfish interest, he should have been allowed to lay down his appointment without any manifestation of honour or respect from those he had served so long and so well. Nor was this indifference confined to Egyptians. It was reflected among the English and other European officials, who pronounced Gordon unpractical and peculiar, while in their hearts they only feared his candour and bluntness. But even public opinion at home, as reflected in the Press, seemed singularly blind to the fresh claim he had established on the admiration of the world. His China campaigns had earned him ungrudging praise, and a fame which, but for his own diffidence, would have carried him to the highest positions in the British army. But his achievements in the Soudan, not less remarkable in themselves, and obtained with far less help from others than his triumph over the Taepings, roused no enthusiasm, and received but scanty notice. The explanation of this difference is not far to seek, and reveals the baser side of human nature. In Egypt he had hurt many susceptibilities, and criticised the existing order of things. His propositions were drastic, and based on the exclusion of a costly European regime and the substitution of a native administration. Even his mode of suppressing the slave trade had been as original as it was fearless. Exeter Hall could not resound with cheers for a man who declared that he had bought slaves himself, and recognised the rights of others in what are called human chattels, even although that man had done more than any individual or any government to kill the slave trade at its root. It was not until his remarkable mission to Khartoum, only four years after he left Egypt, that public opinion woke up to a sense of all he had done before, and realised, in its full extent, the magnitude and the splendour of his work as Governor-General of the Soudan.

CHAPTER 9

Minor Missions—India and China

General Gordon arrived in London at the end of January 1880—having lingered on his home journey in order to visit Rome—resolved as far as he possibly could to take that period of rest which he had thoroughly earned, and which he so much needed. But during these last few years of his life he was to discover that the world would not leave him undisturbed in the tranquillity he desired and sought. Everyone wished to see him usefully and prominently employed for his country's good, and offers, suitable and not suitable to his character and genius, were either made to him direct, or put forward in the public Press as suggestions for the utilization of his experience and energy in the treatment of various burning questions. His numerous friends also wished to do him honour, and he found himself threatened with being drawn into the vortex of London Society, for which he had little inclination, and, at that time, not even the strength and health.

After this incident he left London on 29th February for Switzerland, where he took up his residence at Lausanne, visiting *en route* at Brussels, Mr, afterwards Lord, Vivian, then Minister at the Belgian Court, who had been Consul-General in Egypt during the financial crisis episode. It is pleasant to find that that passage had, in this case, left no ill-feeling behind it on either side, and that Gordon promised to think over the advice Mrs Vivian gave him to get married while he was staying at the Legation. His reply must not be taken as of any serious import, and was meant to turn the subject. About the same time he wrote in a private letter, "Wives! wives! what a trial you are to your husbands! From my experience married men have more or less a cowed look."

It was on this occasion that Gordon was first brought into contact with the King of the Belgians, and had his attention drawn to the prospect of suppressing the slave trade from the side of the Congo, somewhat analogous to his own project of crushing it from Zanzibar. The following unpublished letter gives an amusing account of the circumstances under which he first met King Leopold:

Hotel de Belle-Vue
Bruxelles
Tuesday, 2nd March 1880

I arrived here yesterday at 6 p.m., and found my baggage had not come on when I got to the hotel (having given orders about my boxes which were to arrive today at 9 a.m.). I found I was *detected*, and a huge card of His Majesty awaited me, inviting to dinner at 6.30 p.m. It was then 6.20 p.m. I wrote my excuses, telling the truth. Then I waited. It is now 9.30 a.m., and no baggage. King has just sent to say he will receive me at 11 a.m. I am obliged to say I cannot come if my baggage does not arrive.

I picked up a small book here, the *Souvenirs of Congress of Vienna*, in 1814 and 1815. It is a sad account of the festivities of that time. It shows how great people fought for invitations to the various parties, and how like a bomb fell the news of Napoleon's descent from Elba, and relates the end of some of the great men. The English great man, Castlereagh, cut his throat near Chislehurst; Alexander died mad, etc., etc. They are all in their 6 feet by 2 feet 6 inches. . . . Horrors, it is now 10.20 a.m., and no baggage! King sent to say he will see me at 11 a.m.; remember, too, I have to dress, shave, etc., etc. 10.30 a.m.—No baggage!!! It is getting painful. His Majesty will be furious. 10.48 a.m.—No baggage! Indirectly Mackinnon (late Sir William) is the sinner, for he evidently told the King I was coming. Napoleon said, 'The smallest trifles produce the greatest results.' 12.30 p.m.—Got enclosed note from palace, and went to see the King—a very tall man with black beard. He was very civil, and I stayed with him for one and a half hours. He is quite at sea with his expedition (Congo), and I have to try and get him out of it. I have to go there tomorrow at 11.30 a.m. My baggage has come.

During his stay at Lausanne his health improved, and he lost the numbed feeling in his arms which had strengthened the impression that he suffered from *angina pectoris*. This apprehension, although retained until a very short period before his final departure from England in 1884, was ultimately discovered to be baseless. With restored health returned the old feeling of restlessness. After five weeks he found it impossible to remain any longer in Lausanne. Again he exclaims in his letters: "Inaction is terrible to me!" and on 9th April he left that place for London.

Yet, notwithstanding his desire to return to work, or rather his feeling that he could not live in a state of inactivity, he refused the first definite suggestion that was made to him of employment. While he was still at Lausanne, the Governor of Cape Colony sent the following telegram to the Secretary of State for the Colonies: "My Ministers wish that the post of Commandant of the Colonial Forces should be offered to Chinese Gordon." The reply to this telegram read as follows: "The command of the Colonial Forces would probably be accepted by Chinese Gordon in the event of your Ministers desiring that the offer of it should be made to him." The Cape authorities requested that this offer might be made, and the War Office accordingly telegraphed to him as follows: "Cape Government offer command of Colonial Forces; supposed salary, £1500; your services required early." Everyone seems to have taken it as a matter of course that he would accept; but Gordon's reply was in the negative: "Thanks for telegram just received; I do not feel inclined to accept an appointment." His reasons for not accepting what seemed a desirable post are not known. They were probably due to considerations of health, although the doubt may have presented itself to his mind whether he was qualified by character to work in harmony with the Governor and Cabinet of any colony. He knew very well that all his good work had been done in an independent and unfettered capacity, and at the Cape he must have felt that, as nominal head of the forces, he would have been fettered by red tape and local jealousies, and rendered incapable of doing any good in an anomalous position. But after events make it desirable to state and recollect the precise circumstances of this first offer to him from the Cape Government.

While at Lausanne, General Gordon's attention was much given to the study of the Eastern Question, and I am not at all sure that the real reason of his declining the Cape offer was not the hope and expectation that he might be employed in connection with a subject which he thoroughly understood and had very much at heart. He drew up a memorandum on the Treaties of San Stefano and Berlin, which, for clearness of statement, perfect grasp of a vital international question, and prophetic vision, has never been surpassed among State papers. Although written in March 1880, and in my possession a very short time afterwards, I was not permitted to publish it until September 1885, when it appeared in the *Times* of the 24th of that month. Its remarkable character was at once appreciated by public men, and Sir William Harcourt, speaking in the House four days later, testified to the extraordinary foresight with which "poor Gordon" diagnosed the case of Europe's sick man. I quote here this memorandum in its integrity:

The Powers of Europe assembled at Constantinople, and recommended certain reforms to Turkey. Turkey refused to accede to these terms, the Powers withdrew, and deliberated. Not being able to come to a decision, Russia undertook, on her own responsibility, to enforce them. England acquiesced, provided that her own interests were not interfered with. The Russo-Turkish War occurred, during which time England, in various ways, gave the Turks reason to believe that she would eventually come to their assistance. This may be disputed, but I refer to the authorities in Constantinople whether the Turks were not under the impression during the war *that England would help them, and also save them, from any serious loss eventually.* England, therefore, provided this is true, did encourage Turkey in her resistance.

Then came the Treaty of San Stephano. It was drawn up with the intention of finishing off the rule of Turkey in Europe—there was no disguise about it; but I think that, looking at that treaty from a Russian point of view, it was a very bad one for Russia. Russia, by her own act, had trapped herself.

By it (the Treaty of San Stephano) Russia had created a huge kingdom, or State, south of the Danube, with a port. This new Bulgarian State, being fully satisfied, would have nothing more to desire from Russia, but would have sought, by alliance with other Powers, to keep what she (Bulgaria) possessed, and would have feared Russia more than any other Power. Having a seaport, she would have leant on England and France. Being independent of Turkey, she would wish to be on good terms with her.

Therefore I maintain, that *once* the Russo-Turkish War had been permitted, no greater obstacle could have been presented to Russia than the maintenance of this united Bulgarian State, and I believe that the Russians felt this as well.

I do not go into the question of the Asia Minor acquisitions by Russia, for, to all intents and purposes, the two treaties are alike. By both treaties Russia possesses the strategical points of the country, and though by the Berlin Treaty Russia gave up the strip south of Ararat, and thus does not hold the road to Persia, yet she stretches along this strip, and is only distant two days' march from the road, the value of which is merely commercial.

By both treaties Russia obtained Batoum and the war-like tribes around it. Though the *only port* on the Black Sea between Kertch and Sinope, a distance of 1000 miles, its acquisition by Russia was never contested. It was said to be a worthless possession—'grapes were sour.'

I now come to the changes made in the San Stephano Treaty (which was undoubtedly, and was intended to be, the *coup de grâce* to Turkish rule in Europe) by the Treaty of Berlin.

By the division of the two Bulgarias we prolonged, without alleviating, the agony of Turkey in Europe; we repaired the great mistake of Russia, from a Russian point of view, in making one great State of Bulgaria. We stipulated that Turkish troops, with a hostile Bulgaria to the north, and a hostile Roumelia to the south, should occupy the Balkans. I leave military men, or any men of sense, to consider this step. We restored Russia to her place, as the protector of these lands, which she had by the Treaty of San Stephano given up. We have left the wishes of Bulgarians unsatisfied, and the countries unquiet. We have forced them to look to Russia more than to us and France, and we have lost their sympathies. And for what? It is not doubted that ere long the two States will be united. If Moldavia and Wallachia laughed at the Congress of Paris, and united while it (the Congress) was in session at Paris, is it likely Bulgaria will wait long, or hesitate to unite with Roumelia, because Europe does not wish it?

Therefore the union of the two States is certain, only it is to be regretted that this union will give just the chance Russia wants to interfere again; and though, when the union takes place, I believe Russia will repent it, still it will always be to Russia that they will look till the union is accomplished.

I suppose the Turks are capable of appreciating what they gained by the Treaty of Berlin. They were fully aware that the Treaty of San Stephano was their *coup de grâce*. But the Treaty of Berlin was supposed to be beneficial to them. Why? By it Turkey lost *not only Bulgaria* and *Roumelia* (for she has virtually lost it), but *Bosnia* and *Herzegovina*, while she gained the utterly impossible advantage of occupying the Balkans, with a hostile nation to north and south.

I therefore maintain that the Treaty of Berlin did no good to Turkey, but infinite harm to Europe.

I will now go on to the Cyprus convention, and say a few words on the bag-and-baggage policy. Turkey and Egypt are governed by a ring of Pashas, most of them Circassians, and who are perfect foreigners in Turkey. They are, for the greater part, men who, when boys, have been bought at prices varying from £50 to £70, and who, brought up in the harems, have been pushed on by their purchasers from one grade to another. Some have been dancing boys and drummers, like Riaz and Ismail Eyoub of Egypt. I understand by bag-and-baggage policy the getting rid of, say, two hundred Pashas of this sort in Turkey, and sixty Pashas in Egypt. These men have not the least interest in the welfare of the countries; they are aliens and adventurers, they are hated by the respectable inhabitants of Turkey and Egypt, and they must be got rid of.

Armenia is lost; it is no use thinking of reforms in it. The Russians virtually possess it; the sooner we recognise this fact the better. Why undertake the impossible?

What should be done? Study existing facts, and decide on a definite line of policy, and follow it through. Russia, having a definite line of policy, is strong; we have not one, and are weak and vacillating. 'A double-minded man is unstable in all his ways.'

Supposing such a line of policy as follows was decided upon and followed up, it would be better than the worries of the last four years:

1. The complete purchase of Cyprus.
2. The abandonment of the Asia Minor reforms.
3. The union of Bulgaria and Roumelia, with a port.
4. The increase of Greece.
5. Constantinople, a State, under European guarantees.
6. Increase of Montenegro, and Italy, on that coast.
7. Annexation of Egypt by England, *either directly or by having paramount and entire authority.*
8. Annexation of Syria by France—ditto—ditto—ditto. (By this means France would be as interested in stopping Russian progress as England is.)
9. Italy to be allowed to extend towards Abyssinia.
10. Re-establishment of the Turkish Constitution, and the establishment of a similar one in Egypt (these Constitutions, if not interfered with, would soon rid Turkey and Egypt of their parasite Pashas).

I daresay this programme could be improved, but it has the advantage of being *definite*, and a definite policy, however imperfect, is better than an unstable or hand-to-mouth policy.

I would not press these points at once; I would keep them in view, and let events work themselves out.

I believe, in time, this programme could be worked out without a shot being fired.

I believe it would be quite possible to come to terms with Russia on these questions; I do not think she has sailed under false colours when her acts and words are generally considered. She is the avowed enemy of Turkey, she has not disguised it. Have *we* been the friend of Turkey? How many years have elapsed between the Crimean war and the Russo-Turkish war? What did we do to press Turkey to carry out reforms (as promised by the Treaty of 1856) in those years? *Absolutely nothing.*

What has to be done to prevent the inevitable crash of the Turkish Empire which is impending, imperilling the peace of the world, is *the re-establishment of the Constitution of Midhat, and its maintenance, in spite of the Sultan.* By this means, when the Sultan and the ring of Pashas fall, there would still exist the chambers of representatives of the provinces, who would carry on the Government for a time, and at any rate prevent the foreign occupation of Constantinople, or any disorders there, incident on the exit of the Sultan and his Pashas.

Having partially explained how General Gordon declined one post for which he appeared to be well suited, I have to describe how it was that he accepted another for which neither by training nor by character was he in the least degree fitted. The exact train of trifling circumstances that led up to the proposal that Gordon should accompany the newly-appointed Viceroy, the Marquis of Ripon, to India cannot be traced, because it is impossible to assign to each its correct importance. But it may be said generally, that the prevalent idea was that Lord Ripon was going out to the East on a great mission of reform, and some one suggested that the character of that mission would be raised in the eyes of the public if so well known a philanthropist as Gordon, whose views on all subjects were free from official bias, could be associated with it. I do not know whether the idea originated with Sir Bruce Seton, Lord Ripon's secretary, while at the War Office, but in any case that gentleman first broached the proposition to Sir Henry Gordon, the eldest brother of General Gordon. Sir Henry not merely did not repel the suggestion, but he consented to put it before his brother and to support it. For his responsibility in this affair Sir Henry afterwards took the fullest and frankest blame on himself for his "bad advice." When the matter was put before General Gordon he did not reject it, as might have been expected, but whether from his desire to return to active employment, or biased by his brother's views in favour of the project, or merely from coming to a decision without reflection, he made up his mind at once to accept the offer, and the official announcement of the appointment was made on 1st May, with the additional statement that his departure would take place without delay, as he was to sail with Lord Ripon on the 14th of that month.

It was after his acceptance of this post, and not some months before, as has been erroneously stated, that General Gordon had an interview with the Prince of Wales under circumstances that may be described. The Prince gave a large dinner-party to Lord Ripon before his departure for India, and Gordon was invited. He declined the invitation, and also declined to give any reason for doing so. The Prince of Wales, with his unfailing tact and the genuine kindness with which he always makes allowance for such little breaches of what ought to be done, at least in the cases of exceptional persons like Gordon, sent him a message: "If you won't dine with me, will you come and see me next Sunday afternoon?" Gordon went, and had a very interesting conversation with the Prince, and in the middle of it the Princess came into the room, and then the Princesses, her daughters, who said they would "like to shake hands with Colonel Gordon."

Before even the departure Gordon realised he had made a mistake, and if there had been any way out of the dilemma he would not have been slow to take it. As there was not, he fell back on the hope that he might be able to discharge his uncongenial duties for a brief period, and then seek some convenient opportunity of retiring. But as to his own real views of his mistake, and of his unfitness for the post, there never was any doubt, and they found expression when, in the midst of a family gathering, he exclaimed: "Up to this I have been an independent comet, now I shall be a chained satellite."

The same opinion found expression in a letter he wrote to Sir Halliday Macartney an hour before he went to Charing Cross:

> *My Dear Macartney,*—You will be surprised to hear that I have accepted the Private Secretaryship to Lord Ripon, and that I am just off to Charing Cross. I am afraid that I have decided in haste, to repent at leisure. Goodbye.—Yours,
> C. G. *Gordon*

His own views on this affair were set forth in the following words:

Men at times, owing to the mysteries of Providence, form judgments which they afterwards repent of. This is my case. Nothing could have exceeded the kindness and consideration with which Lord Ripon has treated me. I have never met anyone with whom I could have felt greater sympathy in the arduous task he has undertaken.

And again, writing at greater length to his brother, he explains what took place in the following letter:

In a moment of weakness I took the appointment of Private Secretary to Lord Ripon, the new Governor-General of India. No sooner had I landed at Bombay than I saw that in my irresponsible position I could not hope to do anything really to the purpose in the face of the vested interests out there. Seeing this, and seeing, moreover, that my views were so diametrically opposed to those of the official classes, I resigned. Lord Ripon's position was certainly a great consideration with me. It was assumed by some that my views of the state of affairs were the Viceroy's, and thus I felt that I should do him harm by staying with him. We parted perfect friends. The brusqueness of my leaving was unavoidable, inasmuch as my stay would have put me into the possession of secrets of State that—considering my decision eventually to leave—I ought not to know. Certainly I might have stayed a month or two, had a pain in the hand, and gone quietly; but the whole duties were so distasteful that I felt, being pretty callous as to what the world says, that it was better to go at once.

If a full explanation is sought of the reasons why Gordon repented of his decision, and determined to leave an uncongenial position without delay, it may be found in a consideration of the two following circumstances. His views as to what he held to be the excessive payment of English and other European servants in Asiatic countries were not new, and had been often expressed. They were crystallised in the phrase, "Why pay a man more at Simla than at Hongkong?" and had formed the basis of his projected financial reform in Egypt in 1878, and they often found expression in his correspondence. For instance, in a letter to the present writer, he proposed that the loss accruing from the abolition of the opium trade might be made good by reducing officers' pay from Indian to Colonial allowances. With Gordon's contempt for money, and the special circumstances that led to his not wanting any considerable sum for his own moderate requirements and few responsibilities, it is not surprising that he held these views; but no practical statesman could have attempted to carry them out. During the voyage to India the perception that it would be impossible for Lord Ripon to institute any special reorganisation on these lines led him to decide that it would be best to give up a post he did not like, and he wrote to his sister to this effect while at sea, with the statement that it was arranged that he should leave in the following September or October.

He reached Bombay on the 28th of May, and his resignation was received and accepted on the night of the 2nd June. What had happened in that brief interval of a few days to make him precipitate matters? There is absolutely no doubt, quite apart from the personal explanation given by General Gordon, both verbally and in writing, to myself, that the determining cause was the incident relating to Yakoob Khan.

That Afghan chief had been proclaimed and accepted as Ameer after the death of his father, the Ameer Shere Ali. In that capacity he had signed the Treaty of Gandamak, and received Sir Louis Cavagnari as British agent at his capital. When the outbreak occurred at Cabul, on 1st September, and Cavagnari and the whole of the mission were murdered, it was generally believed that the most guilty person was Yakoob Khan. On the advance of General Roberts, Yakoob Khan took the first opportunity of making his escape from his compatriots and joining the English camp. This voluntary act seemed to justify a doubt as to his guilt, but a Court of Inquiry was appointed to ascertain the facts. The bias of the leading members of that Court was unquestionably hostile to Yakoob, or rather it would be more accurate to say that they were bent on finding the highest possible personage guilty. They were appointed to inquire, not to sentence. Yet they found Yakoob guilty, and they sent a vast mass of evidence to the Foreign Department then at Calcutta. The experts of the Foreign Department examined that evidence. They pronounced it "rubbish," and Lord Lytton was obliged to send Mr (afterwards Sir) Lepel Griffin, an able member of the Indian Civil Service, specially versed in frontier politics, to act as Political Officer with the force in Afghanistan, so that no blunders of this kind might be re-enacted.

But nothing was done either to rehabilitate Yakoob's character or to negotiate with him for the restoration of a central authority in Afghanistan. Any other suitable candidate for the Ameership failing to present himself, the present ruler, Abdurrahman, being then, and indeed until the eve of the catastrophe at Maiwand, on 27th July 1880, an adventurous pretender without any strong following, Lord Lytton had been negotiating on the lines of a division of Afghanistan into three or more provinces. That policy, of which the inner history has still to be written, had a great deal more to be said in its favour than would now be admitted, and only the unexpected genius and success of Abdurrahman has made the contrary policy that was pursued appear the acme of sound sense and high statesmanship. When Lord Ripon reached Bombay at the end of May, the fate of Afghanistan was still in the crucible. Even Abdurrahman, who had received kind treatment in the persons of his imprisoned family at Candahar from the English, was not regarded as a factor of any great importance; while Ayoob, the least known of all the chiefs, was deemed harmless only a few weeks before he crossed the Helmund and defeated our troops in the only battle lost during the war. But if none of the candidates inspired our authorities with any confidence, they were resolute in excluding Yakoob Khan. Having been relieved from the heavier charge of murdering Cavagnari, he was silently cast on the not less fatal one of being a madman.

Such was the position of the question when Lord Ripon and his secretary landed at Bombay. It was known that they would alter the Afghan policy of the Conservative Government, and that, as far as possible, they would revert to the Lawrentian policy of ignoring the region beyond the passes. But it was not known that they had any designs about Yakoob Khan, and this was the bomb they fired on arrival into the camp of Indian officialdom.

The first despatch written by the new secretary was to the Foreign Department, to the effect that Lord Ripon intended to commence negotiations with the captive Yakoob, and Mr (now Sir) Mortimer Durand, then assistant secretary in that branch of the service, was at once sent from Simla to remonstrate against a proceeding which "would stagger every one in India." Lord Ripon was influenced by these representations, and agreed to at least suspend his overtures to Yakoob Khan, but his secretary was not convinced by either the arguments or the facts of the Indian Foreign Department. He still considered that Afghan prince the victim of political injustice, and also that he was the best candidate for the throne of Cabul. But he also saw very clearly from this passage of arms with the official classes that he would never be able to work in harmony with men who were above and before all bureaucrats, and with commendable promptness he seized the opportunity to resign a post which he thoroughly detested. What he thought on the subject of Yakoob Khan is fully set forth in the following memorandum drawn up as a note to my biography of that interesting and ill-starred prince in "Central Asian Portraits."

Whether Gordon was right or wrong in his views about Yakoob Khan is a matter of no very great importance. The incident is only note-worthy as marking the conclusion of his brief secretarial experience, and as showing the hopefulness of a man who thought that he could make the all-powerful administrative system of India decide a political question on principles of abstract justice. The practical comment on such sanguine theories was furnished by Mr Durand being appointed acting private secretary on Gordon's resignation.

General Gordon's memorandum read as follows:

> Yacoob was accused of concealing letters from the Russian Government, and of entering into an alliance with the Rajah of Cashmere to form a Triple Alliance. Where are these letters or proof of this intention? They do not exist.
>
> Yacoob came out to Roberts of his own free will. He was imprisoned. It was nothing remarkable that he was visited by an Afghan leader, although it was deemed evidence of a treacher-ous intention. Roberts and Cavagnari made the Treaty of Gan-damak. It is absurd to say Yacoob wanted an European Resi-dent. It is against all reason to say he did. He was coerced into taking one. He was imprisoned, and a Court of Enquiry was held on him, composed of the President Macgregor, who was chief of the staff to the man who made the Treaty, by which Cavagnari went to Cabul, and who had imprisoned Yacoob. This Court of Enquiry asked for evidence concerning a man in prison, which is in eyes of Asiatics equivalent to being already condemned. This Court accumulated evidence, utterly worth-less in any court of justice, as will be seen if ever published. This Court of *Enquiry* found him guilty and sentenced him to exile. Was that their function? If the secret papers are published, it would be seen that the despatches from the Cabulese chiefs were couched in fair terms. They did not want to fight the English. They wanted their Ameer. Yacoob's defence is splendid. He says in it: 'If I had been guilty, would I not have escaped to Herat, whereas I put myself in your hands?' The following ques-tions arise from this Court of Enquiry. Who fired first shot from the Residency? Was the conduct of Cavagnari and his people discreet in a fanatical city? Were not those who forced Cav-agnari on Yacoob against his protest equally responsible with him? Yacoob was weak and timid in a critical moment, and he failed, but he did not incite this revolt. It was altogether against

his interests to do so. What was the consequence of his unjust exile? Why, all the trouble which happened since that date. Afghanistan was quiet till we took her ruler away. It was an united Afghanistan. This mistake has cost £10,000,000, all from efforts to go on with an injustice. The Romans before their wars invoked all misery on themselves before the Goddess Nemesis if their war was unjust. We did not invoke her, but she followed us. Between the time that the Tory Government went out, and the new Viceroy Ripon had landed at Bombay, Lytton forced the hand of the Liberal Government by entering into negotiations with Abdurrahman, and appointing the Vali at Candahar, so endeavouring to prevent justice to Yacoob. Stokes, Arbuthnot, and another member of Supreme Council all protested against the deposition of Yacoob, also Sir Neville Chamberlain.

Lest it should be thought that Gordon was alone in these opinions, I append this statement, drawn up at the time by Sir Neville Chamberlain:

> An unprejudiced review of the circumstances surrounding the *émeute* of September 1879 clearly indicates that the spontaneous and unpremeditated action of a discontented, undisciplined, and unpaid soldiery had not been planned, directed, or countenanced by the Ameer, his ministers, or his advisers. There is no evidence to prove or even to suspect that the mutiny of his soldiers was in any way not deplored by the Ameer, but was regarded by him with regret, dismay, and even terror. Fully conscious of the very grave misapprehensions and possible accusation of timidity and weakness on our part, I entertain, myself, very strong convictions that we should have first permitted and encouraged the Ameer to punish the mutinous soldiers and rioters implicated in the outrage before we ourselves interfered. The omission to adopt this course inevitably led to the action forced on the Ameer, which culminated in the forced resignation of his power and the total annihilation of the national government. The Ameer in thus resigning reserved to himself the right of seeking, when occasion offered, restoration to his heritage and its reversion to his heir. Nothing has occurred to justify the ignoring of these undeniable rights.

Gordon's resignation was handed in to Lord Ripon on the night of the 2nd of June, the news appeared in the London papers of the 4th, and it had one immediate consequence which no one could have foreseen. But before referring to that matter I must make clear the heavy pecuniary sacrifice his resignation of this post entailed upon Gordon. He repaid every farthing of his expenses as to passage money, etc., to Lord Ripon, which left him very much out of pocket. He wrote himself on the subject:

> All this Private Secretaryship and its consequent expenses are all due to my not acting on my *own* instinct. However, for the future I will be wiser. . . . It was a living crucifixion. . . . I nearly burst with the trammels. . . . A £100,000 a year would not have kept me there. I resigned on 2 June, and never unpacked my official dress.

The immediate consequence referred to was as follows: In the drawer of Mr J. D. Campbell, at the office at Storey's Gate of the Chinese Imperial Customs, had been lying for some little time the following telegram for Colonel Gordon from Sir Robert Hart, the Inspector-General of the Department in China:

> I am directed to invite you here (Peking). Please come and see for yourself. The opportunity of doing really useful work on a large scale ought not to be lost. Work, position, conditions, can all be arranged with yourself here to your satisfaction. Do take six months' leave and come.

As Mr Campbell was aware of Gordon's absence in India, he had thought it useless to forward the message, and it was not until the resignation was announced that he did so. In dealing with this intricate matter, which was complicated by extraneous considerations, it is necessary to clear up point by point. When Gordon received the message he at once concluded that the invitation came from his old colleague Li Hung Chang, and accepted it on that assumption, which in the end proved erroneous. It is desirable to state that since Gordon's departure from China in 1865 at least one communication had passed between these former associates in a great enterprise. The following characteristic letter, dated Tientsin, 22nd March 1879, reached Gordon while he was at Khartoum:

> *Dear Sir,*—I am instructed by His Excellency the Grand Secretary, Li, to answer your esteemed favour, dated the 27th October 1878, from Khartoum, which was duly received. I am right glad to hear from you. It is now over fourteen years since we parted from each other. Although I have not written to you, but I often

speak of you, and remember you with very great interest. The benefit you have conferred on China does not disappear with your person, but is felt throughout the regions in which you played so important and active a part. All those people bless you for the blessings of peace and prosperity which they now enjoy.

Your achievements in Egypt are well known throughout the civilized world. I see often in the papers of your noble works on the Upper Nile. You are a man of ample resources, with which you suit yourself to any kind of emergency. My hope is that you may long be spared to improve the conditions of the people amongst whom your lot is cast. I am striving hard to advance my people to a higher state of development, and to unite both this and all other nations within the 'Four Seas' under one common brotherhood. To the several questions put in your note the following are the answers: Kwoh Sung-Ling has retired from official life, and is now living at home. Yang Ta Jên died a great many years ago. Na Wang's adopted son is doing well, and is the colonel of a regiment, with 500 men under him. The Pa to' Chiaow Bridge, which you destroyed, was rebuilt very soon after you left China, and it is now in very good condition.

Kwoh Ta Jên, the Chinese Minister, wrote to me that he had the pleasure of seeing you in London. I wished I had been there also to see you; but the responsibilities of life are so distributed to different individuals in different parts of the world, that it is a wise economy of Providence that we are not all in the same spot.

I wish you all manner of happiness and prosperity. With my highest regards,—I remain, yours very truly
For Li Hung Chang,
Tsêng Laisun

Under the belief that Hart's telegram emanated from Li Hung Chang, and inspired by loyalty to a friend in a difficulty, as well as by affection for the Chinese people, whom in his own words he "liked best next after his own," Gordon replied to this telegram in the following message:

Inform Hart Gordon will leave for Shanghai first opportunity. As for conditions, Gordon indifferent.

At that moment China seemed on the verge of war with Russia, in consequence of the disinclination of the latter power to restore the province of Kuldja, which she had occupied at the time of the Mahommedan uprising in Central Asia. The Chinese official, Chung How, who had signed an unpopular treaty at Livadia, had been sentenced to death—the treaty itself had been repudiated—and hostilities were even said to have commenced. The announcement that the Chinese Government had invited Gordon to Peking, and that he had promptly replied that he would come, was also interpreted as signifying the resolve to carry matters with a high hand, and to show the world that China was determined to obtain what she was entitled to. Those persons who have a contemptuous disregard for dates went so far even as to assert that Gordon had resigned because of the Chinese invitation. Never was there a clearer case of *post hoc, propter hoc*; but even the officials at the War Office were suspicious in the matter, and their attitude towards Gordon went near to precipitate the very catastrophe they wanted to avoid.

On the same day (8th June) as he telegraphed his reply to the Chinese invitation, he telegraphed to Colonel Grant, Deputy Adjutant-General for the Royal Engineers at the Horse Guards: "Obtain me leave until end of the year; am invited to China; will not involve Government." Considering the position between China and Russia, and the concern of the Russian press and Government at the report about Gordon, it is not surprising that this request was not granted a ready approval. The official reply came back: "Must state more specifically purpose and position for and in which you go to China." To this Gordon sent the following characteristic answer: "Am ignorant; will write from China before the expiration of my leave." An answer like this savoured of insubordination, and shows how deeply Gordon was hurt by the want of confidence reposed in him. In saying this I disclaim all intention of criticising the authorities, for whose view there was some reasonable justification; but the line they took, while right enough for an ordinary Colonel of Engineers, was not quite a considerate one in the case of an officer of such an exceptional position and well-known idiosyncrasies as "Chinese" Gordon. On that ground alone may it be suggested that the blunt decision thus given in the final official telegram—"Reasons insufficient; your going to China is not approved," was somewhat harsh.

It was also impotent, for it rather made Gordon persist in carrying out his resolve than deterred him from doing so. His reply was thus worded: "Arrange retirement, commutation, or resignation of service; ask Campbell reasons. My counsel, if asked, would be for peace, not war. I return by America." Gordon's mind was fully made up to go, even if he had to sacrifice his commission. Without waiting for any further communication he left Bombay. As he had insisted on repaying Lord Ripon his passage-money from England to India which, owing to his resignation, the Viceroy would otherwise have had to pay out of his own pocket, Gordon was quite without funds, and he had to borrow the sum required to defray his passage to China. But having made up his mind, such trifling difficulties were not likely to deter him. He sailed from Bombay, not merely under the displeasure of his superiors and uncertain as to his own status, but also in that penniless condition, which was not wholly out of place in his character of knight-errant. But with that solid good sense, which so often retrieved his reputation in the eyes of the world, he left behind him the following public proclamation as to his mission and intentions. It was at once a public explanation of his proceedings, and a declaration of a pacific policy calculated to appease both official and Russian irritation:

> My fixed desire is to persuade the Chinese not to go to war with Russia, both in their own interests and for the sake of those of the world, especially those of England. In the event of war breaking out I cannot answer how I should act for the present, but I should ardently desire a speedy peace. It is my fixed desire, as I have said, to persuade the Chinese not to go to war with Russia. To me it appears that the question in dispute cannot be of such vital importance that an arrangement could not be come to by concessions upon both sides. Whether I succeed in being heard or not is not in my hands. I protest, however, at being regarded as one who wishes for war in any country, still less in China. Inclined as I am, with only a small degree of admiration for military exploits, I esteem it a far greater honour to promote peace than to gain any paltry honours in a wretched war.

With that message to his official superiors, as well as to the world, Gordon left Bombay on 13th June. His message of the day before saying, "Consult Campbell," had induced the authorities at the Horse Guards to make inquiries of that gentleman, who had no difficulty in satisfying them that the course of events was exactly as has here been set forth, and coupling that with Gordon's own declaration that he was for peace not war, permission was granted to Gordon to do that which at all cost he had determined to do. When he reached Ceylon he found this telegram: "Leave granted on your engaging to take no military service in China," and he somewhat too comprehensively, and it may even be feared rashly if events had turned out otherwise, replied: "I will take no military service in China: I would never embarrass the British Government."

Having thus got clear of the difficulties which beset him on the threshold of his mission, Gordon had to prepare himself for those that were inherent to the task he had taken up. He knew of old how averse the Chinese are to take advice from any one, how they waste time in fathoming motives, and how when they say a thing shall be done it is never performed. Yet the memory of his former disinterested and splendid service afforded a guarantee that if they would take advice and listen to unflattering criticism from any one, that man was Gordon. Still, from the most favourable point of view, the mission was fraught with difficulty, and circumstances over which he had no control, and of which he was even ignorant, added immensely to it. There is no doubt that Peking was at that moment the centre of intrigues, not only between the different Chinese leaders, but also among the representatives of the Foreign Powers. The secret history of these transactions has still to be revealed, and as our Foreign Office never gives up the private instructions it transmits to its representatives, the full truth may never be recorded. But so far as the British Government was concerned, its action was limited to giving the Minister, Sir Thomas Wade, instructions to muzzle Gordon and prevent his doing anything that wasn't strictly in accordance with official etiquette and quite safe, or, in a word, to make him do nothing. The late Sir Thomas Wade was a most excellent Chinese scholar and estimable person in every way, but when he tried to do what the British Government and the whole arrayed body of the Horse Guards, from the Commander-in-Chief down to the Deputy-Adjutant General, had failed to do, viz. to keep Gordon in leading strings, he egregiously failed. Sir Thomas Wade went so far as to order Gordon to stay in the British Legation, and to visit no one without his express permission. Gordon's reply was to ignore the British Legation and to never enter its portals during the whole of his stay in China.

That was one difficulty in the situation apart from the Russian question, but it was not the greatest, and as it was the first occasion on which European politics re-acted in a marked way on the situation in China, such details as are ascertainable are well worth recording at some length.

There is no doubt that the Russian Government was very much disturbed at what seemed an inevitable hostile collision with China. The uncertain result of such a contest along an enormous land-frontier, with which, at that time, Russia had very imperfect means of communication, was the least cause of its disquietude. A war with China signified to Russia something much more serious than this, viz., a breach of the policy of friendship to its vast neighbour, which it had consistently pursued for two centuries, and which it will pursue until it is ready to absorb, and then in the same friendly guise, its share of China. Under these circumstances the Russian Government looked round for every means of averting the catastrophe. It is necessary to guard oneself from seeming to imply that Russia was in any sense afraid, or doubtful as to the result of a war with China; her sole motives were those of astute and far-seeing policy. Whether the Russian Ambassador at Berlin mooted the matter to Prince Bismarck, or whether that statesman, without inspiration, saw his chance of doing Russia a good turn at no cost to himself is not certain, but instructions were sent to Herr von Brandt, the German Minister at Peking, a man of great energy, and in favour of bold measures, to support the Peace Party in every way. He was exactly a man after Prince Bismarck's own heart, prepared to go to any lengths to attain his object, and fully persuaded that the end justifies the means. His plan was startlingly simple and bold. Li Hung Chang, the only prominent advocate of peace, was to rebel, march on Peking with his Black Flag army, and establish a Government of his own. There is no doubt whatever that this scheme was formed and impressed on Li Hung Chang as the acme of wisdom. More than that, it was supported by two other Foreign Ministers at Peking, with greater or less warmth, and one of them was Sir Thomas Wade. These plots were dispelled by the sound sense and candid but firm representations of Gordon. But for him, as will be seen, there would have been a rebellion in the country, and Li Hung Chang would now be either Emperor of China or a mere instance of a subject who had lost his head in trying to be supreme.

Having thus explained the situation that awaited Gordon, it is necessary to briefly trace his movements after leaving Ceylon. He reached Hongkong on 2nd July, and not only stayed there for a day or two as the guest of the Governor, Sir T. Pope Hennessey, but found sufficient time to pay a flying visit to the Chinese city of Canton. Thence he proceeded to Shanghai and Chefoo. At the latter place he found news, which opened his eyes to part of the situation, in a letter from Sir Robert Hart, begging him to come direct to him at Peking, and not to stop *en route* to visit Li Hung Chang at Tientsin. As has been explained, Gordon went to China in the full belief that, whatever names were used, it was his old colleague Li Hung Chang who sent for him, and the very first definite information he received on approaching the Chinese capital was that not Li, but persons whom by inference were inimical to Li, had sent for him. The first question that arises then was who was the real author of the invitation to Gordon that bore the name of Hart. It cannot be answered, for Gordon assured me that he himself did not know; but there is no doubt that it formed part of the plot and counter-plot originated by the German Minister, and responded to by those who were resolved, in the event of Li's rebellion, to uphold the Dragon Throne. Sir Robert Hart is a man of long-proved ability and address, who has rendered the Chinese almost as signal service as did Gordon himself, and on this occasion he was actuated by the highest possible motives, but it must be recorded that his letter led to a temporary estrangement between himself and Gordon, who I am happy to be able to state positively did realise long afterwards that he and Hart were fighting in the same camp, and had the same objects in view—only this was not apparent at the time. Gordon went to China only because he thought Li Hung Chang sent for him, but when he found that powerful persons were inciting him to revolt, he became the first and most strenuous in his advice against so imprudent and unpatriotic a measure. Sir Robert Hart knew exactly what was being done by the German Minister. He wished to save Gordon from being drawn into a dangerous and discreditable plot, and also in the extreme eventuality to deprive any rebellion of the support of Gordon's military genius.

But without this perfect information, and for the best, as in the end it proved, Gordon, hot with disappointment that the original summons was not from Li Hung Chang, went straight to that statesman's *yamen* at Tientsin, ignored Hart, and proclaimed that he had come as the friend of the only man who had given any sign of an inclination to regenerate China. He resided as long as he was in Northern China with Li Hung Chang, whom he found being goaded towards high treason by persons who had no regard for China's interests, and who thought only of the attainment of their own selfish designs. The German Minister, thinking that he had obtained an ally who would render the success of his own plan certain, proposed that Gordon should put himself at the head of Li's army, march on Peking, and depose the Emperor. Gordon's droll comment on this is:

> I told him I was equal to a good deal of filibustering, but that this was beyond me, and that I did not think there was the slightest chance of such a project succeeding, as Li had not a sufficient following to give it any chance of success.

He recorded his views of the situation in the following note:

> The only thing that keeps me in China is Li Hung Chang's safety—if he were safe I would not care—but some people are egging him on to rebel, some to this, and some to that, and all appears in a helpless drift. There are parties at Peking who would drive the Chinese into war for their own ends.

Having measured the position and found it bristling with unexpected difficulties and dangers, Gordon at once regretted the promise he had given his own Government in the message from Ceylon. He thought it was above all things necessary for him to have a free hand, and he consequently sent the following telegram to the Horse Guards:

> I have seen Li Hung Chang, and he wishes me to stay with him. I cannot desert China in her present crisis, and would be free to act as I think fit. I therefore beg to resign my commission in Her Majesty's Service.

Having thus relieved, as he thought, his Government of all responsibility for his acts—although they responded to this message by accusing him of insubordination, and by instructing Sir Thomas Wade to place him under moral arrest—Gordon threw himself into the China difficulty with his usual ardour. Nothing more remained to be done at Tientsin, where he had effectually checked the pernicious counsel pressed on Li Hung Chang most strongly by the German Minister, and in a minor degree by the representatives of France and England. In order to influence the Central Government it was necessary for him to proceed to Peking, and the following unpublished letter graphically describes his views at the particular moment:

> I am on my way to Peking. There are three parties—Li Hung Chang (1), the Court (2), the Literary Class (3). The two first are for peace, but dare not say it for fear of the third party. I have told Li that he, in alliance with the Court, must coerce the third party, and have written this to Li and to the Court Party. By so doing I put my head in jeopardy in going to Peking. I do not wish Li to act alone. It is not good he should do anything except support the Court Party morally. God will overrule for the best. If neither the Court Party nor Li can act, if these two remain and let things drift, then there will be a disastrous war, of which I shall not see the end. You know I do not mourn this. Having given up my commission, I have nothing to look for,

and indeed I long for the quiet of the future. . . . If the third party hear of my recommendation before the Court Party acts, then I may be doomed to a quick exit at Peking. Li Hung Chang is a noble fellow, and worth giving one's life for; but he must not rebel and lose his good name. It is a sort of general election which is going on, but where heads are in gage.

Writing to me some months later, General Gordon entered into various matters relating to this period, and as the letter indirectly throws light on what may be called the Li Hung Chang episode, I quote it here, although somewhat out of its proper place:

> Thanks for your kind note. I send you the two papers which were made public in China, and through the Shen-pao some of it was sent over. Another paper of fifty-two articles I gave Li Hung Chang, but I purposely kept no copy of it, for it went into—
> 1. The contraband of salt and opium at Hongkong.
> 2. The advantages of telegraphs and canals, not railways, which have ruined Egypt and Turkey by adding to the financial difficulties.
> 3. The effeteness of the Chinese representatives abroad, etc., etc., etc.
> I wrote as a Chinaman for the Chinese. I recommended Chinese merchants to do away with middle-men, and to have Government aid and encouragement to create houses or firms in London, etc.; to make their own cotton goods, etc. In fact, I wrote as a Chinaman. I see now and then symptoms that they are awake to the situation, for my object has been always to put myself into the skin of those I may be with, and I like these people as much—well, say nearly as much—as I like my countrymen.
> There are a lot of people in China who would egg on revolts of A and B. All this is wrong. China must *fara da se*. I painted this picture to the Chinese of 1900: 'Who are those people hanging about with *jinrickshas*?' 'The sons of the European merchants.' 'What are those ruins?' 'The Hongs of the European merchants,' etc., etc.
> People have asked me what I thought of the advance of China during the sixteen years I was absent. They looked superficially at the power military of China. I said they are unchanged. You come, I must go; but I go on to say that the stride China has made in commerce is immense, and commerce and wealth are the power of nations, not the troops. Like the Chinese, I

have a great contempt for military prowess. It is ephemeral. I admire administrators, not generals. A military Red-Button mandarin has to bow low to a Blue-Button civil mandarin, and rightly so to my mind.

I wrote the other day to Li Hung Chang to protest against the railway from Ichang to Peking along the Grand Canal. In making it they would enter into no end of expenses, the coin would leave the country and they would not understand it, and would be fleeced by the financial cormorants of Great Britain. They can understand canals. Let them repair the Grand Canal.

Having arrived at Peking, Gordon was received in several councils by Prince Chun, the father of the young Emperor and the recognised leader of the War Party. The leading members of the Grand Council were also present, and Gordon explained his views to them at length. In the first place, he said, if there were war he would only stay to help them on condition that they destroyed the suburbs of Peking, allowed him to place the city in a proper state of defence, and removed the Emperor and Court to a place of safety. When they expressed their opinion that the Taku forts were impregnable, Gordon laughed, and said they could be taken from the rear. The whole gist of his remarks was that "they could not go to war," and when they still argued in the opposite sense, and the interpreter refused to translate the harsh epithets he applied to such august personages, he took the dictionary, looked out the Chinese equivalent for "idiocy," and with his finger on the word, placed it under the eyes of each member of the Council. The end of this scene may be described in Gordon's own words: "I said make peace, and wrote out the terms. They were, in all, five articles; the only one they boggled at was the fifth, about the indemnity. They said this was too hard and unjust. I said that might be, but what was the use of talking about it? If a man demanded your money or your life, you have only three courses open. You must either fight, call for help, or give up your money. Now, as you cannot fight, it is useless to call for help, since neither England nor France would stir a finger to assist you. I believe these are the articles now under discussion at St Petersburg, and the only one on which there is any question is the fifth." This latter statement I may add, without going into the question of the Marquis Tsêng's negotiations in the Russian capital, was perfectly correct.

Gordon drew up several notes or memorandums for the information of the Chinese Government. The first of these was mainly military, and the following extracts will suffice:

China's power lies in her numbers, in the quick moving of her troops, in the little baggage they require, and in their few wants. It is known that men armed with sword and spear can overcome the best regular troops equipped with breech-loading rifles, if the country is at all difficult and if the men with spears and swords outnumber their foe ten to one. If this is the case where men are armed with spears and swords, it will be much truer when those men are themselves armed with breech loaders. China should never engage in pitched battles. Her strength is in quiet movements, in cutting off trains of baggage, and in night attacks *not pushed home*—in a continuous worrying of her enemies. Rockets should be used instead of cannon. No artillery should be moved with the troops; it delays and impedes them. Infantry fire is the most fatal fire; guns make a noise far out of proportion to their value in war. If guns are taken into the field, troops cannot march faster than these guns. The degree of speed at which the guns can be carried dictates the speed at which the troops can march. As long as Peking is the centre of the Government of China, China can never go to war with any first-class power; it is too near the sea.

The second memorandum was of greater importance and more general application. In it he compressed the main heads of his advice into the smallest possible space, and so far as it was at all feasible to treat a vast and complicated subject within the limits of a simple and practical scheme, he therein shows with the greatest clearness how the regeneration of China might be brought about.

In spite of the opinion of some foreigners, it will be generally acknowledged that the Chinese are contented and happy, that the country is rich and prosperous, and that the people are *au fond* united in their sentiments, and ardently desire to remain a nation. At constant intervals, however, the whole of this human hive is stirred by some dispute between the Pekin Government and some foreign Power; the Chinese people, proud of their ancient prestige, applaud the high tone taken up by the Pekin Government, crediting the Government with the power to support their strong words. This goes on for a time, when the Government gives in, and corresponding vexation is felt by the people. The recurrence of these disputes, the inevitable surrender ultimately of the Pekin Government, has the tendency of shaking the Chinese people's confidence in the Central Government. The Central Government appreciates the fact that, little by little, this prestige is being destroyed by their own actions among the Chinese people, each crisis then becomes more accentuated or difficult to surmount, as the Central Government know each concession is another nail in their coffin. The Central Government fear that the taking up of a spirited position by any pre-eminent Chinese would carry the Chinese people with him, and therefore the Central Government endeavour to keep up appearances, and to skirt the precipice of war as near as they possibly can, while never intending to enter into war.

The Central Government residing in the extremity of the Middle Kingdom, away from the great influences which are now working in China, can never alter one iota from what they were years ago: they are being steadily left behind by the people they govern. They know this, and endeavour to stem these influences in all ways in their power, hoping to keep the people backward and in ignorance, and to retard their progress to the same pace they themselves go, if it can be called a pace at all.

It is therefore a maxim that 'no progress can be made by the Pekin Government.' To them any progress, whether slow or quick, is synonymous to slow or quick extinction, for they will never move.

The term 'Pekin Government' is used advisedly, for if the Central Government were moved from Pekin into some province where the pulsations and aspirations of the Chinese people could have their legitimate effect, then the Central Government and the Chinese people, having a unison of thought, would work together.

From what has been said above, it is maintained that, so long as the Central Government of China isolates itself from the Chinese people by residing aloof at Pekin, so long will the Chinese people have to remain passive under the humiliations which come upon them through the non-progressive and destructive disposition of their Government. These humiliations will be the chronic state of the Chinese people until the Central Government moves from Pekin and reunites itself to its subjects. No army, no purchases of ironclad vessels will enable China to withstand a first-class Power so long as China keeps her queen bee at the entrance of her hive. There is, however, the probability that a proud people like the Chinese may sicken at this continual eating of humble pie, that the Pekin Government at some time, by skirting too closely the precipice of war may fall into it, and then that sequence may be anarchy and rebellion throughout the Middle Kingdom which may last for years and cause endless misery.

It may be asked—How can the present state of things be altered? How can China maintain the high position that the wealth, industry, and innate goodness of the Chinese people entitle her to have among the nations of the world? Some may say by the revolt of this Chinaman or of that Chinaman. To me this seems most undesirable, for, in the first place, such action would not have the blessing of God, and, in the second, it would result in the country being plunged into civil war. The fair, upright, and open course for the Chinese people to take is to work, through the Press and by petitions, on the Central Government, and to request them to move from Pekin, and bring themselves thus more into unison with the Chinese people, and thus save that people the constant humiliations they have to put up with, owing to the seat of the Central Government being at Pekin. This recommendation would need no secret societies, no rebellion, no treason; if taken up and persevered in it must succeed, and not one life need be lost.

The Central Government at Pekin could not answer the Chinese people except in the affirmative when the Chinese people say to the Central Government—'By your residing aloof from us in Pekin, where you are exposed to danger, you separate our interests from yours, and you bring on us humiliation, which we would never have to bear if you resided in the interior. Take our application into consideration, and grant our wishes.'

I have been kindly treated by the Central Pekin Government and by the Chinese people; it is for the welfare of both parties that I have written and signed this paper. I may have expressed myself too strongly with respect to the non-progressive nature of the Pekin Government, who may desire the welfare of the Middle Kingdom as ardently as any other Chinese, but as long as the Pekin Government allow themselves to be led and directed by those drones of the hive, the Censors, so long must the Pekin Government bear the blame earned by those drones in plunging China into difficulties. In the insect world the bees get rid of the drones in winter.

There was yet a third memorandum of a confidential nature written to Li Hung Chang himself, of which Gordon did not keep a copy, but he referred to it in the letter written to myself which I have already quoted.

Having thus accomplished his double task, viz.: the prevention of war between Russia and China, and of a rebellion on the part of Li Hung Chang under European advice and encouragement, Gordon left China without any delay. When he reached Shanghai on 16th August he found another official telegram awaiting him: "Leave cancelled, resignation not accepted." As he had already taken his passage home he did not reply, but when he reached Aden he telegraphed as follows: "You might have trusted me. My passage from China was taken days before the arrival of your telegram which states 'leave cancelled.' Do you insist on rescinding the same?" The next day he received a reply granting him nearly six months' leave, and with that message the question of his alleged insubordination may be treated as finally settled. There can be no doubt that among his many remarkable achievements not the least creditable was this mission to China, when by downright candour, and unswerving resolution in doing the right thing, he not merely preserved peace, but baffled the intrigues of unscrupulous diplomatists and selfish governments.

With that incident closed Gordon's connection with China, the country associated with his most brilliant feats of arms, but in concluding this chapter it seems to me that I should do well to record some later expressions of opinion on that subject. The following interesting letter, written on the eve of the war between France and China in 1882, was published by the *New York Herald*:

> The Chinese in their affairs with foreign nations are fully aware of their peculiar position, and count with reason that a war with either France or another Power will bring them perforce allies outside of England. The only Power that could go to war with them with impunity is Russia, who can attack them by land. I used the following argument to them when I was there:—The present dynasty of China is a usurping one—the Mantchou. We may say that it exists by sufferance at Pekin, and nowhere else in the Empire. If you look at the map of China Pekin is at the extremity of the Empire and not a week's marching from the Russian frontier. A war with Russia would imply the capture of Pekin and the fall of the Mantchou dynasty, which would never dare to leave it, for if they did the Chinamen in the south would smite them. I said, 'If you go to war then move the

Queen Bee—*i.e.* the Emperor—into the centre of China and then fight; if not, you must make peace.' The two Powers who can coerce China are Russia and England. Russia could march without much difficulty on Pekin. This much would not hurt trade, so England would not interfere. England could march to Taku and Pekin and no one would object, for she would occupy the Treaty Ports. But if France tried to do so England would object. Thus it is that China will only listen to Russia and England, and eventually she must fear Russia the most of all Powers, for she can never get over the danger of the land journey, but she might, by a great increase of her fleet, get over the fear of England. I say China, but I mean the Mantchou dynasty, for the Mantchous are despised by the Chinese. Any war with China would be for France expensive and dangerous, not from the Chinese forces, which would be soon mastered, but from the certainty of complications with England. As for the European population in China, write them down as identical with those in Egypt in all affairs. Their sole idea is, without any distinction of nationality, an increased power over China for their own trade and for opening up the country as they call it, and any war would be popular with them; so they will egg on any Power to make it. My idea is that no colonial or foreign community in a foreign land can properly, and for the general benefit of the world, consider the questions of that foreign State. The leading idea is how they will benefit themselves. The Isle of Bourbon or Réunion is the cause of the Madagascar war. It is egged on by the planters there, and to my idea they (the planters) want slaves for Madagascar. I have a very mean opinion of the views of any colonial or foreign community: though I own that they are powerful for evil. Who would dare to oppose the European colony in Egypt or China, and remain in those countries?

In a letter to myself, written about this time, very much the same views are expressed:

I do not think I could enlighten *you* about China. Her game is and will be to wait events, and she will try and work so as to embroil us with France if she does go to war. For this there would be plenty of elements in the Treaty Ports. One may say, humanly speaking, China going to war with France must entail our following suit. It would be a bad thing in some ways for civilization, for the Chinese are naturally so bumptious that any success would make them more so, and if allied to us, and they had success, it would be a bad look-out afterwards. This in private. Li Hung Chang as Emperor, if such a thing came to pass, would be worse than the present Emperor, for he is sharp and clever, would unite China under a Chinese dynasty, and be much more troublesome to deal with. Altogether, I cannot think that the world would gain if China went to war with France. Also I think it would be eventually bad for China. China being a queer country, we might expect queer things, and I believe if she did go to war she would contract with Americans for the destruction of French fleet, and she would let loose a horde of adventurers with dynamite. This is essentially her style of action, and Li Hung Chang would take it up, but do not say I think so.

In a further letter from Jaffa, dated 17th November 1883, he wrote finally on this branch of the subject:

I fear I can write nothing of any import, so I will not attempt it. To you I can remark that if I were the Government I would consider the part that should be taken when the inevitable fall of the Mantchou dynasty takes place, what steps they would take, and how they would act in the break-up, which, however, will only end in a fresh cohesion of China, for we, or no other Power, could never for long hold the country. At Penang, Singapore, etc., the Chinese will eventually oust us in another generation.

There was one other question about China upon which Gordon felt very strongly, viz., the opium question, and as he expressed views which I combated, I feel bound to end this chapter by quoting what he wrote on this much-discussed topic. On one point he agrees with myself and his other opponents in admitting that the main object with the Chinese authorities was increased revenue, not morality. They have since attained their object not only by an increased import duty, but also in the far more extensive cultivation of the native drug, to which the Emperor, by Imperial Edict, has given his formal sanction:

Port Louis
3rd February 1882
About the opium article, I think your article—'History of the Opium Traffic,' *Times*, 4th January 1884—reads well. But the question is this. The Chinese *amour propre* as a nation is hurt

by the enforced entry of the drug. This irritation is connected with the remembrance of the wars which led to the Treaties about opium. Had eggs or apples been the cause of the wars, *i.e.* had the Chinese objected to the import of eggs, and we had insisted on their being imported, and carried out such importation in spite of the Chinese wish by force of war, it would be to my own mind the same thing as opium now is to Chinese. We do not give the Chinese credit for being so sensitive as they are. As Black Sea Treaty was to Russia so opium trade is to China.

I take the root of the question to be as above. I do not mean to say that all that they urge is fictitious about morality; and I would go further than you, and say I think they would willingly give up their revenue from opium, indeed I am sure of it, if they could get rid of the forced importation by treaty, but their action in so doing would be simply one of satisfying their *amour propre*. The opium importation is a constant reminder of their defeats, and I feel sure China will never be good friends with us till it is abolished. It is for that reason I would give it up, for I think the only two alliances worth having are France and China.

I have never, when I have written on it, said anything further than this, *i.e. the Chinese Government will not have it*, let us say it is a good drug or not. I also say that it is not fair to force anything on your neighbour, and, therefore, morally, it is wrong, even if it was eggs.

"Further, I say that through our thrusting these eggs on China, this opium, we caused the wars with China which shook the prestige of the Pekin Government, and the outcome of this war of 1842 was the Taeping Rebellion, with its deaths of 13,000,000. The military prestige of the Mantchous was shaken by these defeats, the heavy contributions for war led to thousands of soldiers being disbanded, to a general impoverishment of the people, and this gave the rebel chief, Hung-tsew-tsiuen, his chance.

A wants B to let him import eggs, B refuses, A coerces him; therefore I say it is wrong, and that it is useless discussing whether eggs are good or not.

Can anyone doubt but that, if the Chinese Government had the power, they would stop importation tomorrow? If so, why keep a pressure like this on China whom we need as a friend, and with whom this importation is and ever will be the sole point about which we could be at variance? I know this is the point with Li Hung Chang.

People may laugh at *amour propre* of China. It is a positive fact, they are most-pigheaded on those points. China is the only nation in the world which is forced to take a thing she does not want. England is the only nation which forces another nation to do this, in order to benefit India by this act. Put like this it is outrageous.

Note this, only certain classes of vessels are subject to the Foreign Customs Office at Canton. By putting all vessels under that Office the Chinese Government would make £2,000,000 a year more revenue. The Chinese Government will not do this however, because it would put power in hands of foreigners, so they lose it. Did you ever read the letters of the Ambassador before Marquis Tsêng? His name, I think, was Coh or Kwoh. He wrote home to Pekin about Manchester, telling its wonders, but adding, 'These people are wonderful, but the masses are miserable far beyond Chinese. They think only of money and not of the welfare of the people.'

Any foreign nation can raise the bile of Chinese by saying, 'Look at the English, they forced you to take their opium.'

I should not be a bit surprised did I hear that Li Hung Chang smoked opium himself. I know a lot of the princes do, so they say. I have no doubt myself that what I have said is the true and only reason, or rather root reason. Put our nation in the same position of having been defeated and forced to accept some article which theory used to consider bad for the health, like tea used to be, we would rebel as soon as we could against it, though our people drink tea. The opium trade is a standing, ever-present memento of defeat and heavy payments; and the Chinese cleverly take advantage of the fact that it is a deleterious drug.

The opium wars were not about opium—opium was only a *cheval de bataille*. They were against the introduction of foreigners, a political question, and so the question of opium import is now. As for the loss to India by giving it up, it is quite another affair. On one hand you have gain, an embittered feeling and an injustice; on the other you have loss, friendly nations and justice. Cut down pay of all officers in India to Colonial allowances *above* rank of captains. Do not give them Indian allowances, and you will cover nearly the loss, I expect. Why should officers in India have more than officers in Hongkong?

In a subsequent letter, dated from the Cape, 20th July 1882, General Gordon replied to some objections I had raised as follows:

As for the opium, to which you say the same objection applies as to tea, etc., it is not so, for opium has for ages been a tabooed article among Chinese respectable people. I own reluctance to foreign intercourse applies to what I said, but the Chinese know that the intercourse with foreigners cannot be stopped, and it, as well as the forced introduction of opium, are signs of defeat; yet one, that of intercourse, cannot be stopped or wiped away while the opium question can be. I am writing in a hurry, so am not very clear.

What I mean is that no one country forces another country to take a drug like opium, and therefore the Chinese feel the forced introduction of opium as an intrusion and injustice; thence their feelings in the matter. This, I feel sure, is the case.

What could our Government do *in re* opium? Well, I should say, let the clause of treaty lapse about it, and let the smuggling be renewed. Hongkong is a nest of smugglers.

Pekin would, or rather could, never succeed in cutting off foreign intercourse. The Chinese are too much mixed up (and are increasingly so every year) with foreigners for Pekin even to try it. Also I do not think China would wish to stop its importation altogether. All they ask is an increased duty on it.

CHAPTER 10

Mauritius, the Cape and the Congo

There was a moment of hesitation in Gordon's mind as to whether he would come home or not. His first project on laying down the Indian Secretaryship had been to go to Zanzibar and attack the slave trade from that side. Before his plans were matured the China offer came, and turned his thoughts in a different channel. On his arrival at Aden, on the way back, he found that the late Sir William Mackinnon, a truly great English patriot of the type of the merchant adventurers of the Elizabethan age, had sent instructions that the ships of the British India Steam Packet Company were at his disposal to convey him wherever he liked, and for a moment the thought occurred to him to turn aside to Zanzibar. But a little reflection led him to think that, as he had been accused of insubordination, it would be better for him to return home and report himself at headquarters. When he arrived in London at the end of October 1880, he found that his letters, written chiefly to his sister during his long sojourn in the Soudan, were on the eve of publication by Dr Birkbeck Hill. That exceedingly interesting volume placed at the disposal of the public the evidence as to his great work in Africa, which might otherwise have been buried in oblivion. It was written under considerable difficulties, for Gordon would not see Dr Hill, and made a stringent proviso that he was not to be praised, and that nothing unkind was to be said about anyone. He did, however, stipulate for a special tribute of praise to be given to his Arab secretary, Berzati Bey, "my only companion for these years—my adviser and my counsellor." Berzati was among those who perished with the ill-fated expedition of Hicks Pasha at the end of 1883. To the publication of this work must be attributed the establishment of Gordon's reputation as the authority on the Soudan, and the prophetic character of many of his statements became clear when events confirmed them.

After a stay at Southampton and in London of a few weeks, Gordon was at last induced to give himself a short holiday, and, strangely enough, he selected Ireland as his recreation ground. I have been told that Gordon had a strain of Irish blood in him, but I have failed to discover it genealogically, nor was there any trace of its influence on his character. He was not fortunate in the season of the year he selected, nor in the particular part of the country he chose for his visit. There is scenery in the south-west division of Ireland, quite apart from the admitted beauty of the Killarney district, that will vie with better known and more highly lauded places in Scotland and Switzerland, but no one would recommend a stranger to visit that quarter of Ireland at the end of November, and the absence of cultivation, seen under the depressing conditions of Nature, would strike a visitor with all the effect of absolute sterility. Gordon was so impressed, and it seemed to him that the Irish peasants of a whole province were existing in a state of wretchedness exceeding anything he had seen in either China or the Soudan. If he had seen the same places six months earlier, he would have formed a less extreme view of their situation. It was just the condition of things that appealed to his sympathy, and with characteristic promptitude he put his views on paper, making one definite offer on his own part, and sent them to a friend, the present General James Donnelly, a distinguished engineer officer and old comrade, and moreover a member of a well-known Irish family. Considering the contents of the letter, and the form in which Gordon threw out his suggestions, it is not very surprising that General Donnelly sent it to *The Times*, in which it was published on 3rd December 1880; but Gordon himself was annoyed at this step being taken, because he realised that he had written somewhat hastily on a subject with which he could scarcely be deemed thoroughly acquainted. The following is its text:

You are aware how interested I am in the welfare of this country, and, having known you for twenty-six years, I am sure I may say the same of you.

I have lately been over to the south-west of Ireland in the hope of discovering how some settlement could be made of the Irish question, which, like a fretting cancer, eats away our vitals as a nation.

I have come to the conclusion that—

1. A gulf of antipathy exists between the landlords and tenants of the north-west, west, and south-west of Ireland. It is a gulf which is not caused alone by the question of rent; there

is a complete lack of sympathy between these two classes. It is useless to inquire how such a state of things has come to pass. I call your attention to the pamphlets, letters, and speeches of the landlord class, as a proof of how little sympathy or kindness there exists among them for the tenantry, and I am sure that the tenantry feel in the same way towards the landlords.

2. No half-measured Acts which left the landlords with any say to the tenantry of these portions of Ireland will be of any use. They would be rendered—as past Land Acts in Ireland have been—quite abortive, for the landlords will insert clauses to do away with their force. Any half-measures will only place the Government face to face with the people of Ireland as the champions of the landlord interest. The Government would be bound to enforce their decision, and with a result which none can foresee, but which certainly would be disastrous to the common weal.

3. My idea is that, seeing—through this cause or that, it is immaterial to examine—a deadlock has occurred between the present landlords and tenants, the Government should purchase up the rights of the landlords over the whole or the greater part of Longford, Westmeath, Clare, Cork, Kerry, Limerick, Leitrim, Sligo, Mayo, Cavan, and Donegal. The yearly rental of these districts is some four millions; if the Government give the landlords twenty years' purchase, it would cost eighty millions, which at three and a half per cent. would give a yearly interest of £2,800,000, of which £2,500,000 could be recovered; the lands would be Crown lands; they would be administered by a Land Commission, who would be supplemented by an Emigration Commission, which might for a short time need £100,000. This would not injure the landlords, and, so far as it is an interference with proprietary rights, it is as just as is the law which forces Lord A. to allow a railway through his park for the public benefit. I would restrain the landlords from any power or control in these Crown land districts. Poor-law, roads, schools, etc., should be under the Land Commission.

4. For the rest of Ireland, I would pass an Act allowing free sale of leases, fair rents, and a Government valuation.

In conclusion, I must say, from all accounts and my own observation, that the state of our fellow-countrymen in the parts

I have named is worse than that of any people in the world, let alone Europe. I believe that these people are made as we are, that they are patient beyond belief, loyal, but, at the same time, broken-spirited and desperate, living on the verge of starvation in places in which we would not keep our cattle.

The Bulgarians, Anatolians, Chinese, and Indians are better off than many of them are. The priests alone have any sympathy with their sufferings, and naturally alone have a hold over them. In these days, in common justice, if we endow a Protestant University, why should we not endow a Catholic University in a Catholic country? Is it not as difficult to get a £5 note from a Protestant as from a Catholic or Jew? Read the letters of—— and of——, and tell me if you see in them any particle of kind feeling towards the tenantry; and if you have any doubts about this, investigate the manner in which the Relief Fund was administered, and in which the sums of money for improvements of estates by landlords were expended.

In 1833 England gave freedom to the West Indian slaves at a cost of twenty millions—worth now thirty millions. This money left the country. England got nothing for it. By an expenditure of eighty millions she may free her own people. She would have the hold over the land, and she would cure a cancer. I am not well off, but I would offer——or his agent £1000, if either of them would live one week in one of these poor devil's places, and feed as these people do. Our comic prints do an infinity of harm by their caricatures—firstly, the caricatures are not true, for the crime in Ireland is not greater than that in England; and, secondly, they exasperate the people on both sides of the Channel, and they do no good. It is ill to laugh and scoff at a question which affects our existence.

This heroic mode of dealing with an old and very complicated difficulty scarcely came within the range of practical achievement. The Irish question is not to be solved by any such simple cut-and-dried procedure. It will take time, sympathy, and good-will. When the English people have eradicated their opinion that the Irish are an inferior race, and when the Irish realise that the old prejudice has vanished, the root-difficulty will be removed. At least Gordon deserves the credit of having seen that much from his brief observation on the spot, and his plea for them as "patient beyond belief and loyal," may eventually carry conviction to the hearts of the more powerful and prosperous kingdom.

The Irish question was not the only one on which he recorded a written opinion. The question of retaining Candahar was very much discussed during the winter of 1880-81, and as the Liberal Government was very much put to it to get high military opinion to support their proposal of abandonment, they were very glad when Gordon wrote to *The Times* expressing a strong opinion on their side. I think the writing of that letter was mainly due to a sense of obligation to Lord Ripon, although the argument used as to the necessity of Candahar being held by any *single* ruler of Afghanistan was, and is always, unanswerable. But the question at that time was this: Could any such single ruler be found, and was Abdurrahman, recognised in the August of 1880 as Ameer of Cabul, the man?

On 27th July 1880, less than eight weeks after Gordon's resignation of his Indian appointment, occurred the disastrous battle of Maiwand, when Yakoob's younger brother, Ayoob, gained a decisive victory over a British force. That disaster was retrieved six weeks later by Lord Roberts, but Ayoob remained in possession of Herat and the whole of the country west of the Helmund. It was well known that the rivalry between him and his cousin Abdurrahman did not admit of being patched up, and that it could only be settled by the sword. At the moment there was more reason to believe in the military talent of Ayoob than of the present Ameer, and it was certain that the instant we left Candahar the two opponents would engage in a struggle for its possession. The policy of precipitate evacuation left everything to the chapter of accidents, and if Ayoob had proved the victor, or even able to hold his ground, the situation in Afghanistan would have been eminently favourable for that foreign intervention which only the extraordinary skill and still more extraordinary success of the Ameer Abdurrahman has averted. In giving the actual text of Gordon's letter, it is only right, while frankly admitting that the course pursued has proved most successful and beneficial, to record that it might well have been otherwise, and that as a mere matter of argument the probability was quite the other way. Neither Gordon nor any other supporter of the evacuation policy ventured to predict that Abdurrahman, who was then not a young man, and whose early career had been one of failure, was going to prove himself the ablest administrator and most astute statesman in Afghan history.

Those who advocate the retention of Candahar do so generally on the ground that its retention would render more difficult the advance of Russia on, and would prevent her fomenting rebellion in, India, and that our prestige in India would suffer by its evacuation.

I think that this retention would throw Afghanistan, in the hope of regaining Candahar, into alliance with Russia, and that thereby Russia would be given a temptation to offer which she otherwise would not have. Supposing that temptation did not exist, what other inducement could Russia offer for this alliance? The plunder of India. If, then, Russia did advance, she would bring her auxiliary tribes, who, with their natural predatory habits, would soon come to loggerheads with their natural enemies, the Afghans, and that the sooner when these latter were aided by us. Would the Afghans in such a case be likely to be tempted by the small share they would get of the plunder of India to give up their secure, independent position and our alliance for that plunder, and to put their country at the mercy of Russia, whom they hate as cordially as they do us? If we evacuate Candahar, Afghanistan can only have this small inducement of the plunder of India for Russia to offer her. Some say that the people of Candahar desire our rule. I cannot think that any people like being governed by aliens in race or religion. They prefer their own bad native governments to a stiff, civilized government, in spite of the increased worldly prosperity the latter may give.

We may be sure that at Candahar the spirit which induced children to kill, or to attempt to kill our soldiers in 1879, etc., still exists, though it may be cowed. We have trouble enough with the fanatics of India; why should we go out of our way to add to their numbers?

From a military point of view, by the retention we should increase the line we have to defend by twice the distance of Candahar to the present frontier, and place an objective point to be attacked. Naturally we should make good roads to Candahar, which on the loss of a battle there—and such things must be always calculated as within possibility—would aid the advance of the enemy to the Indus. The *débouché* of the defiles, with good lateral communications between them, is the proper line of defence for India, not the entry into those defiles, which cannot have secure lateral communications. If the entries of the defiles are held, good roads are made through them; and these aid the enemy, if you lose the entries or have them turned. This does not prevent the passage of the defiles being disputed.

The retention of Candahar would tend to foment rebellion in India, and not prevent it; for thereby we should obtain an additional number of fanatical malcontents, who as British subjects would have the greatest facility of passing to and fro in India, which they would not have if we did not hold it.

That our prestige would suffer in India by the evacuation I doubt; it certainly would suffer if we kept it and forsook our word—*i.e.* that we made war against Shere Ali, and not against his people. The native peoples of India would willingly part with any amount of prestige if they obtained less taxation.

India should be able, by a proper defence of her present frontier and by the proper government of her peoples, to look after herself. If the latter is wanting, no advance of frontier will aid her.

I am not anxious about Russia; but, were I so, I would care much more to see precautions taken for the defence of our Eastern colonies, now that Russia has moved her Black Sea naval establishment to the China Sea, than to push forward an outstretched arm to Candahar. The interests of the Empire claim as much attention as India, and one cannot help seeing that they are much more imperilled by this last move of Russia than by anything she can do in Central Asia.

Politically, militarily, and morally, Candahar ought not to be retained. It would oblige us to keep up an interference with the internal affairs of Afghanistan, would increase the expenditure of impoverished India, and expose us chronically to the reception of those painfully sensational telegrams of which we have had a surfeit of late.

During these few months Gordon wrote on several other subjects—the Abyssinian question, in connection with which he curiously enough styled "the Abyssinians the best of mountaineers," a fact not appreciated until their success over the Italians many years later, the registration of slaves in Egypt, and the best way of carrying on irregular warfare in difficult country and against brave and active races. His remarks on the last subject were called forth by our experiences in the field against the Zulus in the first place, and the Boers in the second, and quite exceptional force was given to them by the occurrence of the defeat at Majuba Hill one day after they appeared in the *Army and Navy Gazette*. For this reason I quote the article in its entirety:

The individual man of any country in which active outdoor life, abstinence, hunting of wild game, and exposure to all weathers are the habits of life, is more than a match for the private soldier of a regular army, who is taken from the plough or from cities, and this is the case doubly as much when the field of operations is a difficult country, and when the former is, and the latter is not, acclimatised. On the one hand, the former is accustomed to the climate, knows the country, and is trained to long marches and difficulties of all sorts inseparable from his daily life; the latter is unacclimatised, knows nothing of the country, and, accustomed to have his every want supplied, is at a loss when any extraordinary hardships or difficulties are encountered; he has only his skill in his arms and discipline in his favour, and sometimes that skill may be also possessed by his foe. The native of the country has to contend with a difficulty in maintaining a long contest, owing to want of means and want of discipline, being unaccustomed to any yoke interfering with individual freedom. The resources of a regular army, in comparison to those of the natives of the country, are infinite, but it is accustomed to discipline. In a difficult country, when the numbers are equal, and when the natives are of the description above stated, the regular forces are certainly at a very great disadvantage, until, by bitter experience in the field, they are taught to fight in the same irregular way as their foes, and this lesson may be learnt at a great cost. I therefore think that when regular forces enter into a campaign under these conditions, the former ought to avoid any unnecessary haste, for time does not press with them, while every day increases the burden on a country without resources and unaccustomed to discipline, and as the forces of the country, unprovided with artillery, never ought to be able to attack fortified posts, any advance should be made by the establishment of such posts. All engagements in the field ought, if possible, to be avoided, except by corps raised from people who in their habits resemble those in arms, or else by irregular corps raised for the purpose, apart from the routine and red-tape inseparable from regular armies. The regular forces will act as the back-bone of the expedition, but the rock and cover fighting will be done better by levies of such specially raised irregulars. For war with native countries, I think that, except for the defence of posts, artillery is a great encumbrance, far beyond its value. It is a continual source of anxiety. Its transport regulates the speed of the march, and it forms a target for the enemy, while its effects on the scattered enemy is almost *nil*. An advance of regular troops, as at present organised, is just the sort of march that suits an active native foe. The regulars' column must be heaped together, covering its transport and artillery. The enemy knows the probable point of its destination on a particular day, and then, knowing that the regulars cannot halt definitely where it may be chosen to attack, it hovers round the column like wasps. The regulars cannot, from not being accustomed to the work, go clambering over rocks, or beating covers after their foes. Therefore I conclude that in these wars[1] regular troops should only act as a reserve; that the real fighting should be done either by native allies or by special irregular corps, commanded by special men, who would be untrammelled by regulations; that, except for the defence of posts, artillery should be abandoned. It may seem egotistical, but I may state that I should never have succeeded against native foes had I not had flanks, and front, and rear covered by irregular forces. Whenever either the flanks, or rear, or front auxiliaries were barred in their advance, we turned the regular forces on that point, and thus strengthening the hindered auxiliaries, drove back the enemy. We owed defeats, when they occurred, to the absence of these auxiliaries, and on two occasions to having cannon with the troops, which lost us 1600 men. The Abyssinians, who are the best of mountaineers, though they have them, utterly despise cannon, as they hinder their movements. I could give instance after instance where, in native wars, regular troops could not hold their own against an active guerrilla, and where, in some cases, the disasters of the regulars were brought about by being hampered by cannon. No one can deny artillery may be most efficient in the contention of two regular armies, but it is quite the reverse in guerrilla warfare. The inordinate haste which exists to finish off these wars throws away many valuable aids which would inevitably accrue to the regular army if time was taken to do the work, and far greater expense is caused by this hurry than otherwise would be necessary. All is done on the 'Veni, vidi, vici' principle. It may be very fine, but it is bloody and expensive, and not scientific. I am sure it will occur to many, the times we have advanced, without proper breaches, bridges, etc., and with what loss, assaulted. It would seem that

---

1. In allusion more particularly to the Cape and China.

military science should be entirely thrown away when combating native tribes. I think I am correct in saying that the Romans always fought with large auxiliary forces of the invaded country or its neighbours, and I know it was the rule of the Russians in Circassia.

Perhaps Gordon was influenced by the catastrophes in South Africa when he sent the following telegram at his own expense to the Cape authorities on 7th April 1881:

Gordon offers his services for two years at £700 per annum to assist in terminating war and administering Basutoland.

To this telegram he was never accorded even the courtesy of a negative reply. It will be remembered that twelve months earlier the Cape Government had offered him the command of the forces, and that his reply had been to refuse. The incident is of some interest as showing that his attention had been directed to the Basuto question, and also that he was again anxious for active employment. His wish for the latter was to be realised in an unexpected manner.

He was staying in London when, on visiting the War Office, he casually met the late Colonel Sir Howard Elphinstone, an officer of his own corps, who began by complaining of his hard luck in its just having fallen to his turn to fill the post of Engineer officer in command at the Mauritius, and such was the distastefulness of the prospect of service in such a remote and unattractive spot, that Sir Howard went on to say that he thought he would sooner retire from the service. In his impulsive manner Gordon at once exclaimed: "Oh, don't worry yourself, I will go for you; Mauritius is as good for me as anywhere else."

The exact manner in which this exchange was brought about has been variously described, but this is the literal version given me by General Gordon himself, and there is no doubt that, as far as he could regret anything that had happened, he bitterly regretted the accident that caused him to become acquainted with the Mauritius. In a letter to myself on the subject from Port Louis he said: "It was not over cheerful to go out to this place, nor is it so to find a deadly sleep over all my military friends here." In making the arrangements which were necessary to effect the official substitution of himself for Colonel Elphinstone, Gordon insisted on only two points: first, that Elphinstone should himself arrange the exchange; and secondly that no payment was to be made to him as was usual—in this case about £800—on an exchange being effected. Sir Howard Elphinstone was thus saved by Gordon's peculiarities a disagreeable experience and a considerable sum of money. Some years after Gordon's death Sir Howard met with a tragic fate, being washed overboard while taking a trip during illness to Madeira.

Like everything else he undertook, Gordon determined to make his Mauritius appointment a reality, and although he was only in the island twelve months, and during that period took a trip to the interesting group of the Seychelles, he managed to compress an immense amount of work into that short space, and to leave on record some valuable reports on matters of high importance. He found at Mauritius the same dislike for posts that were outside the ken of headquarters, and the same indifference to the dry details of professional work that drove officers of high ability and attainments to think of resigning the service sooner than fill them, and, when they did take them, to pass their period of exile away from the charms of Pall Mall in a state of inaction that verged on suspended animation. In a passage already quoted, he refers to the deadly sleep of his military friends, and then he goes on to say in a sentence, which cannot be too much taken to heart by those who have to support this mighty empire, with enemies on every hand—

> We are in a perfect Fools' Paradise about our power. We have plenty of power if we would pay attention to our work, but the fault is, to my mind, the military power of the country is eaten up by selfishness and idleness, and we are trading on the reputation of our forefathers. When one sees by the newspapers the Emperor of Germany sitting, old as he is, for two long hours inspecting his troops, and officers here grudging two hours a week for their duties, one has reason to fear the future.

During his stay at Mauritius he wrote three papers of first-rate importance. One of them on Egyptian affairs after the deposition of Ismail may be left for the next chapter, and the two others, one on coaling stations in the Indian Ocean, and the second on the comparative merits of the Cape and Mediterranean routes come within the scope of this chapter, and are, moreover, deserving of special consideration. With regard to the former of these two important subjects, Gordon wrote as follows, but I cannot discover that anything has been done to give practical effect to his recommendations:

> I spoke to you concerning Borneo and the necessity for coaling stations in the Eastern seas. Taking Mauritius with its large French population, the Cape with its conflicting ele-

ments, and Hongkong, Singapore, and Penang with their vast Chinese populations, who may be with or against us, but who are at any time a nuisance, I would select such places where no temptation would induce colonists to come, and I would use them as maritime fortresses. For instance, the only good coaling place between Suez and Adelaide would be in the Chagos group, which contain a beautiful harbour at San Diego. My object is to secure this for the strengthening of our maritime power. These islands are of great strategical importance *vis à vis* with India, Suez, and Singapore. Remember Aden has no harbour to speak of, and has the need of a garrison, while Chagos could be kept by a company of soldiers. It is wonderful our people do not take the views of our forefathers. They took up their positions at all the salient points of the routes. We can certainly hold these places, but from the colonial feelings they have almost ceased to be our own. By establishing these coaling stations no diplomatic complications could arise, while by their means we could unite all our colonies with us, for we could give them effective support. The spirit of no colony would bear up for long against the cutting off of its trade, which would happen if we kept watching the Mediterranean and neglected the great ocean routes. The cost would not be more than these places cost now, if the principle of heavily-armed, light-draught, swift gunboats with suitable arsenals, properly (not over) defended, were followed.

Chagos as well as Seychelles forms part of the administrative group of the Mauritius. The former with, as Gordon states, an admirable port in San Diego, lies in the direct route to Australia from the Red Sea, and the latter contains an equally good harbour in Port Victoria Mahé. The Seychelles are remarkably healthy islands—thirty in number— and Gordon recommended them as a good place for "a man with a little money to settle in." He also advanced the speculative and somewhat imaginative theory that in them was to be found the true site of the Garden of Eden.

The views Gordon expressed in 1881 as to the diminished importance of the Mediterranean as an English interest, and the relative superiority of the Cape over the Canal route, on the ground of its security, were less commonly held then than they have since become. Whether they are sound is not to be taken on the trust of even the greatest of reputations; and in so complicated and many-sided a problem it will be well to consider all contingencies, and to remember that there is no reason why England should not be able in war-time to control them both, until at least the remote epoch when Palestine shall be a Russian possession.

I think Malta has very much lost its importance. The Mediterranean now differs much from what it was in 1815. Other nations besides France possess in it great dockyards and arsenals, and its shores are backed by united peoples. Any war with Great Britain in the Mediterranean with any one Power would inevitably lead to complications with neutral nations. Steam has changed the state of affairs, and has brought the Mediterranean close to every nation of Europe. War in the Mediterranean is *war in a basin*, the borders of which are in the hands of other nations, all pretty powerful and interested in trade, and all likely to be affected by any turmoil in that basin, and to be against the makers of such turmoil. In fact, the Mediterranean trade is so diverted by the railroads of Europe, that it is but of small importance. The trade which is of value is the trade east of Suez, which, passing through the Canal, depends upon its being kept open. If the entrance to the Mediterranean were blocked at Gibraltar by a heavy fleet, I cannot see any advantage to be gained against us by the fleets blocked up in it—at any rate I would say, let our *first care* be for the Cape route, and secondly for the Mediterranean and Canal. The former route entails no complications, the latter endless ones, coupled with a precarious tenure. Look at the Mediterranean, and see how small is that sea on which we are apparently devoting the greater part of our attention. Aden should be made a Crown colony. The Resident, according to existing orders, reports to Bombay, and Bombay to *that* Simla Council, which knows and cares nothing for the question. A special regiment should be raised for its protection.

While stationed in the Mauritius, Gordon attained the rank of Major-General in the army, and another colonel of Engineers was sent out to take his place. During the last three months of his residence he filled, in addition to his own special post, that of the command of all the troops on the station, and at one time it seemed as if he might have been confirmed in the appointment. But this was not done, owing, as he suggested, to the "determination not to appoint officers of the Royal Artillery or Engineers to any command;" but a more probable reason was that Gordon had been inquiring about and had discovered that the colonists were not only a little discontented, but had some ground for their discontent. By this time Gordon's uncompromising sense of justice was beginning to be known in high official quarters, and the then responsible Government had far too many cares on its shoulders that could not be shirked to invite others from so remote and unimportant a possession as the Mauritius.

Even before any official decision could have been arrived at in this matter, fate had provided him with another destination.

Two passages have already been cited, showing the overtures first made by the Cape Government, and then by Gordon himself, for his employment in South Africa. Nothing came of those communications. On 23rd February 1882, when an announcement was made by myself that Gordon would vacate his command in a few weeks' time, the Cape Government again expressed its desire to obtain the use of his services, and moreover recollected the telegram to which no reply had been sent. Sir Hercules Robinson, then Governor of the Cape, sent the following telegram to the Colonial Secretary, the Earl of Kimberley:

> Ministers request me to inquire whether H.M.'s Government would permit them to obtain the services of Colonel Charles Gordon. Ministers desire to invite Colonel Gordon to come to this Colony for the purpose of consultation as to the best measures to be adopted with reference to Basutoland, in the event of Parliament sanctioning their proposals as to that territory, and to engage his services, should he be willing to renew the offer made to their predecessors in April 1881, to assist in terminating the war and administering Basutoland.

Lord Kimberley then sent instructions by telegraph to Durban, and thence by steamer, sanctioning Gordon's employment and his immediate departure from the Mauritius. The increasing urgency of the Basuto question induced the Cape Government to send a message by telegraph to Aden, and thence by steamer direct to Gordon. In this message they stated that "the services of some one of proved ability, firmness, and energy," were required; that they did not expect Gordon to be bound by the salary named in his own telegram, and that they begged him to visit the Colony "at once"—repeating the phrase twice. All these messages reached Gordon's hands on 2nd April. Two days later he started in the sailing vessel *Scotia*, no other ship being obtainable.

The Cape authorities had therefore no ground to complain of the dilatoriness of the man to whom they appealed in their difficulty, although their telegram was despatched 3rd of March, and Gordon did not reach Cape Town before the 3rd of May. It will be quite understood that Gordon had offered in the first place, and been specially invited in the second place, to proceed to the Cape, for the purpose of dealing with the difficulty in Basutoland. He was to find that, just as his mission to China had been complicated by extraneous circumstances, so was his visit to the Cape to be rendered more difficult by Party rivalries, and by work being thrust upon him which he had several times refused to accept, and for the efficient discharge of which, in his own way, he knew he would never obtain the requisite authority.

Before entering upon this matter a few words may be given to the financial agreement between himself and the Cape Government. The first office in 1880 had carried with it a salary of £1500; in 1881 Gordon had offered to go for £700; in 1882 the salary was to be a matter of arrangement, and on arrival at Cape Town he was offered £1200 a year. He refused to accept more than £800 a year; but as he required and insisted on having a secretary, the other £400 was assigned for that purpose. In naming such a small and inadequate salary Gordon was under the mistaken belief that his imperial pay of £500 a year would continue, but, unfortunately for him, a new regulation, 25th June 1881, had come into force while he was buried away in the Mauritius, and he was disqualified from the receipt of the income he had earned. Gordon was very indignant, more especially because it was clear that he was doing public service at the Cape, while, as he said with some bitterness, if he had started an hotel or become director of a company, his pay would have gone on all the same. The only suggestion the War Office made was that he should ask the Cape Government to compensate him, but this he indignantly refused. In the result all his savings during the Mauritius command were swallowed up, and I believe I understate the amount when I say that his Cape experience cost him out of his own pocket from first to last five hundred pounds. That sum was a very considerable one to a man who never inherited any money, and who went through life scorning all opportunities of making it. But on this occasion he vindicated a principle, and showed that "money was not his object."

As Gordon went to the Cape specially for the purpose of treating the Basutoland question, it may be well to describe briefly what that question was. Basutoland is a mountainous country, difficult of access, but in resources self-sufficing, on the eastern side of the Orange

Free State, and separated from Natal and Kaffraria, or the Transkei division of Cape Colony, by the sufficiently formidable Drakensberg range. Its population consisted of 150,000 stalwart and freedom-loving Highlanders, ruled by four chiefs—Letsea, Masupha, Molappo, and Lerothodi, with only the three first of whom had Gordon in any way to deal. Notwithstanding their numbers, courage, and the natural strength of their country, they owed their safety from absorption by the Boers to British protection, especially in 1868, and they were taken over by us as British subjects without any formality three years later. They do not seem to have objected so long as the tie was indefinite, but when in 1880 it was attempted to enforce the regulations of the Peace Preservation Act by disarming these clans, then the Basutos began a pronounced and systematic opposition. Letsea and Lerothodi kept up the pretence of friendliness, but Masupha fortified his chief residence at Thaba Bosigo, and openly prepared for war. That war had gone on for two years without result, and the total cost of the Basuto question had been four millions sterling when Gordon was summoned to the scene. Having given this general description of the question, it will be well to state the details of the matters in dispute, as set forth by Gordon after he had examined all the papers and heard the evidence of the most competent and well-informed witnesses.

His memorandum, dated 26th May 1882, read as follows:

In 1843 the Basuto chiefs entered into a treaty with Her Majesty's Government, by which the limits of Basutoland were recognised roughly in 1845. The Basuto chiefs agreed by convention with Her Majesty's Government to a concession of land on terminable leases, on the condition that Her Majesty's Government should protect them from Her Majesty's subjects.

In 1848 the Basuto chiefs agreed to accept the Sovereignty of Her Majesty the Queen, on the understanding that Her Majesty's Government would restrain Her Majesty's subjects in the territories they possessed.

Between 1848 and 1852, notwithstanding the above treaties, a large portion of Basutoland was annexed by the proclamation of Her Majesty's Government, and this annexation was accompanied by hostilities, which were afterwards decided by Sir George Cathcart as being undertaken in support of unjustifiable aggression.

In 1853, notwithstanding the treaties, Basutoland was abandoned, leaving its chiefs to settle as they could with the Europeans of the Free State who were settled in Basutoland and were mixed up with the Basuto people.

In 1857, the Basutos asked Her Majesty's Government to arbitrate and settle their quarrels. This request was refused.

In 1858 the Free State interfered to protect their settlers, and a war ensued, and the Free State was reduced to great extremities, and asked Her Majesty's Government to mediate. This was agreed to, and a frontier line was fixed by Her Majesty's Government.

In 1865 another war broke out between the Free State and the Basutos, at the close of which the Basutos lost territory, and were accepted as British subjects by Her Majesty's Government for the second time, being placed under the direct government of Her Majesty's High Commissioner.

In 1871 Basutoland was annexed to the *Crown* Colony of the Cape of Good Hope, without the Basutos having been consulted.

In 1872 the *Crown* Colony became a colony with a responsible Government, and the Basutos were placed virtually under another power. The Basutos asked for representation in the Colonial Parliament, which was refused, and to my mind here was the mistake committed which led to these troubles.

Then came constant disputes, the Disarmament Act, the Basuto War, and present state of affairs. From this chronology there are four points that stand out in relief:—

1. That the Basuto people, who date back generations, made treaties with the British Government, which treaties are equally binding, whether between two powerful states, or between a powerful state and a weak one.

2. That, in defiance of the treaties, the Basutos lost land.

3. That, in defiance of the treaties, the Basutos, without being consulted or having their rights safeguarded, were handed over to another power—the Colonial Government.

4. That that other power proceeded to enact their disarmament, a process which could only be carried out with a servile race, like the Hindoos of the plains of India, and which any one of understanding must see would be resisted to the utmost by any people worth the name; the more so in the case of the Basutos, who realised the constant contraction of their frontiers in defiance of the treaties made with the British Government, and who could not possibly avoid the conclusion that this disarmament was only a prelude to their extinction.

The necessary and inevitable result of the four deductions was that the Basutos resisted, and remain passively resisting to this day.

The fault lay in the British Government not having consulted the Basutos, their co-treaty power, when they handed them over to the Colonial Government. They should have called together a national assembly of the Basuto people, in which the terms of the transfer could have been quietly arranged, and this I consider is the root of all the troubles, and expenses, and miseries which have sprung up; and therefore, as it is always best to go to the root of any malady, I think it would be as well to let bygones be bygones, and to commence afresh by calling together by proclamation a Pitso of the whole tribe, in order to discuss the best means of sooner securing the settlement of the country. I think that some such proclamation should be issued. By this Pitso we would know the exact position of affairs, and the real point in which the Basutos are injured or considered themselves to be injured.

To those who wish for the total abandonment of Basutoland, this course must be palatable; to those who wish the Basutos well, and desire not to see them exterminated, it must also be palatable; and to those who hate the name of Basutoland it must be palatable, for it offers a solution which will prevent them ever hearing the name again.

This Pitso ought to be called at once. All Colonial officials ought to be absent, for what the colony wants is to know what is the matter; and the colony wishes to know it from the Basuto people, irrespective of the political parties of the Government.

Such a course would certainly recommend itself to the British Government, and to its masters—the British people.

Provided the demands of the Basutos—who will, for their own sakes, never be for a severing of their connection with the colony, in order to be eventually devoured by the Orange Free State—are such as will secure the repayment to the colony of all expenses incurred by the Colonial Government in the maintenance of this connection, and I consider that the Colonial Government should accept them.

With respect to the Loyals, there are some 800 families, the cost of keeping whom is on an average one shilling per diem each family, that is £40 per diem, or £1200 per month, and they have been rationed during six months at cost of £7200. Their claims may therefore be said to be some £80,000. Now, if these 800 families (some say half) have claims amounting to £30 each individually (say 400 families at £30), £12,000 paid at once would rid the colony of the cost of subsistence of these families, *viz.* £600 a month (the retention of them would only add to the colonial expenditure, and tend to pauperise them).

I believe that £30,000 paid at once to the Loyals would reduce their numbers to one-fourth what they are now. It is proposed to send up a Commission to examine into their claims; the Commission will not report under two months, and there will be the delay of administration at Cape Town, during all which time £1200 a month are being uselessly expended by the colony, detrimentally to the Loyals. Therefore I recommend (1) that the sum of £30,000 should be at once applied to satisfy the minor claims of the Loyals; (2) that this should be done at once, at same time as the meeting of the National Pitso.

The effect of this measure in connection with the meeting of the National Pitso would be very great, for it would be a positive proof of the good disposition of the Colonial Government. The greater claims could, if necessary, wait for the Parliamentary Commission, but I would deprecate even this delay, and though for the distribution of the £30,000 I would select those on whom the responsibility of such distribution could be put, without reference to the Colonial Government, for any larger sums perhaps the colonial sanction should be taken.

I urge that this measure of satisfying the Loyals is one that presses and cannot well wait months to be settled.

In conclusion, I recommend (1) that a National Pitso be held; (2) that the Loyals should at once be paid off.

I feel confident that by the recommendation No. 1 nothing could be asked for detrimental to colonial interests, whose Government would always have the right of amending or refusing any demands, and that by recommendation No. 2 a great moral effect would be produced at once, and some heavy expenses saved.

Attached to this memorandum was the draft of a proclamation to the chiefs, etc., of Basutoland, calling on them to meet in Pitso or National Assembly without any agent of the Colonial Government being present. It was not very surprising that such a policy of fairness and consideration for Basuto opinion, because so diametrically opposite to everything that Government had been doing, should have completely taken the Cape authorities aback, nor were its chances of being accepted increased by Gordon entrusting it to Mr Orpen, whose policy in the matter had been something more than criticised by the Ministers at that moment in power at the Cape. Gordon's despatch was in the hands of the Cape Premier early in June, and the embarrassment he felt at the ability and force with which the Basuto side of the question was put by the officer, who was to settle the matter for the Cape Government, was so great that, instead of making any reply, he passed it on to Lord Kimberley and the Colonial Office for solution. It was not until the 7th of August that an answer was vouchsafed to Gordon on what was, after all, the main portion of his task in South Africa. In the interval Gordon was employed on different military and administrative matters, for he had had thrust on him as a temporary charge the functions of Commandant-General of the Cape forces, which he had never wished to accept, but it will be clearer to the reader to follow to the end the course of his Basuto mission, which was the essential cause of his presence in South Africa.

On the 18th July the Ministers requested Gordon to go up to Basutoland. At that moment, and indeed for more than three weeks later, Gordon had received no reply to the detailed memorandum already quoted. He responded to this request with the draft of a convention that would "save the susceptibilities of Mr Orpen between whom and Masupha any *entente* would seem impossible." The basis of that convention was to be the semi-independence of the Basutos, but its full text must be given in order to show the consistency, as well as the simplicity, of Gordon's proposed remedy of a question that had gone on for years without any prospect of termination.

Convention Between
Colony, Cape of Good Hope and the
Chief and People of Basutoland

The Colonial Government having nominated as their representatives, Colonel C. Griffiths and Dr J. W. Matthews, the Basuto nation having nominated the Chief Letsea Moshesh and Masupha Moshesh as their representatives, the following convention has been agreed upon between these representatives:—

Art. 1. There shall be a complete amnesty on both sides to all who have taken part in the late hostilities.

Art. 2. The question of the succession to Molappo Moshesh's chieftainship shall be decided by the Chief of the Basuto Nation.

Art. 3. The Colonial Government engages to respect the integrity of the Basuto nation within the limits to be hereafter decided upon, and also to use its best endeavours to have these limits respected by the Orange Free State.

Art. 4. The Colonial Government will appoint a Resident to the Basuto nation, with two sub-residents. The Resident will consult with the leading Chief of the Basuto Nation on all measures concerning the welfare of that country, but the government of the Basutos in all internal affairs will remain under the jurisdiction of the chiefs.

Art. 5. The Supreme Council of Basutoland will consist of the leading chiefs and the Resident; the minor chiefs of Basutoland will form a council with the sub-residents. These minor councils can be appealed against by any non-content to the Supreme Council.

Art. 6. A hut-tax will be collected of 10s. per hut by the chiefs, and will be paid to the Resident and sub-resident. The sum thus collected will be used in paying the Resident £2000 a year, all included: the sub-residents £1200 a year, all included; in providing for the education of people (now costing £3320 a year); in making roads, etc.

Art. 7. The chiefs collecting hut-tax will be paid 10 per cent. of the sums they collect.

Art. 8. The frontier line will be placed under headmen, who will be responsible that no thieving be permitted, that spoors are followed up. For this these headmen will be paid at the rate of £20 to £60 per annum, according to the length of frontier they are responsible for.

Art. 9. All passes must be signed by Residents or sub-residents for the Orange Free State, or for the Cape Colony.

Query—Would it be advisable to add chiefs and missionaries after sub-residents?

Art. 10. Colonial warrants will be valid in Basutoland, the chiefs being responsible that prisoners are given up to Resident or sub-residents.

Art. 11. All communications between Basutoland and the Orange Free State to be by and through the Resident.

Art. 12. This Convention to be in quadruplicate, two copies being in possession of the Colonial Government, and two copies in possession of the Basuto chiefs.

Art. 13. On signature of this Convention, and on the fulfilment of Art. 1, amnesty clause, the Colonial Government agrees to withdraw the military forces and the present magisterial administration.

To this important communication no answer was ever vouchsafed, but on 7th August, long after it was in the hands of Ministers, Mr Thomas Scanlan, the Premier, wrote a long reply to the earlier memorandum of 26th May. The writer began by quoting Lord Kimberley's remarks on that memorandum, which were as follows:

I have received the memorandum on the Basuto question by Major-General Gordon. I do not think it necessary to enter upon a discussion of the policy suggested in this memorandum, but it will doubtless be borne in mind by your Ministers that, as I informed you by my telegram of the 6th of May last, H.M.'s Government cannot hold out any expectation that steps will be taken by them to relieve the colony of its responsibilities in Basutoland.

The interpretation placed, and no doubt correctly placed, on that declaration of Government policy was that under no circumstances was it prepared to do anything in the matter, and that it had quite a sufficient number of troubles and worries without the addition of one in remote and unimportant Basutoland. Having thus got out of the necessity of discussing this important memorandum, under the cloak of the Colonial Office's decision in favour of inaction, the Premier went on to say that he was "most anxious to avoid the resumption of hostilities on the one hand or the abandonment of the territory on the other." There was an absolute ignoring in this statement of Gordon's deliberate opinion that the only way to solve the difficulty was by granting Basutoland semi-independence on the terms of a Convention providing for the presence of a British Resident, through whom all external matters were to be conducted. At the same time Mr Scanlan informed Gordon that he was sending up Mr Sauer, then Secretary for Native Affairs, who was a nominee of Mr Orpen, the politician whose policy was directly impugned.

On Mr Sauer reaching King William's Town, where Gordon was in residence at the Grand Depot of the Cape forces, he at once asked him to accompany him to Basutoland. Gordon at first declined to do this on two grounds, viz. that he saw no good could ensue unless the convention were granted, and also that he did not wish Mr Sauer, or any other representative of the Cape Government, as a companion, because he had learnt that "Masupha would only accept his proposed visit as a private one, and then only with his private secretary and two servants."

After some weeks' hesitation Gordon was induced by Mr Sauer to so far waive his objection as to consent to accompany him to Letsea's territory. This Basuto chief kept up the fiction of friendly relations with the Cape, but after Gordon had personally interviewed him, he became more than ever convinced that all the Basuto chiefs were in league. Mr Sauer was of opinion that Letsea and the other chiefs might be trusted to attack and able to conquer Masupha. There was no possibility of reconciling these clashing views, but Gordon also accompanied Mr Sauer to Leribe, the chief town of Molappo's territory, north of, and immediately adjoining that of, Masupha. Here Gordon found fresh evidence as to the correctness of his view, that all the Basuto leaders were practically united, and he wrote a memorandum, dated 16th September, which has not been published, showing the hopelessness of getting one chief to coerce the others. Notwithstanding the way he had been treated by the Cape Government, which had ignored all his suggestions, Gordon, in his intense desire to do good, and his excessive trust in the honour of other persons, yielded to Mr Sauer's request to visit Masupha, and not only yielded but went without any instructions or any prior agreement that his views were to prevail. The consequence was that Mr Sauer deliberately resolved to destroy Gordon's reputation as a statesman, and to ensure the triumph of his own policy by an act of treachery that has never been surpassed.

While Gordon went as a private visitor at the special invitation of Masupha to that chief's territory, Mr Sauer, who was well acquainted with Gordon's views, and also the direct author of Gordon's visit at that particular moment, incited Letsea to induce Lerothodi to attack Masupha. At the moment that the news of this act of treachery reached Masupha's ears, Gordon was a guest in Masupha's camp, and the first construction placed upon events by that chief was, that Gordon had been sent up to hoodwink and keep him quiet, while a formidable invasion was plotted of his territory. When Masupha reported this news to Gordon, he asked what he advised him to do, and it has been established that the object of the question was to ascertain how far Gordon was privy to the plot. Gordon's candid reply—"Refuse to have any dealings with the Government until the forces are withdrawn," and his general demeanour, which showed unaffected indignation, convinced Masupha of his good faith and innocence of all participation in the plot.

A very competent witness, Mr Arthur Pattison (letter in *The Times*, 20th August 1885), bears this testimony:

Gordon divined his character marvellously, and was the only man Masupha had the slightest regard for. Masupha, if you treat him straightforwardly, is as nice a man as possible, and even kind and thoughtful; but, if you treat him the other way, he is a fiend incarnate.

Had Masupha not been thus convinced, Gordon's death was decided on, and never in the whole course of his career, not even when among the Taepings on the day of the Wangs' murder in Soochow, nor among Suleiman's slave-hunters at Shaka, was he in greater peril than when exposed by the treacherous proceedings of Sauer and Orpen to the wrath of Masupha. On his return in safety he at once sent in his resignation, but those who played him false not merely never received their deserts for an unpardonable breach of faith to a loyal colleague, but have been permitted by a lax public opinion at the Cape to remain in the public service, and are now discharging high and responsible duties.

Gordon's mission to the leading Basuto chief, and the policy of conciliation which he consistently and ably advocated from the beginning to the end of his stay at the Cape, were thus failures, but they failed, as an impartial writer like Mr Gresswell says, solely because "of Mr Sauer's intrigues behind his back." It is only necessary to add what Gordon himself wrote on this subject on his return, and to record that practically the very policy he advocated was carried into force, not by the Cape Government, but over its head by the British Government, two years later, in the separation of Basutoland from the Cape Colony, and by placing it in its old direct dependence under the British Crown.

I have looked over the Cape papers; the only thing that is misrepresented, so far as I could see in a ten minutes' glance at them, is that Sauer says I knew of his intentions of sending an expedition against Masupha. He puts it thus: 'Gordon knew that an expedition was being organised against Masupha.' He gives apparently three witnesses that I knew well. It is quite true; but read the words. *I knew Sauer was going* to try the useless expedient of an expedition against Masupha, and *before he did so we agreed I should go and try and make peace.* While carrying on this peace mission, Sauer sends the expedition. So you see he is verbally correct; yet the deduction is false; in fact, who would ever go up with peace overtures to a man who was to be attacked during those overtures, as Masupha was? Garcia knew well enough what a surprise it was to him and me when we heard Sauer was sending the expedition. Garcia was with me at the time.

And again, when at Jaffa, General Gordon adds further, on the 27th of July 1883:

> I saw Masupha one day at 10 a.m., and spoke to him; Sauer was twenty miles away. At 1 p.m. I came back, and wrote to Sauer an account of what had passed; before I sent it off I received a letter from Sauer. I believe it is wished to be made out that Sauer wrote this letter after he had heard what had passed between Masupha and me. This is not the case, for Sauer, having let me go to Masupha, changed his mind and wrote the letter, but this letter had nothing to do with my interview with Masupha.

With this further quotation of Gordon's own words I may conclude the description of the Basuto mission, which, although deemed a failure at the time, was eventually the direct cause of the present administrative arrangement in that important district of South Africa.

In order you should understand the position of affairs, I recall to your memory the fact that Scanlan, Merriman, and yourself all implied to me doubts of Orpen's policy and your desire to remove him; that I deprecated any such change in my favour; that I accepted the post of Commandant-General on Merriman's statement that the Government desired me to eradicate the red-tape system of the colonial forces; that I made certain reports to the Government upon the settlement of the Basuto question in May and July, showing my views; that the Government were aware of the great difference between my views and those of Orpen, both by letter and verbally to Merriman; also to my objections to go up. Sauer was told by me the same thing. I conversed with him *en route*, and I told him if I visited Masupha I could not afterwards fight him, for I would not go and spy upon his defences. Sauer asked me to go to Masupha; he knew my views; yet when I was there negotiating, he, or rather Orpen, moved Lerothodi to attack Masupha, who would, I believe, have come to terms respecting the acceptance of magistrates, a modified hut-tax, and border police. The reported movement of Lerothodi prevented my coming to any arrangement. I told Masupha, when he sent and told me of Lerothodi's advance, not to answer the Government until the hostile movements had ceased. The Government sent me up, knowing my views, and against my wish, and knowing I was not likely to mince matters. There are not more than two Europeans in Basutoland who believe in Orpen or his policy, while the natives have lost all confidence in him. Sauer shut his eyes to all this, and has thrown in his lot with Orpen. Masupha is a sincere man, and he does not care to have placed with him magistrates, against whom are complaints, which Sauer ignores. To show you I was in earnest, I offered to remain as magistrate with Masupha for two years, so much did I desire a settlement of the Basuto question. I did not want nor would I have taken the post of Governor's Agent. The chiefs and people desire peace, but not at any price. They have intelligence enough to see through wretched magistrates like some of those sent up into the native territories. They will accept a convention like the one I sent down to the Colonial Secretary on the 19th of July, and no other. I do not write this to escape being a scapegoat—in fact, I like the altar—only that you may know my views. As long as the present magistrates stay there, no chance exists for any arrangement. As to the Premier's remark that I would not fight against Masupha, is it likely I could fight against a man with whom I am life and soul? Would I fight against him because he would not be controlled by some men like —— and ——? Even suppose I could sink my conscience to do so, what issue would result from the action of undisciplined and insubordinate troops, who are difficult to keep in order during peace-time, and about whom, when I would have made an example of one officer, a Minister telegraphs to me to let him down easy. I beg to recall to you that Her Majesty's Government disapproved of the former Basuto war; therefore, why should I, who am an outsider to the colony, even pretend I could make war against a noble people, who resist magistrates of no capacity? The Government were well warned by me, and they cannot, therefore, plead being led astray.

Intimately connected with the Basuto question was the larger one of the right treatment to be generally extended to the natives, and on that subject General Gordon drew up, on 19th October 1882, the following masterly note, which elicited the admiration of one of the Cape Premiers, Mr Merriman, who said—"As a Colony we must try to follow out the ideas sketched by General Gordon."

The following is the full text of this interesting and valuable state paper:

The Native Question

1. The native question of South Africa is not a difficult one to an outsider. The difficulty lies in procuring a body of men who will have strength of purpose to carry out a definite policy with respect to the natives.

2. The strained relations which exist between the colonist and the native are the outcome of employing, as a rule, magistrates lacking in tact, sympathy, and capacity to deal with the natives, in the Government not supervising the action of these magistrates, and in condoning their conduct, while acknowledging those faults which come to their cognisance.

3. The Colonial Government act in the nomination of native magistrates as if their duties were such as any one could fulfil, instead of being, as they are, duties requiring the greatest tact and judgment. There can be no doubt but that in a great measure, indeed one may say entirely, disturbances among the natives are caused by the lack of judgment, or of honesty, or of tact, on the part of the magistrates in the native territories. There may be here and there good magistrates, but the defects of the bad ones re-act on the good ones. Revolt is contagious and spreads rapidly among the natives.

4. One may say no supervision, in the full sense of the term, exists over the actions of magistrates in native territories. They report to headquarters what suits them, but unless some very flagrant injustice is brought to light, which is often condoned, the Government know nothing. The consequence is that a continual series of petty injustices rankle in the minds of the natives, eventually breaking out into a revolt, in the midst of which Government does not trouble to investigate the causes of such revolt, but is occupied in its suppression. The history of the South African wars is essentially, as Sir G. Cathcart puts it, Wars undertaken in support of unjustifiable acts. Sir Harry Smith was recalled for supporting an inefficient official of the now Free State Territory. Any one who chooses can investigate the causes of the late wars, and will find out that they arose in a great measure from the ignorance of the Government, their support of incapable officials, and their weakness in not investigating causes before they proceeded to coercion.

5. Government by coercion is essentially rotten. The Duke of Wellington said that any fool could govern by that means. And it

is still more rotten when Government governs by the rule of coercion without the power of coercion except at great expense.

6. A properly constituted Commission of independent men proceeding to the native territories, not accepting the hospitality of those whose conduct they *go* to investigate, not driving through the territories in hot haste, as is the manner of some Ministers, but a Commission who would patiently and fearlessly inquire into every detail of administration, into every grievance, is the *sine quâ non* of any quiet in the native territories. This Commission should detail on brass plates the *modus vivendi*, the limits of territory of each district chief, and a body of trustees should be appointed to watch over any infraction of such charter.

7. It must be borne in mind that these native territories cost the Colony for administration some £9000 per annum for administration of magistracies; the receipts are some £3000, leaving a deficit of some £6000 per annum. To this deficit has to be added some £150,000 for regular troops. The last rebellion of Transkei ended in capture of some £60,000 worth of cattle, and that from natives of Colony driven into rebellion, and cost Government of Colony with Basuto war nearly £4,000,000. It is surely worth while, from a financial point of view, to investigate the administration of the Transkei.

8. The present state of the Transkei is one of seething discontent and distrust which the rivalry of the tribes alone prevents breaking out into action, to be quelled again at great expense and by the ruin of the people, and upset of all enterprise to open up the country. Throughout the Transkei is one general clamour against the Government for broken promises, for promises made and never kept. Magistrates complain no answers are given to their questions; things are allowed to drift along as best they can. A fair open policy towards the Pondos would obtain from them all the Colony could require, but as things are now, the Pondos are full of distrust, and only want the chance to turn against the Colony. There are in Transkei 399,000 natives, and 2800 Europeans. Therefore, for the benefit of these 2800 Europeans, 399,000 natives are made miserable, and an expenditure of £210,000 is incurred by the Colony with the probability of periodical troubles.

9. However disagreeable it might be, the Commission of Investigation should inquire into the antecedents of each magistrate, and also his capabilities.

10. With respect to Basutoland, it is understood that no revenue from that country is to go to the Colony, therefore it can be no object to Colony to insist on the installation of magistrates in that country. If the magistrates of Transkei are the cause of discontent among the natives, then what object is there in insisting on their installation in Basutoland? The Pondos, a far inferior people, are happy under their own chiefs—far happier than the natives of Transkei. Why should the Colony insist on sending men who are more likely to goad the Basutos into rebellion than anything else? The administration of Basutoland is on a scale costing £30,000 per annum.

11. It is argued that should the Colony go to war with Masupha the other chiefs would hold aloof. This is quite erroneous. A war with Masupha means a war with the Basuto nation, with a rising in the Transkei, and perhaps in Pondoland, and would affect Natal and Her Majesty's Government.

12. The only remedy is the sending up of his Excellency the Governor, or of some high neutral officer, to Basutoland, and the calling together of the people to decide on their future government and connection with Colony. Or, should the British Government refuse this small concession, which could not involve it, then the Colony should send up an independent Commission to meet the Basuto people, and arrange a *modus vivendi*. Whichever course is followed it is a *sine quâ non* that the present officials in Basutoland should be relieved at once, as they have lost the confidence both of Europeans and natives. The Basutos desire peace, and it is an error to describe their demeanour as aggressive. It is not unnatural that after what they have suffered from the hands of Colonial Government they should desire at least as nearly as much self-government as the Pondos enjoy. Certainly the present magisterial administration of the Transkei is very far from being a blessing, or conducive to peace.

13. Nothing can possibly be worse than the present state of affairs in native administration, and the interests of the Colony demand a vertebrate government of some sort, whoever it may be composed of, instead of the invertebrate formation that is now called a government, and which drifts into and creates its own difficulties.

C. G. Gordon
October 19, 1882

P.S.—Should Her Majesty's Government manage to arrange with Basutos in a satisfactory manner, 10,000 splendid cavalry could be counted on as allies in any contingencies in Natal, etc.

The vital part of Gordon's Cape experiences was the Basuto mission, and as it is desirable that it should not be obscured by other matters, I will only touch briefly on his work as Commandant-General, apart from that he performed as Adviser to the Cape Government in the Basuto difficulty. The post of Commandant-General was forced upon him in the first weeks of his arrival from the Mauritius by the combined urgency of Sir Hercules Robinson, the Governor, and Mr Merriman, then Premier. Much against his inclination, Gordon agreed to fill the post thus thrust upon him, but only for a time. It entailed an infinity of work and worry. His instructions were to break up a red-tape system, and such a task converted every place-holder into his enemy. Still that opposition rather made his task attractive than otherwise, but in a little time he found that this opposition would not stop short of insubordination, and that to achieve success it would be necessary to cashier a good many officers as a wholesome example. It was while matters were in this preliminary stage that Mr Merriman's ministry went out of office, and was succeeded by another under Mr Scanlan. The measures which were favoured by the one were opposed by the other, and Gordon soon saw that the desire for a thorough reorganisation of the Cape forces, which, if properly supported, he could have carried out, was no longer prevalent among the responsible Ministers. Still he drew up an elaborate programme for the improvement of the Colonial Regular forces, by which they might be increased in numbers and improved in efficiency, at the same time that the annual expenditure was reduced. This document shows that mastery of detail which was one of his most striking characteristics, and if his advice had been taken, the Cape would have acquired nearly 4000 troops at no greater cost than it already expended on 1600. In a second memorandum, he not only showed the necessity existing for that larger force, but also how, by administrative alterations in the Transkeian provinces, its cost might be diminished and most conveniently discharged. Although I do not quote these two documents, I cannot help saying that Gordon, in the whole course of his life, never wrote anything more convincing than the advice he gave the Cape Government, which, owing to local jealousies and the invincible bulwark of vested interests, was never carried into effect, although the Basuto question was subsequently composed on Gordon's lines by the Imperial Government, and there has been peace there during all the other South African troubles.

The closing passages between Gordon and the Cape Ministers need only be briefly referred to. Gordon resigned because he saw he could do no good in Basutoland; the Cape Premier accepted his resignation because Gordon "would not fight the Basutos." The intercommunications were much more numerous, but that is their pith. Gordon came down to Cape Town and sailed for England on 14th October, after having been five and a half months in South Africa. He had been treated by the Cape authorities without any regard for justice, and little for courtesy. The leading paper even admitted this much when it observed that "at least General Gordon was entitled to the treatment of a gentleman." But the plain truth was that Gordon was summoned to South Africa and employed by the Government, not as was ostentatiously proclaimed, and as he himself believed, for the attainment of a just solution of the Basuto difficulty, and for the execution of much-needed military reforms, but in order that his military experience and genius might be invoked for the purpose of overthrowing Masupha and of annexing Basutoland, which two years of war and five millions of money had failed to conquer. Hence their disappointment and resentment when Gordon proclaimed that justice was on the side of Masupha; that under no circumstances would he wage war with him; and that the whole origin of the trouble lay in the bad policy, the incompetent magistrates, and the insubordinate military officers of the Cape Government. The indictment was a terrible one; it was also true in every line and every particular.

Having thus vindicated his own character, as well as the highest principles of Government, Gordon left the Cape a poorer and a wiser man than he was on his arrival. I have explained the personal loss he incurred through the inadequacy of his pay and the cutting-off of his army allowance. It has been stated that when he had taken his passage for England he was without any money in his pocket, and that he quaintly said to a friend: "Do you think it is right for a Major-General of the British Army to set out on a journey like this without sixpence in his pocket?" There is nothing improbable in such an occurrence, and it was matched only sixteen months later, when he was on the point of starting for Khartoum in the same impecunious condition.

Gordon arrived in England on 8th November, and after some correspondence with the King of the Belgians, which will be referred to later in connection with the Congo mission, he again left England on

26th December. On this occasion he was going to carry out a long-cherished desire to visit and reside in the Holy Land, so that he might study on the spot the scenes with which his perfect knowledge of the Bible—his inseparable companion—had made him in an extraordinary degree familiar. In the best sense of the word, he was going to take a holiday. There was to be absolute quiet and rest, and at the same time a congenial occupation. He sailed for Jaffa as a guest on one of Sir William Mackinnon's steamers, but he at once proceeded to Jerusalem, where he lived alone, refusing to see any one, with his books as companions, and "mystifying people as to what he was doing." During his stay at Jerusalem he entered with much zest and at great length into the questions of the various sites in the old Jewish capital. I do not propose to follow the course of his labours in that pursuit, as several works contain between them, I should say, every line he wrote on the subject, and the general reader cannot be expected to take any interest in abstruse and much-debated theological and topographical questions. But even in the midst of these pursuits he did not lose his quickness of military perception. After a brief inspection he at once declared that the Russian Convent commanded the whole city, and was in itself a strong fortress, capable of holding a formidable garrison, which Russia could despatch in the guise of priests without any one being the wiser. From Jerusalem, when the heat became great, he returned to Jaffa, and his interest aroused in worldly matters by the progress of events in Egypt, and the development of the Soudan danger, which he had all along seen coming, was evoked by a project that was brought under his notice for the construction across Palestine of a canal to the head of the Gulf of Akabah. In a letter to myself he thus dilates upon the scheme:

Here is the subject which I am interested in if it could be done. The reasons are:

1. We are in Egypt supporting an unpopular sovereign, whose tenure ends with departure of our troops. We offer no hope to the people of any solace by this support, and by the supporting of the Turco-Circassian Pashas, who I know by experience are *hopeless*. We neither govern nor take responsibility; yet we support these vampires.

2. We are getting mixed up with the question of whether the interest of £90,000,000 will be paid or not.

3. We are mixed up with the Soudan, where we provoked the rebellion, and of the responsibility of which government we cannot rid ourselves.

4. We are in constant and increasing hot water with the French, and we gain no benefit from it, for the Canal will remain theirs.

* * * * * * * *

On the other hand, if we get a Firman from Sultan for the Palestine Canal—

1. We lose the sacred sites of Jordan River, Capernaum, Bethsaida, and Tiberias, Jericho, not Engedi.

2. We swamp a notoriously unhealthy valley, where there are no missions.

3. We cut off the pest of the country of Palestine, the Bedouins.

4. We are free of all four objections *in re* occupation of Egypt.

5. We gain the fertile lands of Moab and Ammon.

6. Cyprus is 150 miles from the Mediterranean *débouché*.

7. We get a waterway for large ships to within fifty miles of Damascus.

8. We can never be bothered by any internal commotion, except for the twenty-five miles from Haifa to Tiberias, for the waterway of the Canal would be ten miles wide, except in Arabah Valley, where there are on both sides wastes and deserts.

9. We get rid of unhealthiness of a narrow cut with no current, which is the case with Suez Canal now, where the mud is pestilential from ships' refuse and no current.

10. It would isolate Palestine, render it quiet from Bedouins; it would pave the way to its being like Belgium, under no Great Power, for religious views would be against Palestine ever being owned by a Great Power.

11. Up the ladder of Tyre to Gaza would be 10,000 square miles; population 130,000, quite a small country.

Do not quote me if you write this. Oddly enough, Ezekiel xlvii. 10 seems to say the Dead Sea shall have fish like the great Sea (*i.e.* Mediterranean). Zechariah xiv. speaks of two rivers, one going to Dead Sea, the other to Mediterranean. The cost would be—

Canal from Haifa to Jordan	£2,000,000
Compensation to Jordan peoples	£1,000,000
Canal through Akabah	£6,000,000
Ports at Haifa	£1,000,000
Ports at Akabah	£500,000
Total	£10,500,000

Say, twelve to fifteen millions, and what a comfort to be free of Egypt and Soudan for ever!

Revenue, Palestine, £120,000, of which £80,000 goes to Sultan. Do not quote *me*, for I have written part of this to Mr W. (the late Sir William) Mackinnon of B.I.S.N.C., besides which H.M. Government may object. You may say you had a letter from a correspondent.

He wrote in a similar strain to other correspondents, but I have never succeeded in discovering whether, from an engineering point of view, the scheme was at all feasible. It seems to me that its suggestion is somewhat destructive of Gordon's own declarations as to the superior merits of the Cape route, nor does Sir Henry Gordon much strengthen the case when, perceiving the inconsistency, he goes out of his way to declare that Gordon only meant the Palestine canal to be a commercial route. Any attempt to limit its usefulness could not destroy the character claimed for it by its promoters, as an equally short and more secure route than that by Suez. Yet it needs no gift of second sight to predict that when any project of rivalry to the masterpiece of Lesseps is carried out, it will be by rail to the Persian Gulf, whether the starting-point be the Bosphorus or the Levant.

In the midst of his interesting researches near Mount Carmel, a summons from the outer world reached Gordon in the form of a letter from Sir William Mackinnon, telling him that the King of the Belgians now called on him to fulfil a promise he had made some years before.

When Gordon first returned from the Cape the King of the Belgians wrote, reminding him of his old promise, dating from 1880, to enter into his service on the Congo, and stating that the difficulty of having an internationally recognised Congo flag, which Gordon had made a *sine quâ non* of his appointment, could be most speedily solved by Gordon joining him as counsellor at once. This Gordon could not agree to, and he went to Palestine, there to await the King's summons, which came by Sir William Mackinnon's note in October 1883. It then became necessary for Gordon to obtain the official permission of his Government to take up this post, of the exact nature of which the Foreign Office had been already informed, both by General Gordon and King Leopold.

Gordon at once telegraphed to the War Office for the leave rendered necessary by his being on the active list, and that Department replied, asking for particulars. When these were furnished through the Foreign Office the decision was announced that "the Secretary of State declines to sanction your employment on the Congo." The telegraph clerk, more discerning or considerate than Her Majesty's Government, altered "declines" into "decides," and Gordon, in happy ignorance of the truth, proceeded with all possible despatch *via* Acre and Genoa to Brussels, which he reached on New Year's Day, 1884. That very night he wrote me a short note saying, "I go (*D. V.*) next month to the Congo, but keep it secret." Such things cannot be kept secret, and four days later a leading article in *The Times* informed his countrymen of Gordon's new mission.

On reaching Brussels the mistake in the telegram was discovered, and Gordon here learnt that his Congo mission was vetoed. Then came the difficulty to know what was to be done. Without leave he could not go anywhere without resigning his commission; he was not qualified for a pension, and there were engagements he had voluntarily contracted that he would not see broken, and persons who would suffer by his death, whose interests he was in every way bound to safeguard. Therefore, if he was to carry out his engagement with the King of the Belgians, it was obviously necessary that he should resign the British Army, and that the King should compensate him for his loss. The King said at once: "Retire from the army and I will compensate you," but in a matter of such importance to others Gordon felt nothing should be left to chance, and that a definite contract should be made. For this he had neither the patience nor the business knowledge, and he delegated the task of arranging the matter to his brother, Sir Henry Gordon, who negotiated with the late Sir William Mackinnon as representing the King. They agreed that the value of Gordon's pension if commuted would be £7288, and the King of the Belgians was to provide that sum, which was to be paid into a trust fund. In this and every other matter the King behaved towards Gordon in the most generous and cordial manner, furnishing a marked contrast with the grudging and parsimonious spirit of the British Government towards Gordon in China, at the Cape, and now again when destined for the Congo.

All the arrangements connected with this subject were made in three days, and while Gordon gave instructions for his will to be prepared for the disposal of the trust fund after his death, he wrote the same day (6th January) to Mr H. M. Stanley, then acting for the King on the Congo, announcing his own appointment, offering to "serve willingly with or under him," and fixing his own departure from Lisbon for 5th of February. *Dis aliter visum.* For the moment he worked up some enthusiasm in his task. "We will kill the slave-traders in their haunts"; and again, "No such efficacious means of cutting at root of slave trade ever was presented as that which God has, I trust, opened out to us through the kind disinterestedness of His Majesty," are passages in the same letter, yet all the time there is no doubt his heart and his thoughts were elsewhere. They were in the Soudan, not on the Congo.

The night of this letter he crossed from Brussels, and went straight to his sister's house, long the residence, and, practically speaking, the home of his family, 5 Rockstone Place, Southampton. On the 7th of the month—that is, the same day as he arrived—he wrote the formal letter requesting leave to resign his commission in the Queen's army, and also stating, with his usual candour, that King Leopold II. had guaranteed him against any pecuniary loss. To that letter it may at once be stated that no reply was ever sent. Even the least sympathetic official could not feel altogether callous to a voluntary proposition to remove the name of "Chinese" Gordon from the British army list, and the sudden awakening of the public to the extraordinary claims of General Gordon on national gratitude, and his special fitness to deal with the Soudan difficulty warned the authorities that a too rigid application of office rules would not in his case be allowed. By no individual effort, as has been too lightly granted by some writers, but by the voice of the British people was it decided that not only should Gordon have leave to go to the Congo, without resigning his commission, but also that he should be held entitled to draw his pay as a British general while thus employed. But this was not the whole truth, although I have no doubt that the arrangement would have been carried out in any case. In their dilemma the Government saw a chance of extrication in the person of Gordon, the one man recognised by the public and the press as capable of coping with a difficulty which seemed too much for them. The whole truth, therefore, was that the Congo mission was to wait until after Gordon had been sent to, and returned from, the Soudan. He was then to be placed by the British Government entirely at the disposal of the King of the Belgians. As this new arrangement turned on the assent of the King, it was vital to keep it secret during the remainder of the 15th and the whole of the 16th of that eventful January.

When Gordon arrived at Waterloo Station, at a little before two o'clock on 15th January, and was met there by myself, I do not think that he knew definitely what was coming, but he was a man of extraordinary shrewdness, and although essentially unworldly, could see as clearly and as far through a transaction as the keenest man of business. What he did know was that the army authorities were going to treat him well, but his one topic of conversation the whole way to Pall Mall was not the Congo but the Soudan. To the direct question whether he was not really going, as I suspected, to the Nile instead of the Congo, he declared he had no information that would warrant such an idea, but still, if the King of the Belgians would grant the permission, he would certainly not be disinclined to go there first. I have no doubt that those who acted in the name of the Ministry in a few minutes discovered the true state of his mind, and that Gordon then and there agreed, on the express request of the Government of Mr Gladstone, to go and see the King, and beg him to suspend the execution of his promise until he had gone to the Soudan to arrest the Mahdi's career, or to relieve the Egyptian garrisons, if the phrase be preferred. It should also be stated that Gordon's arrangement with the King of the Belgians was always coupled with this proviso, "provided the Government of my own country does not require my services." The generosity of that sovereign in the matter of the compensation for his Commission did not render that condition void, and however irritating the King may have found the circumstances, Gordon broke neither the spirit nor the letter of his engagement with his Majesty by obeying the orders of his own Government.

Late the same evening I was present at his brother's house to receive an account for publication of his plans on the Congo, but surrounded by so large a number of his relatives summoned to see their hero, many of them for the last time, it was neither convenient nor possible to carry out this task, which was accordingly postponed till the following morning, when I was to see him at the Charing Cross Hotel, and accompany him by the early boat train to Dover. On that night his last will was signed and witnessed by his uncle, Mr George Enderby, and myself. The next morning I was at the hotel before seven, but instead of travelling by this early train, he postponed his departure till ten o'clock, and the greater part of those three hours were given to an explanation, map in hand, of his plans on the Congo. The article, based on his information, appeared in *The Times* of 17th January 1884, but several times during our conversation he exclaimed, "There may be a respite," but he refused to be more definite. Thus he set out for Brussels, whether he was accompanied by his friend Captain (now Colonel) F. Brocklehurst, who was undoubtedly acting as the representative of the authorities. I believe I may say with confidence that if he did not actually see the King of the Belgians on the evening of the same day, some communication passed indirectly, which showed the object of his errand, for although his own letter communicating the event is dated 17th, from Brussels, it is a fact within my own knowledge that late in the evening of the 16th a telegram was received—"Gordon goes to the Soudan."

The first intimation of something having happened that his brother Sir Henry Gordon received, was in a hurried letter, dated 17th January, which arrived by the early post on Friday, 18th, asking him to "get his uniform ready and some patent leather boots," but adding, "I saw King Leopold today; he is furious." Even then Sir Henry, although he guessed his destination, did not know that his departure would be so sudden, for Gordon crossed the same night, and was kept at Knightsbridge Barracks in a sort of honourable custody by Captain Brocklehurst, so that the new scheme might not be prematurely revealed. Sir Henry, a busy man, went about his own work, having seen to his brother's commission, and it was not until his return at five o'clock that he learnt all, and that Gordon was close at hand. He at once hurried off to see him, and on meeting, Gordon, in a high state of exhilaration, exclaimed, "I am off to the Soudan." Sir Henry asked "When?" and back came the reply, "Tonight!" He had got his respite.

To him at that moment it meant congenial work and the chance of carrying out the thoughts that had been surging through his mind ever since Egyptian affairs became troubled and the Mahdi's power rose on the horizon of the Soudan. The reality was to prove far different. He was to learn in his own person the weakness and falseness of his Government, and to find himself betrayed by the very persons who had only sought his assistance in the belief that by a miracle— and nothing less would have sufficed—he might relieve them from responsibilities to which they were not equal. Far better would it have been, not only for Gordon's sake, but even for the reputation of England, if he had carried out his original project on the Congo, where, on a less conspicuous scene than the Nile, he might still have fought and won the battle of humanity.

I am placed in a position to state that on the morning of the 17th, at 10 a.m., he wrote to his sister from Brussels, as follows—"Do not mention it, but there is just a chance I may have to go to Soudan for two months, and then go to Congo," and again in a second letter at two o'clock, "Just got a telegram from Wolseley saying, 'Come back to London by evening train,' so when you get this I shall be in town, *but keep it a dead secret*, for I hope to leave it again the same evening. I will not take Governor-Generalship again, I will only report on situation." After this came a post-card—18th January, 6 a.m. "Left B., am now in London; I hope to go back again tonight." That very night he left for Egypt.

That he was not detained the whole day in the Barracks is shown in the following letter, now published for the first time, which gives the only account of his interview with the members of the Government that sent him out:

19th January, 1884

My Dear Augusta,—I arrived in town very tired, at 6 a.m. yesterday, went with Brocklehurst to Barracks, washed, and went to Wolseley. He said Ministers would see me at 3 p.m. I went back to Barracks and reposed. At 12.30 p.m. Wolseley came for me. I went with him and saw Granville, Hartington, Dilke, and Northbrook. They said, 'Had I seen Wolseley, and did I understand their ideas?' I said 'Yes,' and repeated what Wolseley had said to me as to their ideas, which was *they would evacuate Soudan.*' They were pleased, and said 'That was their idea; would I go?' I said 'Yes.' They said 'When?' I said 'Tonight,' and it was over. I started at 8 p.m. H.R.H. The Duke of Cambridge and Lord Wolseley came to see me off. I saw Henry and Bob (R. F. Gordon); no one else except Stokes—all very kind. I have taken Stewart with me, a nice fellow. We are now in train near Mont Cenis. I am not moved a bit, and hope to do the people good. Lord Granville said Ministers were very much obliged to me. I said I was much honoured by going. I telegraphed King of the Belgians at once, and told him 'Wait a few months.' Kindest love to all.—Your affectionate brother,
C. G. Gordon

As further evidence of the haste of his departure, I should like to mention that he had hardly any clothes with him, and that Mrs Watson, wife of his friend Colonel Watson, procured him all he required—in fact, fitted him out—during the two days he stayed at Cairo. These kindly efforts on his behalf were thrown away, for all his baggage—clothes, uniforms, orders, etc.—was captured with the money at Berber and never reached him. His only insignia of office at Khartoum was the Fez, and the writer who described him as putting on his uniform when the Mahdists broke into the town was gifted with more imagination than love of truth.

CHAPTER 11

The Last Nile Mission

When Gordon left Egypt, at the end of the year 1879, he was able to truthfully declare in the words of his favourite book: "No man could lift his hand or his foot in the land of the Soudan without me." Yet he was fully alive to the dangers of the future, although then they were no more than a little cloud on the horizon, for he wrote in 1878:

> Our English Government lives on a hand-to-mouth policy. They are very ignorant of these lands, yet some day or other, they or some other Government, will have to know them, for things at Cairo cannot stay as they are. The Khedive will be curbed in, and will no longer be absolute Sovereign. Then will come the question of these countries. . . . There is no doubt that if the Governments of France and England do not pay more attention to the Soudan—if they do not establish at Khartoum a branch of the mixed tribunals, and see that justice is done— the disruption of the Soudan from Cairo is only a question of time. This disruption, moreover, will not end the troubles, for the Soudanese through their allies in Lower Egypt—the black soldiers I mean—will carry on their efforts in Cairo itself. Now these black soldiers are the only troops in the Egyptian service that are worth anything.

The gift of prophecy could scarcely have been demonstrated in a more remarkable degree, yet the Egyptian Government and every-body else went on acting as if there was no danger in the Soudan, and treated it like a thoroughly conquered province inhabited by a satisfied, or at least a thoroughly subjected population. From this dream there was to be a rude and startling awakening.

It is impossible to say whether there was any connection direct or indirect between the revolt of Arabi Pasha and the military leaders at Cairo and the rebellion in the Soudan, which began under the auspices of the so-called Mahdi. At the very least it may be asserted that the spectacle of successful insubordination in the Delta—for it was completely successful, and would have continued so but for the intervention of British arms—was calculated to encourage those who entertained a desire to upset the Khedive's authority in the upper regions of the Nile. That Gordon held that the authors of the Arabi rising and of the Mahdist movement were the same in sympathy, if not in person, cannot be doubted, and in February 1882, when the Mahdi had scarcely begun his career, he wrote:

> If they send the Black regiment to the Soudan to quell the revolt, they will inoculate all the troops up there, and the Soudan will revolt against Cairo, whom they all hate.

It will be noted that that letter was written more than twenty months before the destruction of the Hicks Expedition made the Mahdi master of the Soudan.

It was in the year 1880 that the movements of a Mahommedan dervish, named Mahomed Ahmed, first began to attract the attention of the Egyptian officials. He had quarrelled with and repudiated the authority of the head of his religious order, because he tolerated such frivolous practices as dancing and singing. His boldness in this matter, and his originality in others, showed that he was pursuing a course of his own, and to provide for his personal security, as well as for convenience in keeping up his communications with Khartoum and other places, he fixed his residence on an islet in the White Nile near Kawa. Mahomed Ahmed was a native of the lower province of Dongola, and as such was looked upon with a certain amount of contempt by the other races of the Soudan. When he quarrelled with his religious leader he was given the opprobrious name of "a wretched Dongolawi," but the courage with which he defied and exposed an arch-priest for not rigidly abiding by the tenets of the Koran, redounded so much to his credit that the people began to talk of this wonderful dervish quite as much as of the Khedive's Governor-General. Many earnest and energetic Mahommedans flocked to him, and among these was the present Khalifa Abdullah, whose life had been spared by Zebehr, and who in return had wished to proclaim that leader of the slave-hunters Mahdi. To his instigation was probably due not merely the assumption of that title by Mahomed Ahmed, but the addition of a worldly policy to what was to have been a strictly religious propaganda.

Little as he deemed there was to fear from this ascetic, the Egyptian

Governor-General Raouf, Gordon's successor, and stigmatised by him as the Tyrant of Harrar, became curious about him, and sent someone to interview and report upon this new religious teacher. The report brought back was that he was "a madman," and it was at once considered safe to treat him with indifference. Such was the position in the year 1880, and the official view was only modified a year later by the receipt of information that the gathering on the island of Abba had considerably increased, and that Mahomed Ahmed was attended by an armed escort, who stood in his presence with drawn swords. It was at this time too that he began to declare that he had a divine mission, and took unto himself the style of Mahdi—the long-expected messenger who was to raise up Islam—at first secretly among his chosen friends, but not so secretly that news of his bold step did not reach the ears of Raouf. The assumption of such a title, which placed its holder above and beyond the reach of such ordinary commands as are conveyed in the edicts of a Khedive or a Sultan, convinced Raouf that the time had come to put an end to these pretensions. That conviction was not diminished when Mahomed Ahmed made a tour through Kordofan, spreading a knowledge of his name and intentions, and undoubtedly winning over many adherents to his cause. On his return to Abba he found a summons from the Governor-General to come to Khartoum. That summons was followed by the arrival of a steamer, the captain of which had orders to capture the False Mahdi alive or dead.

Mahomed Ahmed received warning from his friends and sympathisers that if he went to Khartoum he might consider himself a dead man. He probably never had the least intention of going there, and what he had seen of the state of feeling in the Soudan, where the authority of the Khedive was neither popular nor firmly established, rendered him more inclined to defy the Egyptians. When the delegate of Raouf Pasha therefore appeared before him, Mahomed Ahmed was surrounded by such an armed force as precluded the possibility of a violent seizure of his person, and when he resorted to argument to induce him to come to Khartoum, Mahomed Ahmed, throwing off the mask, and standing forth in the self-imposed character of Mahdi, exclaimed: "By the grace of God and His Prophet I am the master of this country, and never shall I go to Khartoum to justify myself."

After this picturesque defiance it only remained for him and the Egyptians to prove which was the stronger.

It must be admitted that Raouf at once recognised the gravity of the affair, and without delay he sent a small force on Gordon's old steamer, the *Ismailia*, to bring Mahomed Ahmed to reason. This was in

August 1881. By its numbers and the superior armament of the troops this expedition should have proved a complete success, and a competent commander would have strangled the Mahdist phenomenon at its birth. Unfortunately the Egyptian officers were grossly incompetent, and divided among themselves. They attempted a night attack, and as they were quite ignorant of the locality, it is not surprising that they fell into the very trap they thought to set for their opponents.

In the confusion the divided Egyptian forces fired upon each other, and the Mahdists with their swords and short stabbing spears completed the rest. Of two whole companies of troops only a handful escaped by swimming to the steamer, which returned to Khartoum with the news of this defeat. Even this reverse was very far from ensuring the triumph of Mahomed Ahmed, or the downfall of the Egyptian power; and, indeed, the possession of steamers and the consequent command of the Nile navigation rendered it extremely doubtful whether he could long hold his own on the island of Abba. He thought so himself, and, gathering his forces together, marched to the western districts of Kordofan, where, at Jebel Gedir, he established his headquarters. A special reason made him select that place, for it is believed by Mahommedans that the Mahdi will first appear at Jebel Masa in North Africa, and Mahomed Ahmed had no scruple in declaring that the two places were the same. To complete the resemblance he changed with autocratic pleasure the name Jebel Gedir into Jebel Masa.

During this march several attempts were made to capture him by the local garrisons, but they were all undertaken in such a half-hearted manner, and so badly carried out, that the Mahdi was never in any danger, and his reputation was raised by the failure of the Government.

Once established at Jebel Gedir the Mahdi began to organise his forces on a larger scale, and to formulate a policy that would be likely to bring all the tribes of the Soudan to his side. While thus employed Rashed Bey, Governor of Fashoda, resolved to attack him. Rashed is entitled to the credit of seeing that the time demanded a signal, and if possible, a decisive blow, but he is to be censured for the carelessness and over-confidence he displayed in carrying out his scheme. Although he had a strong force he should have known that the Mahdi's followers were now numbered by the thousand, and that he was an active and enterprising foe. But he neglected the most simple precautions, and showed that he had no military skill. The Mahdi fell upon him during his march, killed him, his chief officers, and 1400 men, and the small body that escaped bore testimony to the formidable character of the victor's fighting power. This battle was fought on 9th

December 1881, and the end of that year therefore beheld the firm establishment of the Mahdi's power in a considerable part of the Soudan; but even then the superiority of the Egyptian resources was so marked and incontestable that, properly handled, they should have sufficed to speedily overwhelm him.

At this juncture Raouf was succeeded as Governor-General by Abd-el-Kader Pasha, who had held the same post before Gordon, and who had gained something of a reputation from the conquest of Darfour, in conjunction with Zebehr. At least he ought to have known the Soudan, but the dangers which had been clear to the eye of Gordon were concealed from him and his colleagues. Still, the first task he set himself—and indeed it was the justification of his re-appointment—was to retrieve the disaster to Rashed, and to destroy the Mahdi's power. He therefore collected a force of not less than 4000 men, chiefly trained infantry, and he entrusted the command to Yusuf Pasha, a brave officer, who had distinguished himself under Gessi in the war with Suleiman. This force left Khartoum in March 1882, but it did not begin its inland march from the Nile until the end of May, when it had been increased by at least 2000 irregular levies raised in Kordofan. Unfortunately, Yusuf was just as over-confident as Rashed had been. He neglected all precautions, and derided the counsel of those who warned him that the Mahdi's followers might prove a match for his well-armed and well-drilled troops. After a ten days' march he reached the neighbourhood of the Mahdi's position, and he was already counting on a great victory, when, at dawn of day on 7th June, he was himself surprised by his opponent in a camp that he had ostentatiously refused to fortify in the smallest degree. The Egyptian force was annihilated. Some of the local irregulars escaped, but of the regular troops and their commanders not one. This decisive victory not merely confirmed the reputation of the Mahdi, and made most people in the Soudan believe that he was really a heaven-sent champion, but it also exposed the inferiority of the Government troops and the Khedive's commanders.

The defeat of Yusuf may be said to have been decisive so far as the active forces of the Khedive in the field were concerned, but the towns held out, and El Obeid, the capital of Kordofan, in particular defied all the Mahdi's efforts to take it. The possession of this and other strong places furnished the supporters of the Government with a reasonable hope that on the arrival of fresh troops the ground lost might be recovered, and an end put to what threatened to become a formidable rebellion. A lull consequently ensued in the struggle. Unfortunately, it was one that the Mahdi turned to the best advantage by drilling and arming his troops, and summoning levies from the more distant parts of the provinces, while the Khedive's Government, engrossed in troubles nearer home—the Arabi revolt and the intervention of England in the internal administration—seemed paralysed in its efforts to restore its authority over the Soudan, which at that moment would have been comparatively easy. The only direct result of Yusuf's defeat in June 1882 was that two of the Black regiments were sent up to Khartoum, and as their allegiance to the Government was already shaken, their presence, as Gordon apprehended, was calculated to aggravate rather than to improve the situation.

Matters remained very much in this state until the Mahdi's capture of the important town of El Obeid. Notwithstanding the presence within the walls of an element favourable to the Mahdi, the Commandant, Said Pasha, made a valiant and protracted defence. He successfully repelled all the Mahdi's attempts to take the place by storm, but he had to succumb to famine after all the privations of a five months' siege. If there had been other men like Said Pasha, especially at Khartoum, the power of the Mahdi would never have risen to the height it attained. The capture of an important place like El Obeid did more for the spread of the Mahdi's reputation and power than the several victories he had gained in the field. This important event took place in January 1883. Abd-el-Kader was then removed from the Governor-Generalship, and a successor found in Alla-ed-din, a man of supposed energy and resource. More than that, an English officer—Colonel Hicks—was given the military command, and it was decided to despatch an expedition of sufficient strength, as it was thought, to crush the Mahdi at one blow.

The preparations for this fresh advance against the Mahdi were made with care, and on an extensive scale. Several regiments were sent from Egypt, and in the spring of the year a permanent camp was established for their accommodation at Omdurman, on the western bank of the Nile, opposite Khartoum. Here, by the end of June 1883, was assembled a force officially computed to number 7000 infantry, 120 cuirassiers, 300 irregular cavalry, and not fewer than 30 pieces of artillery, including rockets and mortars. Colonel Hicks was given the nominal command, several English and other European officers were appointed to serve under him, and the Khedive specially ordered the Governor-General to accompany the expedition that was to put an end to the Mahdi's triumph. Such was the interest, and, it may be added, confidence, felt in the expedition, that two special correspondents, one of whom was Edmond O'Donovan, who had made himself famous a few years earlier by reaching the Turcoman stronghold of Merv, were ordered to accompany it, and report its achievements.

The Mahdi learnt in good time of the extensive preparations being made for this expedition, but he was not dismayed, because all the fighting tribes of Kordofan, Bahr Gazelle, and Darfour were now at his back, and he knew that he could count on the devotion of 100,000 fanatical warriors. Still, he and his henchman Abdullah, who supplied the military brains to the cause, were not disposed to throw away a chance, and the threatening appearance of the Egyptian military preparations led them to conceive the really brilliant idea of stirring up trouble in the rear of Khartoum. For this purpose a man of extraordinary energy and influence was ready to their hand in Osman Digma, a slave-dealer of Souakim, who might truly be called the Zebehr of the Eastern Soudan. This man hastened to Souakim as the delegate of the Mahdi, from whom he brought special proclamations, calling on the tribes to rise for a Holy War. Although this move subsequently aggravated the Egyptian position and extended the military triumphs of the Mahdi, it did not attain the immediate object for which it was conceived, as the Hicks Expedition set out on its ill-omened march before Osman had struck a blow.

The power of the Mahdi was at this moment so firmly established, and his reputation based on the double claim of a divine mission and military success so high that it may be doubted whether the 10,000 men, of which the Hicks force consisted when the irregulars raised by the Governor-General had joined it at Duem, would have sufficed to overcome him even if they had been ably led, and escaped all the untoward circumstances that first retarded their progress and then sealed their fate. The plan of campaign was based on a misconception of the Mahdi's power, and was carried out with utter disregard of prudence and of the local difficulties to be encountered between the Nile and El Obeid. But the radical fault of the whole enterprise was a strategical one. The situation made it prudent and even necessary for the Government to stand on the defensive, and to abstain from military expeditions, while the course pursued was to undertake offensive measures in the manner most calculated to favour the chances of the Mahdi, and to attack him at the very point where his superiority could be most certainly shown.

But quite apart from any original error as to the inception of the campaign, which may fairly be deemed a matter of opinion, there can be no difference between any two persons who have studied the facts that the execution of it was completely mismanaged. In the first place the start of the expedition was delayed, so that the Mahdi got ample warning of the coming attack. The troops were all in the camp at Omdurman in June, but they did not reach Duem till September, and a further delay of two months occurred there before they began their march towards El Obeid. That interval was chiefly taken up with disputes between Hicks and his Egyptian colleagues, and it is even believed that there was much friction between Hicks and his European lieutenants.

The first radical error committed was the decision to advance on El Obeid from Duem, because there were no wells on that route, whereas had the northern route *via* Gebra and Bara been taken, a certain supply of water could have been counted on, and still more important, the co-operation of the powerful Kabbabish tribe, the only one still hostile to the Mahdi, might have been secured. The second important error was not less fatal. When the force marched it was accompanied by 6000 camels and a large number of women. Encumbered in its movements by these useless impedimenta, the force never had any prospect of success with its active enemy. As it slowly advanced from the Nile it became with each day's march more hopelessly involved in its own difficulties, and the astute Mahdi expressly forbade any premature attack to be made upon an army which he clearly saw was marching to its doom.

On the 1st November 1883, when the Egyptians were already disheartened by the want of water, the non-arrival of reinforcements from the garrisons near the Equator, which the Governor-General had rashly promised to bring up, and the exhausting nature of their march through a difficult country, the Mahdi's forces began their attack. Concealed in the high grass, they were able to pour in a heavy fire on the conspicuous body of the Egyptians at short range without exposing themselves. But notwithstanding his heavy losses, Hicks pressed on, because he knew that his only chance of safety lay in getting out of the dense cover in which he was at such a hopeless disadvantage. But this the Mahdi would never permit, and on 4th November, when Hicks had reached a place called Shekan, he gave the order to his impatient followers to go in and finish the work they had so well begun. The Egyptian soldiers seem to have been butchered without resistance. The Europeans and the Turkish cavalry fought well for a short time, but in a few minutes they were overpowered by superior numbers. Of the whole force of 10,000 men, only a few individuals escaped by some special stroke of fortune, for nearly the whole of the 300 prisoners taken were subsequently executed. Such was the complete and appalling character of the destruction of Hicks's army, which seemed to shatter at a single blow the whole fabric of the Khedive's power in the Soudan, and riveted the attention of Europe on that particular quarter of the Dark Continent.

The consequences of that decisive success, which became known in London three weeks after it happened, were immediate throughout the region wherein it occurred. Many Egyptian garrisons, which had been holding out in the hope of succour through the force that Hicks Pasha was bringing from Khartoum, abandoned hope after its destruction at Shekan, and thought only of coming to terms with the conqueror. Among these was the force at Dara in Darfour under the command of Slatin Pasha. That able officer had held the place for months under the greatest difficulty, and had even obtained some slight successes in the field, but the fate of the Hicks expedition convinced him that the situation was hopeless, and that his duty to the brave troops under him required the acceptance of the honourable terms which his tact and reputation enabled him to secure at the hands of the conqueror. Slatin surrendered on 23rd December 1883; Lupton Bey, commander in the Bahr Gazelle, about the same time, and these successes were enhanced and extended by those achieved by Osman Digma in the Eastern Soudan, where, early in February 1884, while Gordon was on his way to Khartoum, that leader inflicted on Baker Pasha at Tokar a defeat scarcely less crushing than that of Shekan.

By New Year's Day, 1884, therefore, the power of the Mahdi was triumphantly established over the whole extent of the Soudan, from the Equator to Souakim, with the exception of Khartoum and the middle course of the Nile from that place to Dongola. There were also some outlying garrisons, such as that at Kassala, but the principal Egyptian force remaining was the body of 4000 so-called troops, the less efficient part, we may be sure, of those available, left behind at Khartoum, under Colonel de Coetlogon, by Hicks Pasha, when he set out on his unfortunate expedition. If the power of the Mahdi at this moment were merely to be measured by comparison with the collapse of authority, courage, and confidence of the titular upholders of the Khedive's Government, it might be pronounced formidable. It had sufficed to defeat every hostile effort made against it, and to practically annihilate all the armies that Egypt could bring into the field. Its extraordinary success was no doubt due to the incompetency, over-confidence, and deficient military spirit and knowledge of the Khedive's commanders and troops. But, while making the fullest admission on these points, it cannot be disputed that some of the elements in the Mahdi's power would have made it formidable, even if the cause of the Government had been more worthily and efficiently sustained. There is no doubt that, in the first place, he appealed to races which thought they were overtaxed, and to classes whose only tangible property had been assailed and diminished by the Anti-Slavery policy of the Government. Even if it would be going too far to say that Mahomed Ahmed, the long-looked-for Mahdi, was only a tool in the hands of secret conspirators pledged to avenge Suleiman, to restore Zebehr, and to bring back the good old times, when a fortune lay in the easy acquisition of human ivory, there is no doubt that the backbone of his power was provided by those followers of Suleiman, whom Gordon had broken up at Shaka and driven from Dara. But the Mahdi had supplied them in religious fanaticism with a more powerful incentive than pecuniary gain, and when he showed them how easily they might triumph over their opponents, he inspired them with a confidence which has not yet lost its efficacy.

In 1884 all these inducements for the tribes of the Soudan to believe in their religious leader were in their pristine strength. He had succeeded in every thing he undertook, he had armed his countless warriors with the weapons taken from the armies he had destroyed, and he had placed at the disposal of his supporters an immense and easily-acquired spoil. The later experiences of the Mahdists were to be neither so pleasant nor so profitable, but at the end of 1883 they were at the height of their confidence and power. It was at such a moment and against such a powerful adversary that the British Government thought it right to take advantage of the devotion and gallantry of a single man, to send him alone to grapple with a difficulty which several armies had, by their own failure and destruction, rendered more grave, at the same time that they established the formidable nature of the rebellion in the Soudan as an unimpeachable fact instead of a disputable opinion. I do not think his own countrymen have yet quite appreciated the extraordinary heroism and devotion to his country which Gordon showed when he rushed off single-handed to oppose the ever-victorious Mahdi at the very zenith of his power.

In unrolling the scroll of events connected with an intricate history, it next becomes necessary to explain why Gordon voluntarily, and it may even be admitted, enthusiastically, undertook a mission that, to any man in his senses, must have seemed at the moment at which it was undertaken little short of insanity. Whatever else may be said against the Government and the military authorities who suggested his going, and availed themselves of his readiness to go, to Khartoum, I do not think there is the shadow of a justification for the allegation that they forced him to proceed on that romantic errand, although of course it is equally clear that he insisted as the condition of his going at all that he should be ordered by his Government to proceed on this mission. Beyond this vital principle, which he held to all his life in never volunteering, he was far too eager to go himself to require any real stirring-up or compulsion. It was even a secret and unexpressed grievance that he should not be called upon to hasten to the spot, which had always been in his thoughts since the time he had left it. He could think of nothing else; in the midst of other work he would turn aside to discuss the affairs of Egypt and the Soudan as paramount to every other consideration; and when a great mission, like that to the Congo, which he could have made a turning-point in African history, was placed in his hands, he could only ask for "a respite," and, with the charm of the Sphinx strong upon him, rushed on his fate in a chivalrous determination to essay the impossible. But was it right or justifiable that wise politicians and experienced generals should take advantage of such enthusiasm and self-sacrifice, and let one man go unaided to achieve what thousands had failed to do?

It is necessary to establish clearly in the first place, and beyond dispute, the frame of mind which induced Gordon to take up his last Nile mission in precisely the confiding manner that he did. Gordon left Egypt at the end of 1879. Although events there in 1880 were of interest and importance, Gordon was too much occupied in India and China to say anything, but in October 1881 he drew up an important memorandum on affairs in Egypt since the deposition of Ismail. Gordon gave it to me specially for publication, and it duly appeared in *The Times*, but its historical interest is that it shows how Gordon's thoughts were still running on the affairs of the country in which he had served so long. The following is the full text:

> On the 16th of August 1879, the Firman installing Tewfik as Khedive was published in Cairo. From the 26th of June 1879, when Ismail was deposed, to this date, Cherif Pasha remained Prime Minister; he had been appointed on the dismissal of the Rivers-Wilson and de Blignières Ministry in May. Between June and August Cherif had been working with the view of securing to the country a representative form of government, and had only a short time before August 16 laid his proposition before Tewfik. Cherif's idea was that, the representation

being in the hands of the people, there would be more chance of Egypt maintaining her independence than if the Government was a personal one. It will be remembered that, though many states have repudiated their debts, no other ruler of those states was considered responsible except in the case of Ismail of Egypt. Europe considered Ismail responsible personally. She did not consider the rulers of Turkey, Greece, Spain, etc., responsible, so that Cherif was quite justified in his proposition. Cherif has been unjustly considered opposed to any reform. This is not so. Certainly he had shown his independence in refusing to acknowledge Rivers-Wilson as his superior, preferring to give up his position to doing so, but he knew well that reform was necessary, and had always advised it. Cherif is perhaps the only Egyptian Minister whose character for strict integrity is unimpeachable.

A thoroughly independent man, caring but little for office or its emoluments, of a good family, with antecedents which would bear any investigation, he was not inclined to be questioned by men whose social position was inferior to his own, and whose *parti pris* was against him. In the Council Chamber he was in a minority because he spoke his mind; but this was not so with other Ministers, whose antecedents were dubious. Had his advice been taken, Ismail would have now been Khedive of Egypt. Any one who knows Cherif will agree to this account of him, and will rate him as infinitely superior to his other colleagues. He is essentially not an intriguer.

To return, immediately after the promulgation of the Firman on August 16, Tewfik dismisses suddenly Cherif, and the European Press considers he has done a bold thing, and, misjudging Cherif, praise him for having broken with the advisers who caused the ruin of Ismail. My opinion is that Tewfik feared Cherif's proposition as being likely to curtail his power as absolute ruler, and that he judged that he would by this dismissal gain *kudos* in Europe, and protect his absolute power.

After a time Riaz is appointed in Cherif's place, and then Tewfik begins his career. He concedes this and that to European desires, but in so doing claims for his youth and inexperience exemption from any reform which would take from his absolute power. Knowing that it was the bondholders who upset his father he conciliates them; they in their turn leave him to act as he wished with regard to the internal government of the country.

Riaz was so placed as to be between two influences—one, the bondholders seeking their advantages; the other, Tewfik, seeking to retain all power. Riaz of course wavers. Knowing better than Tewfik the feeling of Europe, he inclines more to the bondholders than to Tewfik, to whom, however, he is bound to give some sops, such as the Universal Military Service Bill, which the bondholders let pass without a word, and which is the root of the present troubles. After a time Tewfik finds that Riaz will give no more sops, for the simple reason he dares not. Then Tewfik finds him *de trop*, and by working up the military element endeavours to counterbalance him. The European Powers manage to keep the peace for a time, but eventually the military become too strong for even Tewfik, who had conjured them up, and taking things into their own hands upset Riaz, which Tewfik is glad of, and demand a Constitution, which Tewfik is not glad of. Cherif then returns, and it is to be hoped will get for the people what he demanded before his dismissal.

It is against all reason to expect any straightforward dealings in any Sultan, Khedive, or Ameer; the only hope is in the people they govern, and the raising of the people should be our object.

There is no real loyalty towards the descendants of the Sandjak of Salonica in Egypt; the people are Arabs, they are Greeks. The people care for themselves. It is reiterated over and over again that Egypt is prosperous and contented. I do not think it has altered at all, except in improving its finances for the benefit of the bondholders. The army may be paid regularly, but the lot of the fellaheen and inhabitants of the Soudan is the same oppressed lot as before. The prisons are as full of unfortunates as ever they were, the local tribunals are as corrupt, and Tewfik will always oppose their being affiliated to the mixed tribunals of Alexandria, and thus afford protection to the judges of the local tribunals, should they adjudicate justly. Tewfik is essentially one of the Ameer class. I believe he would be willing to act uprightly, if by so doing he could maintain his absolute power. He has played a difficult game, making stock of his fear of his father and of Halim, the legitimate heir according to the Moslem, to induce the European Governments to be gentle with him, at the same time resisting all measures which would benefit his people should these measures touch his absolute power. He is liberal only in measures which do not interfere with his prerogative.

It was inevitable that the present sort of trouble should arise.

The Controllers had got the finances in good order, and were bound to look to the welfare of the people, which could only be done by the curtailment of Tewfik's power. The present arrangement of Controllers and Consul-Generals is defective. The Consul-Generals are charged with the duty of seeing that the country is quiet and the people well treated. They are responsible to their Foreign Offices. The Controllers are charged with the finances and the welfare of the country, but to whom are they responsible? Not to Tewfik; though he pays them, he cannot remove them; yet they must get on well with him. Not to the Foreign Office, for it is repeatedly said that they are Egyptian officials, yet they have to keep on good terms with these Foreign Offices. Not to the bondholders, though they are bound, considering their power, to be on good terms with them. Not to the inhabitants of Egypt, though these latter are taught to believe that every unpopular act is done by the Controllers' advice.

The only remedy is by the formation of a Council of Notables, having direct access to Tewfik, and independent of his or of the Ministers' goodwill, and the subjection of the Controllers to the Consul-Generals responsible to the Foreign Office—in fact, Residents at the Court. This would be no innovation, for the supervision exists now, except under the Controllers and Consul-Generals. It is simply proposed to amalgamate Controllers with Consul-Generals, and to give these latter the position of Residents. By this means the continual change of French Consul-Generals would be avoided, and the consequent ill-feeling between France and England would disappear. Should the Residents fall out, the matter would be easily settled by the Governments. As it is at present, a quadruple combat goes on; sometimes it is one Consul-General against the other Consul-General, aided by the two Controllers, or a Consul-General and one Controller against the other Consul-General and the other Controller, in all of which combats Tewfik gains and the people lose.

One thing should certainly be done—the giving of concessions ought not to be in the power of Controllers, nor if Consul-Generals are amalgamated with Controllers as Residents should these Residents have this power. It ought to be exercised by the Council of Notables, who would look to the welfare of the people.

The progress of events in Lower Egypt during 1881 and 1882 was watched with great care, whether he was vegetating in the Mauritius or absorbed in the anxieties and labours of his South African mission. Commenting on the downfall of Arabi, he explained how the despatch of troops to the Soudan, composed of regiments tainted with a spirit of insubordination, would inevitably aggravate the situation there. Later on, in 1883, when he heard of Hicks being sent to take the command and repair the defeat of Yusuf, he wrote:

> Unless Hicks is given supreme command he is lost; it can never work putting him in a subordinate position. Hicks must be made Governor-General, otherwise he will never end things satisfactorily.

At the same time, he came to the conclusion that there was only one man who could save Egypt, and that was Nubar Pasha. He wrote:—"If they do not make Nubar Pasha Prime Minister or Regent in Egypt they will have trouble, as he is the only man who can rule that country." This testimony to Nubar's capacity is the more remarkable and creditable, as in earlier days Gordon had not appreciated the merit of a statesman who has done more for Egypt than any other of his generation. But at a very early stage of the Soudan troubles Gordon convinced himself that the radical cause of these difficulties and misfortunes was not the shortcomings and errors of any particular subordinate, but the complete want of a definite policy on the part, not of the Khedive and his advisers, but of the British Government itself. He wrote on this point to a friend (2nd September 1883), almost the day that Hicks was to march from Khartoum:

> Her Majesty's Government, right or wrong, will not take a decided step *in re* Egypt and the Soudan; they drift, but at the same time cannot avoid the *onus* of being the real power in Egypt, with the corresponding advantage of being so. It is undoubtedly the fact that they maintain Tewfik and the Pashas in power against the will of the people; this alone is insufferable from disgusting the people, to whom also Her Majesty's Government have given no inducement to make themselves popular. Their present action is a dangerous one, for without any advantage over the Canal or to England, they keep a running sore open with France, and are acting in a way which will justify Russia to act in a similar way in Armenia, and Austria in Salonica. Further than that, Her Majesty's Government must eventually gain the odium which will fall upon them when

the interest of the debt fails to be paid, which will soon be the case. Also, Her Majesty's Government cannot possibly avoid the responsibility for the state of affairs in the Soudan, where a wretched war drags on in a ruined country at a cost of half a million per annum at least. I say therefore to avoid all this, *if Her Majesty's Government will not act firmly and strongly and take the country* (which, if I were they, I would not do), let them attempt to get the Palestine Canal made, and quit Egypt to work out its own salvation. In doing so lots of anarchy will take place. This anarchy is inseparable from a peaceful solution; it is the travail in birth. Her Majesty's Government do not prevent anarchy now; therefore better leave the country, and thus avoid a responsibility which gives no advantage, and is mean and dangerous.

In a letter to myself, dated 3rd January 1884, from Brussels, he enters into some detail on matters that had been forgotten or were insufficiently appreciated, to which the reported appointment of Zebehr to proceed to the Soudan and stem the Mahdi's advance lent special interest:

I send you a small note which you can make use of, but I beg you will not let my name appear under any circumstances. When in London I had printed a pamphlet in Arabic, with all the papers (official) concerning Zebehr Pasha and his action in pushing his son to rebel. It is in Arabic. My brother has it. It is not long, and would repay translating and publishing. It has all the history and the authentic letters found in the divan of Zebehr's son when Gessi took his stockade. It is in a cover, blue and gold. It was my address to people of Soudan—Apologia. Isaiah XIX. 19, 20, 21 has a wonderful prophecy about Egypt and the saviour who will come from the frontier.

The note enclosed was published in *The Times* of 5th January, and read as follows:

A correspondent writes that it may seem inexplicable why the Mahdi's troops attacked Gezireh, which, as its name signifies, is an isle near Berber, but there is an old tradition that the future ruler of the Soudan will be from that isle. Zebehr Rahama knew this, but he fell on leaving his boat at this isle, and so, though the Soudan people looked on him as a likely saviour, this omen shook their confidence in him. He was then on his way to Cairo after swearing his people to rebel (if he was retained there), under a tree at Shaka. Zebehr will most probably be taken prisoner by the Mahdi, and will then take the command of the Mahdi's forces. The peoples of the Soudan are very superstitious, and the fall of the flag by a gust of wind, on the proclamation of Tewfik at Khartoum, was looked on as an omen of the end of Mehemet Ali's dynasty. There is an old tree opposite Cook's office at Jerusalem in Toppet, belonging to an old family, and protected by Sultan's Firman, which the Arabs consider will fall when the Sultan's rule ends. It lost a large limb during the Turko-Russian war, and is now in a decayed state. There can be no doubt but that the movement will spread into Palestine, Syria, and Hedjaz. At Damascus already proclamations have been posted up, denouncing Turks and Circassians, and this was before Hicks was defeated. It is the beginning of the end of Turkey. Austria backed by Germany will go to Salonica, quieting Russia by letting her go into Armenia—England and France neutralising one another.

If not too late, the return of the ex-Khedive Ismail to Egypt, and the union of England and France to support and control the Arab movement, appears the only chance. Ismail would soon come to terms with the Soudan, the rebellion of which countries was entirely due to the oppression of the Turks and Circassians.

These expressions of opinion about Egypt and the Soudan may be said to have culminated in the remarkable pronouncement Gordon made to Mr W. T. Stead, the brilliant editor of the *Pall Mall Gazette*, on 8th January 1884, which appeared in his paper on the following day. The substance of that statement is as follows:

So you would abandon the Soudan? But the Eastern Soudan is indispensable to Egypt. It will cost you far more to retain your hold upon Egypt proper if you abandon your hold of the Eastern Soudan to the Mahdi or to the Turk than what it would to retain your hold upon Eastern Soudan by the aid of such material as exists in the provinces. Darfour and Kordofan must be abandoned. That I admit; but the provinces lying to the east of the White Nile should be retained, and north of Sennaar. The danger to be feared is not that the Mahdi will march northward through Wady Halfa; on the contrary, it is very improbable that he will ever go so far north. The danger is altogether of a different nature. It arises from the influence which the spectacle of a conquering Mahommedan Power established close to your frontiers will exercise upon the population which you govern. In all the cities in Egypt it will be felt that what the Mahdi has done they may do; and, as he has driven out the intruder and the infidel, they may do the same. Nor is it only England that has to face this danger. The success of the Mahdi has already excited dangerous fermentation in Arabia and Syria. Placards have been posted in Damascus calling upon the population to rise and drive out the Turks. If the whole of the Eastern Soudan is surrendered to the Mahdi, the Arab tribes on both sides of the Red Sea will take fire. In self-defence the Turks are bound to do something to cope with so formidable a danger, for it is quite possible that if nothing is done the whole of the Eastern Question may be reopened by the triumph of the Mahdi. I see it is proposed to fortify Wady Halfa, and prepare there to resist the Mahdi's attack. You might as well fortify against a fever. Contagion of that kind cannot be kept out by fortifications and garrisons. But that it is real, and that it does exist, will be denied by no one cognisant with Egypt and the East. In self-defence the policy of evacuation cannot possibly be justified.

There is another aspect of the question. You have 6000 men in Khartoum. What are you going to do with them? You have garrisons in Darfour, in Bahr el Gazelle, and Gondokoro. Are they to be sacrificed? Their only offence is their loyalty to their Sovereign. For their fidelity you are going to abandon them to their fate. You say they are to retire upon Wady Halfa. But Gondokoro is 1500 miles from Khartoum, and Khartoum is only 350 from Wady Halfa. How will you move your 6000 men from Khartoum—to say nothing of other places—and all the Europeans in that city through the desert to Wady Halfa? Where are you going to get the camels to take them away? Will the Mahdi supply them? If they are to escape with their lives, the garrison will not be allowed to leave with a coat on their backs. They will be plundered to the skin, and even then their lives may not be spared. Whatever you may decide about evacuation, you cannot evacuate, because your army cannot be moved. You must either surrender absolutely to the Mahdi or defend Khartoum at all hazards. The latter is the only course which ought to be entertained. There is no serious difficulty about it. The Mahdi's forces will fall to pieces of themselves; but if in a moment of panic orders are issued for the abandonment of the whole of the Eastern Soudan, a blow will be struck against the security of Egypt and the peace of the East, which may have fatal consequences.

The great evil is not at Khartoum, but at Cairo. It is the weakness of Cairo which produces disaster in the Soudan. It is because Hicks was not adequately supported at the first, but was thrust forward upon an impossible enterprise by the men who had refused him supplies when a decisive blow might have been struck, that the Western Soudan has been sacrificed. The Eastern Soudan may, however, be saved if there is a firm hand placed at the helm in Egypt. Everything depends on that.

What then, you ask, should be done? I reply, Place Nubar in power! Nubar is the one supremely able man among Egyptian Ministers. He is proof against foreign intrigue, and he thoroughly understands the situation. Place him in power; support him through thick and thin; give him a free hand; and let it be distinctly understood that no intrigues, either on the part of Tewfik or any of Nubar's rivals, will be allowed for a moment to interfere with the execution of his plans. You are sure to find that the energetic support of Nubar will, sooner or later, bring you into collision with the Khedive; but if that Sovereign really desires, as he says, the welfare of his country, it will be necessary for you to protect Nubar's Administration from any direct or indirect interference on his part. Nubar can be depended upon: that I can guarantee. He will not take office without knowing that he is to have his own way; but if he takes office, it is the best security that you can have for the restoration of order to the country. Especially is this the case with the Soudan. Nubar should be left untrammelled by any stipulations concerning the evacuation of Khartoum. There is no hurry. The garrisons can hold their own at present. Let them continue to hold on until disunion and tribal jealousies have worked their natural results in the camp of the Mahdi. Nubar should be free to deal with the Soudan in his own way. How he will deal with the Soudan, of course, I cannot profess to say; but I should imagine that he would appoint a Governor-General at Khartoum, with full powers, and furnish him with two millions sterling—a large sum, no doubt, but a sum which had much better be spent now than wasted in a vain attempt to avert the consequences of an ill-timed surrender. Sir Samuel Baker, who possesses the essential energy and single tongue requisite for the office, might be appointed Governor-General of the Soudan, and he might take his brother as Commander-in-Chief.

It should be proclaimed in the hearing of all the Soudanese, and engraved on tablets of brass, that a permanent Constitution was granted to the Soudanese, by which no Turk or Circassian would ever be allowed to enter the province to plunder its inhabitants in order to fill his own pockets, and that no immediate emancipation of slaves would be attempted. Immediate emancipation was denounced in 1833 as confiscation in England, and it is no less confiscation in the Soudan today. Whatever is done in that direction should be done gradually, and by a process of registration. Mixed tribunals might be established, if Nubar thought fit, in which European judges would co-operate with the natives in the administration of justice. Police inspectors also might be appointed, and adequate measures taken to root out the abuses which prevail in the prisons.

With regard to Darfour, I should think that Nubar would probably send back the family and the heir of the Sultan of Darfour. If subsidized by the Government, and sent back with Sir Samuel Baker, he would not have much difficulty in regaining possession of the kingdom of Darfour, which was formerly one of the best governed of African countries. As regards Abyssinia, the old warning should not be lost sight of—"Put not your trust in princes;" and place no reliance upon the King of Abyssinia, at least outside his own country. Zeylah and Bogos might be ceded to him with advantage, and the free right of entry by the port of Massowah might be added; but it would be a mistake to give him possession of Massowah which he would ruin. A Commission might also be sent down with advantage to examine the state of things in Harrar, opposite Aden, and see what iniquities are going on there, as also at Berbera and Zeylah. By these means, and by the adoption of a steady, consistent policy at headquarters, it would be possible—not to say easy—to re-establish the authority of the Khedive between the Red Sea and Sennaar.

As to the cost of the Soudan, it is a mistake to suppose that it will necessarily be a charge on the Egyptian Exchequer. It will cost two millions to relieve the garrisons and to quell the revolt; but that expenditure must be incurred any way; and in all probability, if the garrisons are handed over to be massacred and the country evacuated, the ultimate expenditure would exceed that sum. At first, until the country is pacified, the Soudan will need a subsidy of £200,000 a year from Egypt. That, however, would be temporary. During the last years of my administration the Soudan involved no charge upon the Egyptian Exchequer. The bad provinces were balanced against the good, and an equilibrium was established. The Soudan will never be a source of revenue to Egypt, but it need not be a source of expense. That deficits have arisen, and that the present disaster has occurred, is entirely attributable to a single cause, and that is, the grossest misgovernment.

The cause of the rising in the Soudan is the cause of all popular risings against Turkish rule, wherever they have occurred. No one who has been in a Turkish province, and has witnessed the results of the Bashi-Bazouk system, which excited so much indignation some time ago in Bulgaria, will need to be told why the people of the Soudan have risen in revolt against the Khedive. The Turks, the Circassians, and the Bashi-Bazouks have plundered and oppressed the people in the Soudan, as they plundered and oppressed them in the Balkan peninsula. Oppression begat discontent; discontent necessitated an increase of the armed force at the disposal of the authorities; this increase of the army force involved an increase of expenditure, which again was attempted to be met by increasing taxation, and that still further increased the discontent. And so things went on in a dismal circle, until they culminated, after repeated deficits, in a disastrous rebellion. That the people were justified in rebelling, nobody who knows the treatment to which they were subjected will attempt to deny. Their cries were absolutely unheeded at Cairo. In despair, they had recourse to the only method by which they could make their wrongs known; and, on the same principle that Absalom fired the corn of Joab, so they rallied round the Mahdi, who exhorted them to revolt against the Turkish yoke. I am convinced that it is an entire mistake to regard the Mahdi as in any sense a religious leader: he personifies popular discontent. All the Soudanese are potential Mahdis, just as all the Egyptians are potential Arabis. The movement is not religious, but an outbreak of despair. Three times over I warned the late Khedive that it would be impossible to govern the Soudan on the old system, after my appointment to the Governor-Generalship. During the three years that I wielded full powers in the Soudan, I taught the natives that they had a right to exist. I waged war against the Turks and Circassians, who had harried the population. I had taught them something of the meaning of liberty and justice, and accustomed them to a higher ideal of government than that with which they had previously been acquainted. As soon as I had gone, the Turks and Circassians returned in full force; the old Bashi-Bazouk system was re-established; my old employees were persecuted; and a population which had begun to appreciate something like decent government was flung back to suffer the worst excesses of Turkish rule. The inevitable result followed; and thus it may be said that the egg of the present rebellion was laid in the three years during which I was allowed to govern the Soudan on other than Turkish principles.

The Soudanese are a very nice people. They deserve the sincere compassion and sympathy of all civilised men. I got on very well with them, and I am sincerely sorry at the prospect of seeing them handed over to be ground down once more by their Turkish and Circassian oppressors. Yet, unless an attempt is made to hold on to the present garrisons, it is inevitable that the Turks, for the sake of self-preservation, must attempt to crush them. They deserve a better fate. It ought not to be impossible to come to terms with them, to grant them a free amnesty for the past, to offer them security for decent government in the future. If this were done, and the government entrusted to a man whose word was truth, all might yet be re-established. So far from believing it impossible to make an arrangement with the Mahdi, I strongly suspect that he is a mere puppet, put forward by Elias, Zebehr's father-in-law, and the largest slave-owner in Obeid, and that he had assumed a religious title to give colour to his defence of the popular rights.

There is one subject on which I cannot imagine any one can differ about. That is the impolicy of announcing our intention to evacuate Khartoum. Even if we were bound to do so we should have said nothing about it. The moment it is known that we have given up the game, every man will go over to the Mahdi. All men worship the rising sun. The difficulties of evacuation will be enormously increased, if, indeed, the withdrawal of our garrison is not rendered impossible.

The late Khedive, who is one of the ablest and worst-used men in Europe, would not have made such a mistake, and under him the condition of Egypt proper was much better than it is today. Now, with regard to Egypt, the same principle should be observed that must be acted upon in the Soudan. Let your foundations be broad and firm, and based upon the contentment and welfare of the people. Hitherto, both in the Soudan and in Egypt, instead of constructing the social edifice like a pyramid, upon its base, we have been rearing an obelisk which a single push may overturn. Our safety in Egypt is to do something for the people. That is to say, you must reduce their rent, rescue them from the usurers, and retrench expenditure. Nine-tenths of the European employees might probably be weeded out with advantage. The remaining tenth—thoroughly efficient—should be retained; but, whatever you do, do not break up Sir Evelyn Wood's army, which is destined to do good work. Stiffen it as much as you please, but with Englishmen, not with Circassians. Circassians are as much foreigners in Egypt as Englishmen are, and certainly not more popular. As for the European population, let them have charters for the formation of municipal councils, for raising volunteer corps, and for organising in their own defence. Anything more shameful than the flight from Egypt in 1882 I never read. Let them take an example from Shanghai, where the European settlement provides for its own defence and its own government. I should like to see a competent special Commissioner of the highest standing—such a man, for instance, as the Right Honourable W. E. Forster, who is free at once from traditions of the elders and of the Foreign Office and of the bondholders, sent out to put Nubar in the saddle, sift out unnecessary employees, and warn evil-doers in the highest places that they will not be allowed to play any tricks. If that were done, it would give confidence everywhere, and I see no reason why the last British soldier should not be withdrawn from Egypt in six months' time.

A perusal of these passages will suffice to show the reader what thoughts were uppermost in Gordon's mind at the very moment when he was negotiating about his new task for the King of the Belgians on the Congo, and those thoughts, inspired by the enthusiasm derived from his noble spirit, and the perfect self-sacrifice with which he would have thrown himself into what he conceived to be a good and necessary work, made him the ready victim of a Government which absolutely did not know what course to pursue, and which was delighted to find that the very man, whom the public designated as the right man for the situation, was ready—nay, eager—to take all the burden on his shoulders whenever his own Government called on him to do so, and to proceed straight to the scene of danger without so much as asking for precise instructions, or insisting on guarantees for his own proper treatment. There is no doubt that from his own individual point of view, and as affecting any selfish or personal consideration he had at heart, this mode of action was very unwise and reprehensible, and a worldly censure would be the more severe on Gordon, because he acted with his eyes open, and knew that the gravity of the trouble really arose from the drifting policy and want of purpose of the very Ministers for whom he was about to dare a danger that Gordon himself, in a cooler moment, would very likely have deemed it unnecessary to face.

Into the motives that filled him with a belief that he might inspire a Government, which had no policy, with one created by his own courage, confidence, and success, it would be impossible to enter, but it can be confidently asserted that, although they were drawn after him *sed pede claudo* to expend millions of treasure and thousands of lives, they were never inspired by his exhortations and example to form a definite policy as to the main point in the situation, *viz.*, the defence of the Egyptian possessions. In the flush of the moment, carried along by an irresistible inclination to do the things which he saw could be done, he overlooked all the other points of the case, and especially that he was dealing with politicians tied by their party principles, and thinking more of the passage through the House of some domestic measure of fifth-rate importance than of the maintenance of an Imperial interest and the arrest of an outbreak of Mahommedan fanaticism which, if not checked, might call for a crusade. Gordon overlooked all these considerations. He never thought but that he was dealing with other Englishmen equally mindful with himself of their country's fame.

If Gordon, long before he took up the task, had been engrossed in the development of the Soudan difficulty and the Mahdi's power, those who had studied the question and knew his special qualifications for the task, had, at a very early stage of the trouble, called upon the Government to avail themselves of his services, and there is no doubt that if that advice had been promptly taken instead of slowly, reluctantly, and only when matters were desperate, there is no doubt, I repeat, remembering what he did later on, that Gordon would have been able, without a single English regiment, to have strangled the Mahdi's power in its infancy, and to have won back the Soudan for the Khedive.

But it may be said, where was it ever prominently suggested that General Gordon should be despatched to the Soudan at a time before the Mahdi had become supreme in that region, as he undoubtedly did by the overthrow of Hicks and his force?

I reply by the following quotations from prominent articles written by myself in *The Times* of January and February 1883. Until the capture of El Obeid at that period the movement of the Mahdi was a local affair of the importance of which no one, at a distance, could attempt to judge, but that signal success made it the immediate concern of those responsible in Egypt. On 9th January 1883, in an article in *The Times* on the Soudan, occurs this passage:

> It is a misfortune, in the interests of Egypt, of civilisation, and of the mass of the Soudanese, that we cannot send General Gordon back to the region of the Upper Nile to complete there the good work he began eight years ago. With full powers, and with the assurance that the good fruits of his labours shall not be lost by the subsequent acts of corrupt Pashas, there need be little doubt of his attaining rapid success, while the memory of his achievements, when working for a half-hearted Government, and with incapable colleagues, yet lives in the hearts of the black people of the Soudan, and fills one of the most creditable pages in the history of recent administration of alien races by Englishmen.

Again, on 17th February, in another article on the same subject:

> The authority of the Mahdi could scarcely be preserved save by constant activity and a policy of aggression, which would constitute a standing danger to the tranquillity of Lower Egypt. On the other hand, the preservation of the Khedive's sovereign rights through our instrumentality will carry with it the responsibility of providing the unhappy peoples of Darfour, Dongola, Kordofan, and the adjacent provinces with an equitable administration and immunity from heavy taxation. The obligation cannot be avoided under these, or perhaps under any circumstances, but the acceptance of it is not a matter to be entertained with an easy mind. The one thing that would reconcile us to the idea would be the assurance that General Gordon would be sent back with plenary powers to the old scene of his labours, and that he would accept the charge.

As Gordon was not resorted to when the fall of El Obeid in the early part of the year 1883 showed that the situation demanded some decisive step, it is not surprising that he was left in inglorious inaction in Palestine, while, as I and others knew well, his uppermost thought was to be grappling with the Mahdi during the long lull of preparing Hicks's expedition, and of its marching to its fate. The catastrophe to that force on 4th November was known in London on 22nd November.

I urged in every possible way the prompt employment of General Gordon, who could have reached Egypt in a very short time from his place of exile at Jaffa. But on this occasion I was snubbed, being told by one of the ablest editors I have known, now dead, that "Gordon was generally considered to be mad." However, at this moment the Government seem to have come to the conclusion that General Gordon had some qualifications to undertake the task in the Soudan, for at the end of November 1883, Sir Charles Dilke, then a member of the Cabinet as President of the Local Government Board, but whose special knowledge and experience of foreign affairs often led to his assisting Lord Granville at the Foreign Office, offered the Egyptian Government Gordon's services. They were declined, and when, on 1st December 1883, Lord Granville proposed the same measure in a more formal manner, and asked in an interrogatory form whether General Charles Gordon would be of any use, and if so in what capacity, Sir Evelyn Baring, now Lord Cromer, threw cold water on the project, and stated on 2nd December that "the Egyptian Government were very much averse to employing him." Subsequent events make it desirable to call special attention to the fact that when, however tardily, the British Government did propose the employment of General Gordon, the suggestion was rejected, not on public grounds, but on private. Major Baring did not need to be informed as to the work Gordon had done in the Soudan, and as to the incomparable manner in which it had been performed. No one knew better than he that, with the single exception of Sir Samuel Baker, who was far too prudent to take up a thankless task, and to remove the mountain of blunders others had committed, there was no man living who had the smallest pretension to say that he could cope with the Soudan difficulty, save Charles Gordon. Yet, when his name is suggested, he treats the matter as one that cannot be entertained. There is not a word as to the obvious propriety of suggesting Gordon's name, but the objection of a puppet-prince like Tewfik is reported as fatal to the course. Yet six weeks, with the mighty lever of an aroused public opinion, sufficed to make him withdraw the opposition he advanced to the appointment, not on public grounds, which was simply impossible, but, I fear, from private feelings, for he had not forgotten the scene in Cairo in 1878, when he attempted to control the action of Gordon on the financial question. There would be no necessity to refer to this matter, but for its consequences. Had Sir Evelyn Baring done his duty, and given the only honest answer on 2nd December 1883, that if any one man could save the situation, that man was Charles Gordon, Gordon could have reached Khartoum early in January instead of late in February, and that difference of six weeks might well have sufficed to completely alter the course of subsequent events, and certainly to save Gordon's life, seeing that, after all, the Nile Expedition was only a few days too late. The delay was also attended with fatal results to the civil population of Khartoum. Had Gordon reached there early in January he could have saved them all, for as it was he sent down 2600 refugees, i.e. merchants, old men, women, and children, making all arrangements for their comfort in the very brief period of open communication after his arrival, when the greater part of February had been spent.

The conviction that Gordon's appointment and departure were retarded by personal *animus* and an old difference is certainly strengthened by all that follows. Sir Evelyn Baring and the Egyptian Government would not have Charles Gordon, but they were quite content to entrust the part of Saviour of the Soudan to Zebehr, the king of the slave-hunters. On 13th December Lord Granville curtly informed our representative at Cairo that the employment of Zebehr was inexpedient, and Gordon in his own forcible way summed the matter up thus: "Zebehr will manage to get taken prisoner, and will then head the revolt."

But while Sir Evelyn Baring would not have Gordon and the British Cabinet withheld its approval from Zebehr, it was felt that the situation required that something should be done as soon as possible, for the Mahdi was master of the Soudan, and at any moment tidings might come of his advance on Khartoum, where there was only a small and disheartened garrison, and a considerable defenceless population. The responsible Egyptian Ministers made several suggestions for dealing with the situation, but they one and all deprecated ceding territory to the Mahdi, as it would further alienate the tribes still loyal or wavering and create graver trouble in the future. What they chiefly contended for was the opening of the Berber-Souakim route with 10,000 troops, who should be Turks, as English troops were not available. It is important to note that this suggestion did not shock the Liberal Government, and on 13th December 1883 Lord Granville replied that the Government had no objection to offer to the employment of Turkish troops at Souakim for service in the Soudan. In the following month the Foreign Secretary went one step further, and "concurred in the surrender of the Soudan to the Sultan." In fact the British Government were only anxious about one thing, and that was to get rid of the Soudan, and to be saved any further worry in the matter. No doubt, if the Sultan had had the money to pay for the despatch of the expedition, this last suggestion would have been adopted, but as he had not, the only way to get rid of the responsibility was to thrust it on Gordon, who was soon discovered to be ready to accept it without delay or conditions.

On 22nd December 1883 Sir Evelyn Baring wrote:

> It would be necessary to send an English officer of high authority to Khartoum with full powers to withdraw the garrisons, and to make the best arrangements possible for the future government of the country.

News from Khartoum showed that everything there was in a state verging on panic, that the people thought they were abandoned by the Government, and that the enemy had only to advance for the place to fall without a blow. Lastly Colonel de Coetlogon, the governor after Hicks's death, recommended on 9th January the immediate withdrawal of the garrison from Khartoum, which he thought could be accomplished if carried out with the greatest promptitude, but which involved the desertion of the other garrisons. Abd-el-Kader, ex-Governor-General of the Soudan and Minister of War, offered to proceed to Khartoum, but when he discovered that the abandonment of the Soudan was to be proclaimed, he absolutely refused on any consideration to carry out what he termed a hopeless errand.

All these circumstances gave special point to Sir Evelyn Baring's recommendation on 22nd December that "an English officer of high authority should be sent to Khartoum," and the urgency of a decision was again impressed on the Government in his telegram of 1st January, because Egypt is on the point of losing the Soudan, and moreover possesses no force with which to defend the valley of the Nile downwards. But in the many messages that were sent on this subject during the last fortnight of the year 1883, the name of the one "English officer of high authority" specially suited for the task finds no mention. As this omission cannot be attributed to ignorance, some different motive must be discovered. At last, on 10th January, Lord Granville renews his suggestion to send General Gordon, and asks whether he would not be of some assistance under the altered circumstances. The "altered circumstances" must have been inserted for the purpose of letting down Sir Evelyn Baring as lightly as possible, for the only alteration in the circumstances was that six weeks had been wasted in coming to any decision at all. On 11th January Sir Evelyn Baring replied that he and Nubar Pasha did not think Gordon's services could be utilised, and yet three weeks before he had recommended that "an English officer of high authority" should be sent, and he had even complained because prompter measures were not taken to give effect to his recommendation. The only possible conclusion is that, in Sir Evelyn Baring's opinion, General Gordon was not "an English officer of high authority." As if to make his views more emphatic, Sir Evelyn Baring on 15th January again telegraphed for an English officer with the intentional and conspicuous omission of Gordon's name, which had been three times urged upon him by his own Government. But determined as Sir Evelyn Baring was that by no act or word of his should General Gordon be appointed to the Soudan, there were more powerful influences at work than even his strong will.

The publication of General Gordon's views in the *Pall Mall Gazette* of 9th January 1884 had roused public opinion to the importance and urgency of the matter. It had also revealed that there was at least one man who was not in terror of the Mahdi's power, and who thought that the situation might still be saved. There is no doubt that that publication was the direct and immediate cause of Lord Granville's telegram of 10th January; but Sir Evelyn Baring, unmoved by what people thought or said at home, coldly replied on 11th January that Gordon is not the man he wants. If there had been no other considerations in the matter, I have no doubt that Sir Evelyn Baring would have beaten public opinion, and carried matters in the high, dictatorial spirit he had shown since the first mention of Gordon's name. But he had not made allowance for an embarrassed and purposeless Government, asking only to be relieved of the whole trouble, and willing to adopt any suggestion—even to resign its place to "the unspeakable Turk"—so long as it was no longer worried in the matter.

At that moment Gordon appears on the scene, ready and anxious to undertake single-handed a task for which others prescribe armies and millions of money. Public opinion greets him as the man for the occasion, and certainly he is the man to suit "that" Government. The only obstruction is Sir Evelyn Baring. Against any other array of forces his views would have prevailed, but even for him these are too strong.

On 15th January Gordon saw Lord Wolseley, as described in the last chapter, and then and there it is discovered and arranged that he will go to the Soudan, but only at the Government's request, provided the King of the Belgians will consent to his postponing the fulfilment of his promise, as Gordon knows he cannot help but do, for it was given on the express stipulation that the claim of his own country should always come first. King Leopold, who has behaved throughout with generosity, and the most kind consideration towards Gordon, is naturally displeased and upset, but he feels that he cannot restrain Gordon or insist on the letter of his bond. The Congo Mission is therefore broken off or suspended, as described in the last chapter. In the evening of the 15th Lord Granville despatched a telegram to Sir Evelyn Baring, no longer asking his opinion or advice, but stating that the Government have determined to send General Gordon to the Soudan, and that he will start without delay. To that telegram the British representative could make no demur short of resigning his post, but at last the grudging admission was wrung from him that "Gordon would be the best man." This conclusion, to which anyone conversant with the facts, as Sir Evelyn Baring was, would have come at once, was therefore only arrived at seven weeks after Sir Charles Dilke first brought forward Gordon's name as the right person to deal with the Soudan difficulty. That loss of time was irreparable, and in the end proved fatal to Gordon himself.

In describing the last mission, betrayal, and death of Gordon, the heavy responsibility of assigning the just blame to those individuals who were in a special degree the cause of that hero's fate cannot be shirked by any writer pretending to record history. Lord Cromer has filled a difficult post in Egypt for many years with advantage to his country, but in the matter of General Gordon's last Nile mission he allowed his personal feelings to obscure his judgment. He knew that Gordon was a difficult, let it be granted an impossible, colleague; that he would do things in his own way in defiance of diplomatic timidity and official rigidity; and that, instead of there being in the Egyptian firmament the one planet Baring, there would be only the single sun of Gordon. All these considerations were human, but they none the less show that he allowed his private feelings, his resentment at Gordon's treatment of him in 1878, to bias his judgment in a matter of public moment. It was his opposition alone that retarded Gordon's departure by seven weeks, and indeed the delay was longer, as Gordon was then at Jaffa, and that delay, I repeat it solemnly, cost Gordon his life. Whoever else was to blame afterwards, the first against whom a verdict of Guilty must be entered, without any hope of reprieve at the bar of history, was Sir Evelyn Baring, now Lord Cromer.

Mr Gladstone and his Government are certainly clear of any reflection in this stage of the matter. They did their best to put forward General Gordon immediately on the news coming of the Hicks disaster, and although they might have shown greater determination in compelling the adoption of their plan, which they were eventually obliged to do, this was a very venial fault, and not in any serious way blameworthy. Nor did they ever seek to repudiate their responsibility for sending Gordon to the Soudan, although a somewhat craven statement by Lord Granville, in a speech at Shrewsbury in September 1885, to the effect that "Gordon went to Khartoum at his own request," might seem to infer that they did. This remark may have been a slip, or an incorrect mode of saying that Gordon willingly accepted the task given him by the Government, but Mr Gladstone placed the matter in its true light when he wrote that "General Gordon went to the Soudan at the request of H.M.'s Government."

Gordon, accompanied by Lieutenant-Colonel Donald Stewart, an officer who had visited the Soudan in 1883, and written an able report on it, left London by the Indian mail of 18th January 1884. The decision to send Colonel Stewart with him was arrived at only at the very last moment, and on the platform at Charing Cross Station the acquaintance of the two men bound together in such a desperate partnership practically began. It is worth recalling that in that hurried and stirring scene, when the War Office, with the Duke of Cambridge, had assembled to see him off, Gordon found time to say to one of Stewart's nearest relations, "Be sure that he will not go into any danger which I do not share, and I am sure that when I am in danger he will not be far behind."

Gordon's journey to Egypt was uneventful, but after the exciting events that preceded his departure he found the leisure of his sea-trip from Brindisi beneficial and advantageous, for the purpose of considering his position and taking stock of the situation he had to face. By habit and temperament Gordon was a bad emissary to carry out cut-and-dried instructions, more especially when they related to a subject upon which he felt very strongly and held pronounced views. The instructions which the Government gave him were as follows, and I quote the full text. They were probably not drawn up and in Gordon's hands more than two hours before he left Charing Cross, and personally I do not suppose that he had looked through them, much less studied them. His view of the matter never varied. He went to the Soudan to rescue the garrisons, and to carry out the evacuation of the province after providing for its administration. The letter given in the previous chapter shows how vague and incomplete was the agreement between himself and Ministers. It was nothing more than the expression of an idea that the Soudan should be evacuated, but how and under what conditions was left altogether to the chapter of accidents. At the start the Government's view of the matter and his presented no glaring difference. They sent General Gordon to rescue and withdraw the garrisons if he could do so, and they were also not averse to his establishing any administration that he chose. But the main point on which they laid stress was that they were to be no longer troubled in the affair. Gordon's marvellous qualities were to extricate them from the difficult position in which the shortcomings of the Egyptian Government had placed them, and beyond that they had no definite thought or care as to how the remedy was to be discovered and applied. The following instructions should be read by the light of these reflections, which show that, while they nominally started from the same point, Gordon and the Government were never really in touch, and had widely different goals in view:

Foreign Office
January 18th, 1884
Her Majesty's Government are desirous that you should proceed at once to Egypt, to report to them on the military situation in the Soudan, and on the measures which it may be advisable to take for the security of the Egyptian garrisons still holding positions in that country, and for the safety of the European population in Khartoum.

You are also desired to consider and report upon the best mode of effecting the evacuation of the interior of the Soudan, and upon the manner in which the safety and the good administration by the Egyptian Government of the ports on the sea-coast can best be secured.

In connection with this subject, you should pay especial consideration to the question of the steps that may usefully be taken to counteract the stimulus which it is feared may possibly be given to the Slave Trade by the present insurrectionary movement and by the withdrawal of the Egyptian authority from the interior.

You will be under the instructions of Her Majesty's Agent and Consul-General at Cairo, through whom your Reports to Her Majesty's Government should be sent, under flying seal.

You will consider yourself authorized and instructed to perform such other duties as the Egyptian Government may desire to entrust to you, and as may be communicated to you by Sir E. Baring. You will be accompanied by Colonel Stewart, who will assist you in the duties thus confided to you.

On your arrival in Egypt you will at once communicate with Sir E. Baring, who will arrange to meet you, and will settle with you whether you should proceed direct to Suakin, or should go yourself or despatch Colonel Stewart to Khartoum *viâ* the Nile.

General Gordon had not got very far on his journey before he began to see that there were points on which it would be better for him to know the Government's mind and to state his own. Neither at this time nor throughout the whole term of his stay at Khartoum did Gordon attempt to override the main decision of the Government policy, viz. to evacuate the Soudan, although he left plenty of documentary evidence to show that this was not his policy or opinion. Moreover, his own policy had been well set forth in the *Pall Mall Gazette*, and might be summed up in the necessity to keep the Eastern Soudan, and the impossibility of fortifying Lower Egypt against the advance of the Mahdi. But he had none the less consented to give his services to a Government which had decided on evacuation, and he remained loyal to that purpose, although in a little time it was made clear that there was a wide and impassable gulf between the views of the British Government and its too brilliant agent.

The first doubt that flashed through his mind, strangely enough, was about Zebehr. He knew, of course, that it had been proposed to employ him, and that Mr Gladstone had not altogether unnaturally decided against it. But Gordon knew the man's ability, his influence, and the close connection he still maintained with the Soudan, where his father-in-law Elias was the Mahdi's chief supporter, and the paymaster of his forces. I believe that Gordon was in his heart of the opinion that the Mahdi was only a lay figure, and that the real author of the whole movement in the Soudan was Zebehr, but that the Mahdi, carried away by his exceptional success, had somewhat altered the scope of the project, and given it an exclusively religious or fanatical character. It is somewhat difficult to follow all the workings of Gordon's mind on this point, nor is it necessary to do so, but the fact that should not be overlooked is Gordon's conviction in the great power for good or evil of Zebehr. Thinking this matter over in the train, he telegraphed from Brindisi to Lord Granville on 30th January, begging that Zebehr might be removed from Cairo to Cyprus. There is no doubt as to the wisdom of this suggestion, and had it been adopted the lives of Colonel Stewart and his companions would probably have been spared, for, as will be seen, there is good ground to think that they were murdered by men of his tribe. In Cyprus Zebehr would have been incapable of mischief, but no regard was paid to Gordon's wish, and thus commenced what proved to be a long course of indifference.

During the voyage from Brindisi to Port-Said Gordon drew up a memorandum on his instructions, correcting some of the errors that had crept into them, and explaining what, more or less, would be the best course to follow. One part of his instructions had to go by the board—that enjoining him to restore to the ancient families of the Soudan their long-lost possessions, for there were no such families in existence. One paragraph in that memorandum was almost pathetic, when he begged the Government to take the most favourable view of his shortcomings if he found himself compelled by necessity to deviate from his instructions. Colonel Stewart supported that view in a very sensible letter, when he advised the Government, "as the wisest course, to rely on the discretion of General Gordon and his knowledge of the country."

General Gordon's original plan was to proceed straight to Souakim, and to travel thence by Berber to Khartoum, leaving the Foreign Office to arrange at Cairo what his status should be, but this mode of proceeding would have been both irregular and inconvenient, and it was rightly felt that he ought to hold some definite position assigned by the Khedive, as the ruler of Egypt. On arriving at Port-Said he was met by Sir Evelyn Wood, who was the bearer of a private letter from his old Academy and Crimean chum, Sir Gerald Graham, begging him to "throw over all personal feelings" and come to Cairo. The appeal could not have come from a quarter that would carry more weight with Gordon, who had a feeling of affection as well as respect for General Graham; and, moreover, the course suggested was so unmistakably the right one, that he could not, and did not, feel any hesitation in taking it, although he was well aware of Sir Evelyn Baring's opposition, which showed that the sore of six years before still rankled. Gordon accordingly accompanied Sir Evelyn Wood to Cairo, where he arrived on the evening of 24th January. On the following day he was received by Tewfik, who conferred on him for the second time the high office of Governor-General of the Soudan. It is unnecessary to lay stress on any minor point in the recital of the human drama which began with the interview with Lord Wolseley on 15th January, and thence went on without a pause to the tragedy of 26th January in the following year; but it does seem strange, if the British Government were resolved to stand firm to its evacuation policy, that it should have allowed its emissary to accept the title of Governor-General of a province which it had decided should cease to exist.

This was not the only nor even the most important consequence of his turning aside to go to Cairo. When there, those who were interested for various reasons in the proposal to send Zebehr to the Soudan, made a last effort to carry their project by arranging an interview between that person and Gordon, in the hope that all matters in dispute between them might be discussed, and, if possible, settled. Gordon, whose enmity to his worst foe was never deep, and whose temperament would have made him delight in a discussion with the arch-fiend, said at once that he had no objection to meeting Zebehr, and would discuss any matter with him or any one else. The penalty of this magnanimity was that he was led to depart from the uncompromising but safe attitude of opposition and hostility he had up to this observed towards Zebehr, and to record opinions that were inconsistent with those he had expressed on the same subject only a few weeks and even days before. But even in what follows I believe it is safe to discern his extraordinary perspicuity; for when he saw that the Government would not send Zebehr to Cyprus, he promptly concluded that it would be far safer to take or have him with him in the Soudan, where he could personally watch and control his movements, than to allow him to remain at Cairo, guiding hostile plots with his money and influence in the very region whither Gordon was proceeding.

This view is supported by the following Memorandum, drawn up by General Gordon on 25th January 1884, the day before the interview, and entitled by him *Zebehr Pasha v. General Gordon*:

Zebehr Pasha's first connection with me began in 1877, when I was named Governor-General of Soudan. Zebehr was then at Cairo, being in litigation with Ismail Pasha Eyoub, my predecessor in Soudan. Zebehr had left his son Suleiman in charge of his forces in the Bahr Gazelle. Darfour was in complete rebellion, and I called on Suleiman to aid the Egyptian army in May 1877. He never moved. In June 1877 I went to Darfour, and was engaged with the rebels when Suleiman moved up his men, some 6000, to Dara. It was in August 1877. He and his men assumed an hostile attitude to the Government of Dara. I came down to Dara and went out to Suleiman's camp, and asked them to come and see me at

Dara. Suleiman and his chiefs did so, and I told them I felt sure that they meditated rebellion, but if they rebelled they would perish. I offered them certain conditions, appointing certain chiefs to be governors of certain districts, but refusing to let Suleiman be Governor of Bahr Gazelle. After some days' parleying, some of Suleiman's chiefs came over to my side, and these chiefs warned me that, if I did not take care, Suleiman would attack me. I therefore ordered Suleiman to go to Shaka, and ordered those chiefs who were inclined to accept my terms in another direction, so as to separate them. On this Suleiman accepted my terms, and he and others were made Beys. He left for Shaka with some 4000 men. He looted the country from Dara to Shaka, and did not show any respect to my orders. The rebellion in Darfour being settled, I went down to Shaka with 200 men. Suleiman was there with 4000. Then he came to me and begged me to let him have the sole command in Bahr Gazelle. I refused, and I put him, Suleiman, under another chief, and sent up to Bahr Gazelle 200 regular troops. Things remained quiet in Bahr Gazelle till I was ordered to Cairo in April 1878, about the finances. I then saw Zebehr Pasha, who wished to go up to Soudan, and I refused. I left for Aden in May, and in June 1878 Suleiman broke out in revolt, and killed the 200 regular troops at Bahr Gazelle. I sent Gessi against him in August 1878, and Gessi crushed him in the course of 1879. Gessi captured a lot of letters in the divan of Suleiman, one of which was from Zebehr Pasha inciting him to revolt. The original of this letter was given by me to H.H. the Khedive, and I also had printed a brochure containing it and a sort of *exposé* to the people of Soudan why the revolt had been put down—*viz.* that it was not a question of slave-hunting, but one of revolt against the Khedive's authority. Copies of this must exist. On the production of this letter of Zebehr to Suleiman, I ordered the confiscation of Zebehr's property in Soudan, and a court martial to sit on Zebehr's case. This court martial was held under Hassan Pasha Halmi; the court condemned Zebehr to death; its proceedings were printed in the brochure I alluded to. Gessi afterwards caught Suleiman and shot him. With details of that event I am not acquainted, and I never saw the papers, for I went to Abyssinia. Gessi's orders were to try him, and if guilty to shoot him. This is all I have to say about Zebehr and myself.

Zebehr, without doubt, was the greatest slave-hunter who ever existed. Zebehr is the most able man in the Soudan; he is a capital general, and has been wounded several times. Zebehr has a capacity of government far beyond any statesman in the Soudan. All the followers of the Mahdi would, I believe, leave the Mahdi on Zebehr's approach, for they are ex-chiefs of Zebehr. Personally, I have a great admiration for Zebehr, for he is a man, and is infinitely superior to those poor fellows who have been governors of Soudan; but I question in my mind, 'Will Zebehr ever forgive me the death of his son?' and that question has regulated my action respecting him, for I have been told he bears me the greatest malice, and one cannot wonder at it if one is a father.

I would even now risk taking Zebehr, and would willingly bear the responsibility of doing so, convinced, as I am, that Zebehr's approach ends the Mahdi, which is a question which has its pulse in Syria, the Hedjaz, and Palestine.

It cannot be the wish of H.M.'s Government, or of the Egyptian Government, to have an intestine war in the Soudan on its evacuation, yet such is sure to ensue, and the only way which could prevent it is the restoration of Zebehr, who would be accepted on all sides, and who would end the Mahdi in a couple of months. My duty is to obey orders of H.M.'s Government, *i.e.* to evacuate the Soudan as quickly as possible, *vis-à-vis* the safety of the Egyptian employees.

To do this I count on Zebehr; but if the addenda is made that I leave a satisfactory settlement of affairs, then Zebehr becomes a *sine quâ non*.

Therefore the question resolves itself into this. Does H.M.'s Government or Egyptian Government desire a settled state of affairs in Soudan after the evacuation? Do these Governments want to be free of this religious fanatic? If they do, then Zebehr should be sent; and if the two Governments are indifferent, then do not send him, and I have confidence one will (*D. V.*) get out the Egyptian employees in three or four months, and will leave a cockpit behind us. It is not my duty to dictate what should be done. I will only say, first, I was justified in my action against Zebehr; second, that if Zebehr has no malice personally against me, I should take him at once as a humanly certain settler of the Mahdi and of those in revolt. I have written this Minute, and Zebehr's story may be heard. I only wish that after he has been interrogated, I may be questioned on such subjects as his statements are at variance with mine. I would wish this inquiry to be official, and in such a way that, whatever may be the decision come to, it may be come to in my absence.

With respect to the slave-trade, I think nothing of it, for there will always be slave-trade as long as Turkey and Egypt buy the slaves, and it may be Zebehr will or might in his interest stop it in some manner. I will therefore sum up my opinion, viz. that I would willingly take the responsibility of taking Zebehr up with me if, after an interview with Sir E. Baring and Nubar Pasha, they tell 'the mystic feeling' I could trust him, and which 'mystic feeling' I felt I had for him tonight when I met him at Cherif Pasha's house. Zebehr would have nothing to gain in hunting me, and I would have no fear. In this affair my desire, I own, would be to take Zebehr. I cannot exactly say why I feel towards him thus, and I feel sure that his going would settle the Soudan affair to the benefit of H.M.'s Government, and I would bear the responsibility of recommending it.

C. G. Gordon
Major-General

An interview between Gordon and Zebehr was therefore arranged for 26th January, the day after this memorandum was written. On 25th it should also be remembered that the Khedive had again made Gordon Governor-General of the Soudan. Besides the two principals, there were present at this interview Sir Evelyn Baring, Sir Gerald Graham, Colonel Watson, and Nubar Pasha. Zebehr protested his innocence of the charges made against him; and when Gordon reminded him of his letter, signed with his hand and bearing his seal, found in the divan of his son Suleiman, he called upon Gordon to produce this letter, which, of course, he could not do, because it was sent with the other incriminating documents to the Khedive in 1879. The passage in that letter establishing the guilt of Zebehr may, however, be cited, it being first explained that Idris Ebter was Gordon's governor of the Bahr Gazelle province, and that Suleiman did carry out his father's instructions to attack him.

Now since this same Idris Ebter has not appreciated our kindness towards him, nor shown regard for his duty towards God, therefore do you accomplish his ejection by compulsory force, threats, and menaces, without personal hurt, but with absolute expulsion and deprivation from the Bahr-el-Gazelle, leaving no remnant of him in that region, no son, and no relation. For he is a mischief-maker, and God loveth not them who make mischief.

It is highly probable, from the air of confidence with which Zebehr called for the production of the letter, that, either during the Arabi rising or in some other way, he had recovered possession of the original; but Gordon had had all the documents copied in 1879, and bound in the little volume mentioned in the preceding Memorandum, as well as in several of his letters, and the evidence as to Zebehr's complicity and guilt seems quite conclusive.

In his Memorandum Gordon makes two conditions: first, "if Zebehr bears no malice personally against me, I will take him to the Soudan at once," and this condition is given further force later on in reference to "the mystic feeling." The second condition was that Zebehr was only to be sent if the Government desired a settled state of affairs after the evacuation. From the beginning of the interview it was clear to those present that no good would come of it, as Zebehr could scarcely control his feelings, and showed what they deemed a personal resentment towards Gordon that at any moment might have found expression in acts. After a brief discussion it was decided to adjourn the meeting, on the pretence of having search made for the incriminating document, but really to avert a worse scene. General Graham, in the after-discussion on Gordon's renewed desire to take Zebehr with him, declared that it would be dangerous to acquiesce; and Colonel Watson plainly stated that it would mean the death of one or both of them. Gordon, indifferent to all considerations of personal danger, did not take the same view of Zebehr's attitude towards him personally, and would still have taken him with him, if only on the ground that he would be less dangerous in the Soudan than at Cairo; but the authorities would not acquiesce in a proposition that they considered would inevitably entail the murder of Gordon at an early stage of the journey. They cannot, from any point of view, be greatly blamed in this matter; and when Gordon complains later on, as he frequently did complain, about the matter, the decision must be with his friends at Cairo, for they strictly conformed with the first condition specified in his own Memorandum. At the same time, he was perfectly correct in his views as to Zebehr's power and capacity for mischief, and it was certainly very unfortunate and wrong that his earlier suggestion of removing him to Cyprus or some other place of safety was not adopted.

The following new correspondence will at least suggest a doubt whether Gordon was not more correct in his view of Zebehr's attitude towards himself than his friends. What they deemed strong resentment and a bitter personal feeling towards Gordon on the part of Zebehr, he considered merely the passing excitement from discussing a matter of great moment and interest. He would still have taken Zebehr with him, and for many weeks after his arrival at Khartoum he expected that, in reply to his frequently reiterated messages, "Send me Zebehr," the ex-Dictator of the Soudan would be sent up from Cairo. In one of the last letters to his sister, dated Khartoum, 5th March 1884, he wrote: "I hope *much* from Zebehr's coming up, for he is so well known to all up here." I come now to the correspondence referred to.

Some time after communications were broken off with Khartoum, Miss Gordon wrote to Zebehr, begging him to use his influence with the Mahdi to get letters for his family to and from General Gordon. To that Zebehr replied as follows:

> *To Her Excellency Miss Gordon,*—I am very grateful to you for having had the honour of receiving your letter of the 13th, and am very sorry to say that I am not able to write to the Mahdi, because he is new, and has appeared lately in the Soudan. I do not know him. He is not of my tribe nor of my relations, nor of the tribes with which I was on friendly terms; and for these reasons I do not see the way in which I could carry out your wish. I am ready to serve you in all that is possible all my life through, but please accept my excuse in this matter.
> Please accept my best respects.
> *Zebehr Rahamah*, Pasha
> Cairo
> 22nd January 1885

Some time after the fall of Khartoum, Miss Gordon made a further communication to Zebehr, but, owing to his having been exiled to Gibraltar, it was not until October 1887 that she received the following reply, which is certainly curious; and I believe that this letter and personal conversations with Zebehr induced one of the officers present at the interview on 26th January 1884 to change his original opinion, and to conclude that it would have been safe for General Gordon to have taken Zebehr with him:

> Cairo
> *Honourable Lady,*—I most respectfully beg to acknowledge the receipt of your letter, enclosed to that addressed to me by His Excellency Watson Pasha.

This letter has caused me a great satisfaction, as it speaks of the friendly relations that existed between me and the late Gordon Pasha, your brother, whom you have replaced in my heart, and this has been ascertained to me by your inquiring about me and your congratulating me for my "return to Cairo".

I consider that your poor brother is still alive in you, and for the whole run of my life I put myself at your disposal, and beg that you will count upon me as a true and faithful friend to you.

You will also kindly pay my respects to the whole family of Gordon Pasha, and may you not deprive me of your good news at any time.

My children and all my family join themselves to me, and pay you their best respects.

Further, I beg to inform you that the messenger who had been previously sent through me, carrying Government correspondence to your brother, Gordon Pasha, has reached him, and remitted the letter he had in his own hands, and without the interference of any other person. The details of his history are mentioned in the enclosed report, which I hope you will kindly read.—Believe me, honourable Lady, to remain yours most faithfully,

Zebehr Rahamah

Report Enclosed

When I came to Cairo and resided in it as I was before, I kept myself aside of all political questions connected with the Soudan or others, according to the orders given me by the Government to that effect. But as a great rumour was spread over by the high Government officials who arrived from the Soudan, and were with H.E. General Gordon Pasha at Khartoum before and after it fell, that all my properties in that country had been looted, and my relations ill-treated, I have been bound, by a hearty feeling of compassion, to ask the above said officials what they knew about it, and whether the messenger sent by me with the despatches addressed by the Government to General Gordon Pasha had reached Khartoum and remitted what he had.

These officials informed me verbally that on the 25th Ramadan 1301 (March 1884), at the time they were sitting at Khartoum with General Gordon, my messenger, named Fadhalla Kabileblos, arrived there, and remitted to the General in his proper hands, and without the interference of anyone, all the despatches he had on him. After that the General expressed his greatest content for the receipt of the correspondence, and immediately gave orders to the artillery to fire twenty-five guns, in sign of rejoicing, and in order to show to the enemy his satisfaction for the news of the arrival of British troops. General Gordon then treated my messenger cordially, and requested the Government to pay him a sum of £500 on his return to Cairo, as a gratuity for all the dangers he had run in accomplishing his faithful mission. Besides that, the General gave him, when he embarked with Colonel Stewart, £13 to meet his expenses on the journey. A few days after the arrival of my messenger at Khartoum, H.E. General Gordon thought it proper to appoint Colonel Stewart for coming to Cairo on board a man-of-war with a secret mission, and several letters, written by the General in English and Arabic, were put in two envelopes, one addressed to the British and the other to the Egyptian Government, and were handed over to my messenger, with the order to return to Cairo with Colonel Stewart on board a special steamer.

But when Khartoum fell, and the rebels got into it, making all the inhabitants prisoners, the Government officials above referred to were informed that my messenger had been arrested, and all the correspondence that he had on him, addressed by General Gordon to the Government, was seized; for when the steamer on board of which they were arrived at Abou Kamar she went on rocks, and having been broken, the rebels made a massacre of all those who were on board; and as, on seeing the letters carried by my messenger, they found amongst them a private letter addressed to me by H.E. Gordon Pasha, expressing his thanks for my faithfulness to him, the rebels declared me an infidel, and decided to seize all my goods and properties, comprising them in their *Beit-el-Mal* (that is, Treasury) as it happened in fact.

Moreover, the members of my family who were in the Soudan were treated most despotically, and their existence was rendered most difficult.

Such a state of things being incompatible with the suspicion thrown upon me as regards my faithfulness to the Government, I have requested the high Government officials referred to above to give me an official certificate to that effect, which they all gave; and the enclosed copies will make known to those who take the trouble to read them that I have been honest and faithful in all what has been entrusted to me. This is the summary of the information I have obtained from persons I have reason to believe.

Some further evidence of Zebehr's feelings is given in the following letter from him to Sir Henry Gordon, dated in October 1884:

Your favour of 3rd September has been duly received, for which I thank you. I herewith enclose my photograph, and hope that you will kindly send me yours.

The letter that you wished me to send H.E. General Gordon was sent on the 18th August last, registered. I hope that you will excuse me in delaying to reply, for when your letter arrived I was absent, and when I returned I was very sorry that they had not forwarded the letter to me; otherwise I should have replied at once.

I had closed this letter with the photograph when I received fresh news, to the effect that the messengers we sent to H.E. Gordon Pasha were on their way back. I therefore kept back the letter and photograph till they arrived, and I should see what tidings they brought. . . . You have told me that Lord Northbrook knows what has passed between us. I endeavoured and devised to see His Excellency, but I did not succeed, as he was very busy. I presented a petition to him that he should help to recover the property of which I was robbed unjustly, and which H.E. your brother ordered to be restored, and at the same time to right me for the oppression I had suffered. I have had no answer up to this present moment.

Hoping that H.E. Gordon Pasha will return in safety, accept my best regards, dear Sir, and present my compliments to your sister.
Zebehr
28th October, 1884

To sum up on this important matter. There never was any doubt that the authorities in the Delta took on themselves a grave responsibility when they remained deaf to all Gordon's requests for the co-operation of Zebehr. They would justify themselves by saying that they had a tender regard for Gordon's own safety. At least this was the only point on which they showed it, and they would not like to be deprived of the small credit attached to it; but the evidence I have now adduced renders even this plea of doubtful force. As to the value of Zebehr's co-operation, if Gordon could have obtained it there cannot be two opinions. Gordon did not exaggerate in the least degree when he said that on the approach of Zebehr the star of the Mahdi would at once begin to wane, or, in other words, that he looked to Zebehr's ability and influence as the sure way to make his own mission a success.

On the very night of his interview with Zebehr, and within forty-eight hours of his arrival in Cairo, General Gordon and his English companion, with four Egyptian officers, left by train for Assiout, *en route* to Khartoum.

CHAPTER 12

Khartoum

Before entering on the events of this crowning passage in the career of this hero, I think the reader might well consider on its threshold the exact nature of the adventure undertaken by Gordon as if it
were a sort of everyday experience and duty. At the commencement
of the year 1884 the military triumph of the Mahdi was as complete as
it could be throughout the Soudan. Khartoum was still held by a force
of between 4000 and 6000 men. Although not known, all the other
garrisons in the Nile Valley, except Kassala and Sennaar, both near the
Abyssinian frontier, had capitulated, and the force at Khartoum would
certainly have offered no resistance if the Mahdi had advanced immediately after the defeat of Hicks. Even if he had reached Khartoum before the arrival of Gordon, it is scarcely doubtful that the place would
have fallen without fighting. Colonel de Coetlogon was in command,
but the troops had no faith in him, and he had no confidence in them.
That officer, on 9th January, "telegraphed to the Khedive, strongly
urging an immediate withdrawal from Khartoum. He said that one-
third of the garrison are unreliable, and that even if it were twice as
strong as it is, it would not hold Khartoum against the whole country."
In several subsequent telegrams Colonel de Coetlogon importuned
the Cairo authorities to send him authority to leave with the garrison,
and on the very day that the Government finally decided to despatch
Gordon he telegraphed that there was only just enough time left to
escape to Berber. While the commandant held and expressed these
views, it is not surprising that the garrison and inhabitants were disheartened and decidedly unfit to make any resolute opposition to a
confident and daring foe. There is excellent independent testimony as
to the state of public feeling in the town.

Mr Frank Power had been residing in Khartoum as correspondent of *The Times* from August 1883, and in December, after the Hicks catastrophe, he was appointed Acting British Consul. In a letter written on 12th January he said: "They have done nothing for us yet from Cairo. They are leaving it all to fate, and the rebels around us are growing stronger!" Such was the general situation at Khartoum when General Gordon was ordered, almost single-handed, to save it; and not merely to rescue its garrison, pronounced by its commander to be partly unreliable and wholly inadequate, but other garrisons scattered throughout the regions held by the Mahdi and his victorious legions. A courageous man could not have been charged with cowardice if he had shrunk back from such a forlorn hope, and declined to take on his shoulders the responsibility that properly devolved on the commander on the spot. A prudent man would at least have insisted that his instructions should be clear, and that the part his Government and country were to play was to be as strictly defined and as obligatory on them as his own. But while Gordon's courage was of such a quality that I believe no calculation of odds or difficulties ever entered into his view, his prudence never possessed the requisite amount of suspicion to make him provide against the contingencies of absolute betrayal by those who sent him, or of that change in party convenience and tactics which induced those who first thought his mission most advantageous as solving a difficulty, or at least putting off a trouble, to veer round to the conclusion that his remaining at Khartoum, his honourable but rigid resolve not to return without the people he went to save, was a distinct breach of contract, and a serious offence.

The state of feeling at Khartoum was one verging on panic. The richest townsmen had removed their property and families to Berber. Colonel de Coetlogon had the river boats with steam up ready to commence the evacuation, and while everyone thought that the place was doomed, the telegraph instrument was eagerly watched for the signal to begin the flight. The tension could not have lasted much longer—without the signal the flight would have begun—when on 24th January the brief message arrived: "General Gordon is coming to Khartoum."

The effect of that message was electrical. The panic ceased, confidence was restored, the apathy of the Cairo authorities became a matter of no importance, for England had sent her greatest name as a pledge of her intended action, and the unreliable and insufficient garrison pulled itself together for one of the most honourable and brilliant defences in the annals of military sieges. Yet it was full time. Two months had been wasted, and, as Mr Power said, "the fellows in Lucknow did not look more anxiously for Colin Campbell than we are looking for

Gordon." Gordon, ever mindful of the importance of time, and fully impressed with the sense of how much had been lost by delay, did not let the grass grow under his feet, and after his two days' delay at Cairo sent a message that he hoped to reach Khartoum in eighteen days. Mr Power's comment on that message is as follows: "Twenty-four days is the shortest time from Cairo to Khartoum on record; Gordon says he will be here in eighteen days; but he travels like a whirlwind." As a matter of fact, Gordon took twenty days' travelling, besides the two days he passed at Berber. He thus reached Khartoum on 18th February, and four days later Colonel de Coetlogon started for Cairo.

The entry of Gordon into Khartoum was marked by a scene of indescribable enthusiasm and public confidence. The whole population, men, women, and children, turned out to welcome him as a conqueror and a deliverer, although he really came in his own person merely to cope with a desperate situation. The women threw themselves on the ground and struggled to kiss his feet; in the confusion Gordon was several times pushed down; and this remarkable demonstration of popular confidence and affection was continued the whole way from the landing-place to the *Hukumdaria* or Palace. This greeting was the more remarkable because it was clear that Gordon had brought no troops—only one white officer—and it soon became known that he had brought no money. Even the Mahdi himself made his contribution to the general tribute, by sending General Gordon on his arrival a formal *salaam* or message of respect. Thus hailed on all hands as the one pre-eminently good man who had been associated with the Soudan, Gordon addressed himself to the hard task he had undertaken, which had been rendered almost hopeless of achievement by the lapse of time, past errors, and the blindness of those who should have supported him.

Difficult as it had been all along, it was rendered still more difficult by the decisive defeat of Baker Pasha and an Egyptian force of 4000 men at Tokar, near Souakim. This victory was won by Osman Digma, who had been sent by the Mahdi to rouse up the Eastern Soudan at the time of the threatened Hicks expedition. The result showed that the Mahdi had discovered a new lieutenant of great military capacity and energy, and that the Eastern Soudan was for the time as hopelessly lost to Egypt as Kordofan and Darfour.

The first task to which Gordon addressed himself was to place Khartoum and the detached work at Omdurman on the left bank of the White Nile in a proper state of defence, and he especially supervised the establishment of telegraphic communication between the

Palace and the many outworks, so that at a moment's notice he might receive word of what was happening. His own favourite position became the flat roof of this building, whence with his glass he could see round for many miles. He also laid in considerable stores of provisions by means of his steamers, in which he placed the greatest faith. In all these matters he was ably and energetically assisted by Colonel Stewart; and beyond doubt the other Europeans took some slight share in the incessant work of putting Khartoum in a proper state of defence; but even with this relief, the strain, increased by constant alarms of the Mahdi's hostile approach, was intense, and Mr Power speaks of Gordon as nearly worn out with work before he had been there a month.

When Gordon went to the Soudan his principal object was to effect the evacuation of the country, and to establish there some administration which would be answerable for good order and good neighbourship. If the Mahdi had been a purely secular potentate, and not a fanatical religious propagandist, it would have been a natural and feasible arrangement to have come to terms with him as the conqueror of the country. But the basis of the Mahdi's power forbade his being on terms with anyone. If he had admitted the equal rights of Egypt and the Khedive at any point, there would have been an end to his heavenly mission, and the forces he had created out of the simple but deep-rooted religious feelings of the Mahommedan clans of the Soudan would soon have vanished. It is quite possible that General Gordon had in his first views on the Mahdist movement somewhat undervalued the forces created by that fanaticism, and that the hopes and opinions he first expressed were unduly optimistic. If so, it must be allowed that he lost not a moment in correcting them, and within a week of his arrival at Khartoum he officially telegraphed to Cairo, that "if Egypt is to be quiet the Mahdi must be smashed up."

When the British Government received that message, as they did in a few days, with, moreover, the expression of supporting views by Sir Evelyn Baring, they ought to have reconsidered the whole question of the Gordon mission, and to have defined their own policy. The representative they had sent on an exceptional errand to relieve and bring back a certain number of distressed troops, and to arrange if he could for the formation of a new government through the notabilities and ancient families, reports at an early stage of his mission that in his opinion there is no solution of the difficulty, save by resorting to offensive measures against the Mahdi as the disturber of the peace, not merely for that moment, but as long as he had to discharge the divine task implied by his title. As it was of course obvious that Gordon single-handed could not take the field, the conclusion necessarily followed that he would require troops, and the whole character of his task would thus have been changed. In face of that absolute *volte-face*, from a policy of evacuation and retreat to one of retention and advance, for that is what it signified, the Government would have been justified in recalling Gordon, but as they did not do so, they cannot plead ignorance of his changed opinion, or deny that, at the very moment he became acquainted with the real state of things at Khartoum, he hastened to convey to them his decided conviction that the only way out of the difficulty was to "smash up the Mahdi."

All his early messages show that there had been a change, or at least a marked modification, in his opinions. At Khartoum he saw more clearly than in Cairo or in London the extreme gravity of the situation, and the consequences to the tranquillity of Lower Egypt that would follow from the abandonment of Khartoum to the Mahdi. He therefore telegraphed on the day of his arrival these words:

> To withdraw without being able to place a successor in my seat would be the signal for general anarchy throughout the country, which, though all Egyptian element were withdrawn, would be a misfortune, and inhuman.

In the same message he repeated his demand for the services of Zebehr, through whom, as has been shown, he thought he might be able to cope with the Mahdi. Yet their very refusal to comply with that reiterated request should have made the authorities more willing and eager to meet the other applications and suggestion of a man who had thrust himself into a most perilous situation at their bidding, and for the sake of the reputation of his country. It must be recorded with feelings of shame that it had no such effect, and that apathy and indifference to the fate of its gallant agent were during the first few months the only characteristics of the Government policy.

At the same period all Gordon's telegrams and despatches showed that he wanted reinforcements to some small extent, and at least military demonstrations along his line of communication with Egypt to prove that he possessed the support of his Government, and that he had only to call upon it to send troops, and they were there to come. He, naturally enough, treated as ridiculous the suggestion that he had bound himself to do the whole work without any support; and fully convinced that he had only to summon troops for them to be sent him in the moderate strength he alone cared for, he issued a proclamation in Khartoum, stating that "British troops are now on their way, and in a few days will reach Khartoum." He therefore begged for the despatch of a small force to Wady Halfa, and he went on to declare that it would be "comparatively easy to destroy the Mahdi" if 200 British troops were sent to Wady Halfa, and if the Souakim–Berber route were opened up by Indian-Moslem troops. Failing the adoption of these measures, he asked leave to raise a sum, by appealing to philanthropists, sufficient to pay a small Turkish force and carry on a contest for supremacy with the Mahdi on his own behalf. All these suggestions were more or less supported by Sir Evelyn Baring, who at last suggested in an important despatch, dated 28th February, that the British Government should withdraw altogether from the matter, and "give full liberty of action to General Gordon and the Khedive's Government to do what seems best to them."

Well would it have been for Gordon and everyone whose reputation was concerned if this step had been taken, for the Egyptian Government, the Khedive, his ministers Nubar and Cherif, were opposed to all surrender, and desired to hold on to Khartoum and the Souakim–Berber route. But without the courage and resolution to discharge it, the Government saw the obligation that lay on them to provide for the security and good government of Egypt, and that if they shirked responsibility in the Soudan, the independence of Egypt might be accomplished by its own effort and success. They perceived the objections to giving Egypt a free hand, but they none the less abstained from taking the other course of definite and decisive action on their own initiative. As Gordon quickly saw and tersely expressed: "You will not let Egypt keep the Soudan, you will not take it yourself, and you will not permit any other country to occupy it."

As if to give emphasis to General Gordon's successive requests— Zebehr, 200 men to Wady Halfa, opening of route from Souakim to Berber, presence of English officers at Dongola, and of Indian cavalry at Berber—telegraphic communication with Khartoum was interrupted early in March, less than a fortnight after Gordon's arrival in the town. There was consequently no possible excuse for anyone ignoring the dangerous position in which General Gordon was placed. He had gone to face incalculable dangers, but now the success of Osman Digma and the rising of the riparian tribes threatened him with that complete isolation which no one had quite expected at so early a stage after his arrival. It ought, and one would have expected it, to have produced an instantaneous effect, to have braced the Government to the task of deciding what its policy should be when challenged by its own representative to declare it. Gordon himself soon realised his own position, for he wrote: "I shall be caught in Khartoum; and even if I was mean enough to escape I have not the power to do so." After a month's interruption he succeeded in getting the following message, dated 8th April, through, which is significant as showing that he had abandoned all hope of being supported by his own Government:

> I have telegraphed to Sir Samuel Baker to make an appeal to British and American millionaires to give me £300,000 to engage 3000 Turkish troops from the Sultan and send them here. This would settle the Soudan and Mahdi for ever. For my part, I think you (Baring) will agree with me. I do not see the fun of being caught here to walk about the streets for years as a dervish with sandaled feet. Not that (*D. V.*) I will ever be taken alive. It would be the climax of meanness after I had borrowed money from the people here, had called on them to sell their grain at a low price, etc., to go and abandon them without using every effort to relieve them, whether those efforts are diplomatically correct or not; and I feel sure, whatever you may feel diplomatically, I have your support, and that of every man professing himself a gentleman, in private.

Eight days later he succeeded in getting another message through, to the following effect:

> As far as I can understand, the situation is this. You state your intention of not sending any relief up here or to Berber, and you refuse me Zebehr. I consider myself free to act according to circumstances. I shall hold on here as long as I can, and if I can suppress the rebellion I shall do so. If I cannot, I shall retire to the Equator and leave you the indelible disgrace of abandoning the garrisons of Senaar, Kassala, Berber, and Dongola, with the *certainty* that you will eventually be forced to smash up the Mahdi under greater difficulties if you wish to maintain peace in, and, indeed, to retain Egypt.

Before a silence of five and a half months fell over Khartoum, Gordon had been able to make three things clear, and of these only one could be described as having a personal signification, and that was that the Government, by rejecting all his propositions, had practically abandoned him to his fate. The two others were that any settlement would be a work of time, and that no permanent tranquillity could be attained without overcoming the Mahdi.

Immediately on arriving at Khartoum he perceived that the evacuation of the Soudan, with safety to the garrison and officials, as well as the preservation of the honour of England and Egypt, would necessarily be a work of time, and only feasible if certain measures were taken in his support, which, considerable as they may have appeared at the moment, were small and costless in comparison with those that had subsequently to be sanctioned. Six weeks sufficed to show Gordon that he would get no material help from the Government, and he then began to look elsewhere for support, and to propound schemes for pacifying the Soudan and crushing the Mahdi in which England and the Government would have had no part. Hence his proposal to appeal to wealthy philanthropists to employ Turkish troops, and in the last resort to force his way to the Equator and the Congo. Even that avenue of safety was closed to him by the illusory prospect of rescue held out to him by the Government at the eleventh hour, when success was hardly attainable.

For the sake of clearness it will be well to give here a brief summary of the siege during the six months that followed the arrival of General Gordon and the departure of Colonel Stewart on 10th September. The full and detailed narrative is contained in Colonel Stewart's Journal, which was captured on board his steamer. This interesting diary was taken to the Mahdi at Omdurman, and is said to be carefully preserved in the Treasury. The statement rests on no very sure foundation, but if true the work may yet thrill the audience of the English-speaking world. But even without its aid the main facts of the siege of Khartoum, down at all events to the 14th December, when Gordon's own diary stops, are sufficiently well known for all the purposes of history.

At a very early stage of the siege General Gordon determined to try the metal of his troops, and the experiment succeeded to such a perfect extent that there was never any necessity to repeat it. On 16th March, when only irregular levies and detached bodies of tribesmen were in the vicinity of Khartoum, he sent out a force of nearly 1000 men, chiefly Bashi–Bazouks, but also some regulars, with a field-piece and supported by two steamers. The force started at eight in the morning, under the command of Colonel Stewart, and landed at Halfiyeh, some miles down the stream on the right bank of the Nile. Here the rebels had established a sort of fortified position, which it was desirable to destroy, if it could be done without too much loss. The troops were accordingly drawn up for the attack, and the gun and infantry fire commenced to cover the advance. At this moment about sixty rebel horsemen came out from behind the stockade and charged the Bashi-Bazouks, who fired one volley and fled. The horsemen then charged the infantry drawn up in square, which they broke, and the retreat to the river began at a run. Discouraging as this was for a force of all arms to retire before a few horsemen one-twentieth its number, the disaster was rendered worse and more disheartening by the conduct of the men, who absolutely refused to fight, marching along with shouldered arms without firing a shot, while the horsemen picked off all who straggled from the column. The gun, a considerable quantity of ammunition, and about sixty men represented the loss of Gordon's force; the rebels are not supposed to have lost a single man. "Nothing could be more dismal than seeing these horsemen, and some men even on camels, pursuing close to troops who with shouldered arms plodded their way back." Thus wrote Gordon of the men to whom he had to trust for a successful defence of Khartoum. His most recent experience confirmed his old opinion, that the Egyptian and Arab troops were useless even when fighting to save their own lives, and he could only rely on the very small body left of black Soudanese, who fought as gallantly for him as any troops could, and whose loyalty and devotion to him surpassed all praise. Treachery, it was assumed, had something to do with the easy overthrow of this force, and two Pashas were shot for misconduct on return to Khartoum.

Having no confidence in the bulk of his force, it is not surprising that Gordon resorted to every artifice within engineering science to compensate for the shortcomings of his army. He surrounded Khartoum—which on one side was adequately defended by the Nile and his steamers—on the remaining three sides with a triple line of land mines connected by wires. Often during the siege the Mahdists attempted to break through this ring, but only to meet with repulse, accompanied by heavy loss; and to the very last day of the siege they never succeeded in getting behind the third of these lines. Their efficacy roused Gordon's professional enthusiasm, and in one passage he exclaims that these will be the general form of defence in the future. During the first months of the siege, which began rather in the form of a loose investment, the Nile was too low to allow of his using the nine steamers he possessed, but he employed the time in making two new ones, and in strengthening them all with bulwarks of iron plates and soft wood, which were certainly bullet-proof. Each of these steamers he valued as the equivalent of 2000 men. When it is seen how he employed them the value will not be deemed excessive, and certainly without them he could not have held Khartoum and baffled all the assaults of the Mahdi for the greater part of a year.

After this experience Gordon would risk no more combats on land, and on 25th March he dismissed 250 of the Bashi-Bazouks who had behaved so badly. Absolutely trustworthy statistics are not available as to the exact number of troops in Khartoum or as to the proportion the Black Soudanese bore to the Egyptians, but it approximates to the truth to say that there were about 1000 of the former to 3000 of the latter, and with other levies during the siege he doubled this total. For these and a civilian population of nearly 40,000 Gordon computed that he had provisions for five months from March, and that for at least two months he would be as safe as in Cairo. By carefully husbanding the corn and biscuit he was able to make the supply last much longer, and even to the very end he succeeded in partially replenishing the depleted granaries of the town. There is no necessity to repeat the details of the siege during the summer of 1884. They are made up of almost daily interchanges of artillery fire from the town, and of rifle fire in reply from the Arab lines. That this was not merely child's play may be gathered from two of Gordon's protected ships showing nearly a thousand bullet-marks apiece. Whenever the rebels attempted to force their way through the lines they were repulsed by the mines; and the steamers not only inflicted loss on their fighting men, but often suc-ceeded in picking up useful supplies of food and grain. No further reverses were reported, because Gordon was most careful to avoid all risk, and the only misfortunes occurred in Gordon's rear, when first Berber, through the treachery of the Greek Cuzzi, and then Shendy passed into the hands of the Mahdists, thus, as Gordon said, "completely hemming him in." In April a detached force up the Blue Nile went over to the Mahdi, taking with them a small steamer, but this loss was of no great importance, as the men were of what Gordon called "the Arabi hen or hero type," and the steamer could not force its way past Khartoum and its powerful flotilla. In the four months from 16th March to 30th July Gordon stated that the total loss of the garrison was only thirty killed and fifty or sixty wounded, while half a million cartridges had been fired against the enemy. The conduct of both the people and garrison had been excellent, and this was the more creditable, because Gordon was obliged from the very beginning, owing to the capture of the bullion sent him at Berber, to make all payments in paper money bearing his signature and seal. During that period the total reinforcement to the garrison numbered seven men, including Gordon himself, while over 2600 persons had been sent out of it in safety as far as Berber.

The reader will be interested in the following extracts from a letter written by Colonel Duncan, R.A., M.P., showing the remarkable way in which General Gordon organised the despatch of these refugees from Khartoum. The letter is dated 29th November 1886, and addressed to Miss Gordon:

When your brother, on reaching Khartoum, found that he could commence sending refugees to Egypt, I was sent on the 3rd March 1884 to Assouan and Korosko to receive those whom he sent down. As an instance of your brother's thoughtfulness, I may mention that he requested that, if possible, some motherly European woman might also be sent, as many of the refugees whom he had to send had never been out of the Soudan before, and might feel strange on reaching Egypt. A German, Giegler Pasha, who had been in Khartoum with your brother before, and who had a German wife, was accordingly placed at my disposal, and I stationed them at Korosko, where almost all the refugees arrived. I may mention that I saw and spoke to every one of the refugees who came down, and to many of the women and children. Their references to your brother were invariably couched in language of affection and gratitude, and the adjective most frequently applied to him was 'just.' In sending away the people from Khartoum, he sent away the Governor and some of the other leading Egyptian officials first. I think he suspected they would intrigue; he always had more confidence in the people than in the ruling Turks or Egyptians. The oldest soldiers, the very infirm, the wounded (from Hicks's battles) were sent next, and a ghastly crew they were. But the precautions he took for their comfort were very complete, and although immediately before reaching me they had to cross a very bad part of the desert between Abou Hamed and Korosko, they reached me in wonderful spirits. It was touching to see the perfect confidence they had that the promises of Gordon Pasha would be fulfilled. After the fall of Khartoum, and your brother's death, a good many of the Egyptian officers who had been with your brother managed to escape, and to come down the river disguised in many cases as beggars. I had an opportunity of talking to most of them, and there was no collusion, for they arrived at different times and by different roads. I remember having a talk with one, and when we alluded to your brother's

348

death he burst out crying like a child, and said that though he had lost his wives and children when Khartoum was taken, he felt it as nothing to the loss of 'that just man.'

The letters written at the end of July at Khartoum reached Cairo at the end of September, and their substance was at once telegraphed to England. They showed that, while his success had made him think that after all there might be some satisfactory issue of the siege, he foresaw that the real ordeal was yet to come. "In four months (that is end of November) river begins to fall; before that time you *must* settle the Soudan question." So wrote the heroic defender of Khartoum in words that could not be misunderstood, and those words were in the hands of the British Ministers when half the period had expired. At the same time Mr Power wrote: "We can at best hold out but two months longer." Gordon at least never doubted what their effect would be, for after what seemed to him a reasonable time had elapsed to enable this message to reach its destination, he took the necessary steps to recover Berber, and to send his steamers half-way to meet and assist the advance of the reinforcement on which he thought from the beginning he might surely rely.

On 10th September all his plans were completed, and Colonel Stewart, accompanied by a strong force of Bashi-Bazouks and some black soldiers, with Mr Power and M. Herbin, the French consul, sailed northwards on five steamers. The first task of this expedition was if possible, to retake Berber, or, failing that, to escort the *Abbas* past the point of greatest danger; the second, to convey the most recent news about Khartoum affairs to Lower Egypt; and the third was to lend a helping hand to any force that might be coming up the Nile or across the desert from the Red Sea. Five days after its departure Gordon knew through a spy that Stewart's flotilla had passed Shendy in safety, and had captured a valuable Arab convoy. It was not till November that the truth was known how the ships bombarded Berber, and passed that place not only in safety, but after causing the rebels much loss and greater alarm, and then how Stewart and his European companions went on in the small steamer *Abbas* to bear the tale of the wonderful defence of Khartoum to the outer world—a defence which, wonderful as it was, really only reached the stage of the miraculous after they had gone and had no further part in it. So far as Gordon's military skill and prevision could arrange for their safety, he did so, and with success. When the warships had to return he gave them the best advice against treachery or ambuscade:—"Do not anchor near the bank, do not collect wood at isolated spots, trust nobody." What more could Gordon say? If they had paid strict heed to his advice, there would have been no catastrophe at Dar Djumna. These reflections invest with much force Gordon's own view of the matter:—"If *Abbas* was captured by treachery, then I am not to blame; neither am I to blame if she struck a rock, for she drew under two feet of water; if they were attacked and overpowered, then I am to blame." So perfect were his arrangements that only treachery, aided by Stewart's over-confidence, baffled them.

With regard to the wisdom of the course pursued in thus sending away all his European colleagues—the Austrian consul Hensall alone refusing to quit Gordon and his place of duty—opinions will differ to the end of time, but one is almost inclined to say that they could not have been of much service to Gordon once their uppermost thought became to quit Khartoum. The whole story is told very graphically in a passage of Gordon's own diary:

> I determined to send the *Abbas* down with an Arab captain. Herbin asked to be allowed to go. I jumped at his offer. Then Stewart said he would go if I would exonerate him from deserting me. I said, 'You do not desert me. I cannot go; but if you go you do great service.' I then wrote him an official; he wanted me to write him an order. I said 'No; for, though I fear not responsibility, I will not put you in any danger in which I am not myself.' I wrote them a letter couched thus:—'*Abbas* is going down; you say you are willing to go in her if I think you can do so in honour. You can go in honour, for you can do nothing here; and if you go you do me service in telegraphing my views.'

There are two points in this matter to which I must draw marked attention. The suggestion for any European leaving Khartoum came from M. Herbin, and when Gordon willingly acquiesced, Colonel Stewart asked leave to do likewise. Mr Power, whose calculation was that provisions would be exhausted before the end of September, then followed suit, and not one of these three of the five Europeans in Khartoum seem to have thought for a moment what would be the position of Gordon left alone to cope with the danger from which they ran away. The suggestion as to their going came in every case from themselves. Gordon, in his thought for others, not merely threw no obstacle in their way, but as far as he could provided for their safety as if they were a parcel of women. But he declined all responsibility for their fate, as they went not by his order but of their own free-will. He gave them his ships, soldiers, and best counsel.

They neglected the last, and were taken in in a manner that showed less than a child's suspicion, and were massacred at the very moment they felt sure of safety. It was a cruel fate, and a harsh Nemesis speedily befell them for doing perhaps the one unworthy thing of their lives—leaving their solitary companion to face the tenfold dangers by which he would be beset. But it cannot be allowed any longer that the onus of this matter should rest in any way on Gordon. They went because they wanted to go, and he, knowing well that men with such thoughts would be of no use to him ("you can do nothing here") let them go, and even encouraged them to do so. Under the circumstances he preferred to be alone. Colonel Donald Stewart was a personal friend of mine, and a man whose courage in the ordinary sense of the word could not be aspersed, but there cannot be two opinions that he above all the others should not have left his brother-in-arms alone in Khartoum.

After their departure Gordon had to superintend everything himself, and to resort to every means of husbanding the limited supply of provisions he had left. He had also to anticipate a more vigorous attack, for the Mahdi must quickly learn of the departure of the steamers, the bombardment of Berber, and the favourable chance thus provided for the capture of Khartoum. Nor was this the worst, for on the occurrence of the disaster the Mahdi was promptly informed of the loss of the *Abbas* and the murder of the Europeans, and it was he himself who sent in to Gordon the news of the catastrophe, with so complete a list of the papers on the *Abbas* as left no ground for hope or disbelief. Unfortunately, before this bad news reached Gordon, he had again, on 30th September, sent down to Shendy three steamers—the *Talataween*, the *Mansourah*, and *Saphia*, with troops on board, and the gallant Cassim-el-Mousse, there to await the arrival of the relieving force. He somewhat later reinforced this squadron with the *Bordeen*; and although one or two of these boats returned occasionally to Khartoum, the rest remained permanently at Shendy, and when the English troops reached the Nile opposite that place all five were waiting them. Without entering too closely into details, it is consequently correct to say that during the most critical part of the siege Gordon deprived himself of the co-operation of these vessels, each of which he valued at 2000 men, simply and solely because he believed that reinforcements were close at hand, and that some troops at the latest would arrive before the end of November 1884. As Gordon himself repeatedly said, it would have been far more just if the Government had told him in March, when he first demanded reinforcements as a right, that he must shift for himself. Then he would have kept these boats by him, and triumphantly fought his way in them to the Equator. But his trust in the Government, notwithstanding all his experience, led him to weaken his own position in the hope of facilitating their movements, and he found their aid a broken reed. In only one passage of his journal does Gordon give expression to this view, although it was always present to his mind:—"Truly the indecision of our Government has been, from a military point of view, a very great bore, for we never could act as if independent; there was always the chance of their taking action, which hampered us." But in the telegrams to Sir Evelyn Baring and Mr Egerton, which the Government never dared to publish, and which are still an official secret, he laid great stress on this point, and on Sir Evelyn Baring's message forbidding him to retire to the Equator, so that, if he sought safety in that direction, he would be indictable on a charge of desertion.

The various positions at Khartoum held by Gordon's force may be briefly described. First, the town itself, on the left bank of the Blue Nile, but stretching almost across to the right bank of the White Nile, protected on the land side by a wall, in front of which was the triple line of mines, and on the water side by the river and the steamers. On the right bank of the Blue Nile was the small North Fort. Between the two stretched the island of Tuti, and at each end of the wall, on the White Nile as well as the Blue, Gordon had stationed a *santal* or heavy-armed barge, carrying a gun. Unfortunately, a large part of the western end of the Khartoum wall had been washed away by an inundation of the Nile, but the mines supplied a substitute, and so long as Omdurman Fort was held this weakness in the defences of Khartoum did not greatly signify. That fort itself lay on the left bank of the White Nile. It was well built and fairly strong, but the position was faulty. It lay in a hollow, and the trench of the extensive camp formed for Hicks's force furnished the enemy with cover. It was also 1200 yards from the river bank, and when the enemy became more enterprising it was impossible to keep up communication with it. In Omdurman Fort was a specially selected garrison of 240 men, commanded by a gallant black officer, Ferratch or Faragalla Pasha, who had been raised from a subordinate capacity to the principal command under him by Gordon. Gordon's point of observation was the flat roof of the Palace, whence he could see everything with his telescope, and where he placed his best shots to bear on any point that might seem hard pressed. Still more useful was it for the purpose of detecting the remissness of his own troops and officers, and often his telescope showed him sentries asleep at their posts, and officers absent from the points they were supposed to guard.

From the end of March until the close of the siege scarcely a day passed without the exchange of artillery and rifle fire on one side or the other of the beleaguered town. On special occasions the Khedive's garrison would fire as many as forty or even fifty thousand rounds of Remington cartridges, and the Arab fire was sometimes heavier. This incessant fire, as the heroic defender wrote in his journal, murdered sleep, and at last he became so accustomed to it that he could tell by the sound where the firing was taking place. The most distant points of the defence, such as the *santal* on the White Nile and Fort Omdurman, were two miles from the Palace; and although telegraphic communication existed with them during the greater part of the siege, the oral evidence as to the point of attack was often found the most rapid means of obtaining information. This was still more advantageous after the 12th of November, for on that day communications were cut between Khartoum and Omdurman, and it was found impossible to restore them. The only communications possible after that date were by bugle and flag. At the time of this severance Gordon estimated that the garrison of Omdurman had enough water and biscuit for six weeks, and that there were 250,000 cartridges in the arsenal. Gordon did everything in his power to aid Ferratch in the defence, and his remaining steamer, the *Ismailia*, after the grounding of the *Husseinyeh* on the very day Omdurman was cut off, was engaged in almost daily encounters with the Mahdists for that purpose. Owing to Gordon's incessant efforts, and the gallantry of the garrison led by Ferratch, Omdurman held out more than two months. It was not until 15th January that Ferratch, with Gordon's leave, surrendered, and then when the Mahdists occupied the place, General Gordon had the satisfaction of shelling them out of it, and showing that it was untenable.

The severance of Omdurman from Khartoum was the prelude to fiercer fighting than had taken place at any time during the earlier stages of the siege, and although particulars are not obtainable for the last month of the period, there is no doubt that the struggle was incessant, and that the fighting was renewed from day to day. It was then that Gordon missed the ships lying idle at Shendy. If he had had them Omdurman would not have fallen, nor would it have been so easy for the Mahdi to transport the bulk of his force from the left to the right bank of the White Nile, as he did for the final assault on the fatal 26th January.

At the end of October the Mahdi, accompanied by a far more numerous force than Gordon thought he could raise, described by Slatin as countless, pitched his camp a few miles south of Omdurman. On 8th November his arrival was celebrated by a direct attack on the lines south of Khartoum. The rebels in their fear of the hidden mines, which was far greater than it need have been, as it was found they had been buried too deep, resorted to the artifice of driving forward cows, and by throwing rockets among them Gordon had the satisfaction of spreading confusion in their ranks, repulsing the attack, and capturing twenty of the animals. Four days later the rebels made the desperate attack on Omdurman, when, as stated, communications were cut, and the *Husseinyeh* ran aground. In attempting to carry her off and to check the further progress of the rebels the *Ismailia* was badly hit, and the incident was one of those only too frequent at all stages of the siege, when Gordon wrote: "Every time I hear the gun fire I have a twitch of the heart of gnawing anxiety for my penny steamers." At the very moment that these fights were in progress he wrote, 10th November: "Today is the day I expected we should have had some one of the Expedition here;" and he also recorded that we "have enough biscuit for a month or so"—meaning at the outside six weeks. Throughout the whole of November rumours of a coming British Expedition were prevalent, but they were of the vaguest and most contradictory character. On 25th November Gordon learnt that it was still at Ambukol, 185 miles further away from Khartoum than he had expected, and his only comment under this acute disappointment was, "This is lively!"

Up to the arrival of the Mahdi daily desertions of his Arab and other soldiers to Gordon took place, and by these and levies among the townspeople all gaps in the garrison were more than filled up. Such was the confidence in Gordon that it more than neutralised all the intrigues of the Mahdi's agents in the besieged town, and scarcely a man during the first seven months of the siege deserted him; but after the arrival of the Mahdi there was a complete change in this respect. In the first place there were no more desertions to Gordon, and then men began to leave him, partly, no doubt, from fear of the Mahdi, or awakened fanaticism, but chiefly through the non-arrival of the British Expedition, which had been so much talked about, yet which never came. Still to all the enemy's invitations to surrender on the most honourable terms Gordon gave defiant answers. "I am here like iron, and I hope to see the newly-arrived English;" and when the situation had become little short of desperate, at the end of the year, he still, with bitter agony at his heart, proudly rejected all overtures, and sent the haughty message: "Can hold Khartoum for twelve years." Unfortunately the Mahdi knew better. He had read the truth in all the papers captured on Stewart's steamer, and he knew that Gordon's resources were nearly spent. Even some of the messages Gordon sent out by spies for Lord Wolseley's information fell into his hands, and on one of these Slatin says it was written: "Can hold Khartoum at the outside till the end of January." Although Gordon may be considered to have more than held his own against all the power of the Mahdi down to the capture of Omdurman Fort on 15th January, the Mahdi knew that his straits must be desperate, and that unless the expedition arrived he could not hold out much longer. The first advance of the English troops on 3rd January across the desert towards the Nile probably warned the enemy that now was the time to renew the attack with greater vigour, but it does not seem that there is any justification for the entirely hypothetical view that at any point the Mahdi could have seized the unhappy town. Omdurman Fort itself fell, not to the desperate onset of his Ghazis, but from the want of food and ammunition, and with Gordon's expressed permission to the commandant to surrender. Unfortunately the details of the most tragic part of the siege are missing, but Gordon himself well summed up what he had done up to the end of October when his position was secure, and aid, as he thought, was close at hand:

The news of Hicks's defeat was known in Cairo three weeks after the event occurred; since that date up to this (29th October 1884) nine people have come up as reinforcements—myself, Stewart, Herbin, Hussein, Tongi, Ruckdi, and three servants, and not one penny of money. Of those who came up two, Stewart and Herbin, have gone down, Hussein is dead; so six alone remain, while we must have sent down over 1500 and 700 soldiers, total 2200, including the two Pashas, Coetlogon, etc. The regulars, who were in arrears of pay for three months when I came, are now only owed half a month, while the Bashi-Bazouks are owed only a quarter month, and we have some £500 in the Treasury. It is quite a miracle. We have lost two battles, suffering severe losses in these actions of men and arms, and may have said to have scrambled through, for I cannot say we can lay claim to any great success during the whole time. I believe we have more ammunition (Remington) and more soldiers now than when I came up. We have

£40,000 in Treasury *in paper* and £500. When I came up there was £5000 in Treasury. We have £15,000 out in the town in paper money.

At the point (14th December) when the authentic history of the protracted siege and gallant defence of Khartoum stops, a pause may be made to turn back and describe what the Government and country which sent General Gordon on his most perilous mission, and made use of his extraordinary devotion to the call of duty to extricate themselves from a responsibility they had not the courage to face, had been doing not merely to support their envoy, but to vindicate their own honour. The several messages which General Gordon had succeeded in getting through had shown how necessary some reinforcement and support were at the very commencement of the siege. The lapse of time, rendered the more expressive by the long period of silence that fell over what was taking place in the besieged town, showed, beyond need of demonstration, the gravity of the case and the desperate nature of the situation. But a very little of the knowledge at the command of the Government from a number of competent sources would have enabled it to foresee what was certain to happen, and to have provided some remedy for the peril long before the following despairing message from Gordon showed that the hour when any aid would be useful had almost expired. This was the passage, dated 13th December, in the last (sixth) volume of the Journal, but the substance of which reached Lord Wolseley by one of Gordon's messengers at Korti on 31st December:

> We are going to send down the *Bordeen* the day after tomorrow, and with her I shall send this Journal. *If some effort is not made before ten days' time the town will fall.* It is inexplicable this delay. If the Expeditionary forces have reached the river and met my steamers, one hundred men are all that we require just to show themselves. . . . Even if the town falls under the nose of the Expeditionary forces it will not in my opinion justify the abandonment of Senaar and Kassala, or of the Equatorial Province by H.M.'s Government. All that is absolutely necessary is for fifty of the Expeditionary force to get on board a steamer and come up to Halfiyeh, and thus let their presence be felt. This is not asking much, but it must happen *at once*, or it will (as usual) be too late.

The motives which induced Mr Gladstone's Government to send

General Gordon to the Soudan in January 1884 were, as has been clearly shown, the selfish desire to appease public opinion, and to shirk in the easiest possible manner a great responsibility. They had no policy at all, but they had one supreme wish, *viz.* to cut off the Soudan from Egypt; and if the Mahdi had only known their wishes and pressed on, and treated the Khartoum force as he had treated that under Hicks, there would have been no garrisons to rescue, and that British Government would have done nothing. It recked nothing of the grave dangers that would have accrued from the complete triumph of the Mahdi, or of the outbreak that must have followed in Lower Egypt if his tide of success had not been checked as it was single-handed by General Gordon, through the twelve months' defence of Khartoum. Still it could not quite stoop to the dishonour of abandoning these garrisons, and of making itself an accomplice to the Mahdi's butcheries, nor could it altogether turn a deaf ear to the representations and remonstrances of even such a puppet prince as the Khedive Tewfik. England was then far more mistress of the situation at Cairo than she is now, but a helpless refusal to discharge her duty might have provoked Europe into action at the Porte that would have proved inconvenient and damaging to her position and reputation. Therefore the Government fell back on General Gordon, and the hope was even indulged that, under his exceptional reputation, the evacuation of the Soudan might not only be successfully carried out, but that his success might induce the public and the world to accept that abnegation of policy as the acme of wisdom. In all this they were destined to a complete awakening, and the only matter of surprise is that they should have sent so well-known a character as General Gordon, whose independence and contempt for official etiquette and restraint were no secrets at the Foreign and War Offices, on a mission in which they required him not only to be as indifferent to the national honour as they were, but also to be tied and restrained by the shifts and requirements of an embarrassed executive.

At a very early stage of the mission the Government obtained evidence that Gordon's views on the subject were widely different from theirs. They had evidently persuaded themselves that their policy was Gordon's policy; and before he was in Khartoum a week he not merely points out that the evacuation policy is not his but theirs, and that although he thinks its execution is still possible, the true policy is, "if Egypt is to be quiet, that the Mahdi must be smashed up." The hopes that had been based on Gordon's supposed complaisance in the post of representative on the Nile of the Government policy were thus dispelled, and it became evident that Gordon, instead of being a tool, was resolved to be master, so far as the mode of carrying out the evacuation policy with full regard for the dictates of honour was to be decided. Nor was this all, or the worst of the revelations made to the Government in the first few weeks after his arrival at Khartoum. While expressing his willingness and intention to discharge the chief part of his task, viz. the withdrawal of the garrisons, which was all the Government cared about, he also descanted on the moral duty and the inevitable necessity of setting up a provisional government that should avert anarchy and impose some barrier to the Mahdi's progress. All this was trying to those who only wished to be rid of the whole matter, but Gordon did not spare their feelings, and phrase by phrase he revealed what his own policy would be and what his inner wishes, however repressed his charge might keep them, really were.

Having told them that "the Mahdi must be smashed up," he went on to say that "we cannot hurry over this affair" (the future of the Soudan) "if we do we shall incur disaster," and again that, although "it is a miserable country it is joined to Egypt, and it would be difficult to divorce the two." Within a very few weeks, therefore, the Government learnt that its own agent was the most forcible and damaging critic of the policy of evacuation, and that the worries of the Soudan question for an administration not resolute enough to solve the difficulty in a thorough manner were increased and not diminished by Gordon's mission. At that point the proposition was made and supported by several members of the Cabinet that Gordon should be recalled. There is no doubt that this step would have been taken but for the fear that it would aggravate the difficulties of the English expedition sent to Souakim under the command of General Gerald Graham to retrieve the defeat of Baker Pasha. Failing the adoption of that extreme measure, which would at least have been straightforward and honest, and ignoring what candour seemed to demand if a decision had been come to to render Gordon no support, and to bid him shift for himself, the Government resorted to the third and least justifiable course of all, viz. of showing indifference to the legitimate requests of their emissary, and of putting off definite action until the very last moment.

We have seen that Gordon made several specific demands in the first six weeks of his stay at Khartoum—that is, in the short period before communication was cut off. He wanted Zebehr, 200 troops at Berber, or even at Wady Halfa, and the opening of the route from Souakim to the Nile. To these requests not one favourable answer was given, and the not wholly unnatural rejection of the first rendered it more than ever necessary to comply with the others. They were such as ought to have been granted, and in anticipation they had been suggested and discussed before Gordon felt bound to urge them as necessary for the security of his position at Khartoum. Even Sir Evelyn Baring had recommended in February the despatch of 200 men to Assouan for the moral effect, and that was the very reason why Gordon asked, in the first place, for the despatch of a small British force to at least Wady Halfa. It is possible that one of the chief reasons for the Government rejecting all these suggestions, and also, it must be remembered, doing nothing in their place towards the relief and support of their representative, may have been the hope that this treatment would have led him to resign and throw up his mission. They would then have been able to declare that, as the task was beyond the powers of General Gordon, they were only coming to the prudent and logical conclusion in saying that nothing could be done, and that the garrisons had better come to terms with the Mahdi. Unfortunately for those who favoured the evasion of trouble as the easiest and best way out of the difficulty, Gordon had high notions as to what duty required. No difficulty had terrors for him, and while left at the post of power and responsibility he would endeavour to show himself equal to the charge.

Yet there can be no doubt that those who sent him would have rejoiced if he had formally asked to be relieved of the task he had accepted, and Mr Gladstone stated on the 3rd April that "Gordon was under no orders and no restraint to stay at Khartoum." A significant answer to the fact represented in that statement was supplied, when, ten days later, silence fell on Khartoum, and remained unbroken for more than five months. But at the very moment that the Prime Minister made that statement as to Gordon's liberty of movement, the Government knew of the candid views which he had expressed as to the proper policy for the Soudan. It should have been apparent that, unless they and their author were promptly repudiated, and unless the latter was stripped of his official authority, the Government would, however tardily and reluctantly, be drawn after its representative into a policy of intervention in the Soudan, which it, above everything else, wished to avoid. Gordon concealed nothing. He told them "time," "reinforcements," and a very considerable expenditure was necessary to honourably carry out their policy of evacuation. They were not prepared to concede any of these save the last, and even the money they sent him was lost because they would send it by Berber instead of Kassala. But they knew that "the order and restraint" which kept Gordon at Khartoum was the duty he had contracted towards them when he accepted his mission, and which was binding on a man of his principles until they chose to relieve him of the task. The fear of public opinion had more to do with their abstaining from the step of ordering his recall than the hope that his splendid energy and administrative power might yet provide some satisfactory issue from the dilemma, for at the very beginning it was freely given out that "General Gordon was exceeding his instructions."

The interruption of communications with Khartoum at least suspended Gordon's constant representations as to what he thought the right policy, as well as his demands for the fulfilment by the Government of their side of the contract. It was then that Lord Granville seemed to pluck up heart of grace, and to challenge Gordon's right to remain at Khartoum. On 23rd April Lord Granville asked for explanation of "cause of detention." Unfortunately it was not till months later that the country knew of Gordon's terse and humorous reply, "cause of detention, these horribly plucky Arabs." Lord Granville, thinking this despatch not clear enough, followed it up on 17th May by instructing Mr Egerton, then acting for Sir Evelyn Baring, to send the following remonstrance to Gordon:

> As the original plan for the evacuation of the Soudan has been dropped, and as aggressive operations cannot be undertaken with the countenance of H.M.'s Government, General Gordon is enjoined to consider, and either to report upon, or, if possible, to adopt at the first proper moment measures for his own removal and for that of the Egyptians at Khartoum who have suffered for him, or who have served him faithfully, including their wives and children, by whatever route he may consider best, having especial regard to his own safety and that of the other British subjects.

Then followed suggestions and authority to pay so much a head for refugees safely escorted to Korosko. The comment Gordon made on that, and similar despatches, to save himself and any part of the garrison he could, was that he was not so mean as to desert those who had nobly stood by him and committed themselves on the strength of his word.

It is impossible to go behind the collective responsibility of the Government and to attempt to fix any special responsibility or blame on any individual member of that Government. The facts as I read them show plainly that there was a complete abnegation of policy or purpose on the part of the British Government, that Gordon was then sent as a sort of stop-gap, and that when it was revealed that he had strong views and clear plans, not at all in harmony with those who sent him, it was thought, by the Ministers who had not the courage to recall him, very inconsiderate and insubordinate of him to remain at his post and to refuse all the hints given him, that he ought to resign unless he would execute a *sauve qui peut* sort of retreat to the frontier. Very harsh things have been said of Mr Gladstone and his Cabinet on this point, but considering their views and declarations, it is not so very surprising that Gordon's boldness and originality alarmed and displeased them. Their radical fault in these early stages of the question was not that they were indifferent to Gordon's demands, but that they had absolutely no policy. They could not even come to the decision, as Gordon wrote, "to abandon altogether and not care what happens."

But all these minor points were merged in a great common national anxiety when month after month passed during the spring and summer of 1884, and not a single word issued from the tomb-like silence of Khartoum. People might argue that the worst could not have happened, as the Mahdi would have been only too anxious to proclaim his triumph far and wide if Khartoum had fallen. Anxiety may be diminished, but is not banished, by a calculation of probabilities, and the military spirit and capacity exhibited by the Mahdi's forces under Osman Digma in the fighting with General Graham's well-equipped British force at Teb and Tamanieb revealed the greatness of the peril with which Gordon had to deal at Khartoum where he had only the inadequate and untrustworthy garrison described by Colonel de Coetlogon. During the summer of 1884 there was therefore a growing fear, not only that the worst news might come at any moment, but that in the most favourable event any news would reveal the desperate situation to which Gordon had been reduced, and with that conviction came the thought, not whether he had exactly carried out what Ministers had expected him to do, but solely of his extraordinary courage and devotion to his country, which had led him to take up a thankless task without the least regard for his comfort or advantage, and without counting the odds. There was at least one Minister in the Cabinet who was struck by that single-minded conduct; and as early as April, when his colleagues were asking the formal question why Gordon did not leave Khartoum, the Marquis of Hartington, then Minister of War, and now Duke of Devonshire, began to inquire as to the steps necessary to rescue the emissary, while still adhering to the policy of the Administration of which he formed part. During the whole of that summer the present Duke of Devonshire advocated the special claim of General Gordon on the Government, whose mandate he had so readily accepted, and urged the necessity of special measures being taken at the earliest moment to save the gallant envoy from what seemed the too probable penalty of his own temerity and devotion. But for his energetic and consistent representations the steps that were taken—all too late as they proved—never would have been taken at all, or deferred to such a date as to let the public see by the event that there was no use in throwing away money and precious lives on a lost cause.

If the first place among those in power—for of my own and other journalists' efforts in the Press to arouse public opinion and to urge the Government to timely action it is unnecessary to speak—is due to the Duke of Devonshire, the second may reasonably be claimed by Lord Wolseley. This recognition is the more called for here, because the most careful consideration of the facts has led me to the conclusion, which I would gladly avoid the necessity of expressing if it were possible, that Lord Wolseley was responsible for the failure of the relief expedition. This stage of responsibility has not yet been reached, and it must be duly set forth that on 24th July Lord Wolseley, then Adjutant-General, wrote a noble letter, stating that, as he "did not wish to share the responsibility of leaving Charley Gordon to his fate," he recommended "immediate action," and "the despatch of a small brigade of between three and four thousand British soldiers to Dongola, so that they might reach that place about 15th October." But even that date was later than it ought to have been, especially when the necessity of getting the English troops back as early in the New Year as possible was considered, and in the subsequent recriminations that ensued, the blame for being late from the start was sought to be thrown on the badness of the Nile flood that year. General Gordon himself cruelly disposed of that theory or excuse when he wrote, "It was not a bad Nile; quite an average one. You were too late, that was all." Still, Lord Wolseley must not be robbed of the credit of having said on 24th July that an expedition was necessary to save Gordon, "his old friend and Crimean comrade," towards whom Wolseley himself had contracted a special moral obligation for his prominent share in inducing him to accept the very mission that had already proved so full of peril. In short, if the plain truth must be told, Lord Wolseley was far more responsible for the despatch of General Gordon to Khartoum than Mr Gladstone.

The result of the early representations of the Duke of Devonshire, and the definite suggestion of Lord Wolseley, was that the Government gave in when the public anxiety became so great at the continued silence of Khartoum, and acquiesced in the despatch of an expedition to relieve General Gordon. Having once made the concession, it must be allowed that they showed no niggard spirit in sanctioning the expedition and the proposals of the military authorities. The sum of ten millions was devoted to the work of rescuing Gordon by the very persons who had rejected his demands for the hundredth part of that total. Ten thousand men selected from the elite of the British army were assigned to the task for which he had begged two hundred men in vain. It is impossible here to enter closely into the causes which led to the expansion of the three or four thousand British infantry into a special corps of ten thousand fighting men, picked from the crack regiments of the army, and composed of every arm of the service compelled to fight under unaccustomed conditions. The local authorities—in particular Major Kitchener, now the Sirdar of the Egyptian army, who is slowly recovering from the Mahdi the provinces which should never have been left in his possession—protested that the expedition should be a small one, and if their advice had been taken the cost would have been about one-fourth that incurred, and the force would have reached Khartoum by that 11th November on which Gordon expected to see the first man of it. But Major Kitchener, although, as Gordon wrote, "one of the few really first-class officers in the British army," was only an individual, and his word did not possess a feather's weight before the influence of the Pall Mall band of warriors who have farmed out our little wars—India, of course, excepted—of the last thirty years for their own glorification. So great a chance of fame as "the rescue of Gordon" was not to be left to some unknown brigadiers, or to the few line regiments, the proximity of whose stations entitled them to the task. That would be neglecting the favours of Providence. For so noble a task the control of the most experienced commander in the British army would alone suffice, and when he took the field his staff had to be on the extensive scale that suited his dignity and position. As there would be some reasonable excuse for the dispensation of orders and crosses from a campaign against a religious leader who had not yet known defeat, any friend might justly complain if he was left behind. To justify so brilliant a staff, no ordinary British force would suffice. Therefore our household brigade, our heavy cavalry, and our light cavalry were requisitioned for their best men, and these splendid troops were drafted and amalgamated into special corps—heavy and light camelry—for work that would have been done far better and more efficiently by two regiments of Bengal Lancers. If all this effort and expenditure had resulted in success, it would be possible to keep silent and shrug one's shoulders; but when the mode of undertaking this expedition can be clearly shown to have been the direct cause of its failure, silence would be a crime. When Lord Wolseley told the soldiers at Korti on their return from Metemmah, "It was not *your* fault that Gordon has perished and Khartoum fallen," the positiveness of his assurance may have been derived from the inner conviction of his own stupendous error.

The expedition was finally sanctioned in August, and the news of its coming was known to General Gordon in September, before, indeed, his own despatches of 31st July were received in London, and broke the suspense of nearly half a year. He thought that only a small force was coming, under the command of Major-General Earle, and he at once, as already described, sent his steamers back to Shendy, there to await the troops and convey them to Khartoum. He seems to have calculated that three months from the date of the message informing him of the expedition would suffice for the conveyance of the troops as far as Berber or Metemmah, and at that rate General Earle would have arrived where his steamers awaited him early in November. Gordon's views as to the object of the expedition, which somebody called the Gordon Relief Expedition, were thus clearly expressed:

I altogether decline the imputation that the projected expedition has come to relieve me. It has come to save our National honour in extricating the garrisons, etc., from a position in which our action in Egypt has placed these garrisons. I was Relief Expedition No. 1; they are Relief Expedition No. 2. As for myself, I could make good my retreat at any moment, if I wished. Now realise what would happen if this first relief expedition was to bolt, and the steamers fell into the hands of the Mahdi. This second relief expedition (for the honour of England engaged in extricating garrisons) would be somewhat hampered. We, the first and second expeditions, are equally engaged for the honour of England. This is fair logic. I came up to extricate the garrison, and failed. Earle comes up to extricate garrisons, and I hope succeeds. Earle does not come to extricate me. The extrication of the garrisons was supposed to affect our "National honour." If Earle succeeds, the "National honour" thanks him, and I hope recommends him, but it is altogether independent of me, who, for failing, incurs its blame. I am not *the rescued lamb*, and I will not be.

Lord Wolseley, still possessed with the idea that, now that an expedition had been sanctioned, the question of time was not of supreme importance, and that the relieving expedition might be carried out in a deliberate manner, which would be both more effective and less exposed to risk, did not reach Cairo till September, and had only arrived at Wady Halfa on 8th October, when his final instructions reached him in the following form:

> The primary object of your expedition is to bring away General Gordon and Colonel Stewart, and you are not to advance further south than necessary to attain that object, and when it has been secured, no further offensive operations of any kind are to be undertaken.

These instructions were simple and clear enough. The Government had not discovered a policy. It had, however, determined to leave the garrisons to their fate, despite the National honour being involved, at the very moment that it sanctioned an enormous expenditure to try and save the lives of its long-neglected representatives, Gordon and Colonel Stewart. With extraordinary shrewdness, Gordon detected the hollowness of its purpose, and wrote:—"I very much doubt what is really going to be the policy of our Government, even now that the Expedition is at Dongola," and if they intend ratting out, "the troops had better not come beyond Berber till the question of what will be done is settled."

The receipt of Gordon's and Power's despatches of July showed that there were, at the time of their being written, supplies for four months, which would have carried the garrison on till the end of November. As the greater part of that period had expired when these documents reached Lord Wolseley's hands, it was quite impossible to doubt that time had become the most important factor of all in the situation. The chance of being too late would even then have presented itself to a prudent commander, and, above all, to a friend hastening to the rescue of a friend. The news that Colonel Stewart and some other Europeans had been entrapped and murdered near Merowe, which reached the English commander from different sources before Gordon confirmed it in his letters, was also calculated to stimulate, by showing that Gordon was alone, and had single-handed to conduct the defence of a populous city. Hard on the heels of that intelligence came Gordon's letter of 4th November to Lord Wolseley, who received it at Dongola on 14th of the same month. The letter was a long one, but only two passages need be quoted: "At Metemmah, waiting your orders, are five steamers with nine guns." Did it not occur to anyone how greatly, at the worst stage of the siege, Gordon had thus weakened himself to assist the relieving expedition? Even for that reason there was not a day or an hour to be lost.

But the letter contained a worse and more alarming passage:—"We can hold out forty days with ease; after that it will be difficult." Forty days would have meant till 14th December, one month ahead of the day Lord Wolseley received the news, but the message was really more alarming than the form in which it was published, for there is no doubt that the word "difficult" is the official rendering of Gordon's, a little indistinctly written, word "desperate." In face of that alarming message, which only stated facts that ought to have been surmised, if not known, it was no longer possible to pursue the leisurely promenade up the Nile, which was timed so as to bring the whole force to Khartoum in the first week of March. Rescue by the most prominent general and swell troops of England at Easter would hardly gratify the commandant and garrison starved into surrender the previous Christmas, and that was the exact relationship between Wolseley's plans and Gordon's necessities.

The date at which Gordon's supplies would be exhausted varied not from any miscalculation, but because on two successive occasions he discovered large stores of grain and biscuits, which had been stolen from the public granaries before his arrival. The supplies that would all have disappeared in November were thus eked out, first till the middle of December, and then finally till the end of January, but there is no doubt that they would not have lasted as long as they did if in the last month of the siege he had not given the civil population permission to leave the doomed town. From any and from every point of view, there was not the shadow of an excuse for a moment's delay after the receipt of that letter on 14th November.

With the British Exchequer at a commander's back, it is easy to organise an expedition on an elaborate scale, and to carry it out with the nicety of perfection, but for the realisation of these ponderous plans there is one thing more necessary, and that is time. I have no doubt if Gordon's letter had said "granaries full, can hold out till Easter," that Lord Wolseley's deliberate march—Cairo, September 27; Wady Halfa, October 8; Dongola, November 14; Korti, December 30; Metemmah any day in February, and Khartoum, March 3, and those were the approximate dates of his grand plan of campaign—would have been fully successful, and held up for admiration as a model of skill. Unfortunately, it would not do for the occasion, as Gordon was on the verge of starvation and in desperate straits when the rescuing force reached

Dongola. It is not easy to alter the plan of any campaign, nor to adapt a heavy moving machine to the work suitable for a light one. To feed 10,000 British soldiers on the middle Nile was alone a feat of organisation such as no other country could have attempted, but the effort was exhausting, and left no reserve energy to despatch that quick-moving battalion which could have reached Gordon's steamers early in December, and would have reinforced the Khartoum garrison, just as Havelock and Outram did the Lucknow Residency.

Dongola is only 100 miles below Debbeh, where the intelligence officers and a small force were on that 14th November; Ambukol, specially recommended by Gordon as the best starting-point, is less than fifty miles, and Korti, the point selected by Lord Wolseley, is exactly that distance above Debbeh. The Bayuda desert route by the Jakdul Wells to Metemmah is 170 miles. At Metemmah were the five steamers with nine guns to convoy the desperately needed succour to Khartoum. The energy expended on the despatch of 10,000 men up 150 miles of river, if concentrated on 1000 men, must have given a speedier result, but, as the affair was managed, the last day of the year 1884 was reached before there was even that small force ready to make a dash across the desert for Metemmah.

The excuses made for this, as the result proved, fatal delay of taking six weeks to do what—the forward movement from Dongola to Korti, not of the main force, but of 1000 men—ought to have been done in one week, were the dearth of camels, the imperfect drill of the camel corps, and, it must be added, the exaggerated fear of the Mahdi's power. When it was attempted to quicken the slow forward movement of the unwieldy force confusion ensued, and no greater progress was effected than if things had been left undisturbed. The erratic policy in procuring camels caused them at the critical moment to be not forthcoming in anything approaching the required numbers, and this difficulty was undoubtedly increased by the treachery of Mahmoud Khalifa, who was the chief contractor we employed. Even when the camels were procured, they had to be broken in for regular work, and the men accustomed to the strange drill and mode of locomotion. The last reason perhaps had the most weight of all, for although the Mahdi with all his hordes had been kept at bay by Gordon single-handed, Lord Wolseley would risk nothing in the field. Probably the determining reason for that decision was that the success of a small force would have revealed how absolutely unnecessary his large and costly expedition was. Yet events were to show beyond possibility of contraversion that this was the case, for not less than two-thirds of the force were never in any shape or form actively employed, and, as far as the fate of Gordon went, might just as well have been left at home. They had, however, to be fed and provided for at the end of a line of communication of over 1200 miles.

Still, notwithstanding all these delays and disadvantages, a well-equipped force of 1000 men was ready on 30th December to leave Korti to cross the 170 miles of the Bayuda desert. That route was well known and well watered. There were wells at, at least, five places, and the best of these was at Jakdul, about half-way across. The officer entrusted with the command was Major-General Sir Herbert Stewart, an officer of a gallant disposition, who was above all others impressed with the necessity of making an immediate advance, with the view of throwing some help into Khartoum. Unfortunately he was trammelled by his instructions, which were to this effect—he was to establish a fort at Jakdul; but if he found an insufficiency of water there he was at liberty to press on to Metemmah. His action was to be determined by the measure of his own necessities, not of Gordon's, and so Lord Wolseley arranged throughout. He reached that place with his 1100 fighting men, but on examining the wells and finding them full, he felt bound to obey the orders of his commander, viz. to establish the fort, and then return to Korti for a reinforcement. It was a case when Nelson's blind eye might have been called into requisition, but even the most gallant officers are not Nelsons.

The first advance of General Stewart to Jakdul, reached on 3rd January 1885, was in every respect a success. It was achieved without loss, unopposed, and was quite of the nature of a surprise. The British relieving force was at last, after many months' report, proved to be a reality, and although late, it was not too late. If General Stewart had not been tied by his instructions, but left a free hand, he would undoubtedly have pressed on, and a reinforcement of British troops would have entered Khartoum even before the fall of Omdurman. But it must be recorded also that Sir Herbert Stewart was not inspired by the required flash of genius. He paid more deference to the orders of Lord Wolseley than to the grave peril of General Gordon.

General Stewart returned to Korti on the 7th January, bringing with him the tired camels, and he found that during his absence still more urgent news had been received from Gordon, to the effect that if aid did not come within ten days from the 14th December, the place might fall, and that under the nose of the expedition. The native who brought this intimation arrived at Korti the day after General Stewart left, but a messenger could easily have caught him up and given him orders to press on at all cost. It was not realised at the time, but the neglect to give that order, and the rigid adherence to a preconceived plan, proved fatal to the success of the whole expedition.

The first advance of General Stewart had been in the nature of a surprise, but it aroused the Mahdi to a sense of the position, and the subsequent delay gave him a fortnight to complete his plans and assume the offensive.

On 12th January—that is, nine days after his first arrival at Jakdul—General Stewart reached the place a second time with the second detachment of another 1000 men—the total fighting strength of the column being raised to about 2300 men. For whatever errors had been committed, and their consequences, the band of soldiers assembled at Jakdul on that 12th of January could in no sense be held responsible. Without making any invidious comparisons, it may be truthfully said that such a splendid fighting force was never assembled in any other cause, and the temper of the men was strung to a high point of enthusiasm by the thought that at last they had reached the final stage of the long journey to rescue Gordon. A number of causes, principally the fatigue of the camels from the treble journey between Korti and Jakdul, made the advance very slow, and five days were occupied in traversing the forty-five miles between Jakdul and the wells at Abou Klea, themselves distant twenty miles from Metemmah. On the morning of 17th January it became clear that the column was in presence of an enemy.

At the time of Stewart's first arrival at Jakdul there were no hostile forces in the Bayuda desert. At Berber was a considerable body of the Mahdi's followers, and both Metemmah and Shendy were held in his name. At the latter place a battery or small fort had been erected, and in an encounter between it and Gordon's steamers one of the latter had been sunk, thus reducing their total to four. But there were none of the warrior tribes of Kordofan and Darfour at any of these places, or nearer than the six camps which had been established round Khartoum. The news of the English advance made the Mahdi bestir himself, and as it was known that the garrison of Omdurman was reduced to the lowest straits, and could not hold out many days, the Mahdi despatched some of his best warriors of the Jaalin, Degheim, and Kenana tribes to oppose the British troops in the Bayuda desert. It was these men who opposed the further advance of Sir Herbert Stewart's column at Abou Klea. It is unnecessary to describe the desperate assault these gallant warriors made on the somewhat cumbrous and ill-arranged square of the British force, or the ease and tremendous loss with which these fanatics were beaten off, and never allowed to come to close quarters, save at one point. The infantry soldiers, who formed two sides of the square, signally repulsed the onset, not a Ghazi succeeded in getting within a range of 300 yards; but on another side, cavalrymen, doing infantry soldiers' unaccustomed work, did not adhere to the strict formation necessary, and trained for the close *melée*, and with the *gaudia certaminis* firing their blood, they recklessly allowed the Ghazis to come to close quarters, and their line of the square was impinged upon. In that close fighting, with the Heavy Camel Corps men and the Naval Brigade, the Blacks suffered terribly, but they also inflicted loss in return. Of a total loss on the British side of sixty-five killed and sixty-one wounded, the Heavy Camel Corps lost fifty-two, and the Sussex Regiment, performing work to which it was thoroughly trained, inflicted immense loss on the enemy at hardly any cost to itself. Among the slain was the gallant Colonel Fred. Burnaby, one of the noblest and gentlest, as he was physically the strongest, officers in the British army. There is no doubt that signal as was this success, it shook the confidence of the force. The men were resolute to a point of ferocity, but the leaders' confidence in themselves and their task had been rudely tried; and yet the breaking of the square had been clearly due to a tactical blunder, and the inability of the cavalry to adapt themselves to a strange position.

On the 18th January the march, rendered slower by the conveyance of the wounded, was resumed, but no fighting took place on that day, although it was clear that the enemy had not been dispersed. On the 19th, when the force had reached the last wells at Abou Kru or Gubat, it became clear that another battle was to be fought. One of the first shots seriously wounded Sir Herbert Stewart, and during the whole of the affair many of our men were carried off by the heavy rifle fire of the enemy. Notwithstanding that our force fought under many disadvantages and was not skilfully handled, the Mahdists were driven off with terrible loss, while our force had thirty-six killed and one hundred and seven wounded. Notwithstanding these two defeats, the enemy were not cowed, and held on to Metemmah, in which no doubt those who had taken part in the battles were assisted by a force from Berber. The 20th January was wasted in inaction, caused by the large number of wounded, and when on 21st January Metemmah was attacked, the Mahdists showed so bold a front that Sir Charles Wilson, who succeeded to the command on Sir Herbert Stewart being incapacitated by his, as it proved, mortal wound, drew off his force. This was the more disappointing, because

Gordon's four steamers arrived during the action and took a gallant part in the attack. It was a pity for the effect produced that that attack should have been distinctly unsuccessful. The information the captain of these steamers, the gallant Cassim el Mousse, gave about Gordon's position was alarming. He stated that Gordon had sent him a message informing him that if aid did not come in ten days from the 14th December his position would be desperate, and the volumes of his journal which he handed over to Sir Charles Wilson amply corroborated this statement—the very last entry under that date being these memorable words:

> Now, mark this, if the Expeditionary Force—and I ask for no more than 200 men—does not come in ten days, *the town may fall*, and I have done my best for the honour of our country. Goodbye.

The other letters handed over by Cassim el Mousse amply bore out the view that a month before the British soldiers reached the last stretch of the Nile to Khartoum Gordon's position was desperate. In one to his sister he concluded, "I am quite happy, thank God, and, like Lawrence, have tried to do my duty," and in another to his friend Colonel Watson: "I think the game is up, and send Mrs Watson, yourself, and Graham my adieux. We may expect a catastrophe in the town in or after ten days. This would not have happened (if it does happen) if our people had taken better precautions as to informing us of their movements, but this is 'spilt milk.'" In face of these documents, which were in the hands of Sir Charles Wilson on 21st January, it is impossible to agree with his conclusion in his book "Korti to Khartoum," that "the delay in the arrival of the steamers at Khartoum was unimportant" as affecting the result. Every hour, every minute, had become of vital importance. If the whole Jakdul column had been destroyed in the effort, it was justifiable to do so as the price of reinforcing Gordon, so that he could hold out until the main body under Lord Wolseley could arrive. I am not one of those who think that Sir Charles Wilson, who only came on the scene at the last moment, should be made the scapegoat for the mistakes of others in the earlier stages of the expedition, and I hold now, as strongly as when I wrote the words, the opinion that, "in the face of what he did, any suggestion that he might have done more would seem both ungenerous and untrue." Still the fact remains that on 21st January there was left a sufficient margin of time to avert what actually occurred at daybreak on the 26th, for the theory that the Mahdi could have entered the town one hour before he did was never a serious argument, while the evidence of Slatin Pasha strengthens the view that Gordon was at the last moment only overcome by the Khalifa's resorting to a surprise. On one point of fact Sir Charles Wilson seems also to have been in error. He fixes the fall of Omdurman at 6th January, whereas Slatin, whose information on the point ought to be unimpeachable, states that it did not occur until the 15th of that month.

When Sir Herbert Stewart had fought and won the battle of Abou Klea, it was his intention on reaching the Nile, as he expected to do the next day, to put Sir Charles Wilson on board one of Gordon's own steamers and send him off at once to Khartoum. The second battle and Sir Herbert Stewart's fatal wound destroyed that project. But this plan might have been adhered to so far as the altered circumstances would allow. Sir Charles Wilson had succeeded to the command, and many matters affecting the position of the force had to be settled before he was free to devote himself to the main object of the dash forward, viz. the establishment of communications with Gordon and Khartoum. As the consequence of that change in his own position, it would have been natural that he should have delegated the task to someone else, and in Lord Charles Beresford, as brave a sailor as ever led a cutting-out party, there was the very man for the occasion. Unfortunately, Sir Charles Wilson did not take this step for, as I believe, the sole reason that he was the bearer of an important official letter to General Gordon, which he did not think could be entrusted to any other hands. But for that circumstance it is permissible to say that one steamer—there was more than enough wood on the other three steamers to fit one out for the journey to Khartoum—would have sailed on the morning of the 22nd, the day after the force sheered off from Metemmah, and, at the latest, it would have reached Khartoum on Sunday, the 25th, just in time to avert the catastrophe.

But as it was done, the whole of the 22nd and 23rd were taken up in preparing two steamers for the voyage, and in collecting scarlet coats for the troops, so that the effect of real British soldiers coming up the Nile might be made more considerable. At 8 a.m. on Saturday, the 24th, Sir Charles Wilson at last sailed with the two steamers, *Bordeen* and *Talataween*, and it was then quite impossible for the steamers to cover the ninety-five miles to Khartoum in time. Moreover, the Nile had, by this time, sunk to such a point of shallowness that navigation was specially slow and even dangerous. The

Shabloka cataract was passed at 3 p.m. on the afternoon of Sunday; then the *Bordeen* ran on a rock, and was not got clear till 9 p.m. on the fatal 26th. On the 27th, Halfiyeh, eight miles from Khartoum, was reached, and the Arabs along the banks shouted out that Gordon was killed and Khartoum had fallen. Still Sir Charles Wilson went on past Tuti Island, until he made sure that Khartoum had fallen and was in the hands of the dervishes. Then he ordered full steam down stream under as hot a fire as he ever wished to experience, Gordon's black gunners working like demons at their guns. On the 29th the *Talataween* ran on a rock and sank, its crew being taken on board the *Bordeen*. Two days later the *Bordeen* shared the same fate, but the whole party was finally saved on the 4th February by a third steamer, brought up by Lord Charles Beresford. But these matters, and the subsequent progress of the Expedition which had so ignominiously failed, have no interest for the reader of Gordon's life. It failed to accomplish the object which alone justified its being sent, and, it must be allowed, that it accepted its failure in a very tame and spiritless manner. Even at the moment of the British troops turning their backs on the goal which they had not won, the fate of Gordon himself was unknown, although there could be no doubt as to the main fact that the protracted siege of Khartoum had terminated in its capture by the cruel and savage foe, whom it, or rather Gordon, had so long defied.

I have referred to the official letter addressed to General Gordon, of which Sir Charles Wilson was the bearer. That letter has never been published, and it is perhaps well for its authors that it has not been, for, however softened down its language was by Lord Wolseley's intercession, it was an order to General Gordon to resign the command at Khartoum, and to leave that place without a moment's delay. Had it been delivered and obeyed (as it might have been, because Gordon's strength would probably have collapsed at the sight of English soldiers after his long incarceration), the next official step would have been to censure him for having remained at Khartoum against orders. Thus would the primary, and, indeed, sole object of the Expedition have been attained without regard for the national honour, and without the discovery of that policy, the want of which was the only cause of the calamities associated with the Soudan.

After the 14th of December there is no trustworthy, or at least, complete evidence, as to what took place in Khartoum. A copy of one of the defiant messages Gordon used to circulate for the special purpose of letting them fall into the hands of the Mahdi was dated

29th of that month, and ran to the effect, "Can hold Khartoum for years." There was also the final message to the Sovereigns of the Powers, undated, and probably written, if at all, by Gordon, during the final agony of the last few weeks, perhaps when Omdurman had fallen. It was worded as follows:

> After salutations, I would at once, calling to mind what I have gone through, inform their Majesties, the Sovereigns, of the action of Great Britain and the Ottoman Empire, who appointed me as Governor-General of the Soudan for the purpose of appeasing the rebellion in that country.
>
> During the twelve months that I have been here, these two Powers, the one remarkable for her wealth, and the other for her military force, have remained unaffected by my situation—perhaps relying too much on the news sent by Hussein Pasha Khalifa, who surrendered of his own accord.
>
> Although I, personally, am too insignificant to be taken into account, the Powers were bound, nevertheless, to fulfil the engagement upon which my appointment was based, so as to shield the honour of the Governments.
>
> What I have gone through I cannot describe. The Almighty God will help me.

Although this copy was not in Gordon's own writing, it was brought down by one of his clerks, who escaped from Khartoum, and he declared that the original had been sent in a cartridge case to Dongola. The style is certainly the style of Gordon, and there was no one in the Soudan who could imitate it. It seems safe, as Sir Henry Gordon did, to accept it as the farewell message of his brother.

Until fresh evidence comes to light, that of Slatin Pasha, then a chained captive in the Mahdi's camp, is alone entitled to the slightest credence, and it is extremely graphic. We can well believe that up to the last moment Gordon continued to send out messages—false, to deceive the Mahdi, and true to impress Lord Wolseley. The note of 29th December was one of the former; the little French note on half a cigarette paper, brought by Abdullah Khalifa to Slatin to translate early in January, may have been one of the latter. It said:—"Can hold Khartoum at the outside till the end of January." Slatin then describes the fall of Omdurman on 15th January, with Gordon's acquiescence, which entirely disposes of the assertion that Ferratch, the gallant defender of that place during two months, was a traitor, and of how, on its surrender, Gordon's fire from the western wall of Khartoum prevented the Mahdists occupying it. He also comments on the alarm caused by the first advance of the British force into the Bayuda desert, and of the despatch of thousands of the Mahdi's best warriors to oppose it. Those forces quitted the camp at Omdurman between 10th and 15th January, and this step entirely disposes of the theory that the Mahdi held Khartoum in the hollow of his hand, and could at any moment take it. As late as the 15th of January, Gordon's fire was so vigorous and successful that the Mahdi was unable to retain possession of the fort which he had just captured.

The story had best be continued in the words used by the witness. Six days after the fall of Omdurman loud weeping and wailing filled the Mahdi's camp. As the Mahdi forbade the display of sorrow and grief it was clear that something most unusual had taken place. Then it came out that the British troops had met and utterly defeated the tribes, with a loss to the Mahdists of several thousands. Within the next two or three days came news of the other defeat at Abou Kru, and the loud lamentations of the women and children could not be checked. The Mahdi and his chief emirs, the present Khalifa Abdullah prominent among them, then held a consultation, and it was decided, sooner than lose all the fruits of the hitherto unchecked triumph of their cause, to risk an assault on Khartoum. At night on the 24th, and again on the 25th, the bulk of the rebel force was conveyed across the river to the right bank of the White Nile; the Mahdi preached them a sermon, promising them victory, and they were enjoined to receive his remarks in silence, so that no noise was heard in the beleaguered city. By this time their terror of the mines laid in front of the south wall had become much diminished, because the mines had been placed too low in the earth, and they also knew that Gordon and his diminished force were in the last stages of exhaustion. Finally, the Mahdi or his energetic lieutenant decided on one more arrangement, which was probably the true cause of their success. The Mahdists had always delivered their attack half an hour after sunrise; on this occasion they decided to attack half an hour before dawn, when the whole scene was covered in darkness. Slatin knew all these plans, and as he listened anxiously in his place of confinement he was startled, when just dropping off to sleep, by "the deafening discharge of thousands of rifles and guns; this lasted for a few minutes, then only occasional rifle shots were heard, and now all was quiet again. Could this possibly be the great attack on Khartoum? A wild discharge of firearms and cannon, and in a few minutes complete silence!" He was not left long in doubt. Some hours afterwards three black soldiers approached, carrying in a bloody cloth the head of General Gordon, which he identified. It is unnecessary to add the gruesome details which Slatin picked up as to his manner of death from the gossip of the camp. In this terrible tragedy ended that noble defence of Khartoum, which, wherever considered or discussed, and for all time, will excite the pity and admiration of the world.

There is no need to dwell further on the terrible end of one of the purest heroes our country has ever produced, whose loss was national, but most deeply felt as an irreparable shock, and as a void that can never be filled up by that small circle of men and women who might call themselves his friends. Ten years elapsed after the eventful morning when Slatin pronounced over his remains the appropriate epitaph, "A brave soldier who fell at his post; happy is he to have fallen; his sufferings are over!" before the exact manner of Gordon's death was known, and some even clung to the chance that after all he might have escaped to the Equator, and indeed it was not till long after the expedition had returned that the remarkable details of his single-handed defence of Khartoum became known. Had all these particulars come out at the moment when the public learnt that Khartoum had fallen, and that the expedition was to return without accomplishing anything, it is possible that there would have been a demand that no Minister could have resisted to avenge his fate; but it was not till the publication of the journals that the exact character of his magnificent defence and of the manner in which he was treated by those who sent him came to be understood and appreciated by the nation.

The lapse of time has been sufficient to allow of a calm judgment being passed on the whole transaction, and the considerations which I have put forward with regard to it in the chronicle of events have been dictated by the desire to treat all involved in the matter with impartiality. If they approximate to the truth, they warrant the following conclusions. The Government sent General Gordon to the Soudan on an absolutely hopeless mission for any one or two men to accomplish without that support in reinforcements on which General Gordon thought he could count. General Gordon went to the Soudan, and accepted that mission in the enthusiastic belief that he could arrest the Mahdi's progress, and treating as a certainty which did not require formal expression the personal opinion that the Government, for the national honour, would comply with whatever demands he made upon it. As a simple matter of fact, every one of those demands, some against and some with Sir Evelyn Baring's authority, were rejected. No incident could show more clearly the imperative need of definite arrangements being made even with Governments; and in this case the precipitance with which General Gordon was sent off did not admit of him or the Government knowing exactly what was in the other's mind. Ostensibly of one mind, their views on the matter in hand were really as far as the poles asunder.

There then comes the second phase of the question—the alleged abandonment of General Gordon by the Government which enlisted his services in face of an extraordinary, and indeed unexampled danger and difficulty. The evidence, while it proves conclusively and beyond dispute that Mr Gladstone's Government never had a policy with regard to the Soudan, and that even Gordon's heroism, inspiration, and success failed to induce them to throw aside their lethargy and take the course that, however much it may be postponed, is inevitable, does not justify the charge that it abandoned Gordon to his fate. It rejected the simplest and most sensible of his propositions, and by rejecting them incurred an immense expenditure of British treasure and an incalculable amount of bloodshed; but when the personal danger to its envoy became acute, it did not abandon him, but sanctioned the cost of the expedition pronounced necessary to effect his rescue. This decision, too late as it was to assist in the formation of a new administration for the Soudan, or to bring back the garrisons, was taken in ample time to ensure the personal safety and rescue of General Gordon. In the literal sense of the charge, history will therefore acquit Mr Gladstone and his colleagues of the abandonment of General Gordon personally.

With regard to the third phase of the question—*viz.* the failure of the attempt to rescue General Gordon, which was essentially a military, and not a political question—the responsibility passes from the Prime Minister to the military authorities who decided the scope of the campaign, and the commander who carried it out. In this case, the individual responsible was the same. Lord Wolseley not only had his own way in the route to be followed by the expedition, and the size and importance attached to it, but he was also entrusted with its personal direction. There is consequently no question of the subdivision of the responsibility for its failure, just as there could have been none of the credit for its success. Lord Wolseley decided that the route should be the long one by the Nile Valley, not the short one from Souakim to Berber. Lord Wolseley decreed that there should be no Indian troops, and that the force, instead of being an ordinary one, should be a picked special corps from the elite of the British army; and finally Lord Wolseley insisted that there should be no dash to the rescue of Gordon by a small part of his force, but a slow, impressive, and overpoweringly scientific advance of the whole body. The extremity of Gordon's distress necessitated a slight modification of his plan, when, with qualified instructions, which practically tied his hands, Sir Herbert Stewart made his first appearance at Jakdul.

It was then known to Lord Wolseley that Gordon was in extremities, yet when a fighting force of 1100 English troops, of special physique and spirit, was moved forward with sufficient transport to enable it to reach the Nile and Gordon's steamers, the commander's instructions were such as confined him to inaction, unless he disobeyed his orders, which only Nelsons and Gordons can do with impunity. It is impossible to explain this extraordinary timidity. Sir Herbert Stewart reached Jakdul on 3rd January with a force small in numbers, but in every other respect of remarkable efficiency, and with the camels sufficiently fresh to have reached the Nile on 7th or 8th January had it pressed on. The more urgent news that reached Lord Wolseley after its departure would have justified the despatch of a messenger to urge it to press on at all costs to Metemmah. In such a manner would a Havelock or Outram have acted, yet the garrison of the Lucknow Residency was in no more desperate case than Gordon at Khartoum.

It does not need to be a professor of a military academy to declare that, unless something is risked in war, and especially wars such as England has had to wage against superior numbers in the East, there will never be any successful rescues of distressed garrisons. Lord Wolseley would risk nothing in the advance from Korti to Metemmah, whence his advance guard did not reach the latter place till the 20th, instead of the 7th of January. His lieutenant and representative, Sir Charles Wilson, would not risk anything on the 21st January, whence none of the steamers appeared at Khartoum until late on the 27th, when all was over. Each of these statements cannot be impeached, and if so, the conclusion seems inevitable that in the first and highest degree Lord Wolseley was alone responsible for the failure to reach Khartoum in time, and that in a very minor degree Sir Charles Wilson might be considered blameworthy for not having sent off one of the steamers with a small reinforcement to Khartoum on the 21st January, before even he allowed Cassim el Mousse to take any part in the attack on Metemmah. He could not have done this himself, but he would have had no difficulty in finding a substitute. When, however, there were others far more blameworthy, it seems almost unjust to a gallant officer to say that by a desperate effort he might at the very last moment have snatched the chestnuts out of the fire, and converted the most ignominious failure in the military annals of this country into a creditable success.

* * * * * * * *

The tragic end at Khartoum was not an inappropriate conclusion for the career of Charles Gordon, whose life had been far removed from the ordinary experiences of mankind. No man who ever lived was called upon to deal with a greater number of difficult military and administrative problems, and to find the solution for them with such inadequate means and inferior troops and subordinates. In the Crimea he showed as a very young man the spirit, discernment, energy, and regard for detail which were his characteristics through life. Those qualities enabled him to achieve in China military exploits which in their way have never been surpassed. The marvellous skill, confidence, and vigilance with which he supplied the shortcomings of his troops, and provided for the wants of a large population at Khartoum for the better part of a year, showed that, as a military leader, he was still the same gifted captain who had crushed the Taeping rebellion twenty years before. What he did for the Soudan and its people during six years' residence, at a personal sacrifice that never can be appreciated, has been told at length; but pages of rhetoric would not give as perfect a picture as the spontaneous cry of the blacks: "If we only had a governor like Gordon Pasha, then the country would indeed be contented."

"Such examples are fruitful in the future," said Mr Gladstone in the House of Commons; and it is as a perfect model of all that was good, brave, and true that Gordon will be enshrined in the memory of the great English nation which he really died for, and whose honour was dearer to him than his life. England may well feel proud of having produced so noble and so unapproachable a hero. She has had, and she will have again, soldiers as brave, as thoughtful, as prudent, and as successful as Gordon. She has had, and she will have again, servants of the same public spirit, with the same intense desire that not a spot should sully the national honour. But although this breed is not extinct, there will never be another Gordon. The circumstances that produced him were exceptional; the opportunities that offered themselves for the demonstration of his greatness can never fall to the lot of another; and even if by some miraculous combination the man and the occasions arose, the hero, unlike Gordon, would be spoilt by his own success and public applause. But the qualities which made Gordon superior not only to all his contemporaries, but to all the temptations and weaknesses of success, are attainable; and the student of his life will find that the guiding star he always kept before him was the duty he owed his country. In that respect, above all others, he has left future generations of his countrymen a great example.

LEONAUR

ALSO FROM LEONAUR

AVAILABLE IN SOFTCOVER OR HARDCOVER WITH DUST JACKET

A JOURNAL OF THE SECOND SIKH WAR by *Daniel A. Sandford*—The Experiences of an Ensign of the 2nd Bengal European Regiment During the Campaign in the Punjab, India, 1848-49.

LAKE'S CAMPAIGNS IN INDIA by *Hugh Pearse*—The Second Anglo Maratha War, 1803-1807. Often neglected by historians and students alike, Lake's Indian campaign was fought against a resourceful and ruthless enemy-almost always superior in numbers to his own forces.

BRITAIN IN AFGHANISTAN 1: THE FIRST AFGHAN WAR 1839-42 by *Archibald Forbes*—Following over a century of the gradual assumption of sovereignty of the Indian Sub-Continent, the British Empire, in the form of the Honourable East India Company, supported by troops of the new Queen Victoria's army, found itself inevitably at the natural boundaries that surround Afghanistan. There it set in motion a series of disastrous events-the first of which was to march into the country at all.

BRITAIN IN AFGHANISTAN 2: THE SECOND AFGHAN WAR 1878-80 by *Archibald Forbes*—This the history of the Second Afghan War-another episode of British military history typified by savagery, massacre, siege and battles.

UP AMONG THE PANDIES by *Vivian Dering Majendie*—An outstanding account of the campaign for the fall of Lucknow. This is a vital book of war as fought by the British Army of the mid-nineteenth century, but in truth it is also an essential book of war that will enthral.

BLOW THE BUGLE, DRAW THE SWORD by *W. H. G. Kingston*—The Wars, Campaigns, Regiments and Soldiers of the British & Indian Armies During the Victorian Era, 1839-1898.

INDIAN MUTINY 150th ANNIVERSARY: A LEONAUR ORIGINAL

MUTINY: 1857 by *James Humphries*—It is now 150 years since the 'Indian Mutiny' burst like an engulfing flame on the British soldiers, their families and the civilians of the Empire in North East India. The Bengal Native army arose in violent rebellion, and the once peaceful countryside became a battleground as Native sepoys and elements of the Indian population massacred their British masters and defeated them in open battle. As the tide turned, a vengeful army of British and loyal Indian troops repressed the insurgency with a savagery that knew no mercy. It was a time of fear and slaughter. James Humphries has drawn together the voices of those dreadful days for this commemorative book.

LEONAUR

ALSO FROM LEONAUR

AVAILABLE IN SOFTCOVER OR HARDCOVER WITH DUST JACKET

WELLINGTON AND THE PYRENEES CAMPAIGN VOLUME I: FROM VITORIA TO THE BIDASSOA *by F. C. Beatson*—The final phase of the campaign in the Iberian Peninsula.

WELLINGTON AND THE INVASION OF FRANCE VOLUME II: THE BIDASSOA TO THE BATTLE OF THE NIVELLE *by F. C. Beatson*—The second of Beatson's series on the fall of Revolutionary France published by Leonaur, the reader is once again taken into the centre of Wellington's strategic and tactical genius.

WELLINGTON AND THE FALL OF FRANCE VOLUME III: THE GAVES AND THE BATTLE OF ORTHEZ *by F. C. Beatson*—This final chapter of F. C. Beatson's brilliant trilogy shows the 'captain of the age' at his most inspired and makes all three books essential additions to any Peninsular War library.

NAVAL BATTLES OF THE NAPOLEONIC WARS *by W. H. Fitchett*—Cape St. Vincent, the Nile, Cadiz, Copenhagen, Trafalgar & Others

SERGEANT GUILLEMARD: THE MAN WHO SHOT NELSON? *by Robert Guillemard*—A Soldier of the Infantry of the French Army of Napoleon on Campaign Throughout Europe

WITH THE GUARDS ACROSS THE PYRENEES *by Robert Batty*—The Experiences of a British Officer of Wellington's Army During the Battles for the Fall of Napoleonic France, 1813.

A STAFF OFFICER IN THE PENINSULA *by E. W. Buckham*—An Officer of the British Staff Corps Cavalry During the Peninsula Campaign of the Napoleonic Wars

THE LEIPZIG CAMPAIGN: 1813—NAPOLEON AND THE "BATTLE OF THE NATIONS" *by F. N. Maude*—Colonel Maude's analysis of Napoleon's campaign of 1813.

BUGEAUD: A PACK WITH A BATON *by Thomas Robert Bugeaud*—The Early Campaigns of a Soldier of Napoleon's Army Who Would Become a Marshal of France.

TWO LEONAUR ORIGINALS

SERGEANT NICOL *by Daniel Nicol*—The Experiences of a Gordon Highlander During the Napoleonic Wars in Egypt, the Peninsula and France.

WATERLOO RECOLLECTIONS *by Frederick Llewellyn*—Rare First Hand Accounts, Letters, Reports and Retellings from the Campaign of 1815.

CPSIA information can be obtained at www.ICGtesting.com
Printed in the USA
BVOW08s1206210515

401111BV00001B/302/P